FIGURE SEVENTEEN
Tsubasa and Hikaru

Vol.1

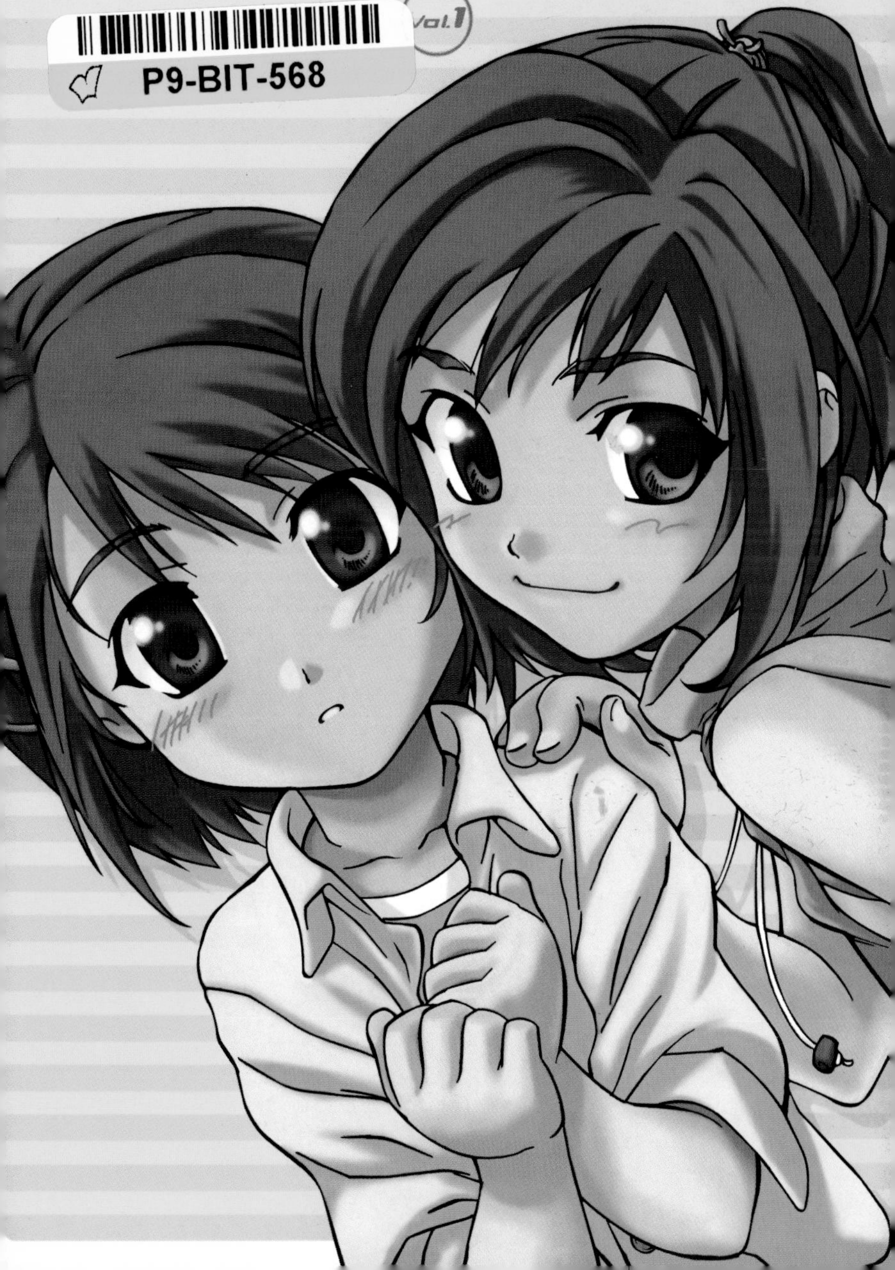

F I G U R E S E V E N T E E N

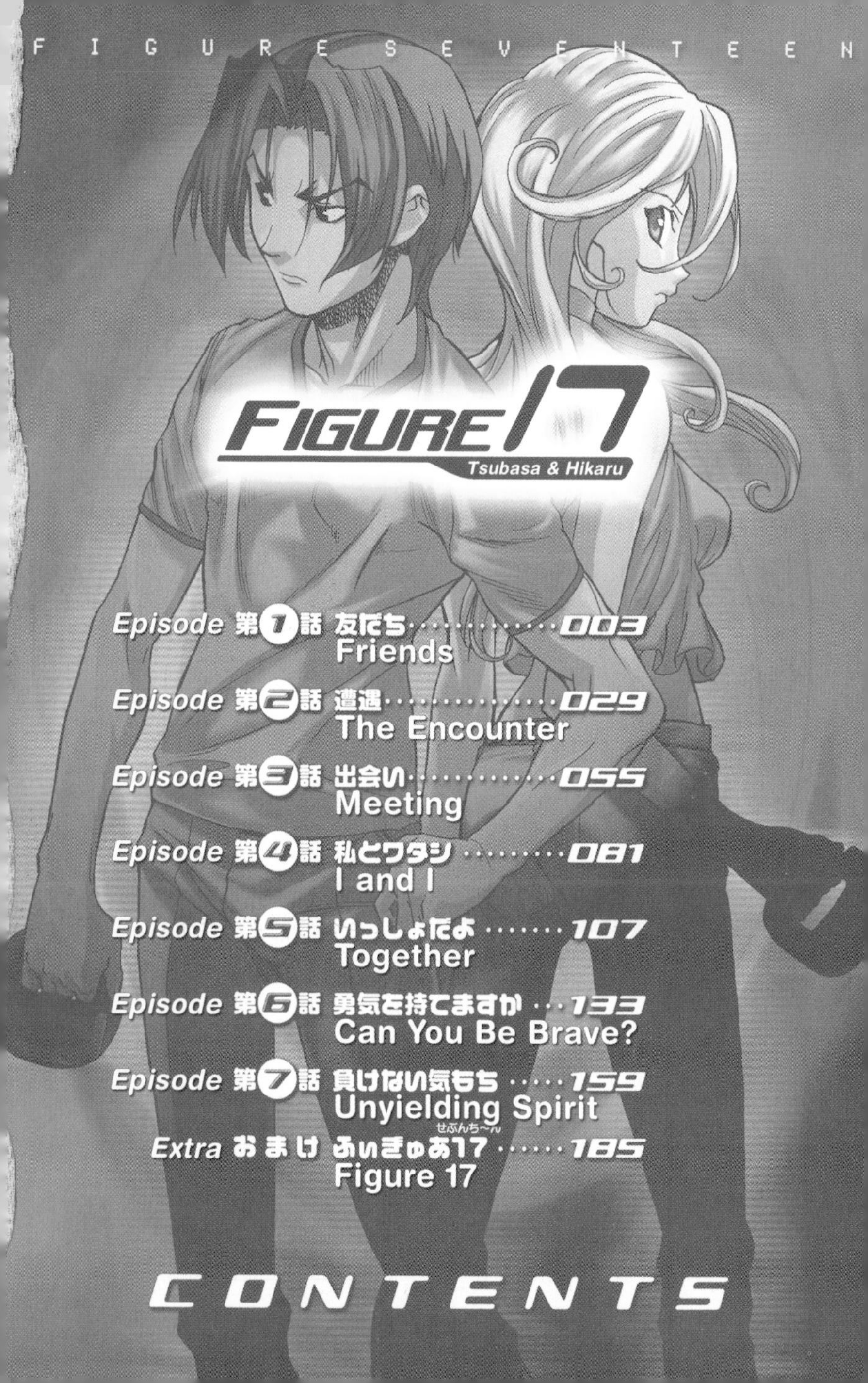

FIGURE 17
Tsubasa & Hikaru

CONTENTS

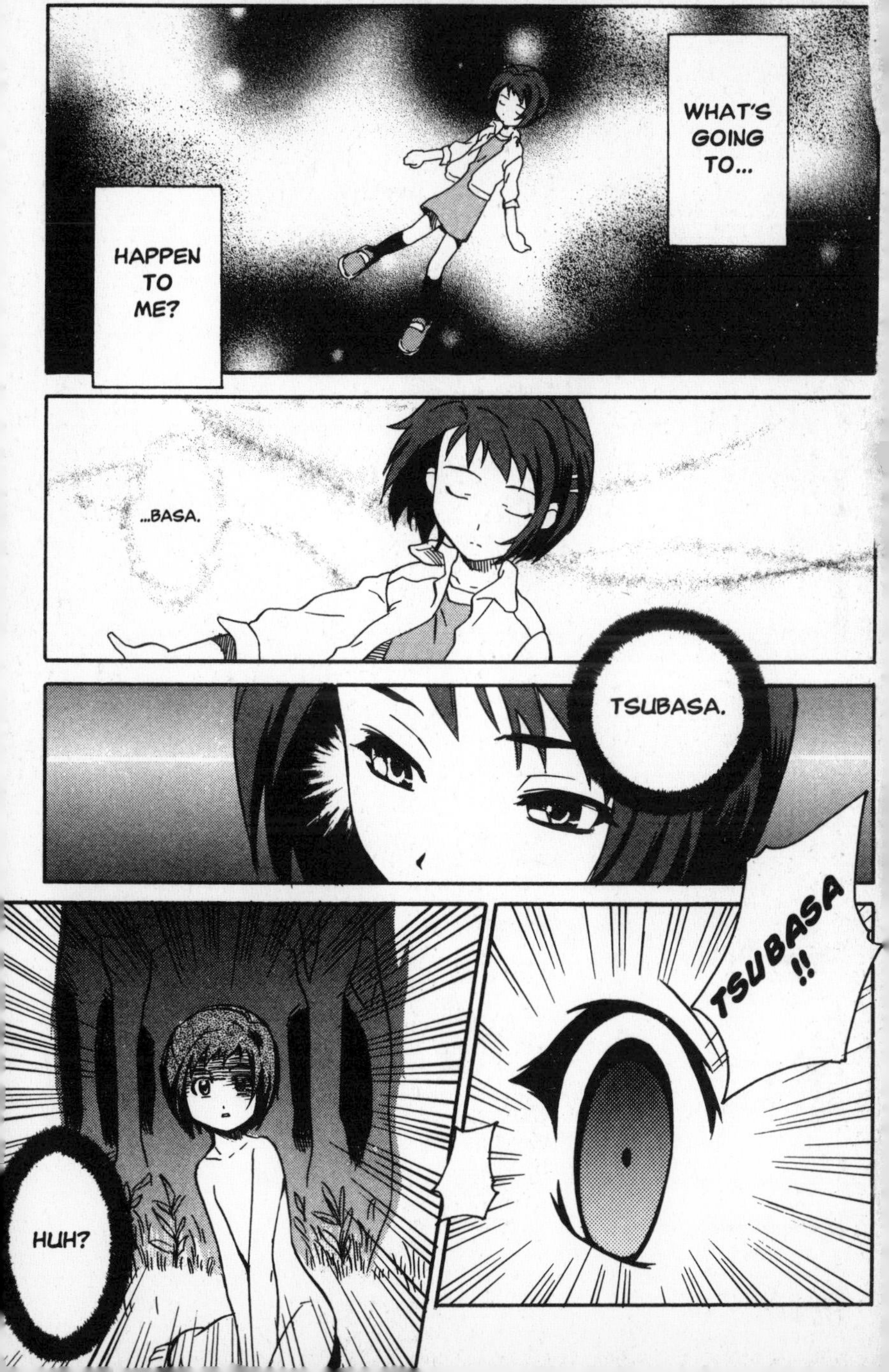
WHAT'S GOING TO...
HAPPEN TO ME?
...BASA.
TSUBASA.
TSUBASA !!
HUH?

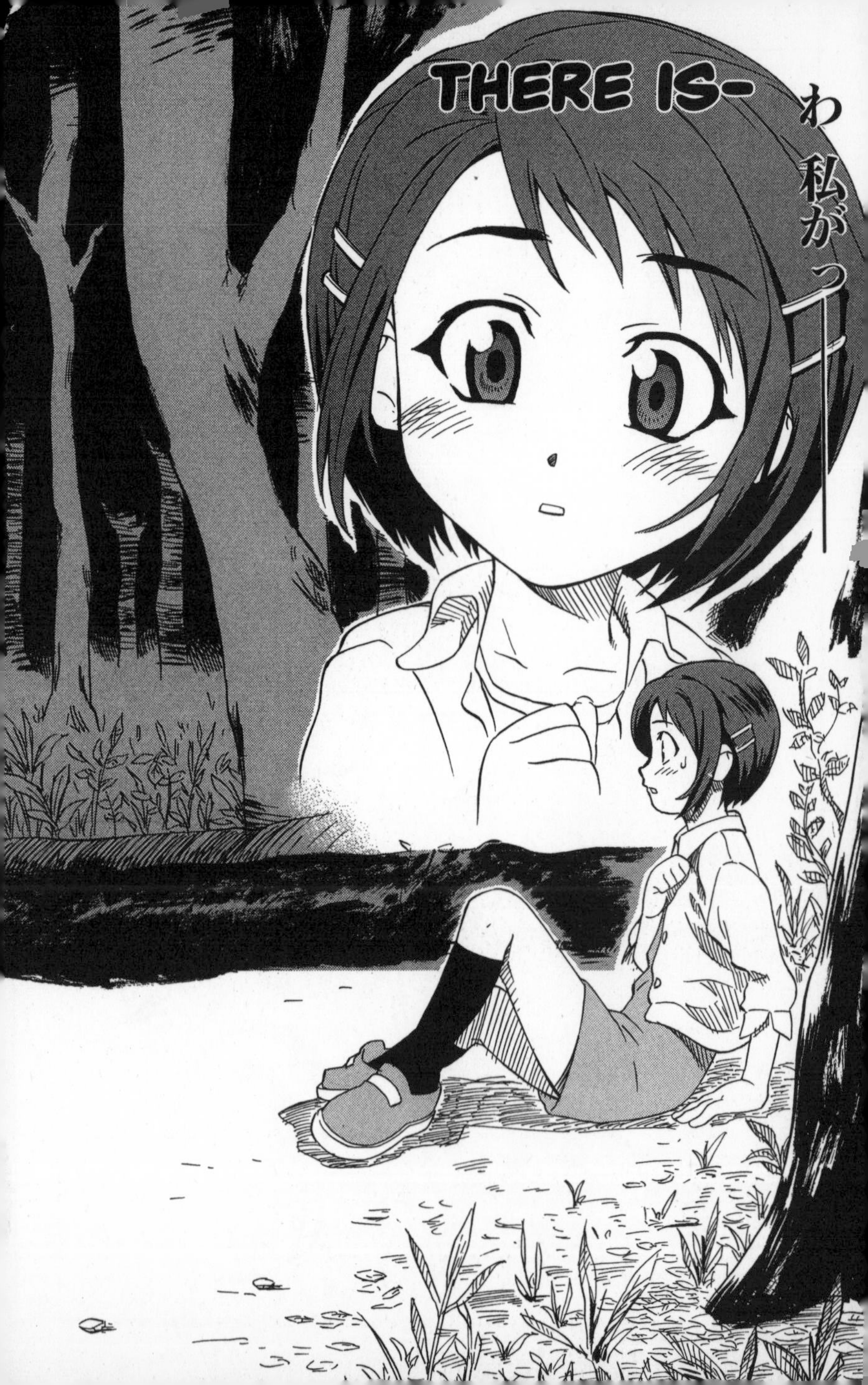
THERE IS-
わ私がっ

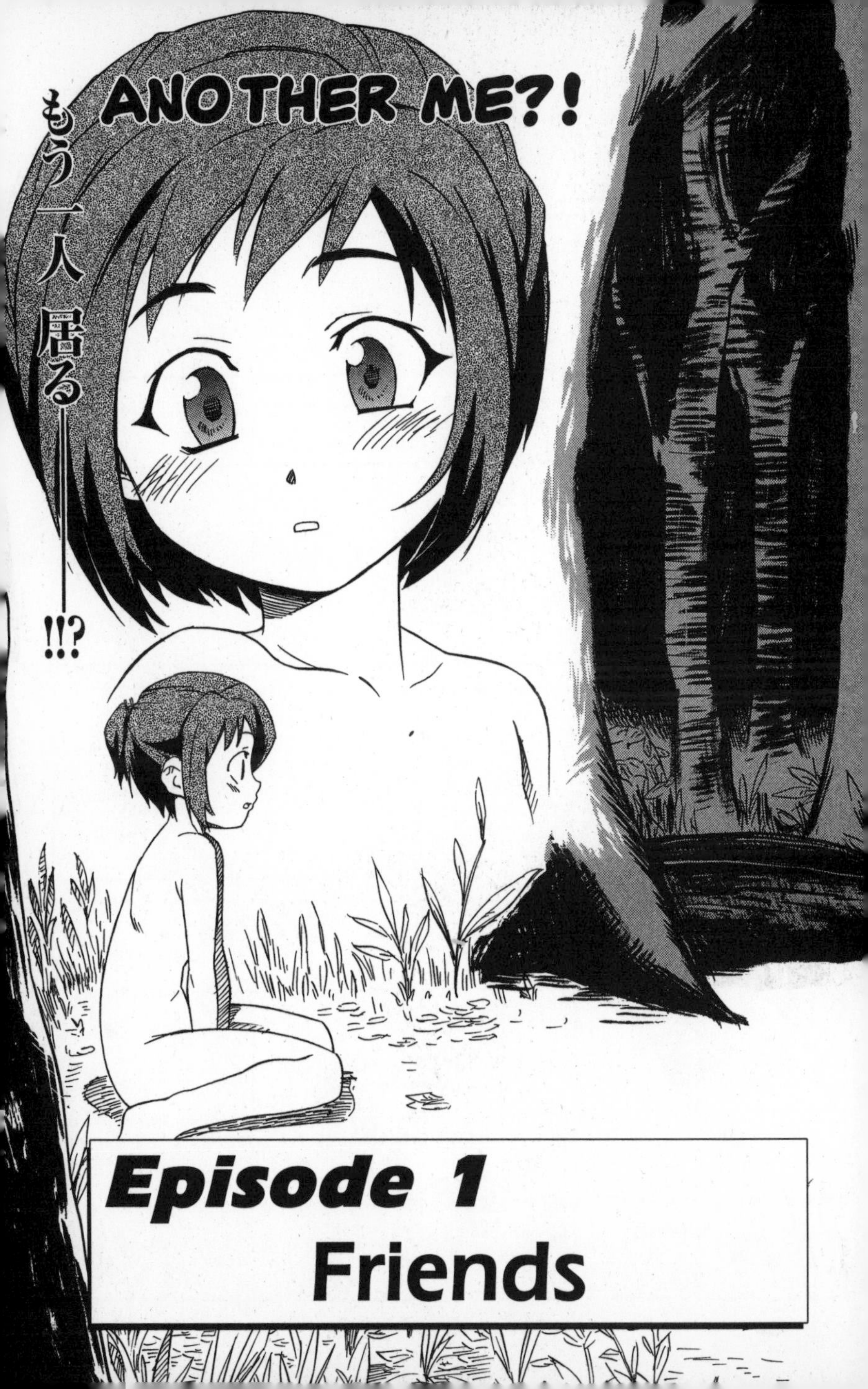
ANOTHER ME?!
もう一人居る——!!?
Episode 1
Friends

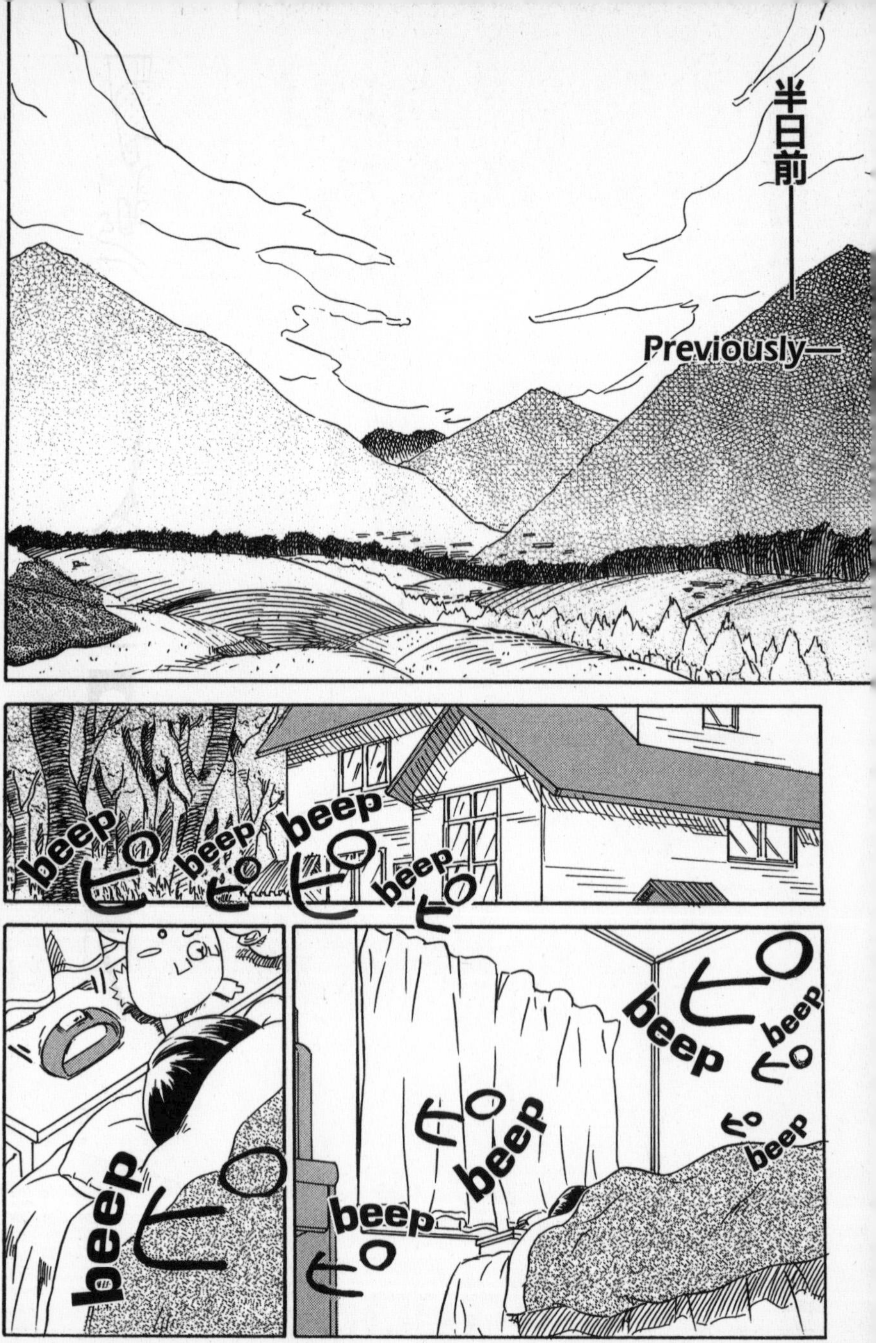
半日前
Previously—
ピ beep
ピ beep
ピ beep
ピ beep
ピ beep
ピ beep
ピ beep
ピ beep
ピ beep
ピ beep

beep

HRNNN...

thmp

thmp

thmp

GUESS IT'S TIME TO GET...

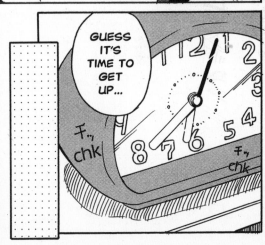

chk

chk

I WONDER IF DADDY SAW THE FLIER ABOUT PARENTS' DAY...

fwip

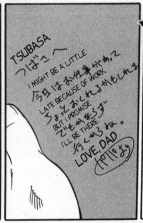

TSUBASA
つばさへ

I MIGHT BE A LITTLE
LATE BECAUSE OF WORK
今日はお仕事があって
ちょっとおくれるかもしれません
BUT I PROMISE
でもやきます
I'LL BE THERE
行くからね。
LOVE, DAD
パパより

Wakaba-News

わかば通信
Open House

授業参観

TSUBASA
つばさへ

パパより
LOVE, DAD

8

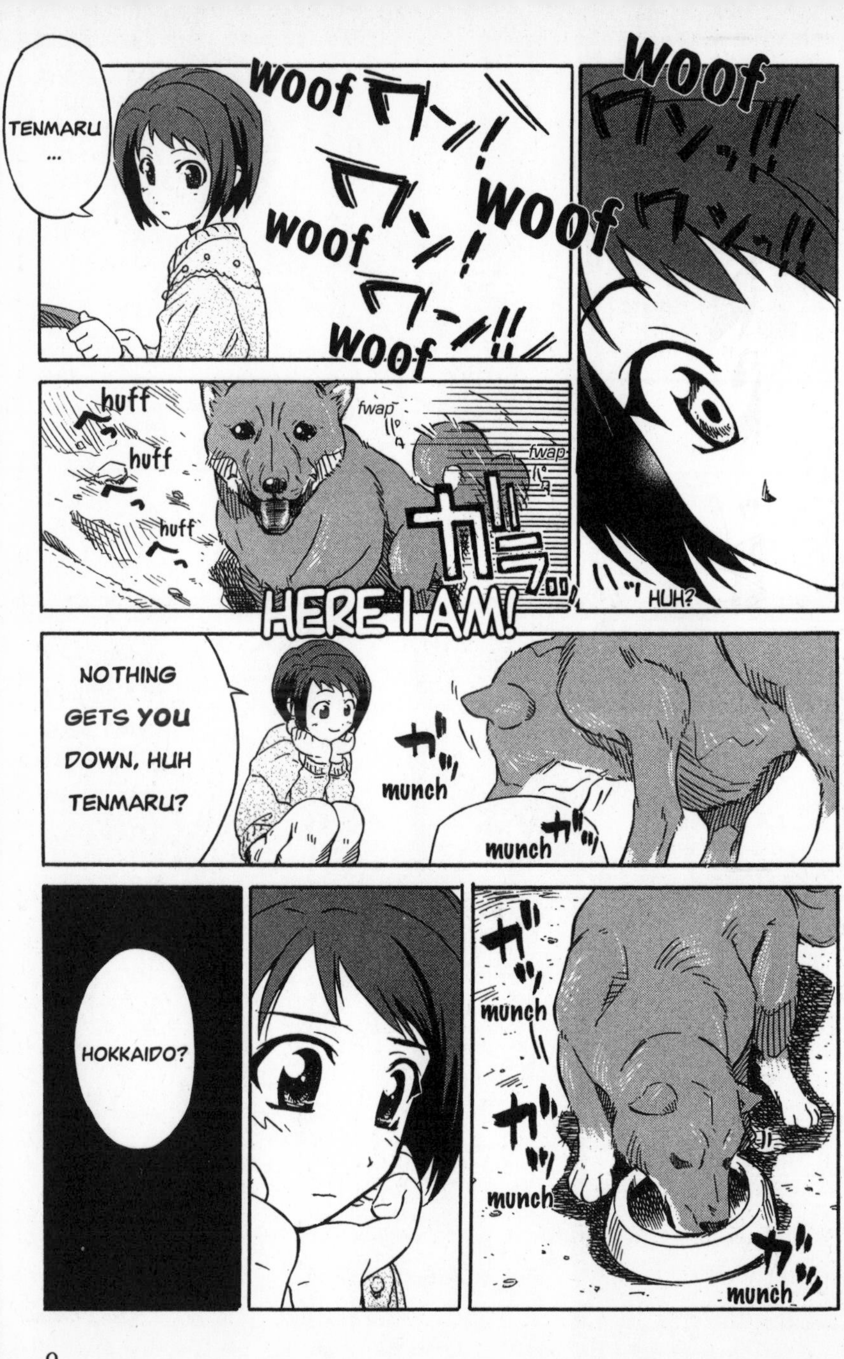
woof
woof
woof
woof
woof
TENMARU ...
woof
HUH?
fwap
fwap
huff
huff
huff
HERE I AM!
munch
munch
NOTHING GETS YOU DOWN, HUH TENMARU?
munch
munch
munch
HOKKAIDO?

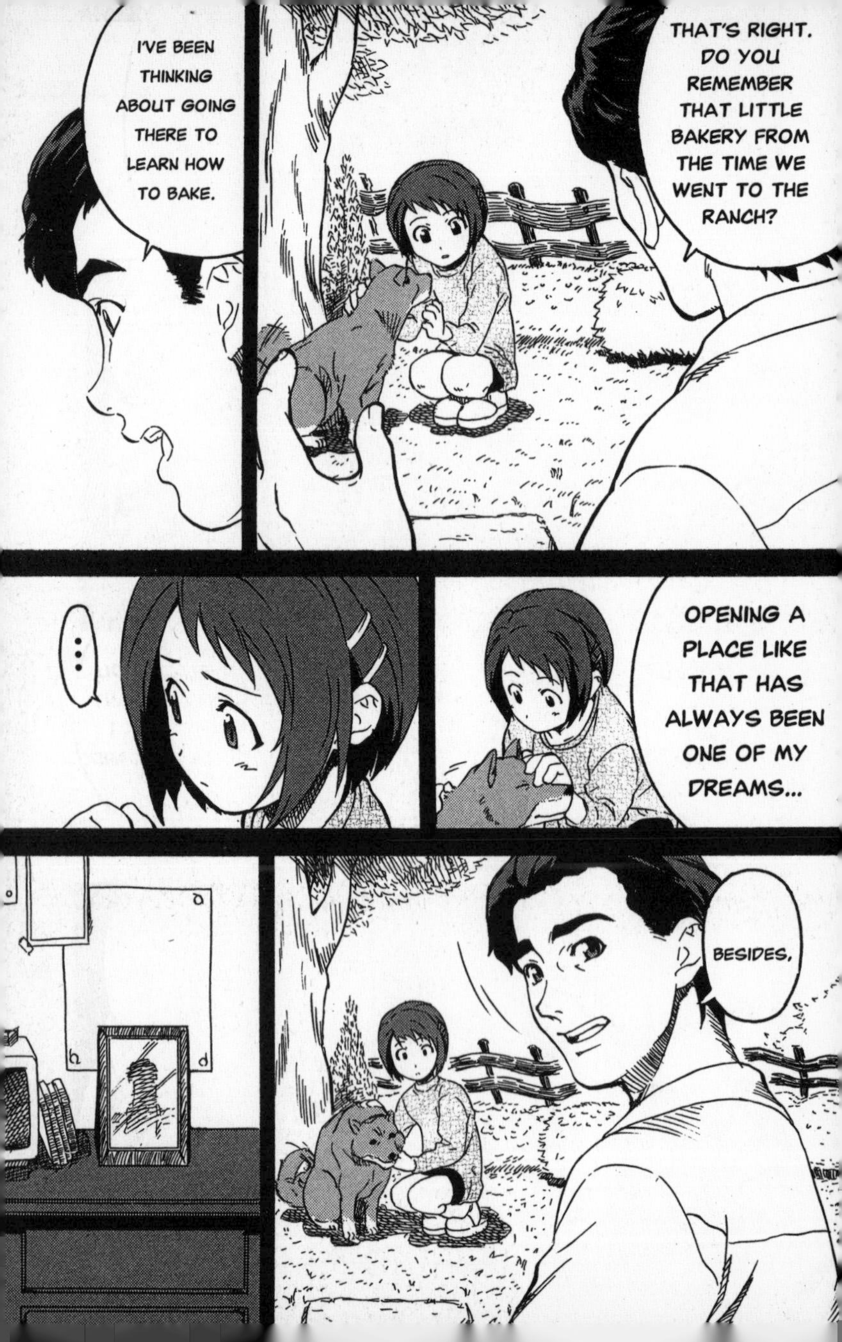
I'VE BEEN THINKING ABOUT GOING THERE TO LEARN HOW TO BAKE.
THAT'S RIGHT. DO YOU REMEMBER THAT LITTLE BAKERY FROM THE TIME WE WENT TO THE RANCH?
...
OPENING A PLACE LIKE THAT HAS ALWAYS BEEN ONE OF MY DREAMS...
BESIDES,

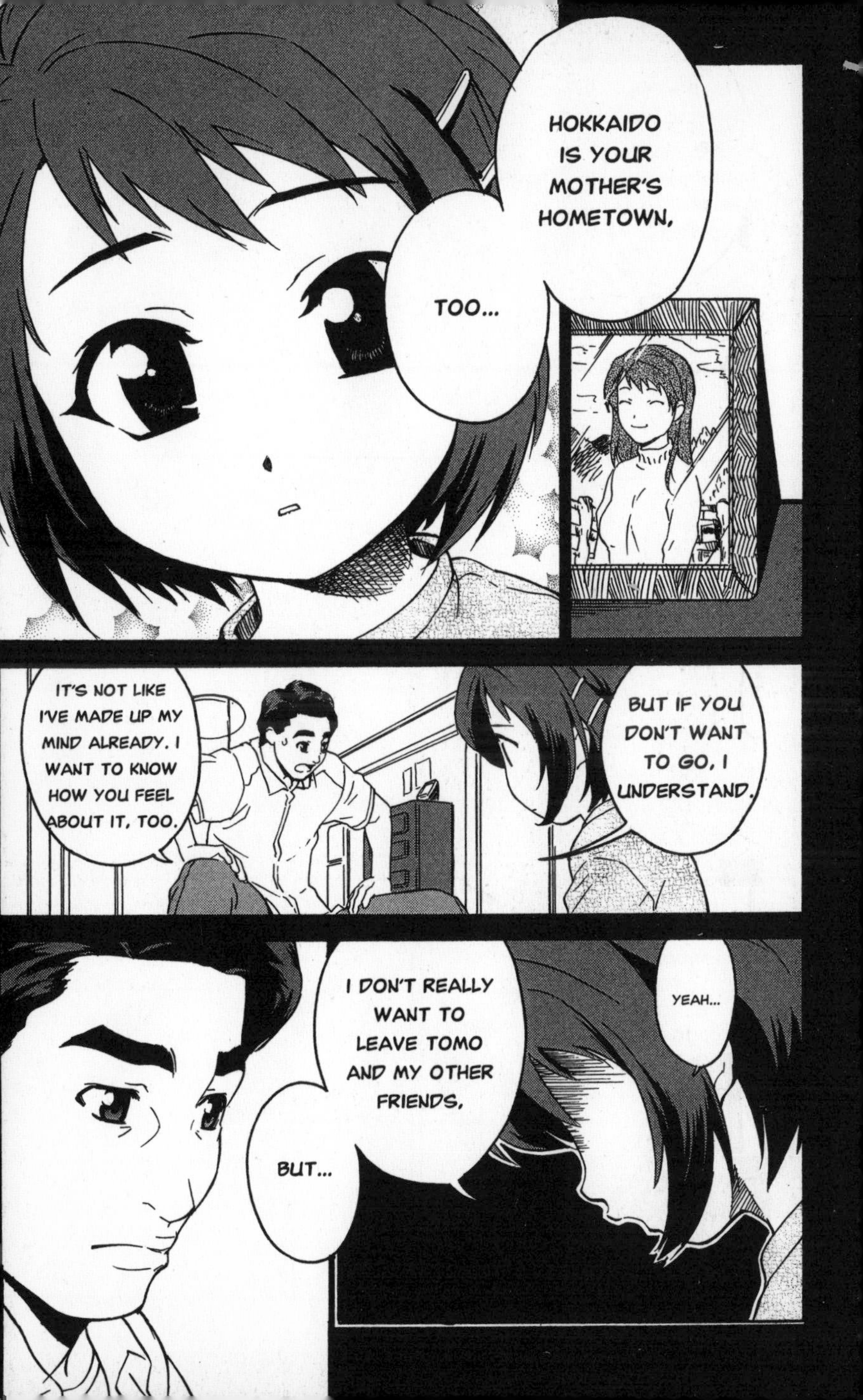
HOKKAIDO IS YOUR MOTHER'S HOMETOWN,
TOO...
IT'S NOT LIKE I'VE MADE UP MY MIND ALREADY. I WANT TO KNOW HOW YOU FEEL ABOUT IT, TOO.
BUT IF YOU DON'T WANT TO GO, I UNDERSTAND.
I DON'T REALLY WANT TO LEAVE TOMO AND MY OTHER FRIENDS,
BUT...
YEAH...

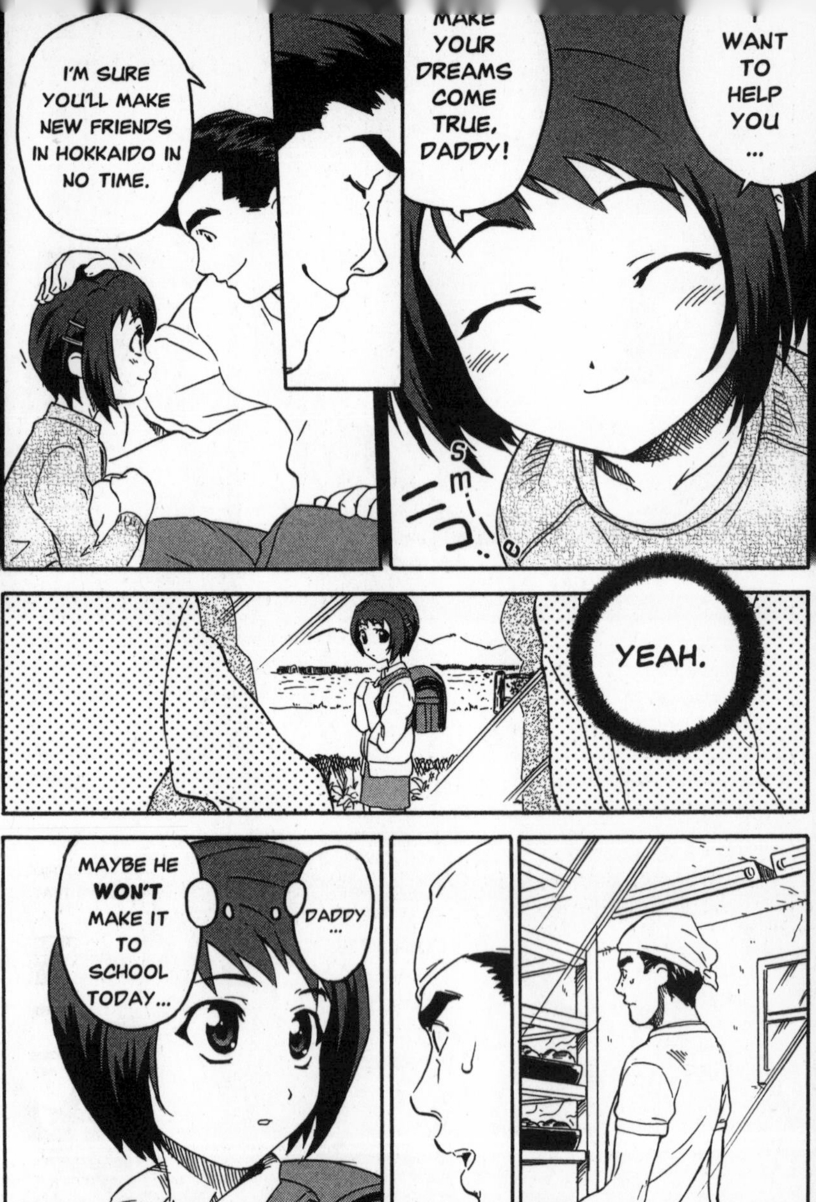
WANT TO HELP YOU ...
MAKE YOUR DREAMS COME TRUE, DADDY!
smile
I'M SURE YOU'LL MAKE NEW FRIENDS IN HOKKAIDO IN NO TIME.
YEAH.
DADDY ...
MAYBE HE **WON'T** MAKE IT TO SCHOOL TODAY...

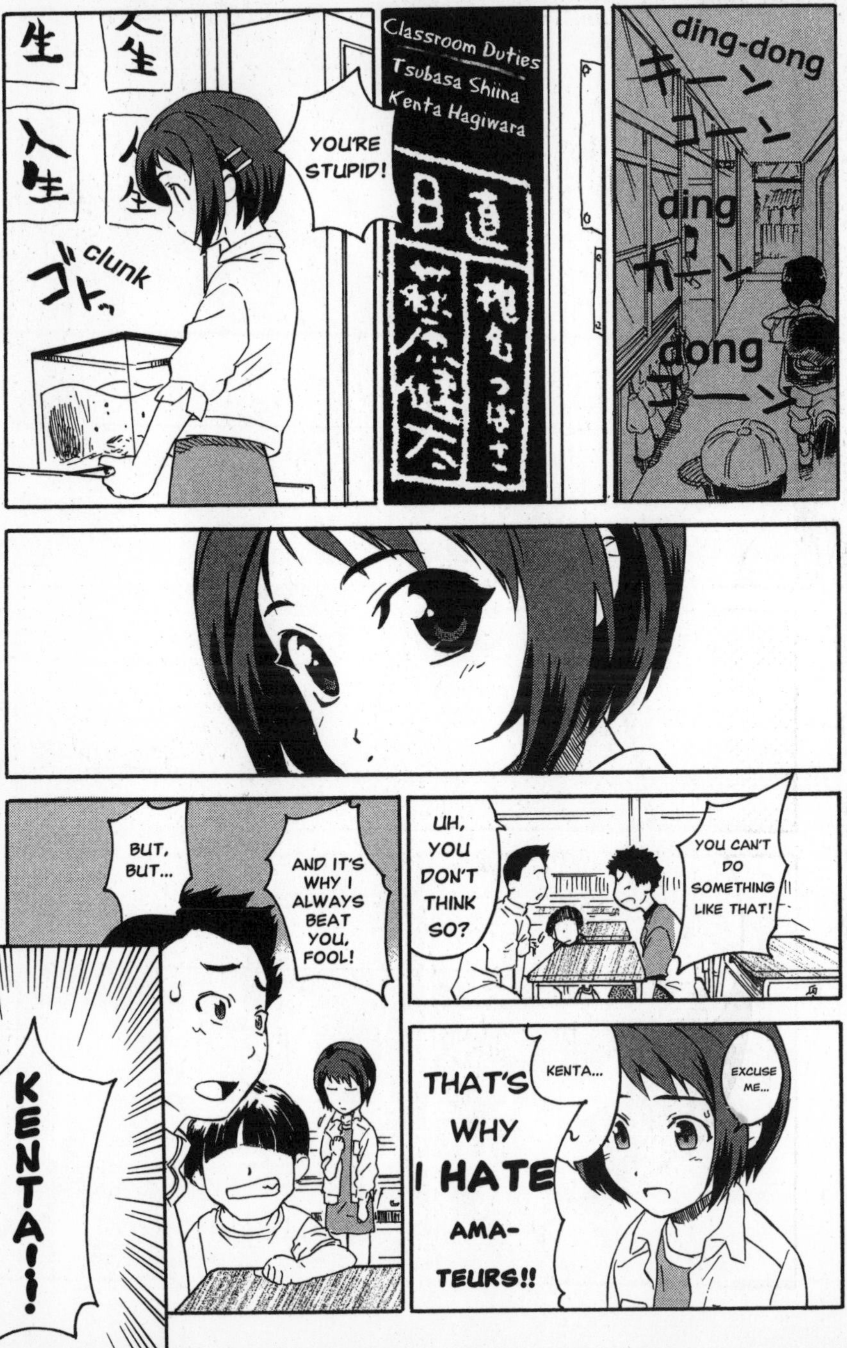
ding-dong
キーンコーン
ding
カーン
dong
コーン
Classroom Duties
Tsubasa Shiina
Kenta Hagiwara
YOU'RE STUPID!
clunk
ゴトッ
YOU CAN'T DO SOMETHING LIKE THAT!
UH, YOU DON'T THINK SO?
AND IT'S WHY I ALWAYS BEAT YOU, FOOL!
BUT, BUT...
EXCUSE ME...
KENTA...
THAT'S WHY I HATE AMA-TEURS!!
KENTA!!!

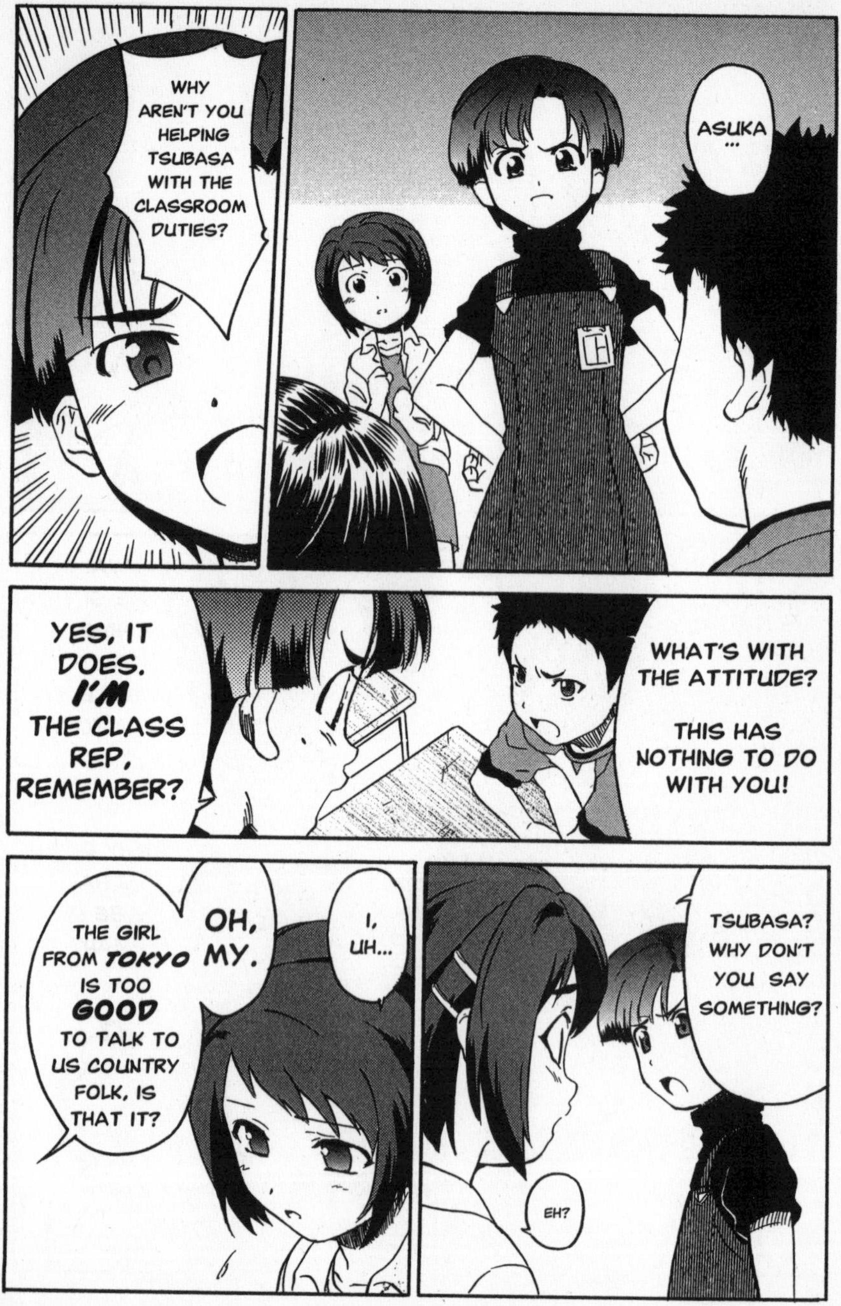
ASUKA ...
WHY AREN'T YOU HELPING TSUBASA WITH THE CLASSROOM DUTIES?
WHAT'S WITH THE ATTITUDE?
THIS HAS NOTHING TO DO WITH YOU!
YES, IT DOES. I'M THE CLASS REP, REMEMBER?
TSUBASA? WHY DON'T YOU SAY SOMETHING?
EH?
I, UH...
OH, MY.
THE GIRL FROM TOKYO IS TOO GOOD TO TALK TO US COUNTRY FOLK, IS THAT IT?

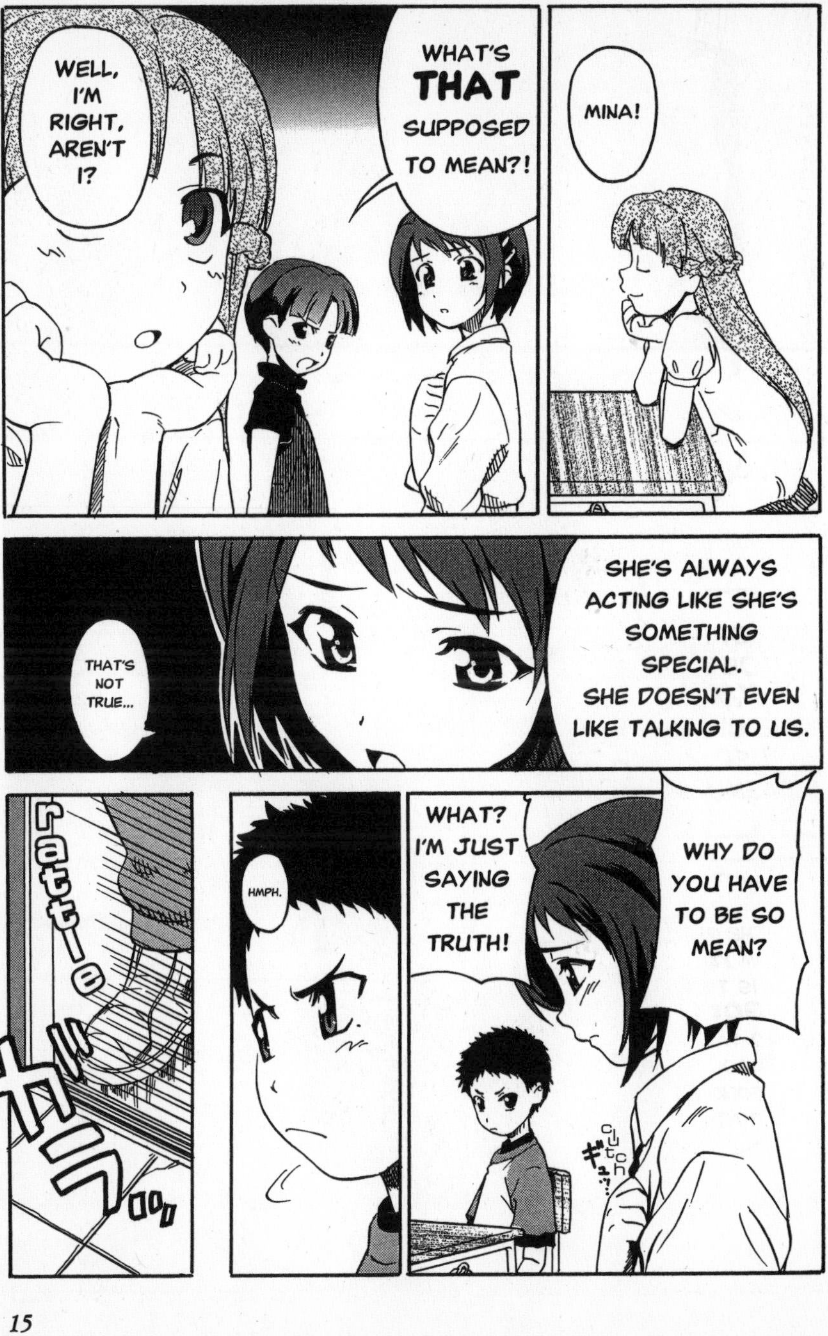
MINA!
WHAT'S THAT SUPPOSED TO MEAN?!
WELL, I'M RIGHT, AREN'T I?
SHE'S ALWAYS ACTING LIKE SHE'S SOMETHING SPECIAL. SHE DOESN'T EVEN LIKE TALKING TO US.
THAT'S NOT TRUE...
WHY DO YOU HAVE TO BE SO MEAN?
clutch
WHAT? I'M JUST SAYING THE TRUTH!
HMPH.
rattle

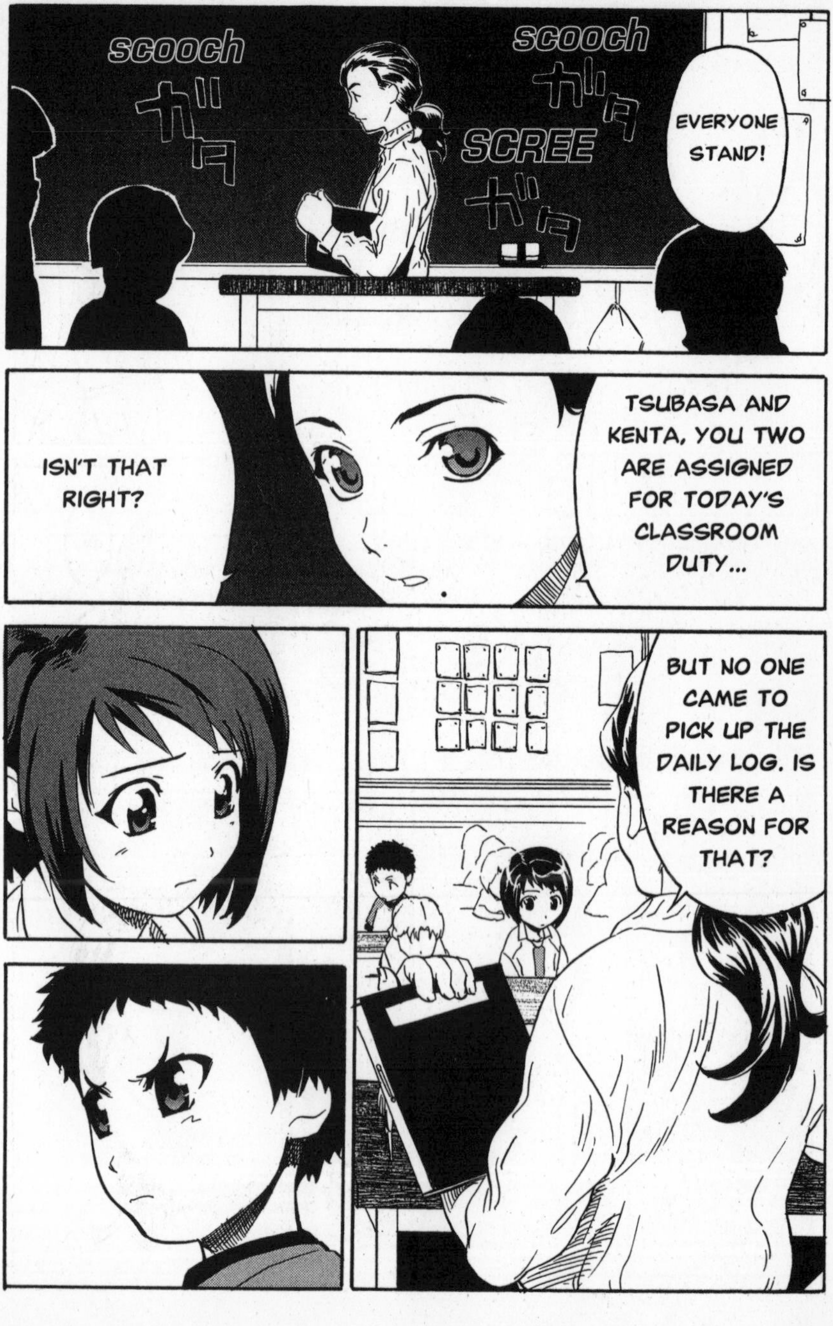
EVERYONE STAND!
scooch
ガタ
SCREE
ガタ
scooch
ガタ
TSUBASA AND KENTA, YOU TWO ARE ASSIGNED FOR TODAY'S CLASSROOM DUTY...
ISN'T THAT RIGHT?
BUT NO ONE CAME TO PICK UP THE DAILY LOG. IS THERE A REASON FOR THAT?

I KNOW WHY! I THINK KENTA MADE TSUBASA DO ALL THE WORK HERSELF.
ガタッ
TSUBASA! KENTA! IS THIS TRUE?
QUIET!
THERE'S THAT BIG MOUTH!
SHUT UP!
Heh heh heh
UM...
...
I WAS GOOFING OFF AND DIDN'T HELP HER. I'M SORRY.
sulk
ムスッ
YOU TWO ARE SUPPOSED TO TAKE CARE OF CLASSROOM DUTIES TOGETHER. UNDERSTAND?
YES.
OKAY.
...AND THAT'S WHAT YASUHIRO SAID.
murmur
ざわ
murmur
ざわ
WELL DONE!
chatter
ざわ

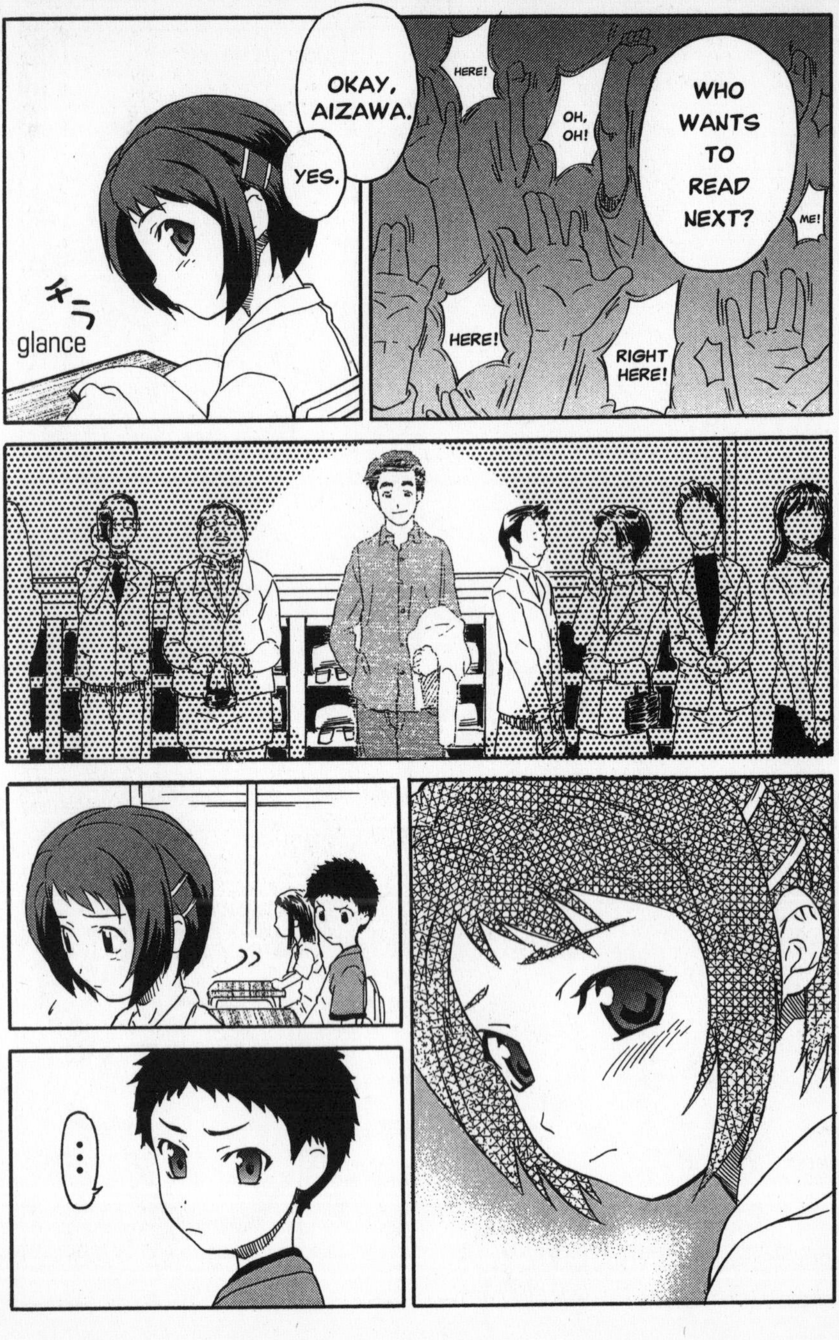
WHO WANTS TO READ NEXT?
ME!
OH, OH!
HERE!
HERE!
RIGHT HERE!
OKAY, AIZAWA.
YES.
チラ
glance
...

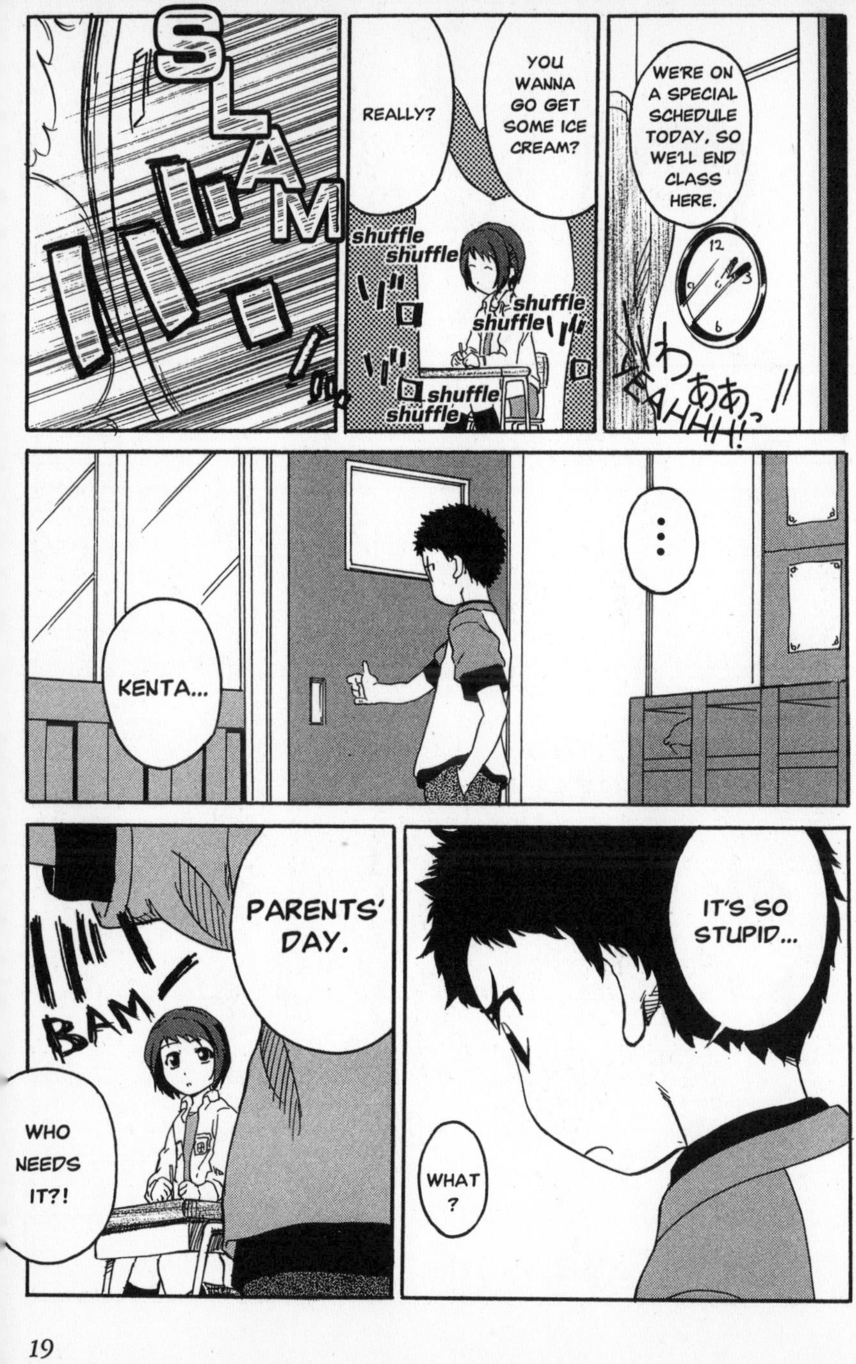
WE'RE ON A SPECIAL SCHEDULE TODAY, SO WE'LL END CLASS HERE.
わぁあっ
EAHHH!
YOU WANNA GO GET SOME ICE CREAM?
REALLY?
shuffle shuffle
shuffle shuffle
shuffle shuffle
SLAM
...
KENTA...
IT'S SO STUPID...
WHAT?
PARENTS' DAY.
BAM
WHO NEEDS IT?!

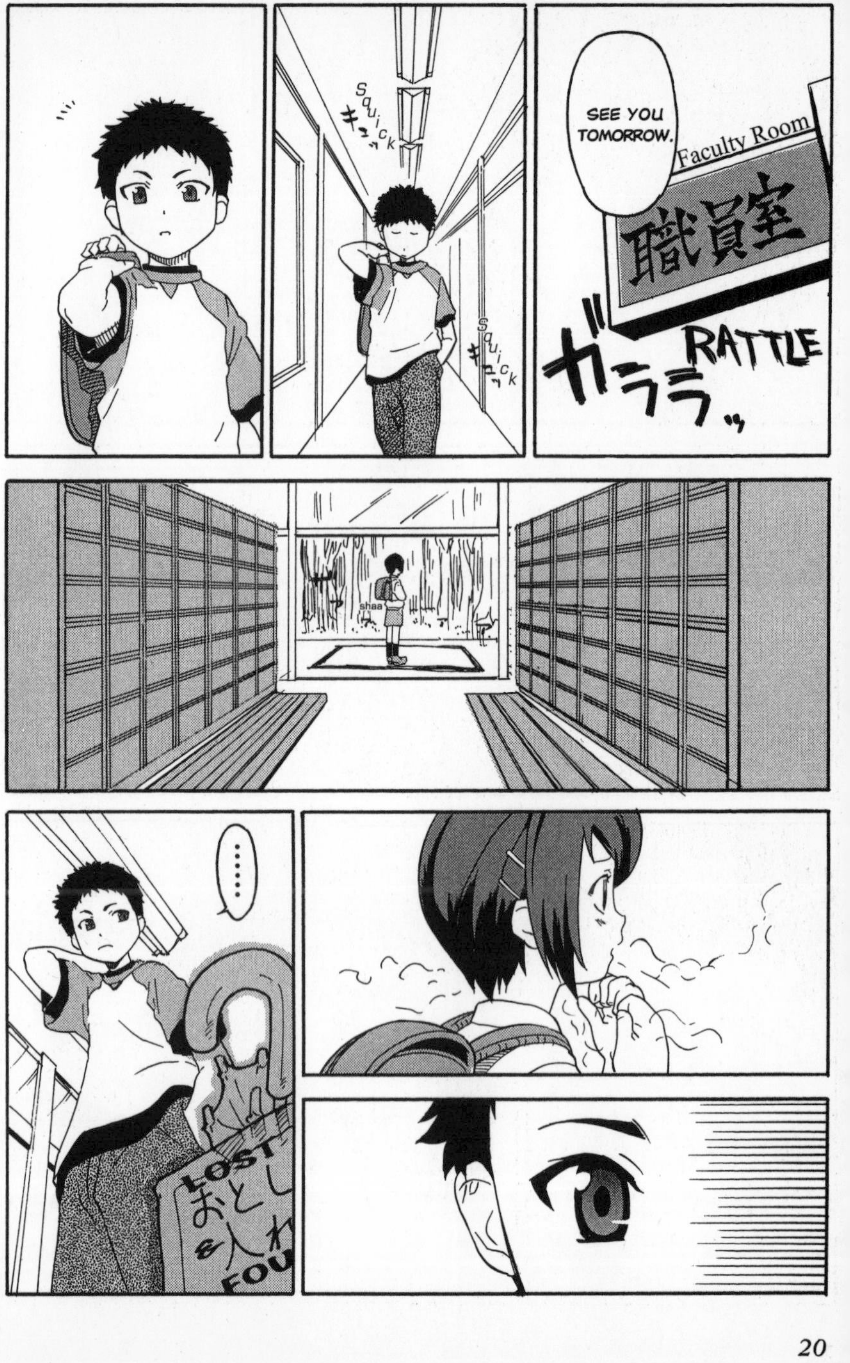
SEE YOU TOMORROW.
Faculty Room
職員室
ガラララッ
RATTLE
squick
キュッ
squick
キュッ
shaa
......
LOST

TSUBASA
!!

fwip

TAKE IT.

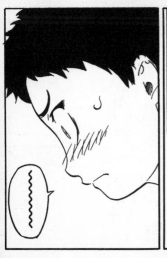

...

YOU WON'T GET
IN TROUBLE 'CUZ

IT'S FROM THE
LOST
&
FOUND

21

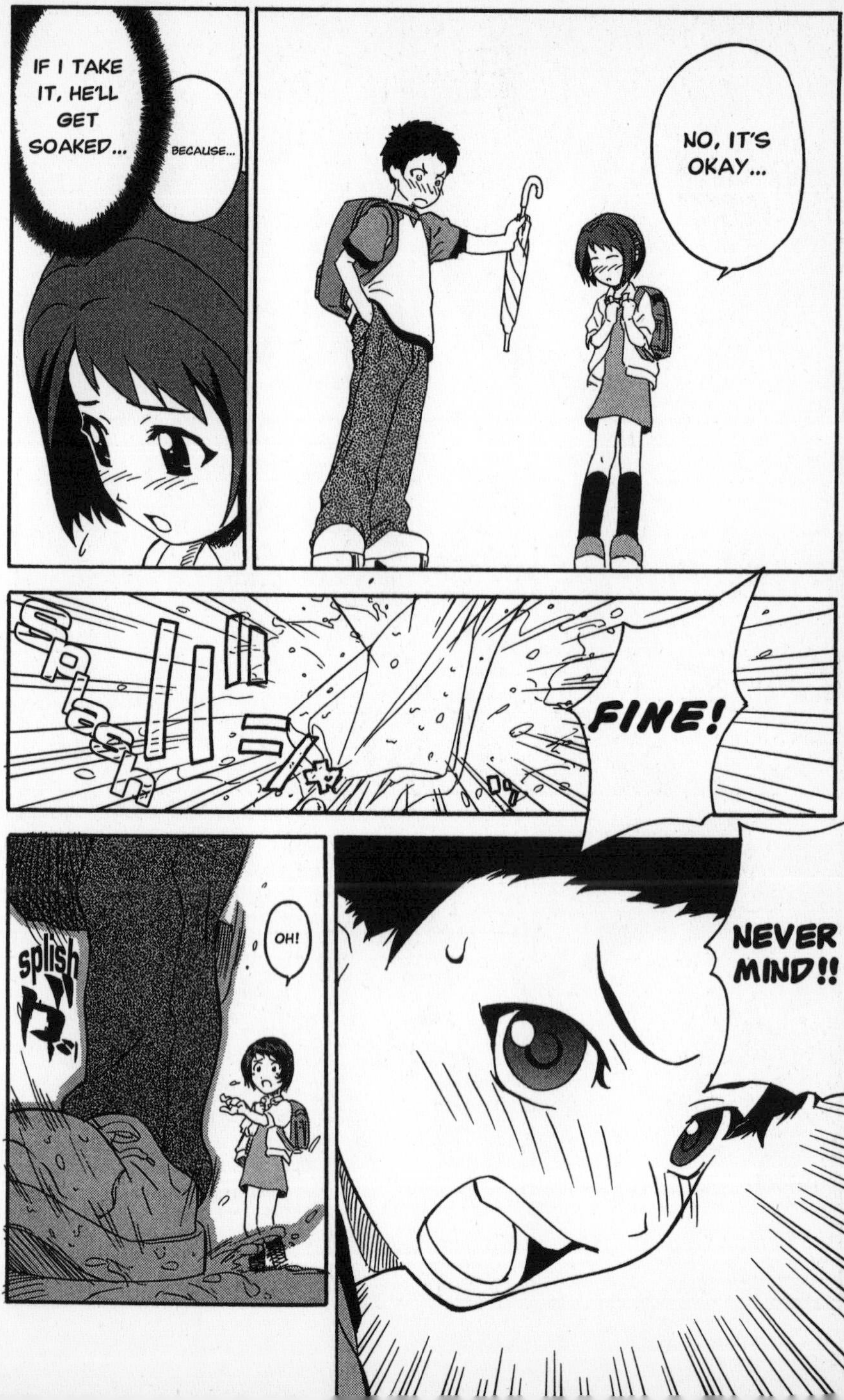
NO, IT'S OKAY...
BECAUSE...
IF I TAKE IT, HE'LL GET SOAKED...
FINE!
Splash
NEVER MIND!!
OH!
splish

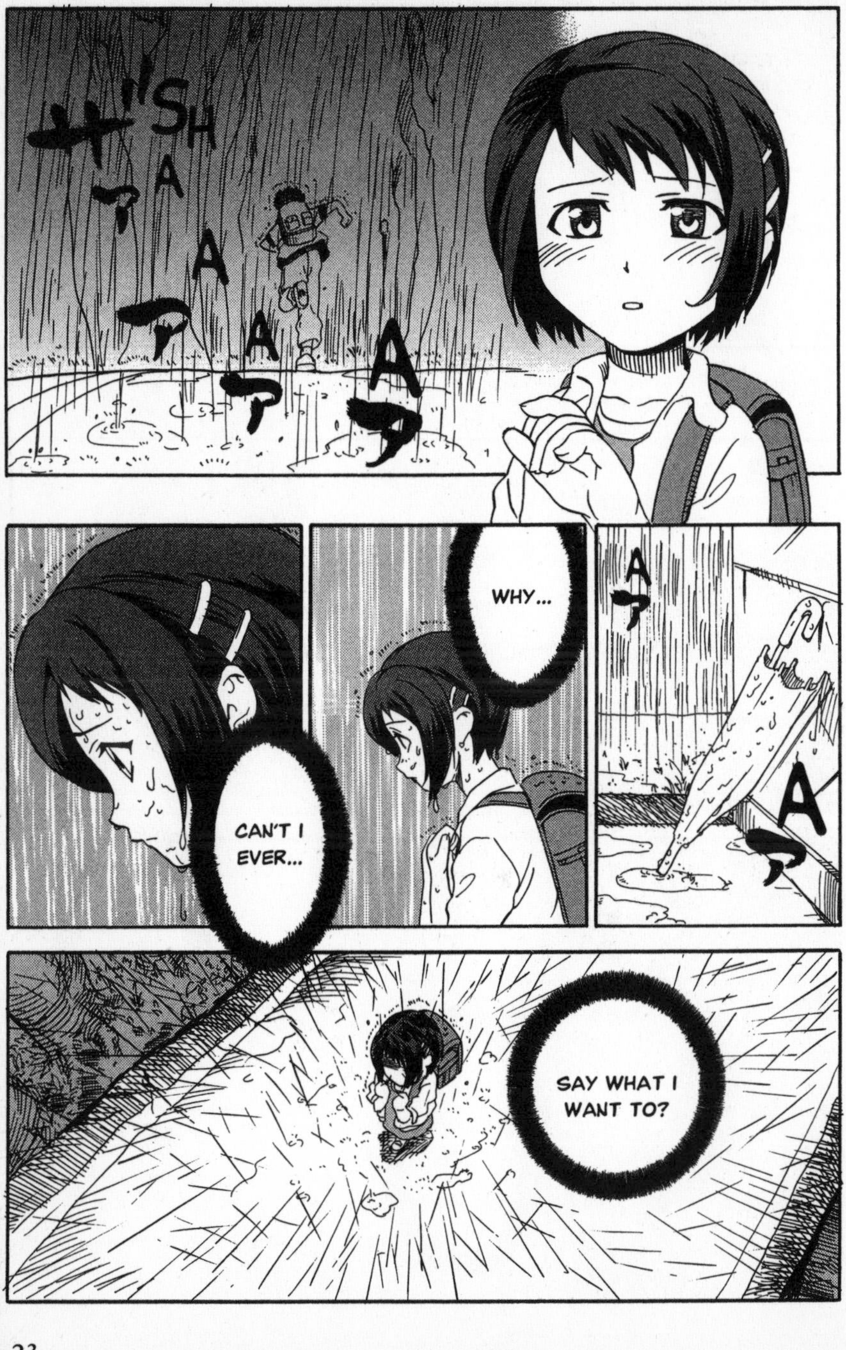
SHAAAA
A
A
WHY...
CAN'T I EVER...
SAY WHAT I WANT TO?

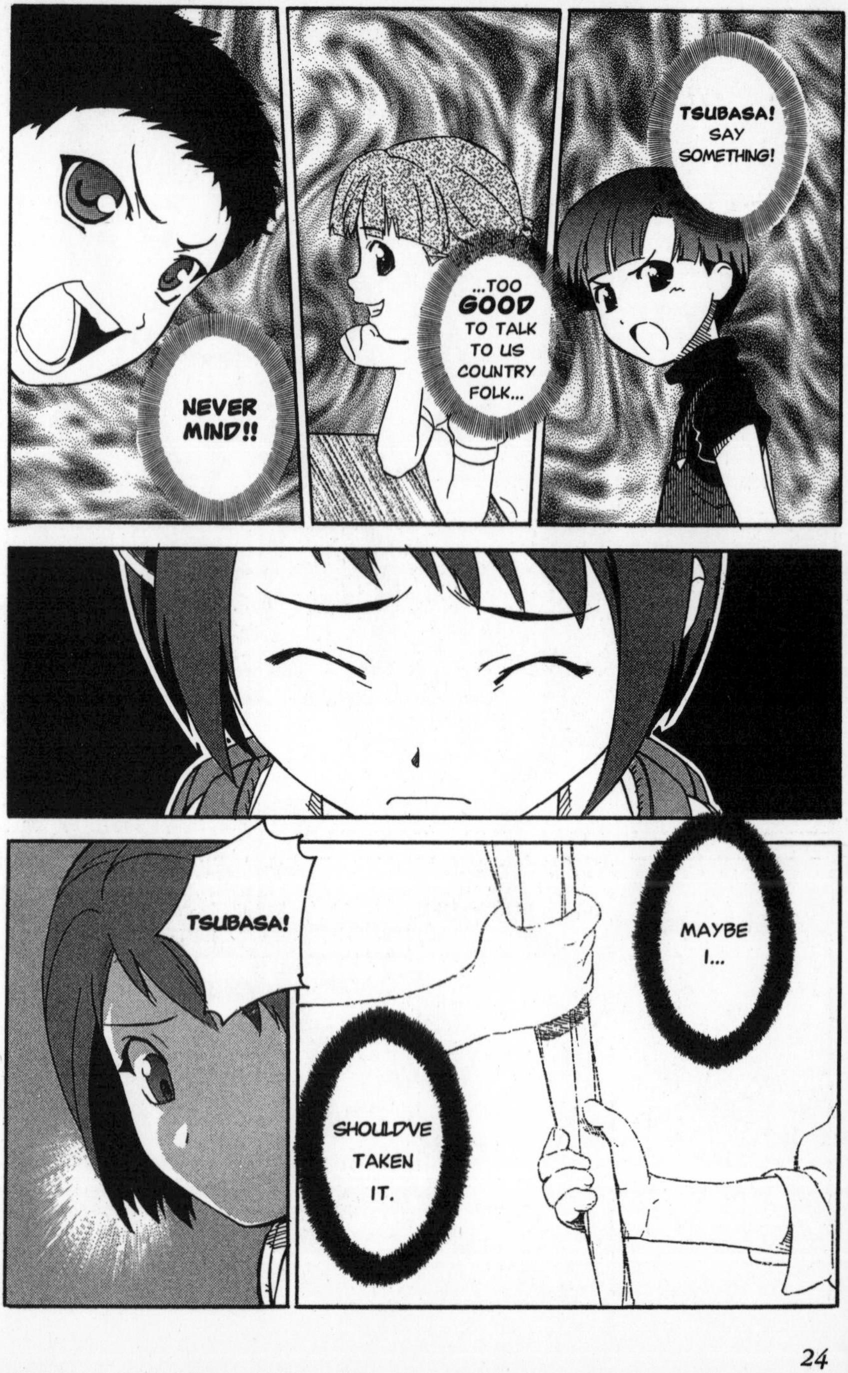
NEVER MIND!!
...TOO GOOD TO TALK TO US COUNTRY FOLK...
TSUBASA! SAY SOMETHING!
TSUBASA!
MAYBE I...
SHOULD'VE TAKEN IT.

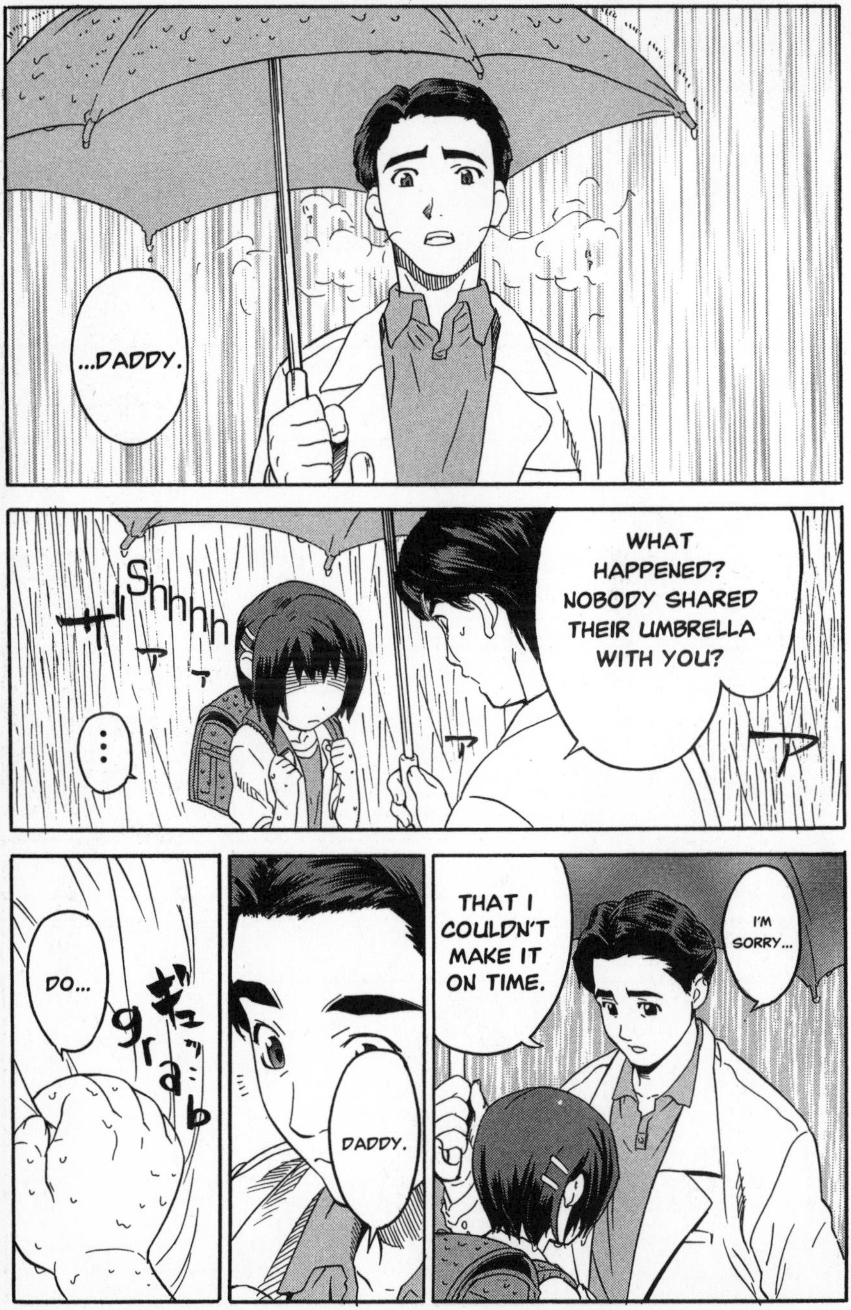
...DADDY.
WHAT HAPPENED? NOBODY SHARED THEIR UMBRELLA WITH YOU?
Shhhh
...
I'M SORRY...
THAT I COULDN'T MAKE IT ON TIME.
DADDY.
DO...
grab

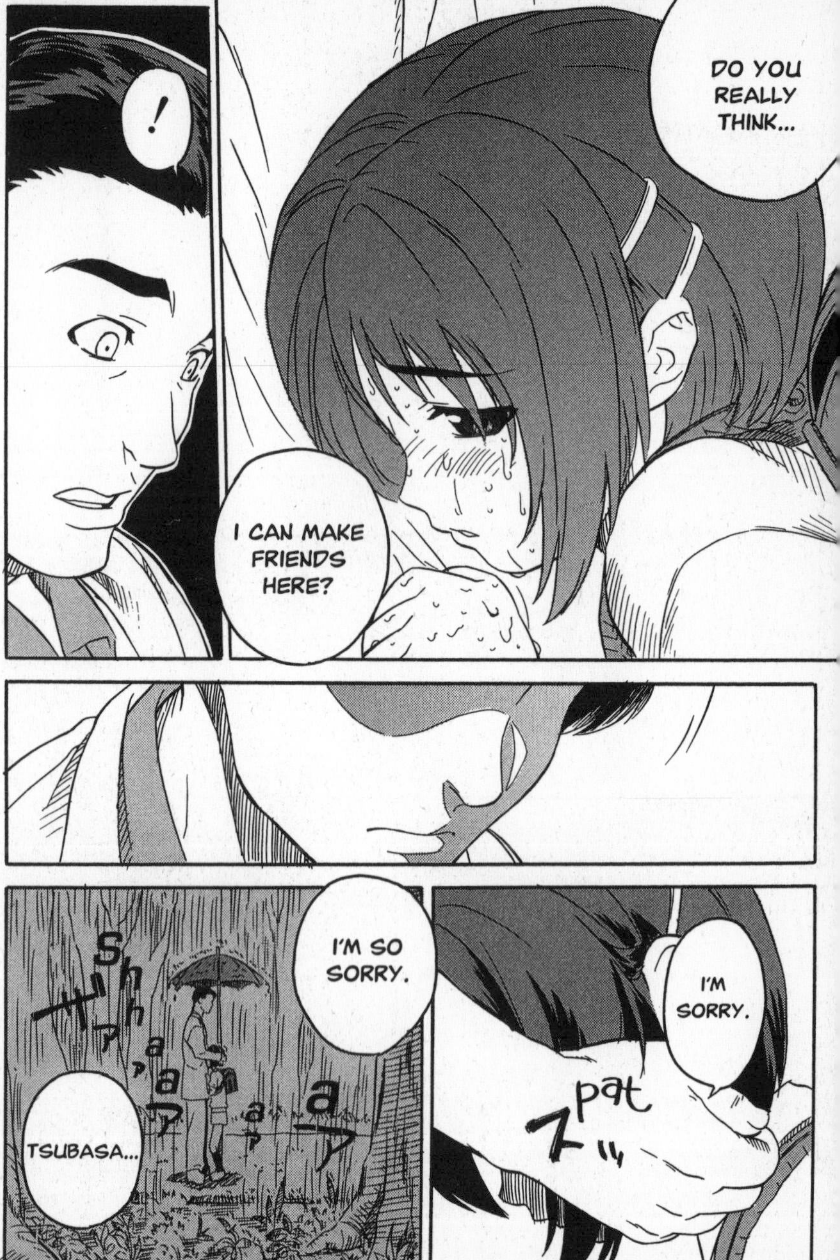
DO YOU REALLY THINK...
I CAN MAKE FRIENDS HERE?
!
I'M SORRY.
pat
I'M SO SORRY.
Shhaaaa
TSUBASA...

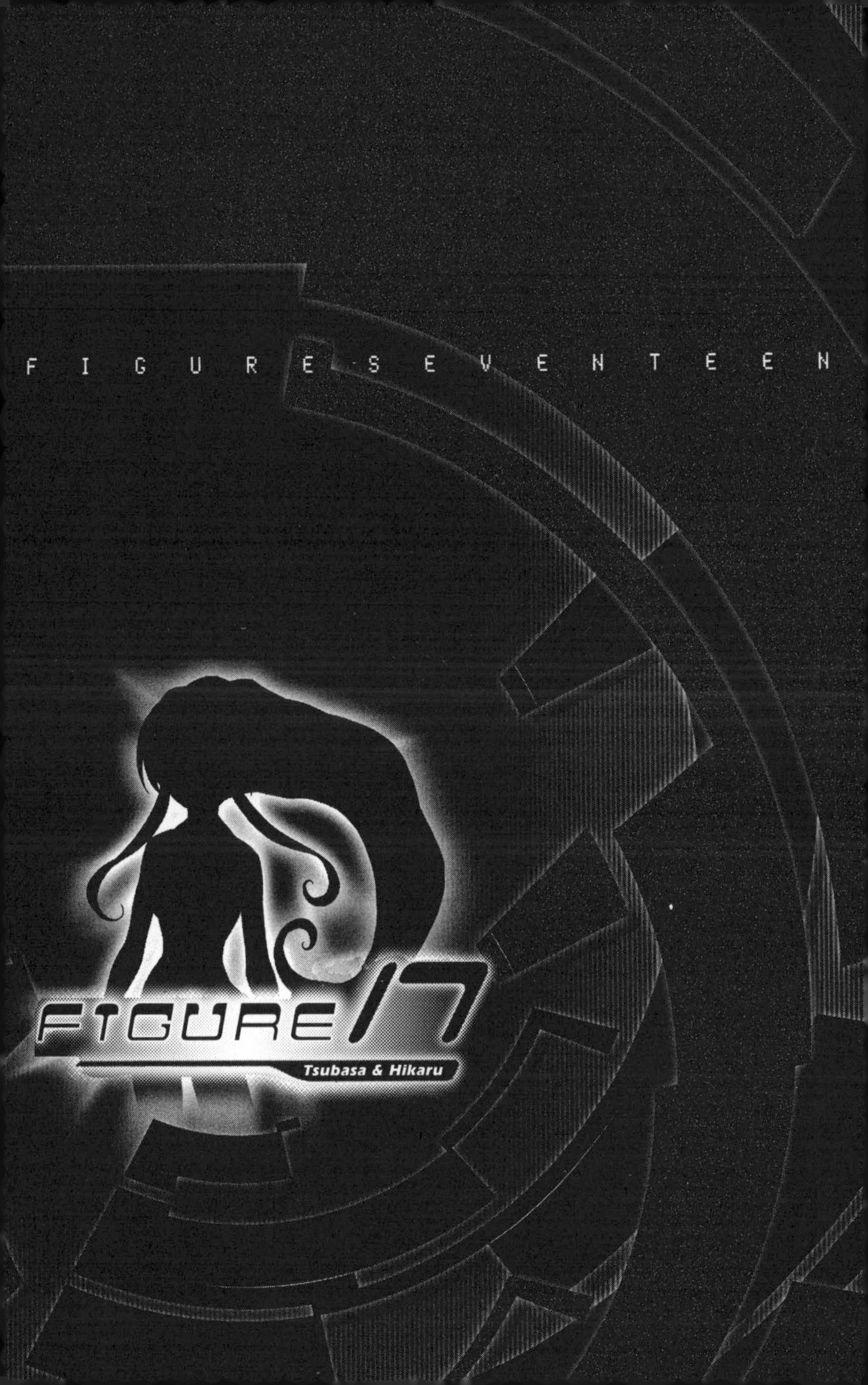
F I G U R E S E V E N T E E N
FIGURE 17
Tsubasa & Hikaru

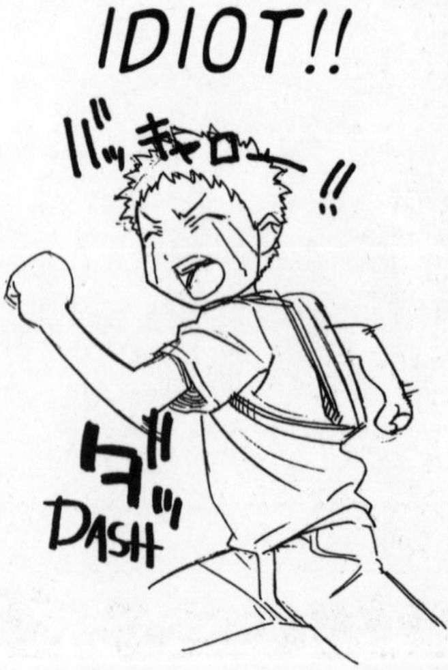
IDIOT!!
バッキャロー!!
ダッ
DASH

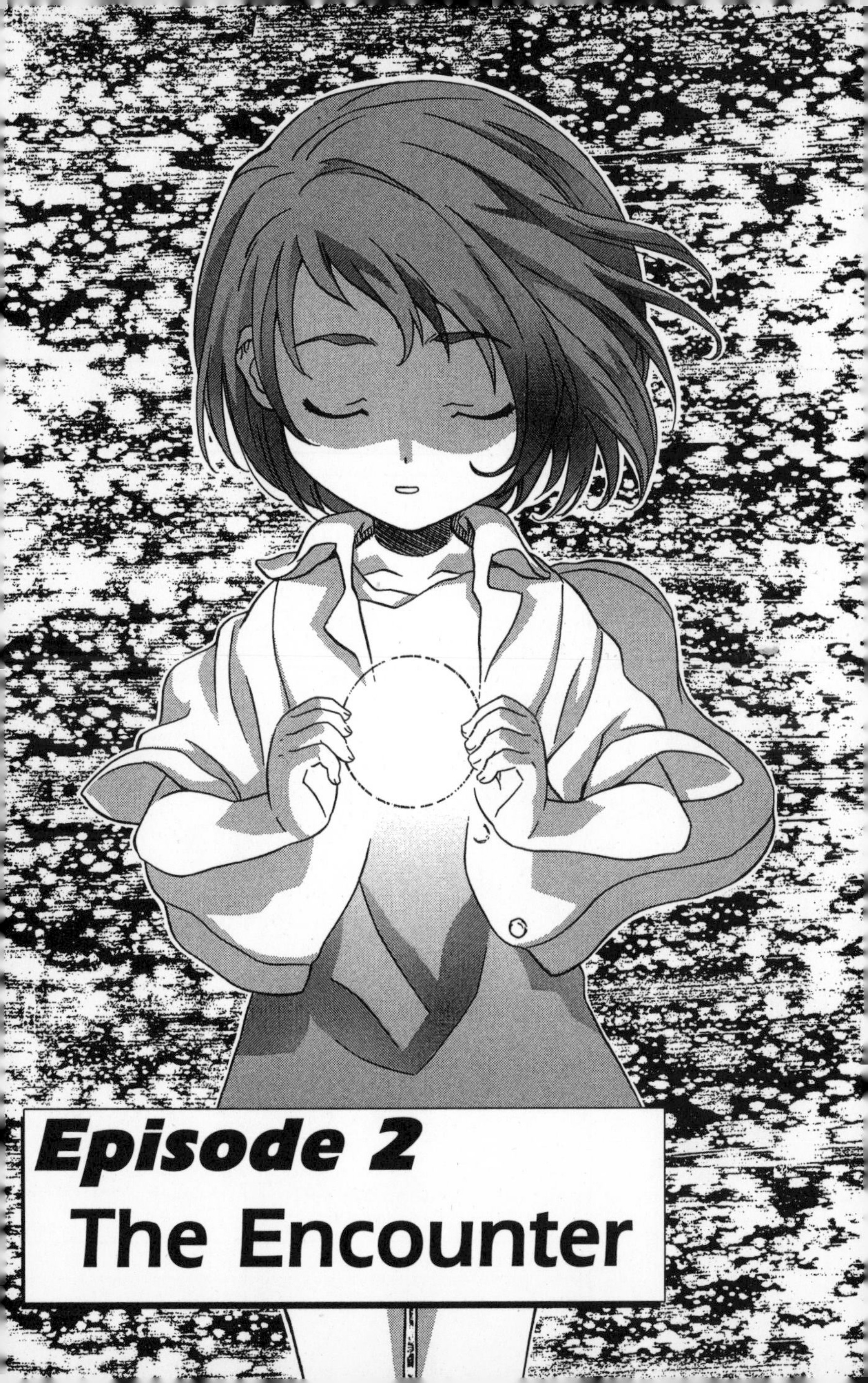

Episode 2
The Encounter

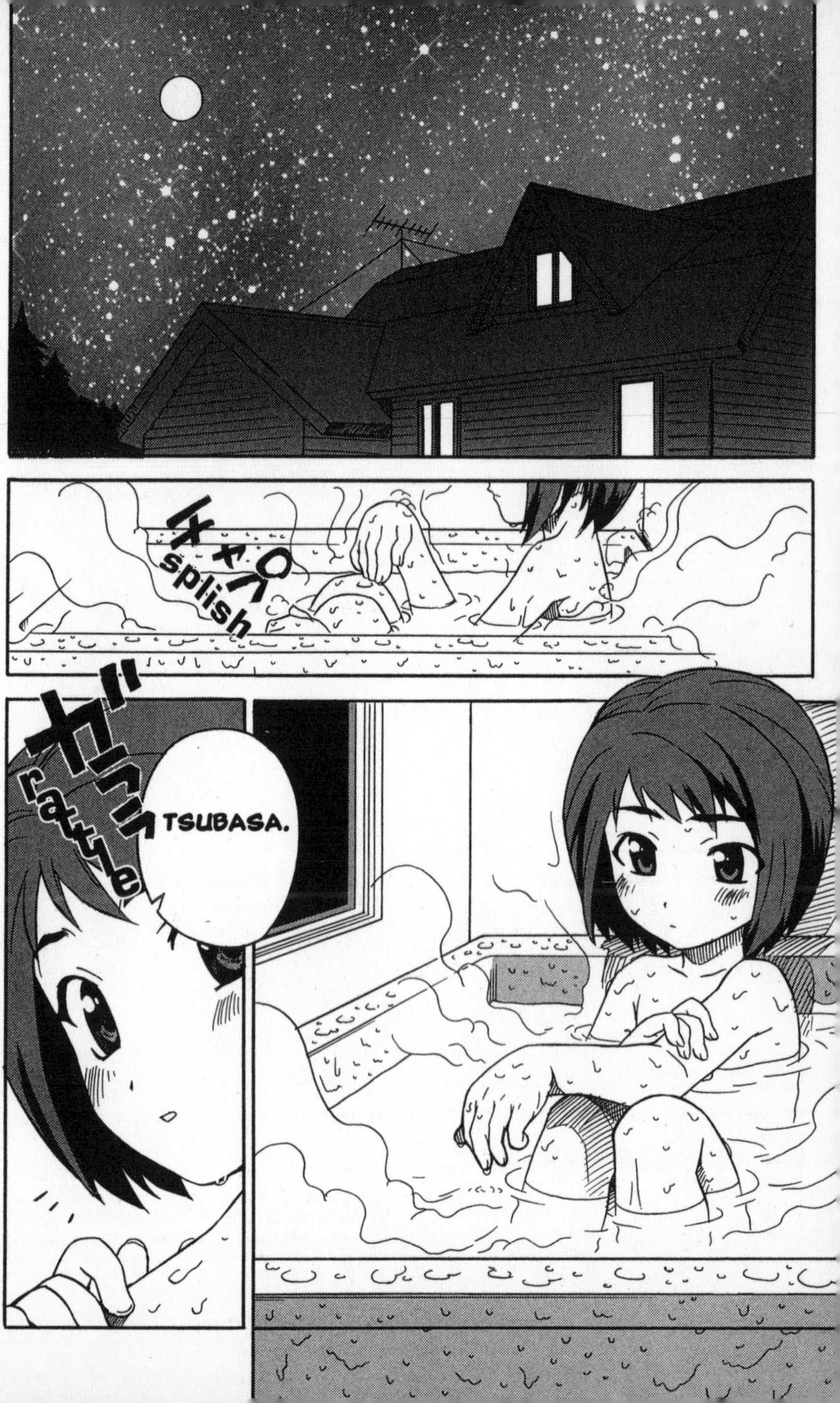
パシャ
splish
rattle
TSUBASA.

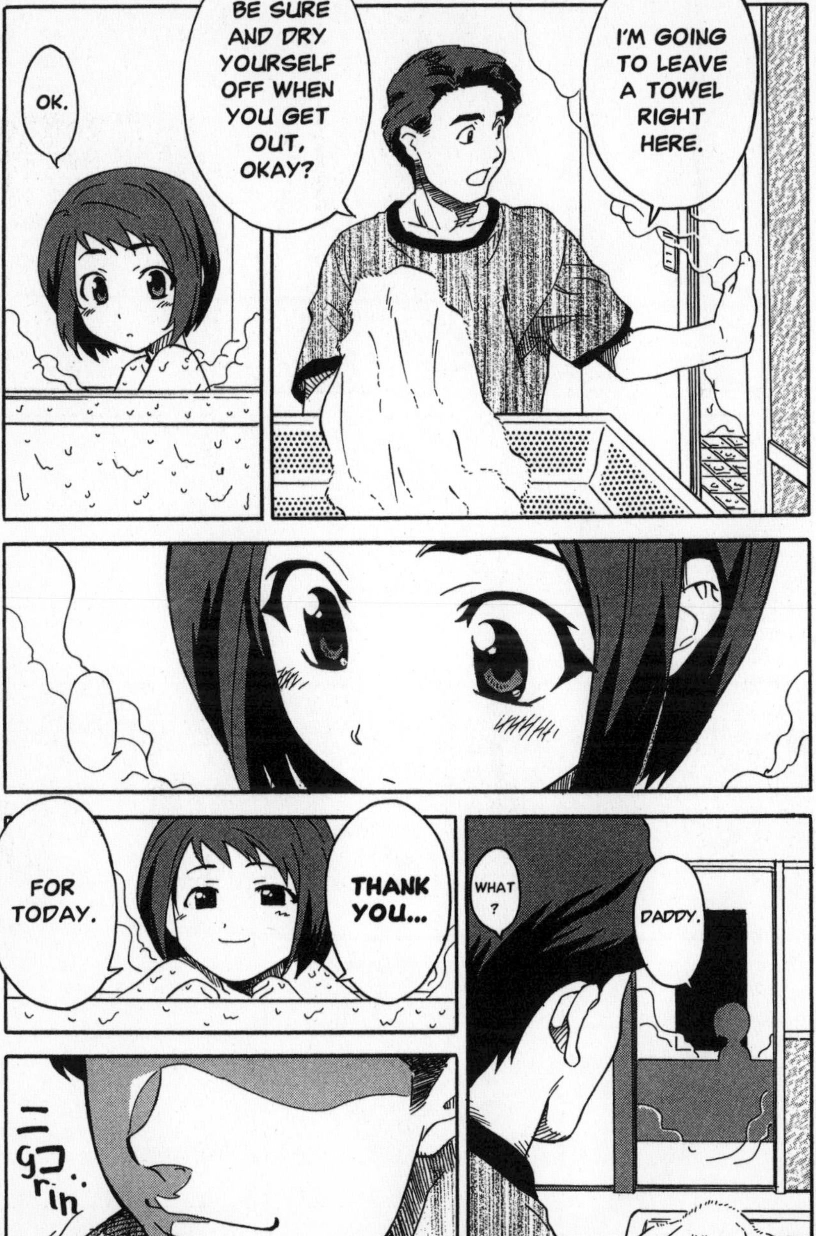
I'M GOING TO LEAVE A TOWEL RIGHT HERE.
BE SURE AND DRY YOURSELF OFF WHEN YOU GET OUT, OKAY?
OK.
THANK YOU...
FOR TODAY.
DADDY.
WHAT?
grin

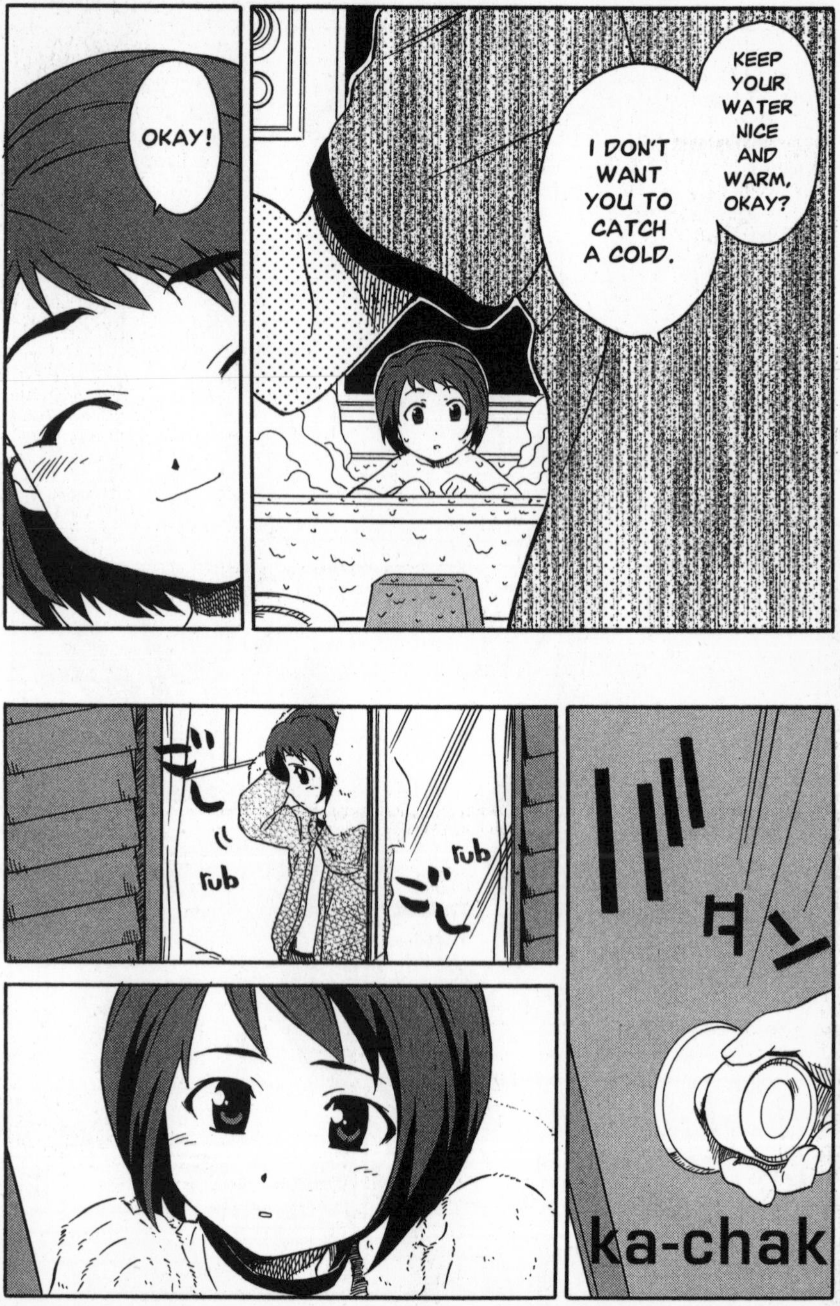
KEEP YOUR WATER NICE AND WARM, OKAY?
I DON'T WANT YOU TO CATCH A COLD.
OKAY!
ka-chak
rub
rub

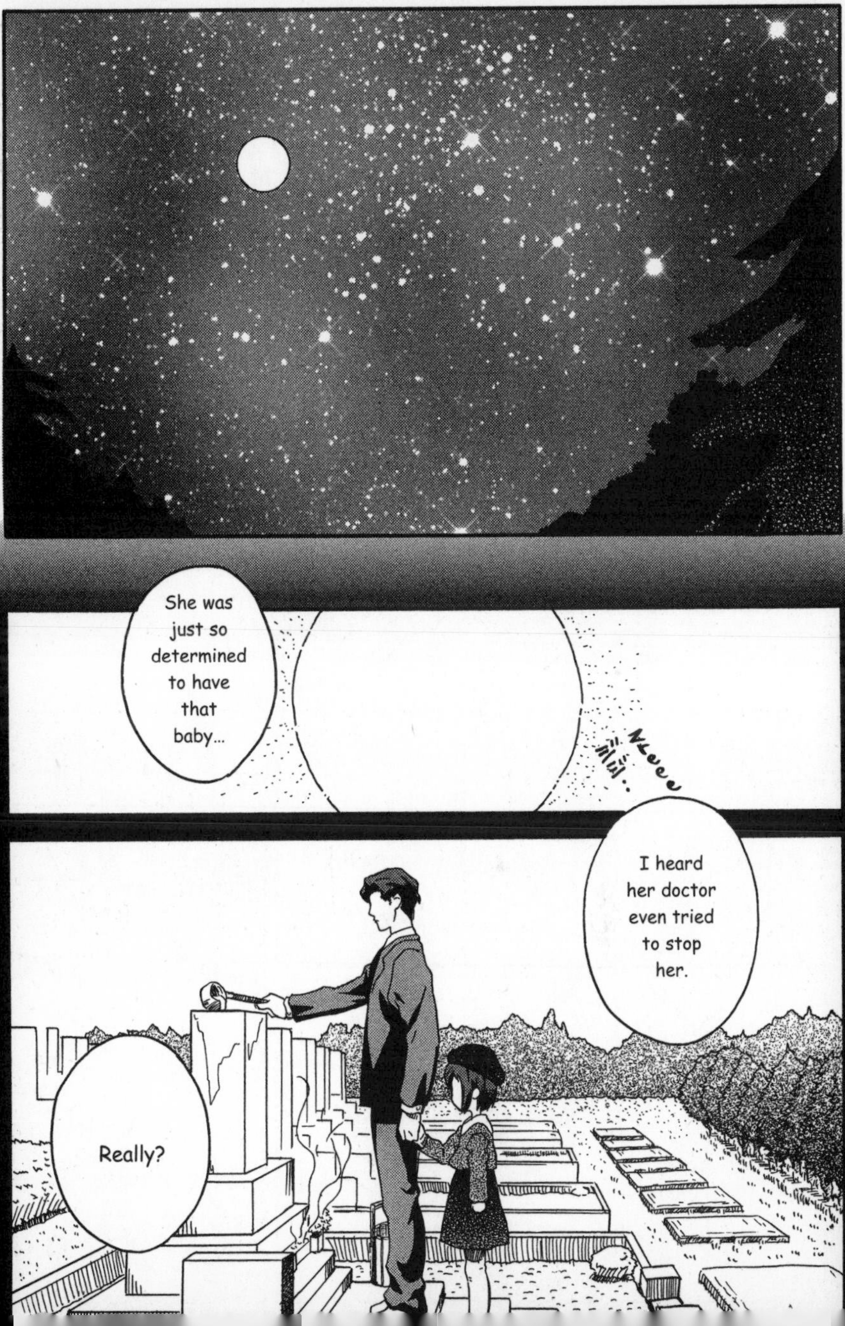
She was just so determined to have that baby...
Neeee
I heard her doctor even tried to stop her.
Really?

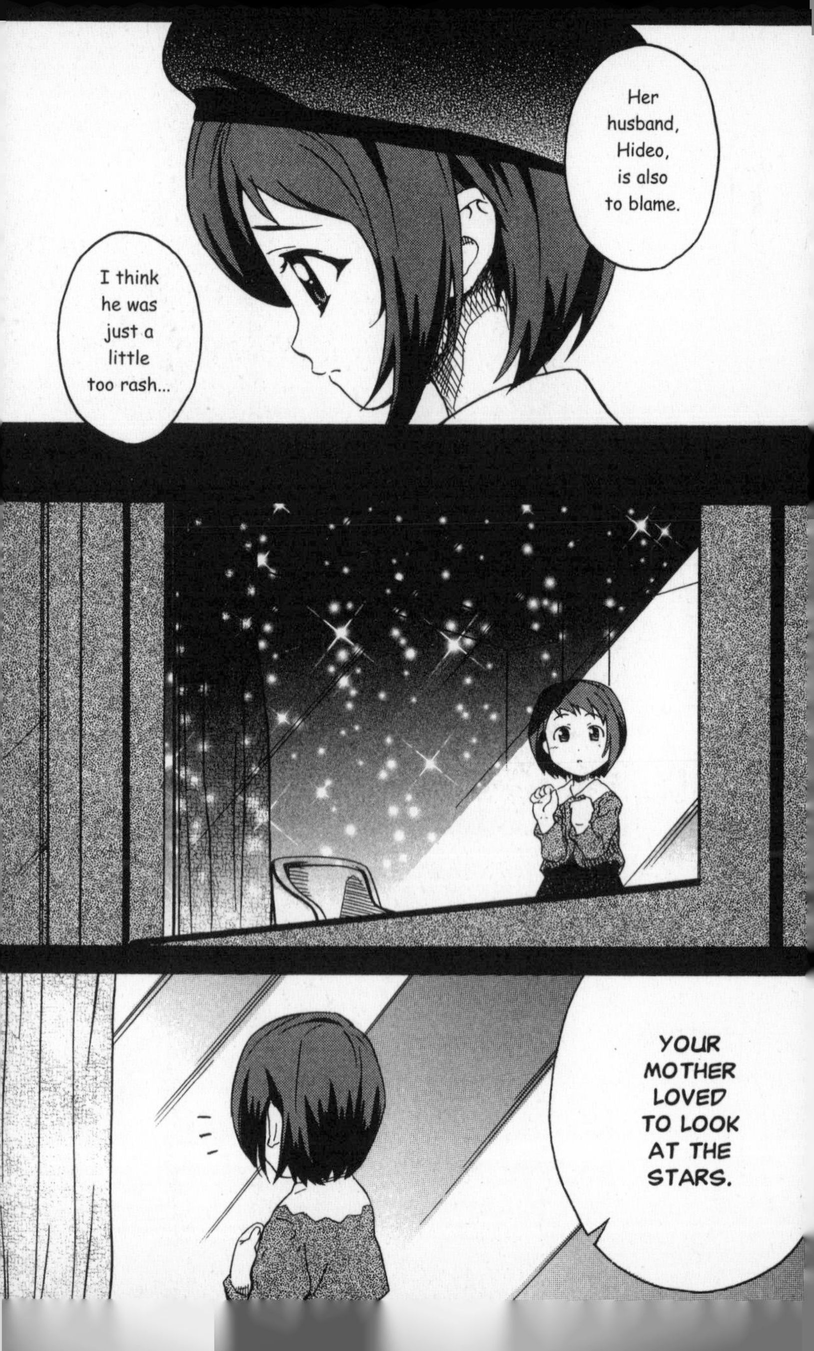
Her husband, Hideo, is also to blame.
I think he was just a little too rash...
YOUR MOTHER LOVED TO LOOK AT THE STARS.

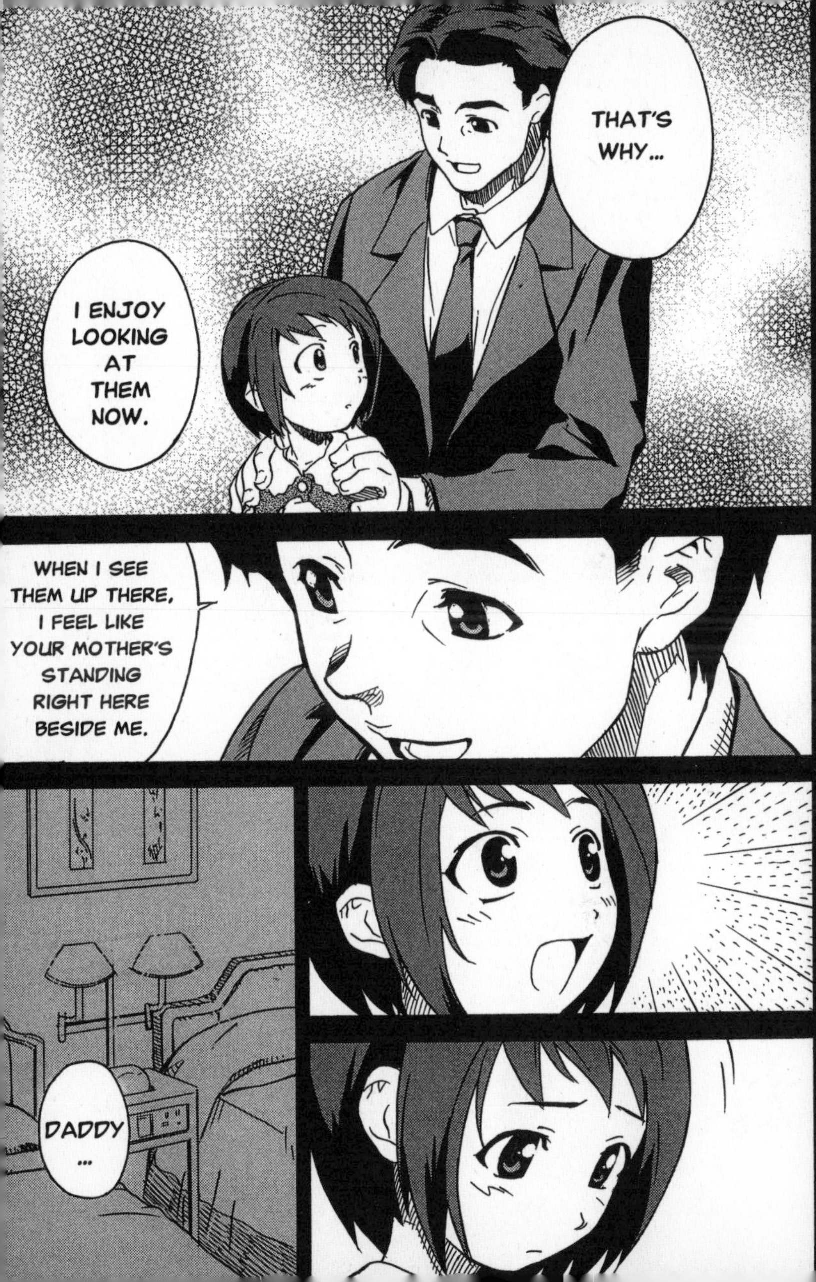
THAT'S WHY...
I ENJOY LOOKING AT THEM NOW.
WHEN I SEE THEM UP THERE, I FEEL LIKE YOUR MOTHER'S STANDING RIGHT HERE BESIDE ME.
DADDY ...

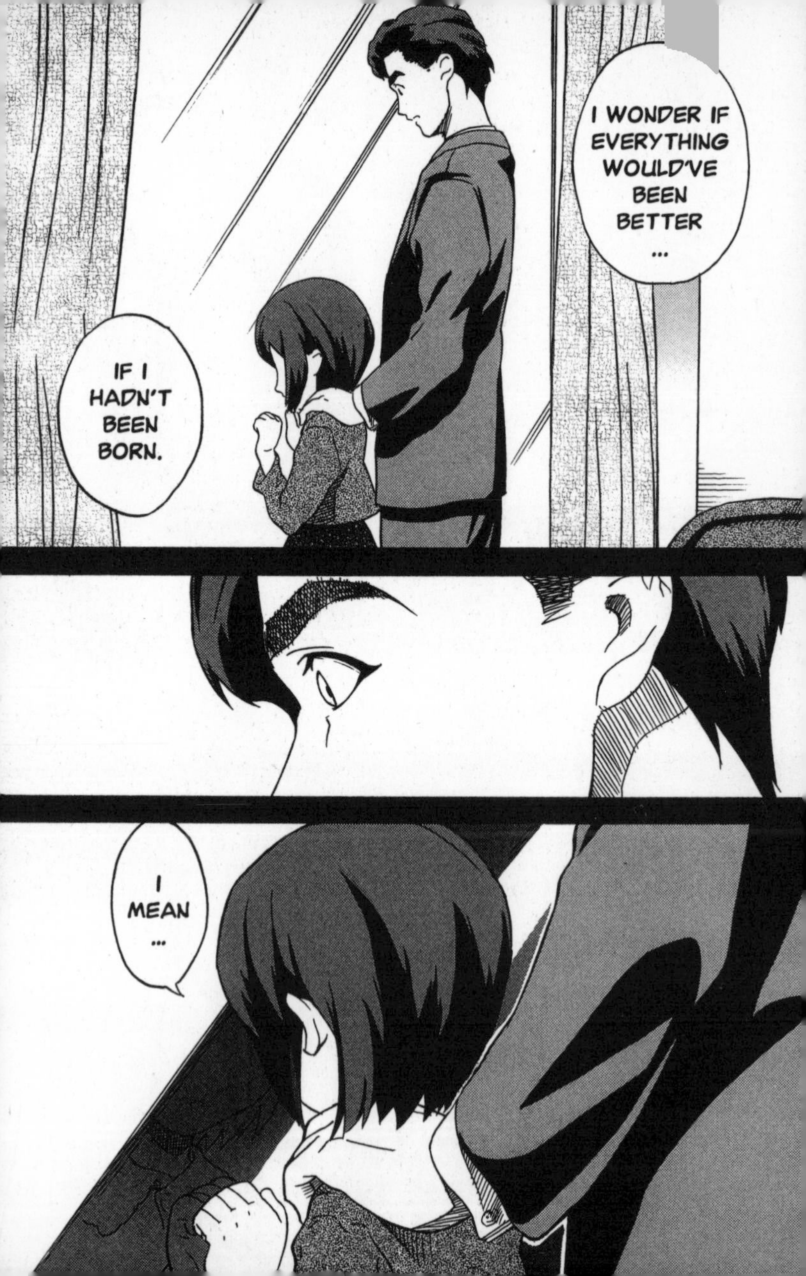
I WONDER IF EVERYTHING WOULD'VE BEEN BETTER ...
IF I HADN'T BEEN BORN.
I MEAN ...

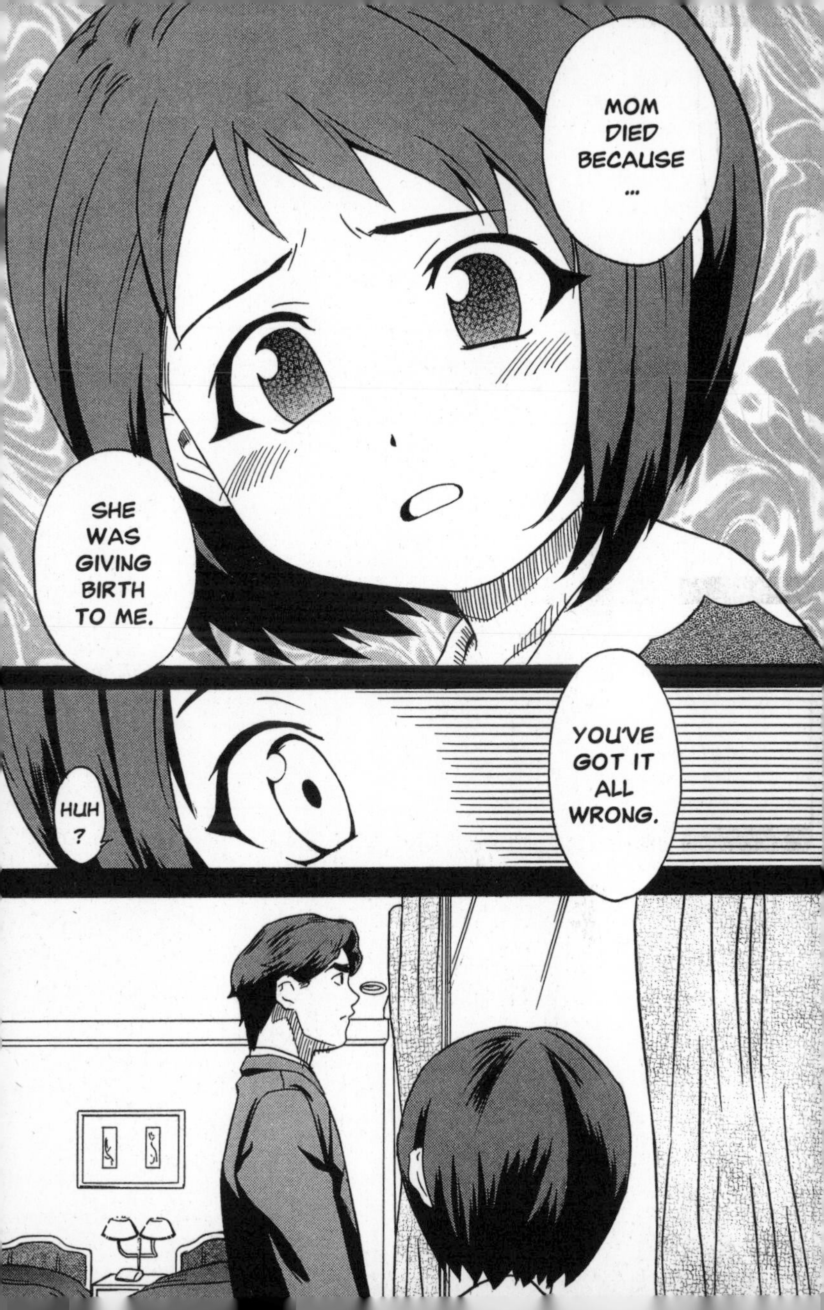
MOM DIED BECAUSE ...
SHE WAS GIVING BIRTH TO ME.
YOU'VE GOT IT ALL WRONG.
HUH?

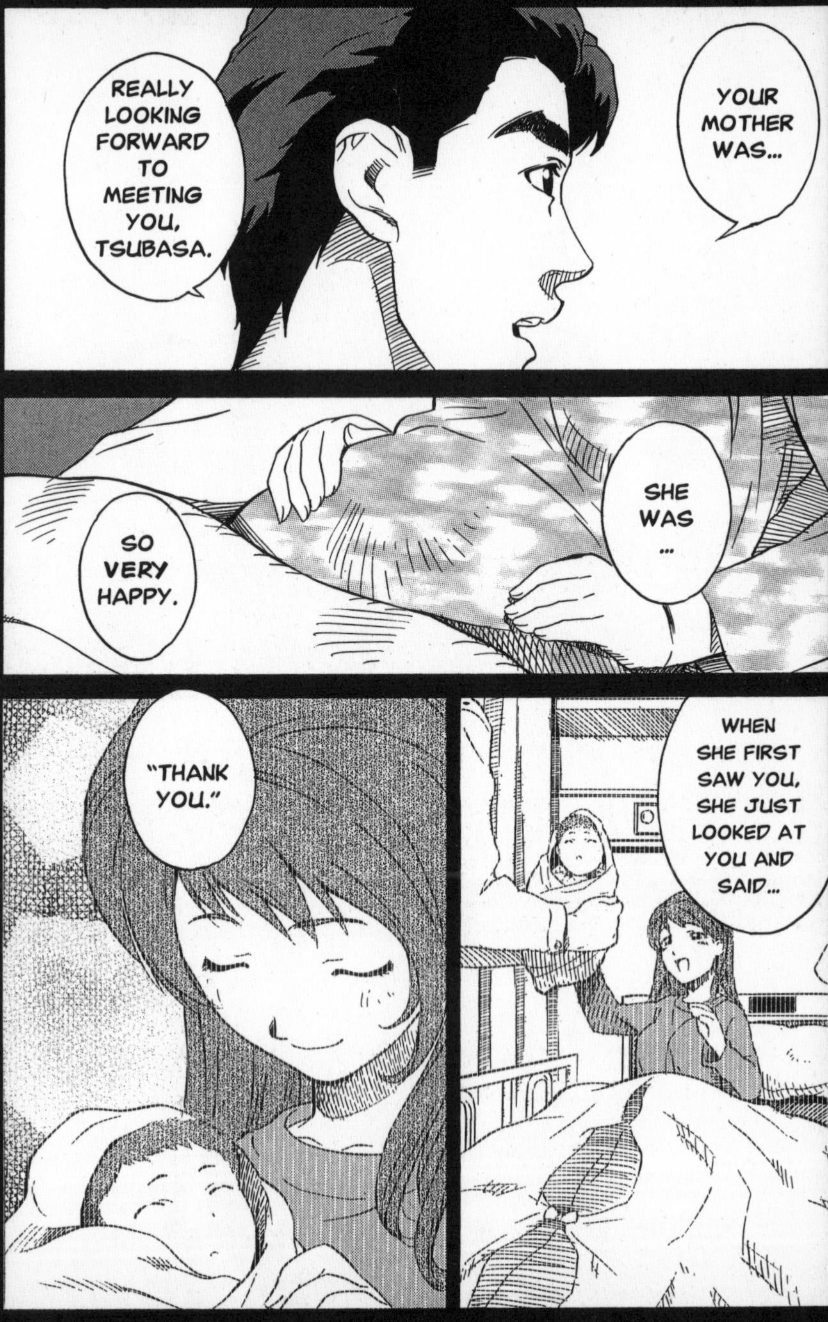
YOUR MOTHER WAS...
REALLY LOOKING FORWARD TO MEETING YOU, TSUBASA.
SHE WAS ...
SO VERY HAPPY.
WHEN SHE FIRST SAW YOU, SHE JUST LOOKED AT YOU AND SAID...
"THANK YOU."

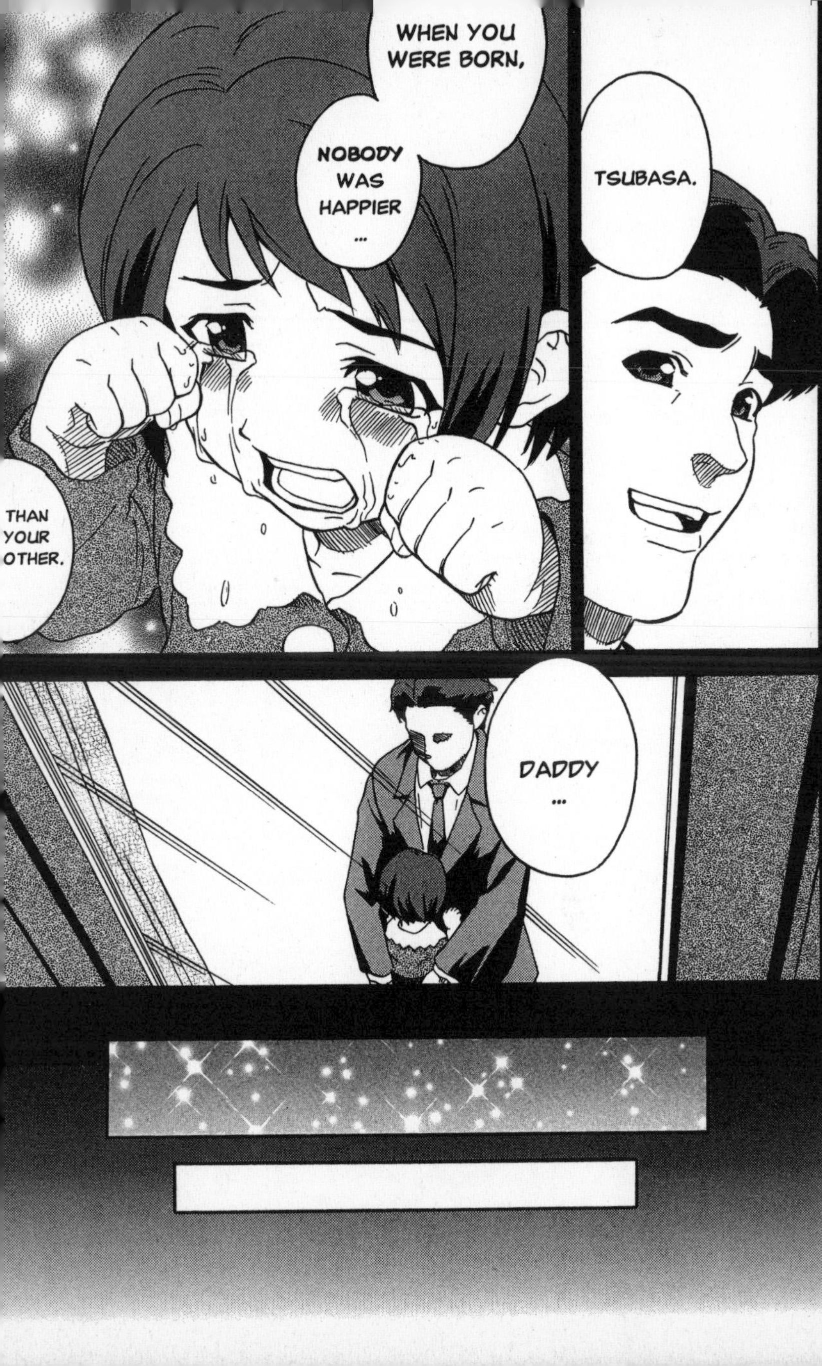
TSUBASA.
WHEN YOU WERE BORN,
NOBODY WAS HAPPIER ...
THAN YOUR OTHER.
DADDY ...

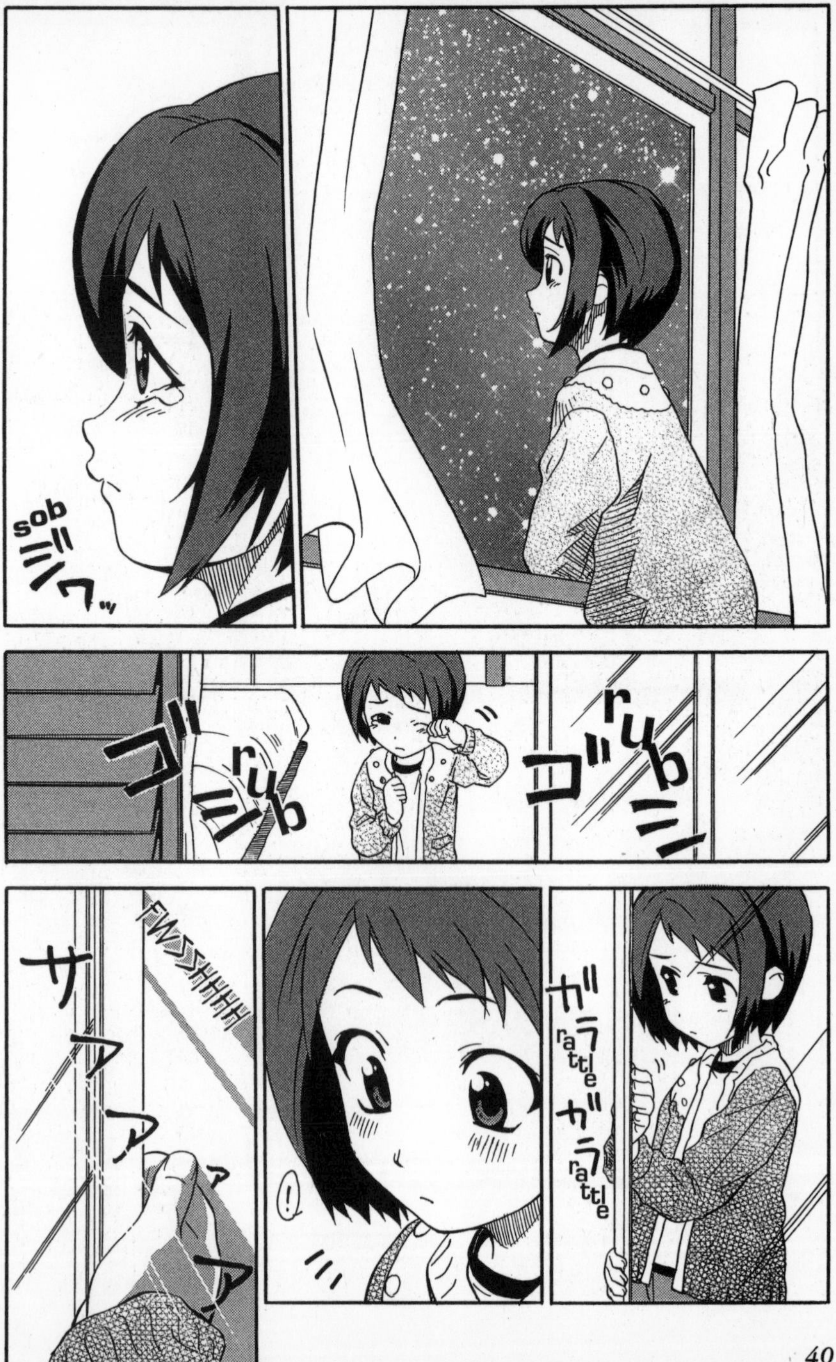
sob
ジワッ
rub
ゴシ
rub
ゴシ
ガラ
rattle
ガラ
rattle
!
FWSSHHHH
サァァァァ

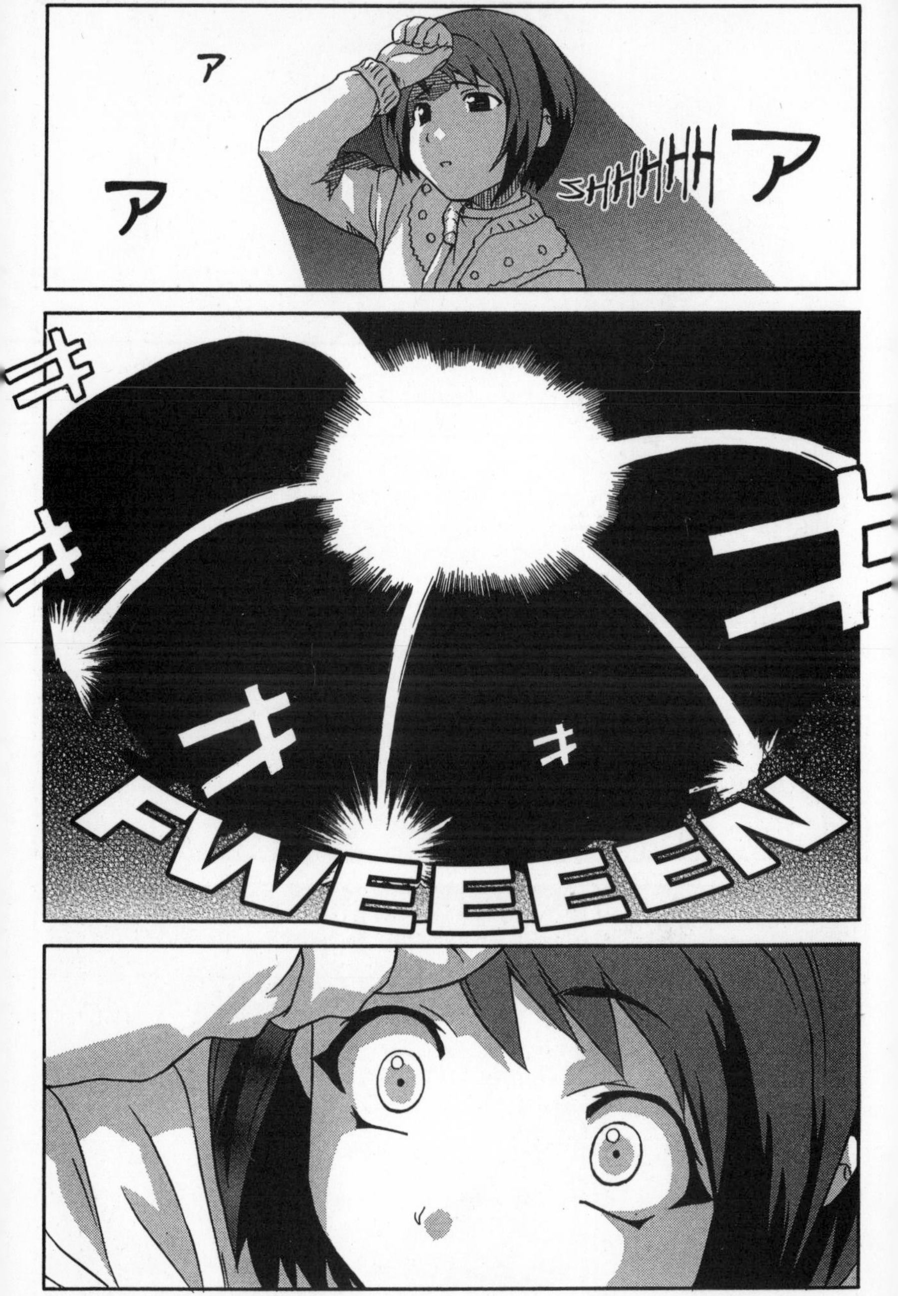
アアア
SHHHHHH
キキキキキ
FWEEEEN

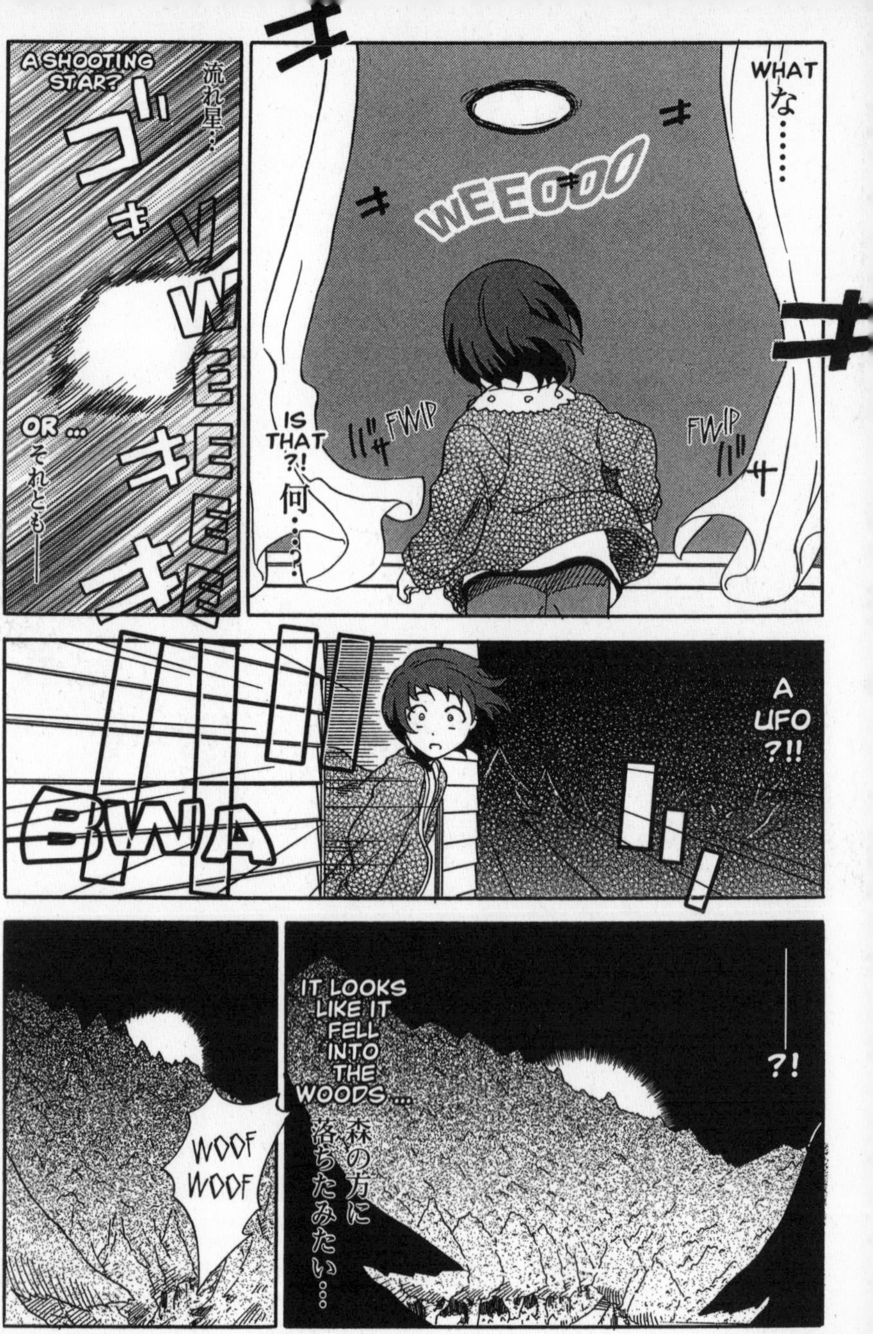
WHAT
な……
WEEOOO
FWIP
FWIP
IS THAT?!
何…?
A SHOOTING STAR?
流れ星…
WHEEE
OR…
それとも——
A UFO?!!
BWA
——?!
IT LOOKS LIKE IT FELL INTO THE WOODS…
森の方に落ちたみたい…
WOOF WOOF

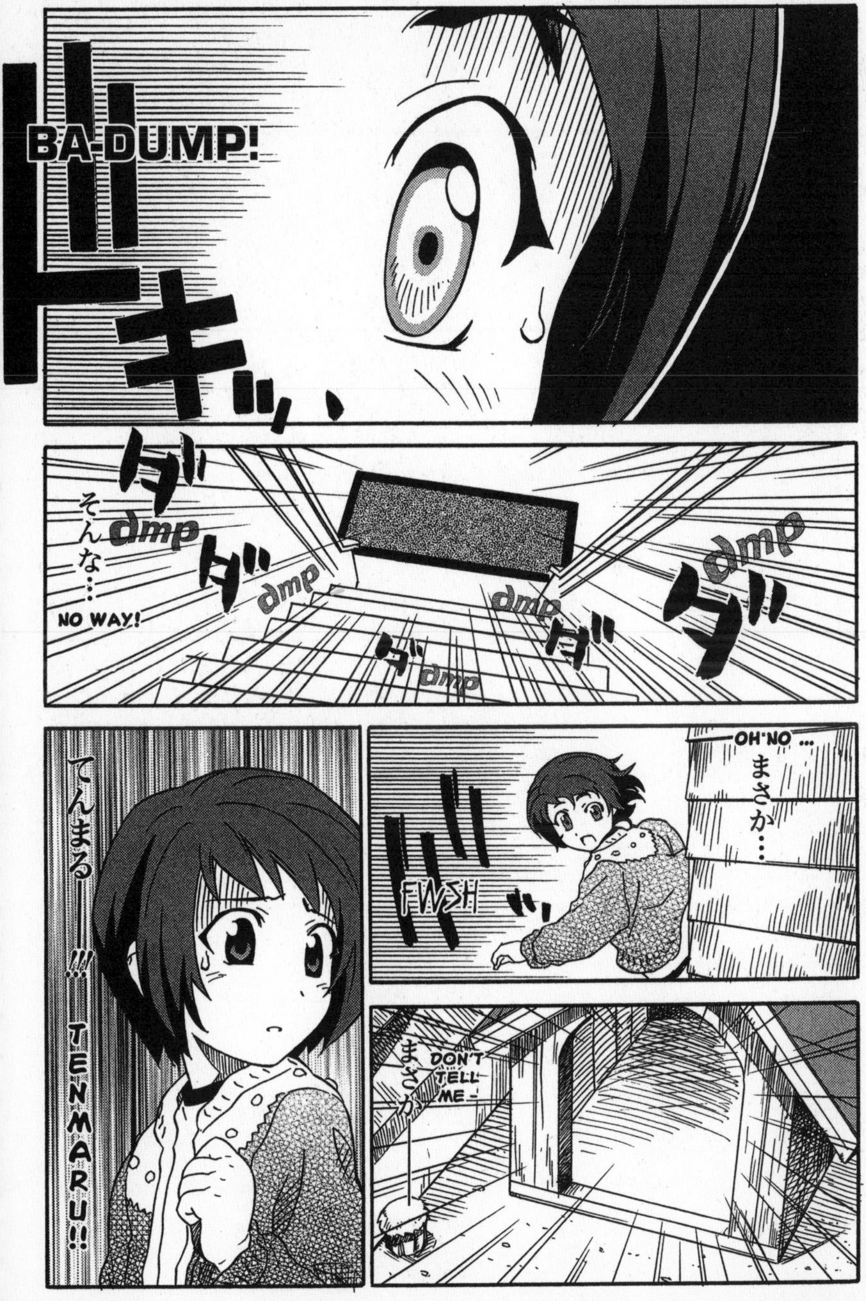

BA-DUMP!
dmp
dmp
dmp
dmp
dmp
そんな…
NO WAY!
OH NO ...
まさか…
FWSH
てんまる
!!!
TENMARU!!
まさか
DON'T TELL ME -

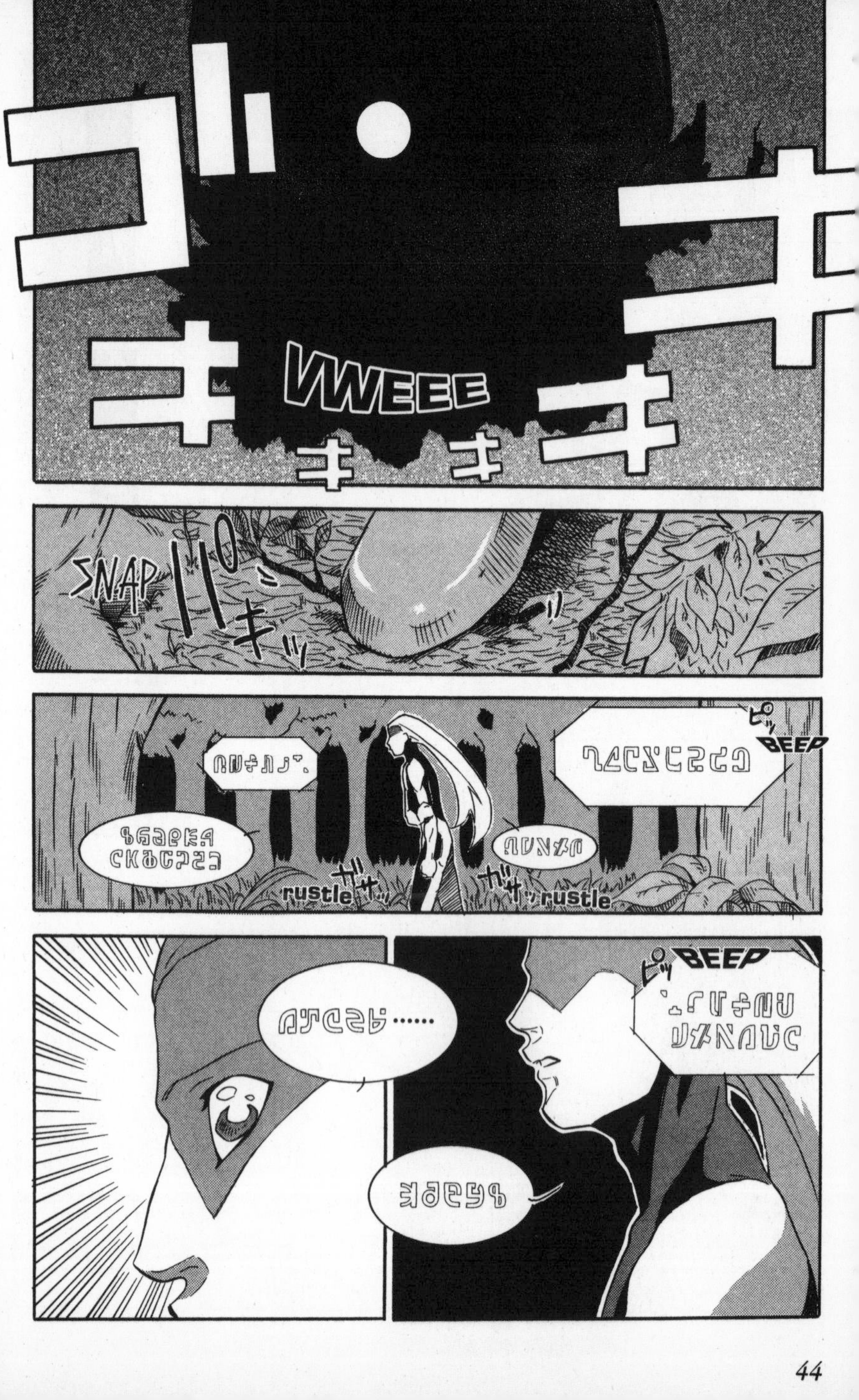

VWEEE
SNAP
パキッ
ピッ BEEP
ガサッ rustle
ガサッ rustle
ピッ BEEP

VMmMMmmmM
WHHHHHH
SHORR
kaTHUNK

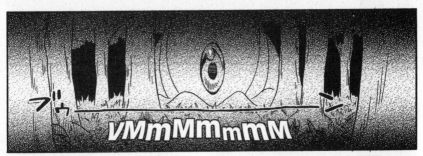

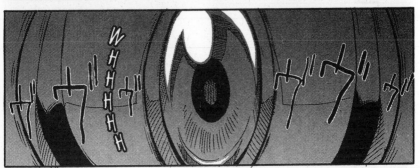

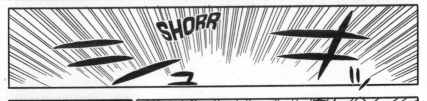

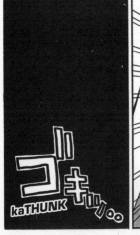

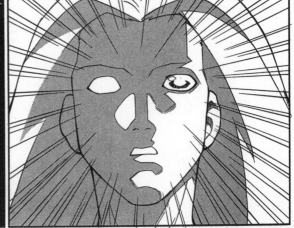

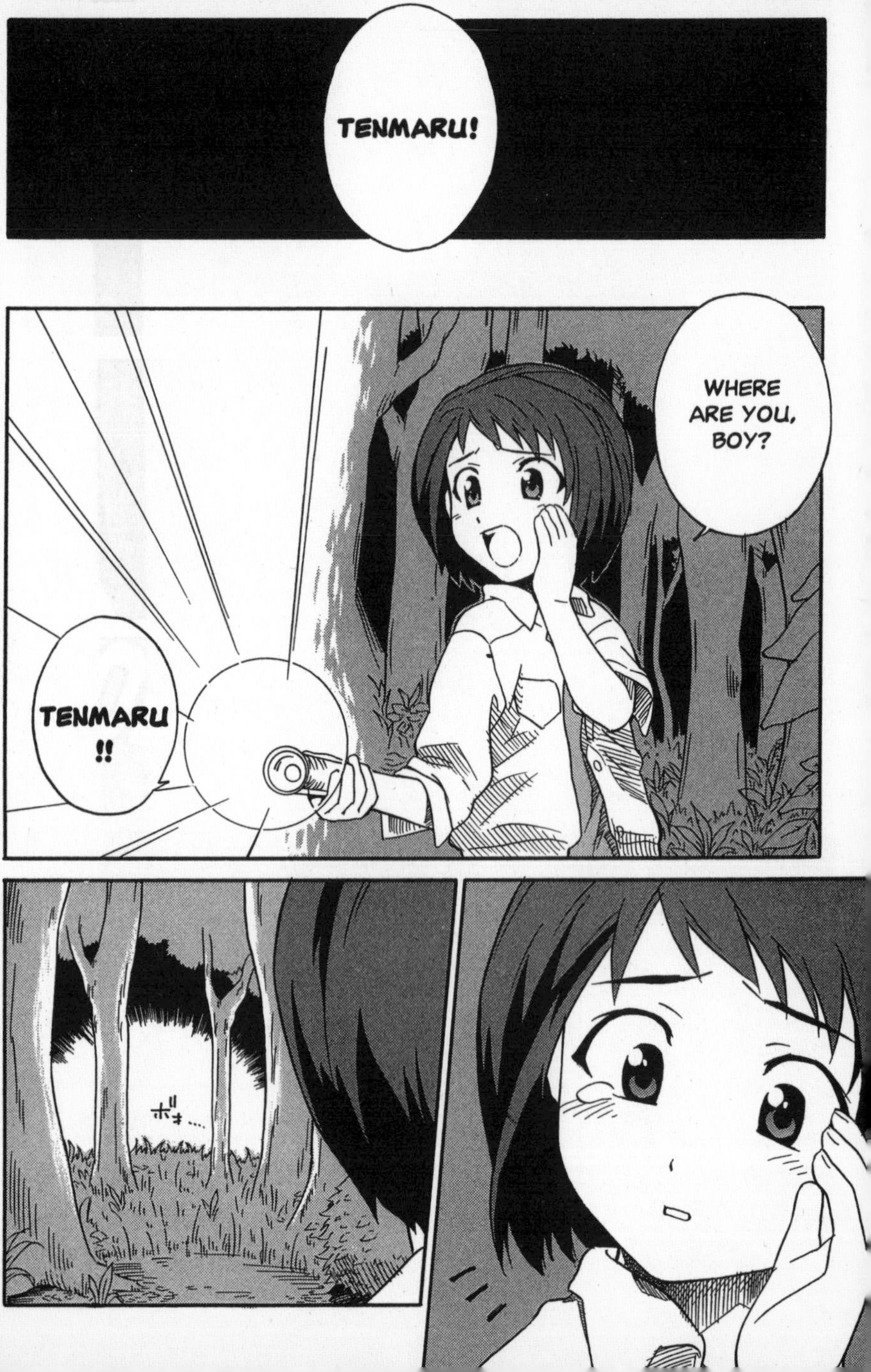
TENMARU!
WHERE ARE YOU, BOY?
TENMARU !!
ボォ....

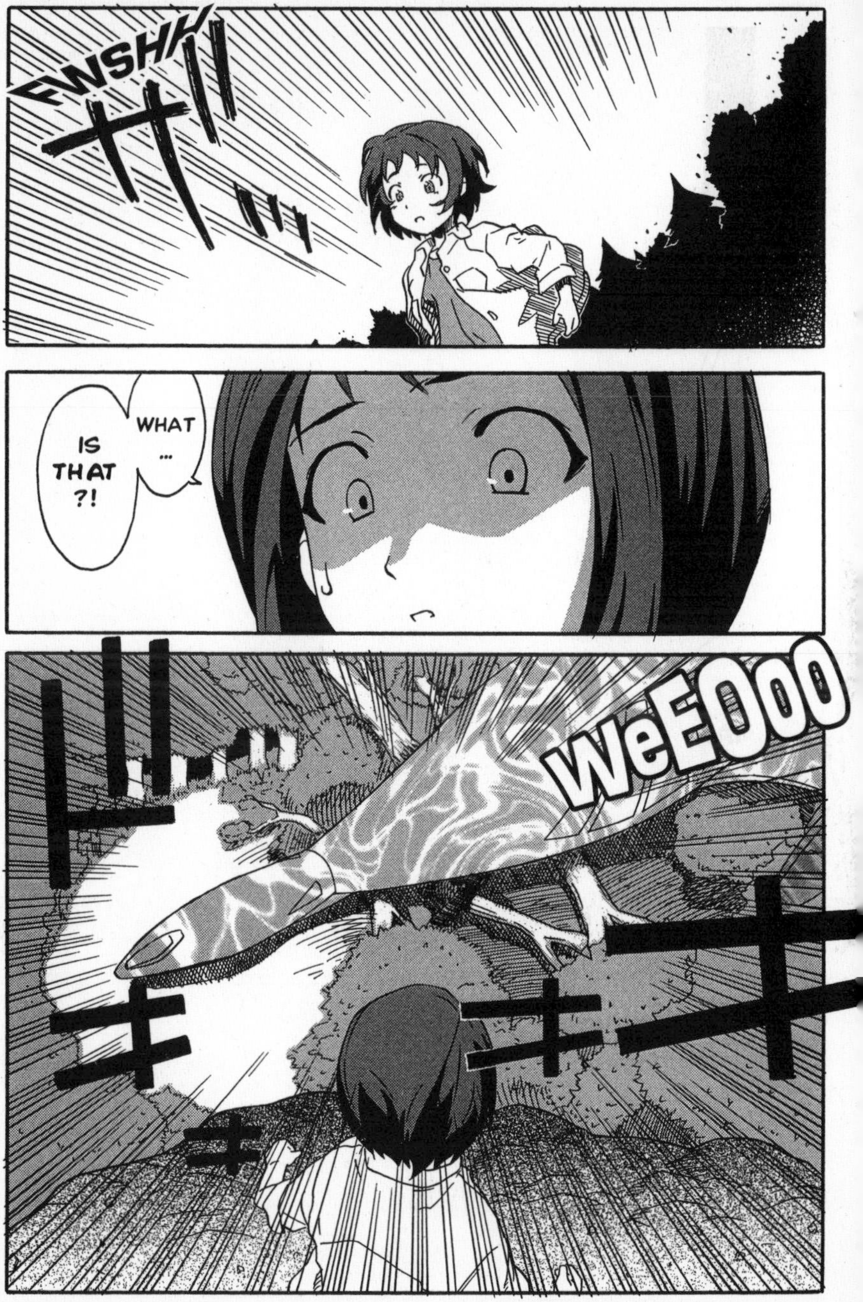
FWSHH
WHAT ...
IS THAT ?!
WeEOOO

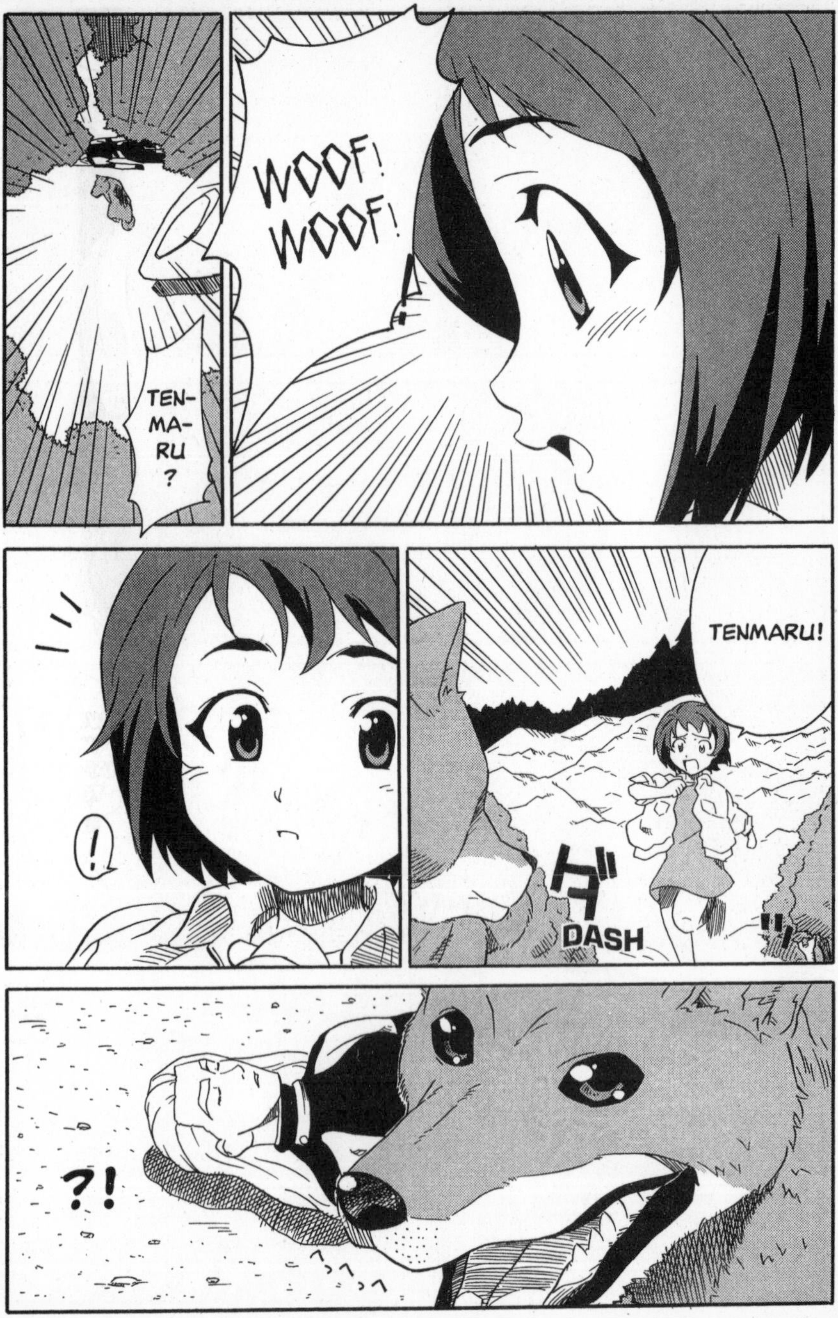
WOOF! WOOF!
!
TEN-MA-RU ?
TENMARU!
ダ
DASH
!
?!

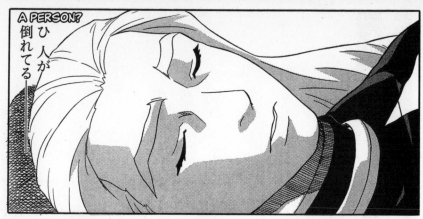

A PERSON?

ひ人が倒れてる——

...!

UM...

ARE YOU OKAY?

もしかして何かに巻き込まれたんじゃ...

I WONDER WHAT HAPPENED TO HIM

TWITCH ピク

ケガしてる... HE'S HURT

スピ スピ スピ

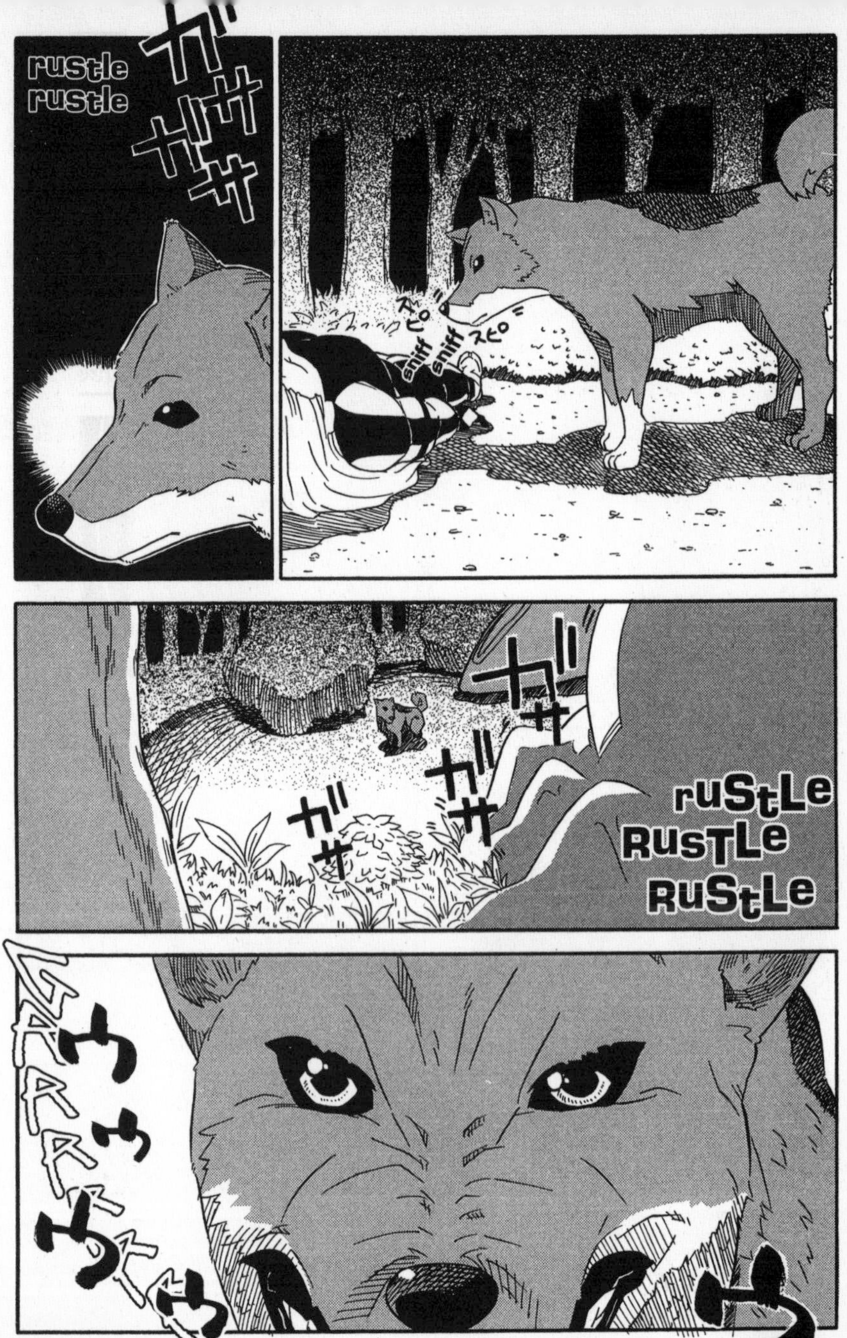
スピ スピ
sniff sniff
ガサガサ
rustle rustle
ガサ ガサ ガサ
rustle rustle rustle
ウゥゥゥ
GRRRRRR

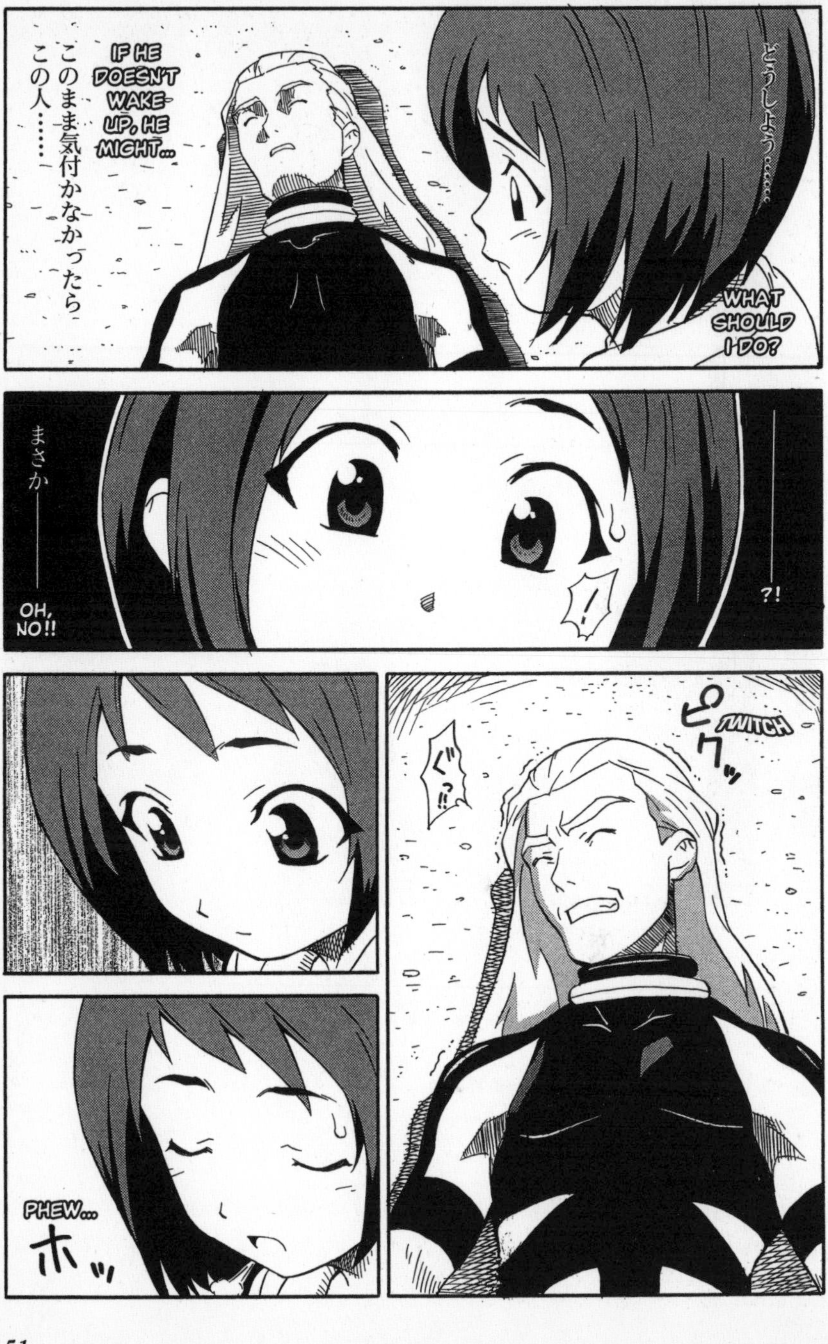
どうしよう……
WHAT SHOULD I DO?
このまま気付かなかったらこの人……
IF HE DOESN'T WAKE UP, HE MIGHT...
——
?!
まさか——
OH, NO!!
!
ピクッ
TWITCH
ぐっ?!
ホッ
PHEW...

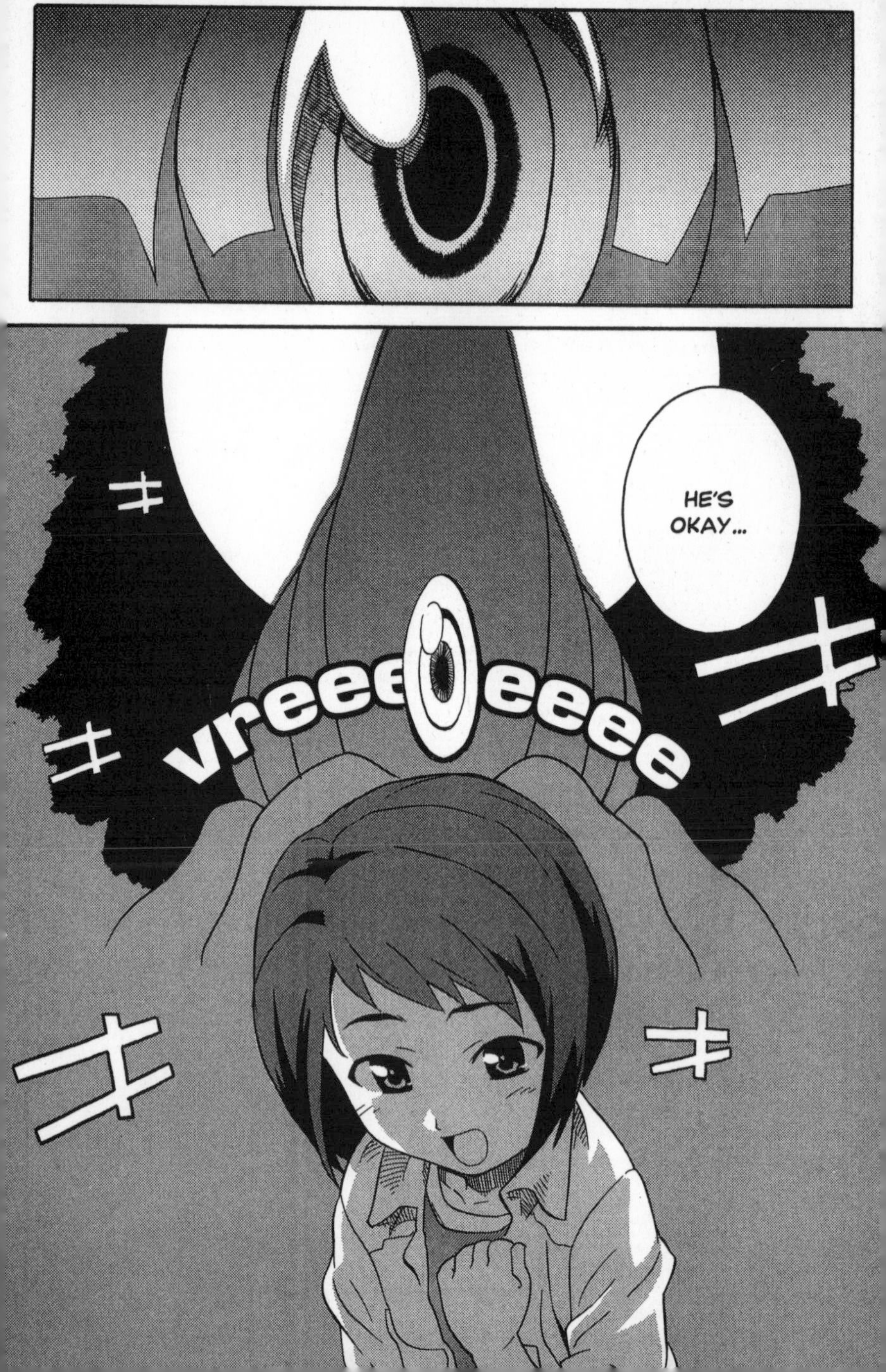
HE'S OKAY...
vreeeeeeee

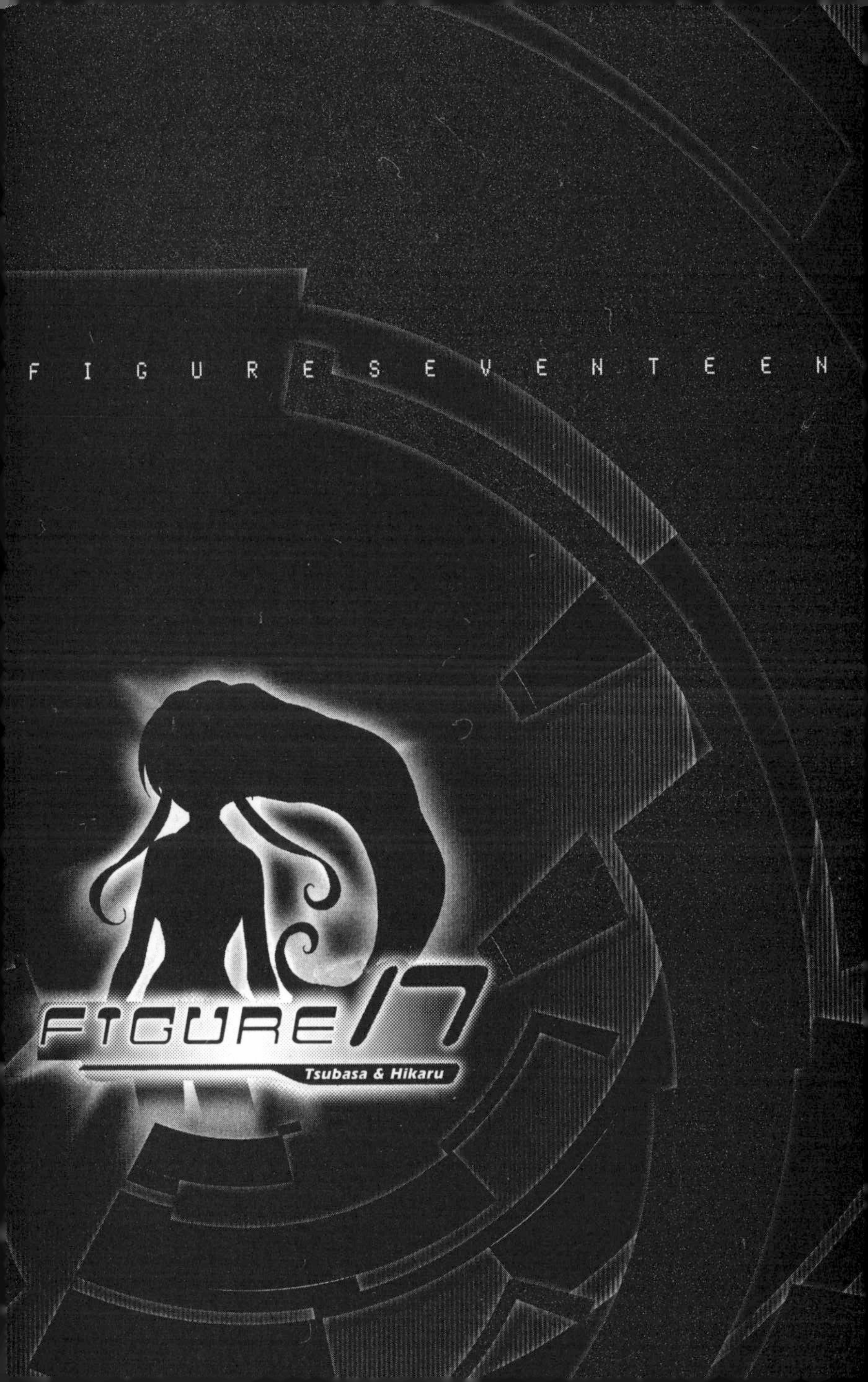
F I G U R E S E V E N T E E N
FIGURE 17
Tsubasa & Hikaru

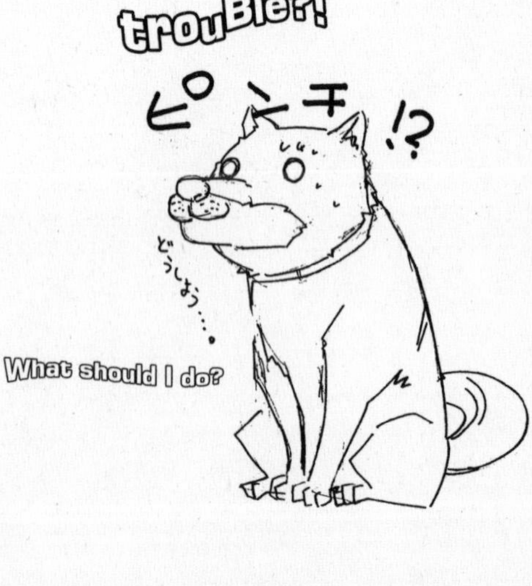

troUBle?!
ピンチ!?
どうしよう…。
What should I do?

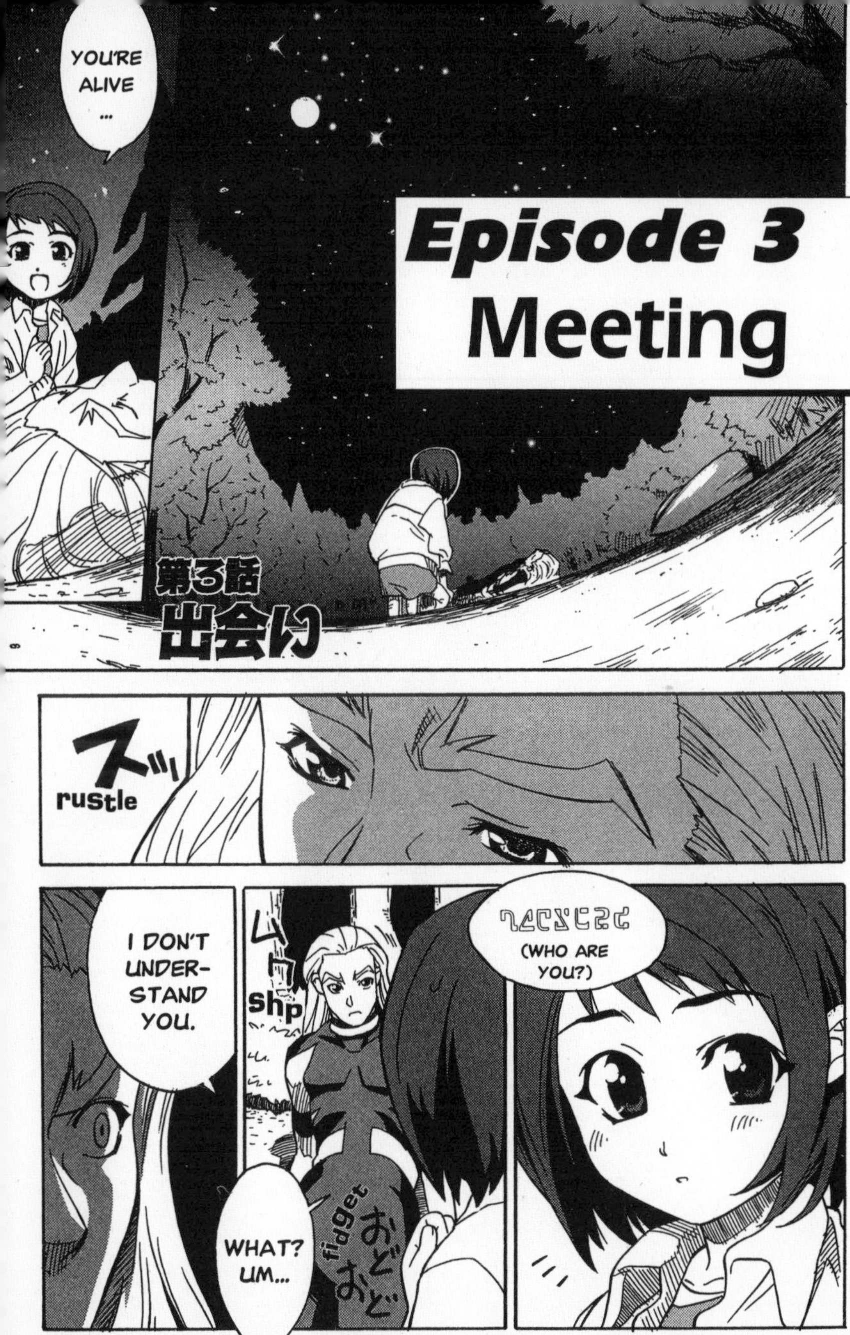
Episode 3
Meeting
第3話 出会い
YOU'RE ALIVE ...
スッ rustle
(WHO ARE YOU?)
shp
WHAT? UM...
fidget おどおど
I DON'T UNDER-STAND YOU.

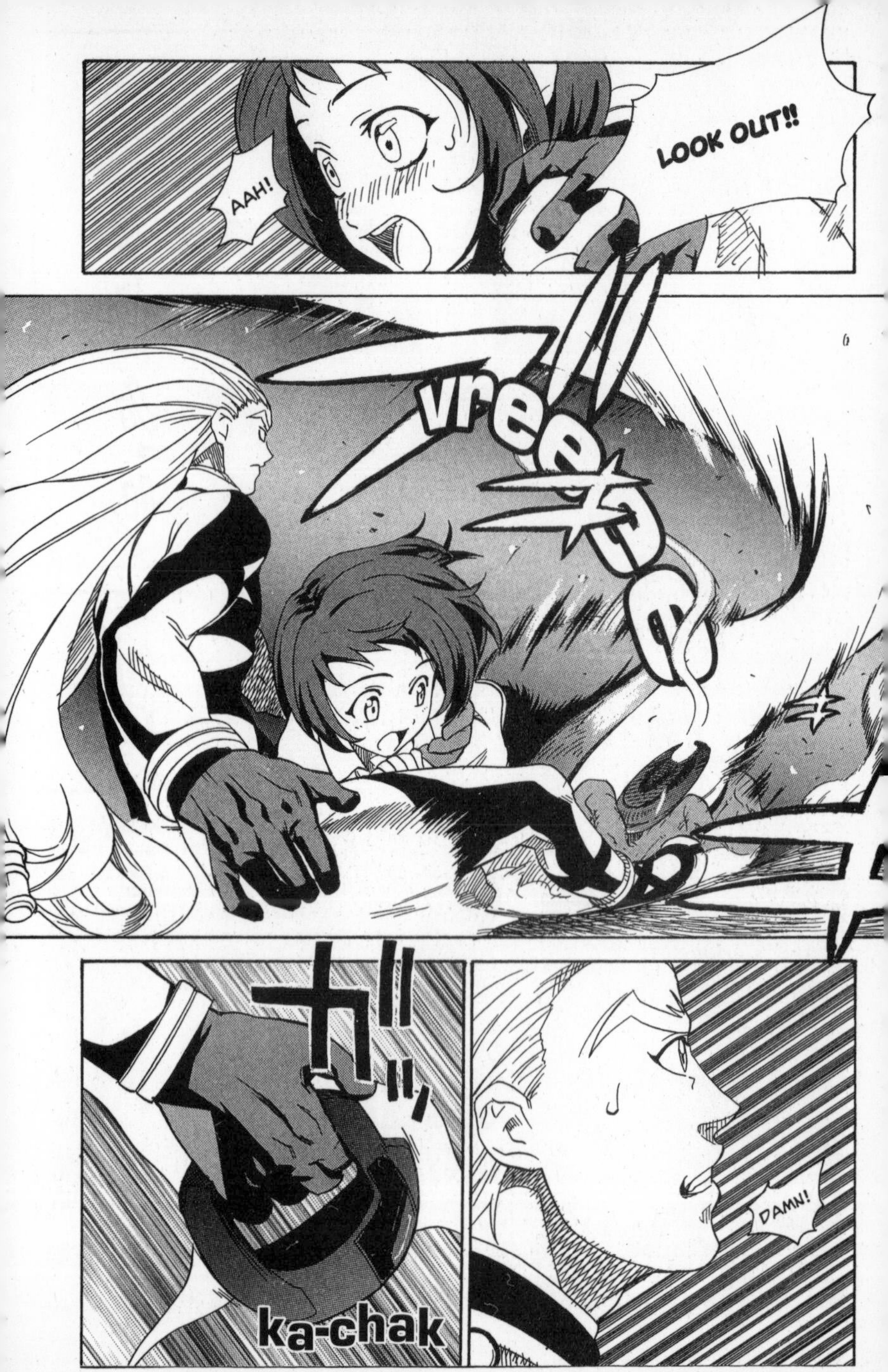
LOOK OUT!!
AAH!
vreeeee
ka-chak
DAMN!

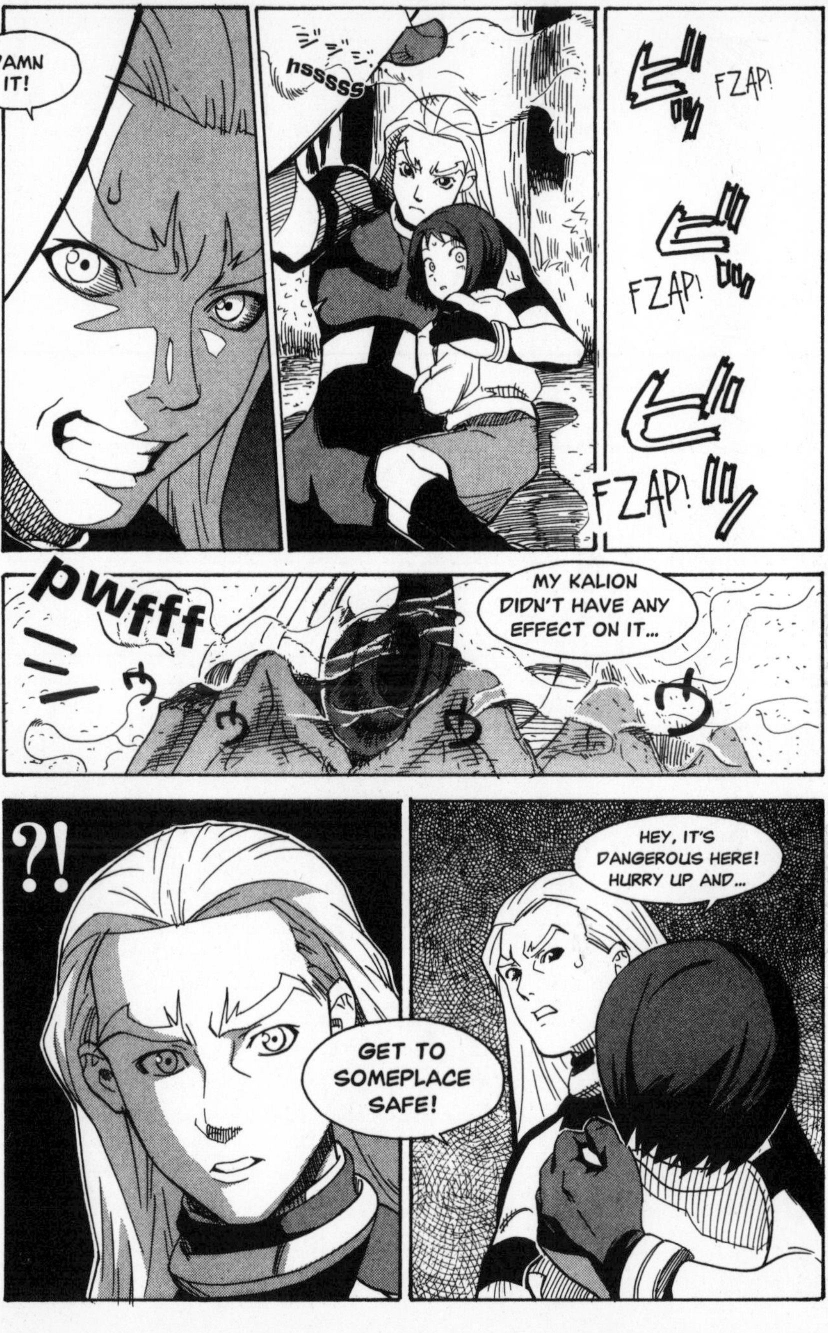
DAMN IT!
hssssss
FZAP!
FZAP!
FZAP!
pwfff
MY KALION DIDN'T HAVE ANY EFFECT ON IT...
?!
GET TO SOMEPLACE SAFE!
HEY, IT'S DANGEROUS HERE! HURRY UP AND...

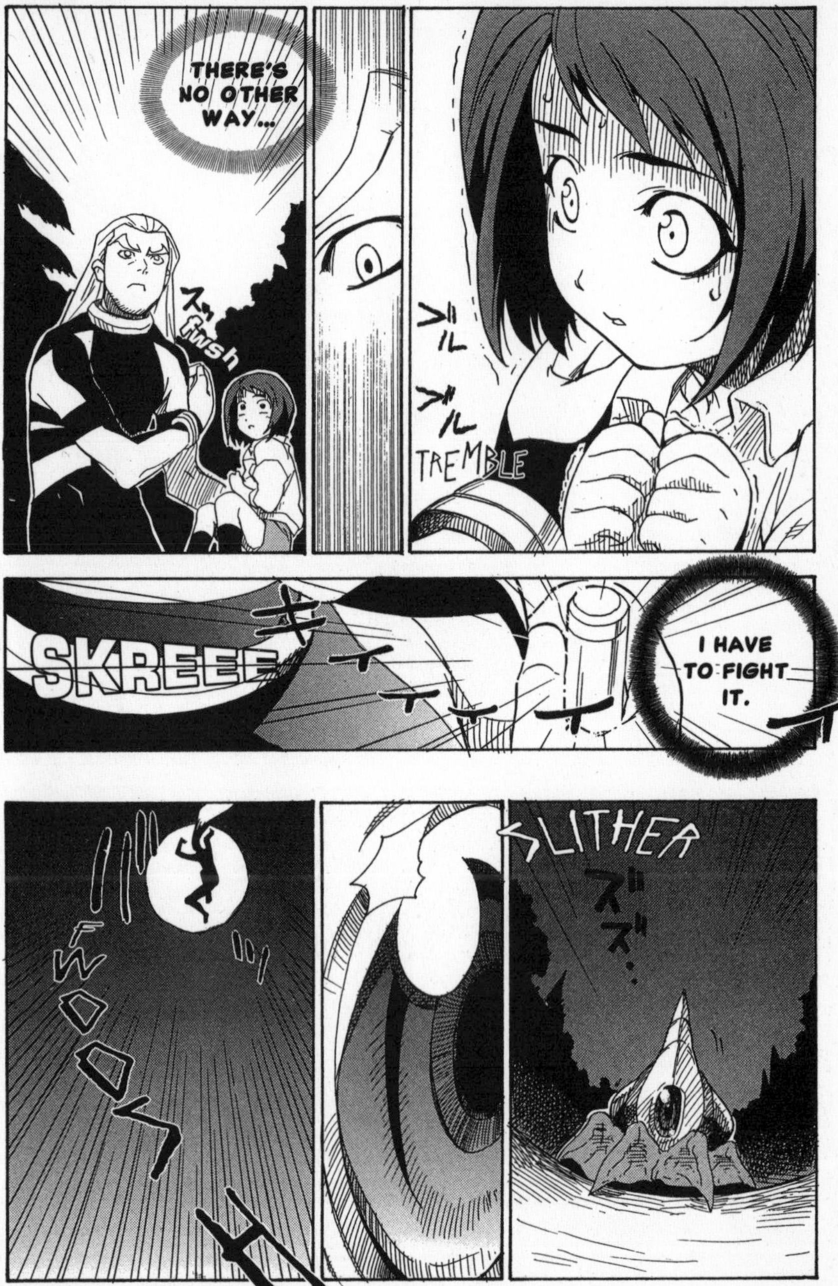
THERE'S NO OTHER WAY...
fwsh
TREMBLE
SKREEE
I HAVE TO FIGHT IT.
SLITHER

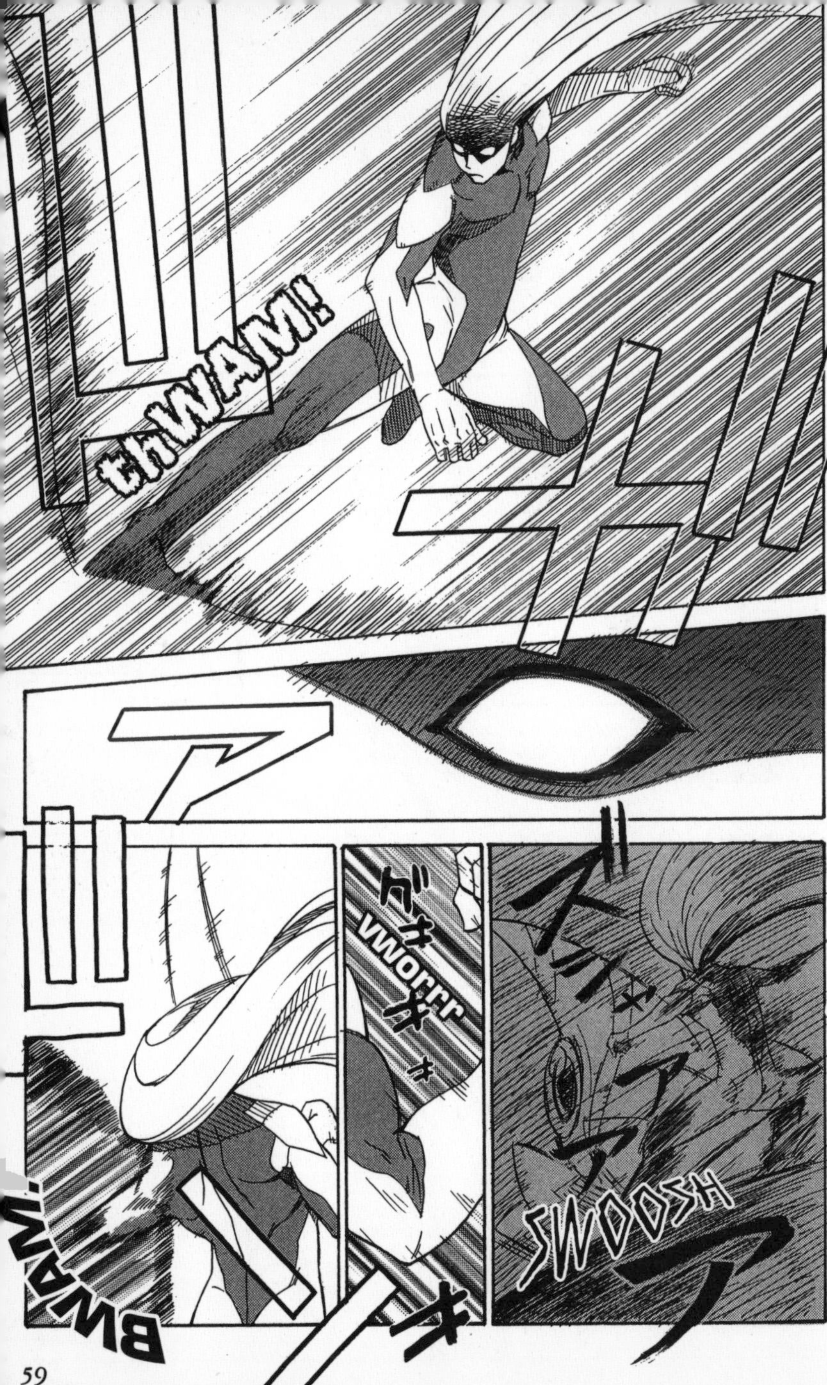

thWAM!
BWAM!
vworrr
SWOOSH

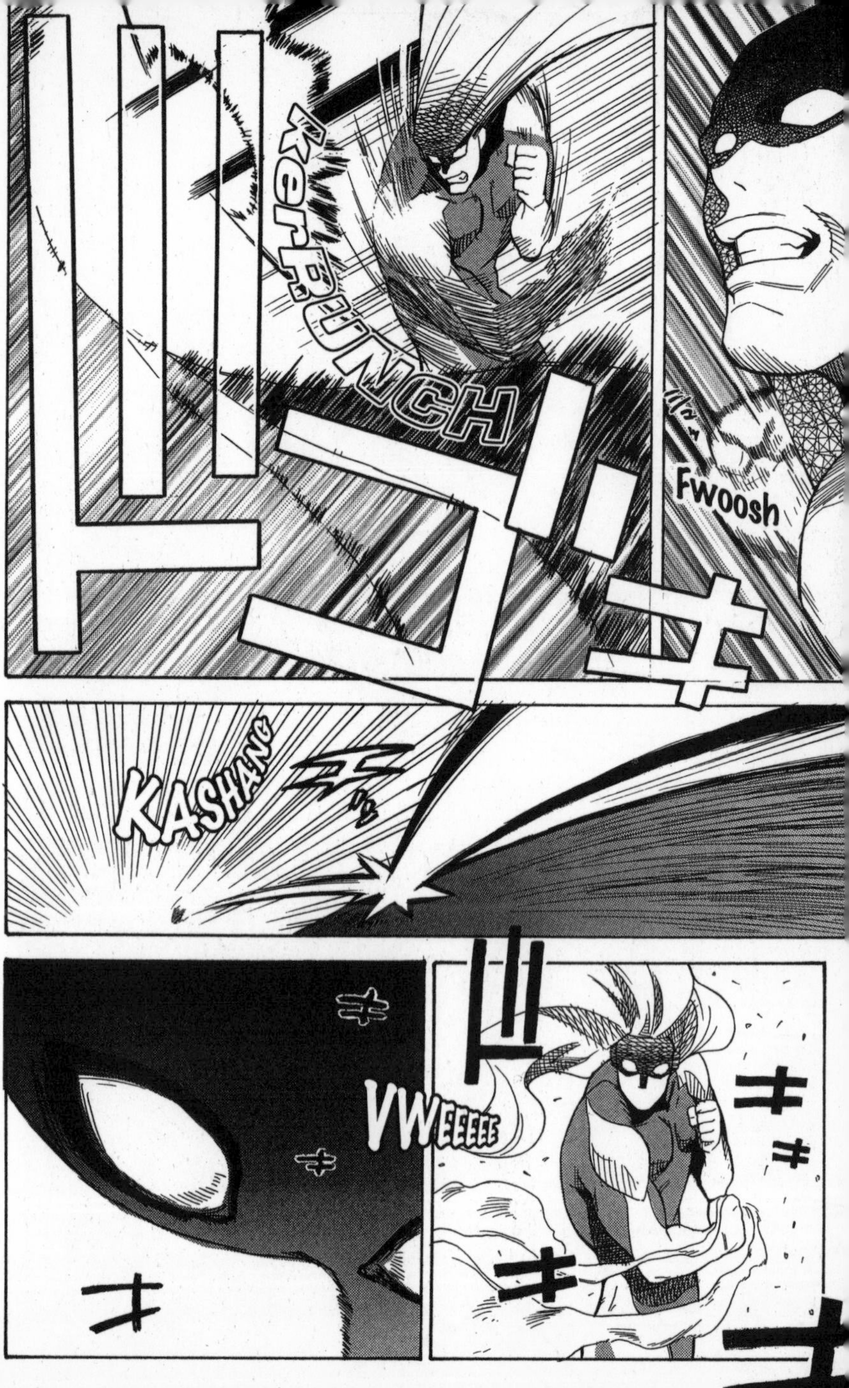

Fwoosh
KerRUNCH
KASHANG
VWEEEEE

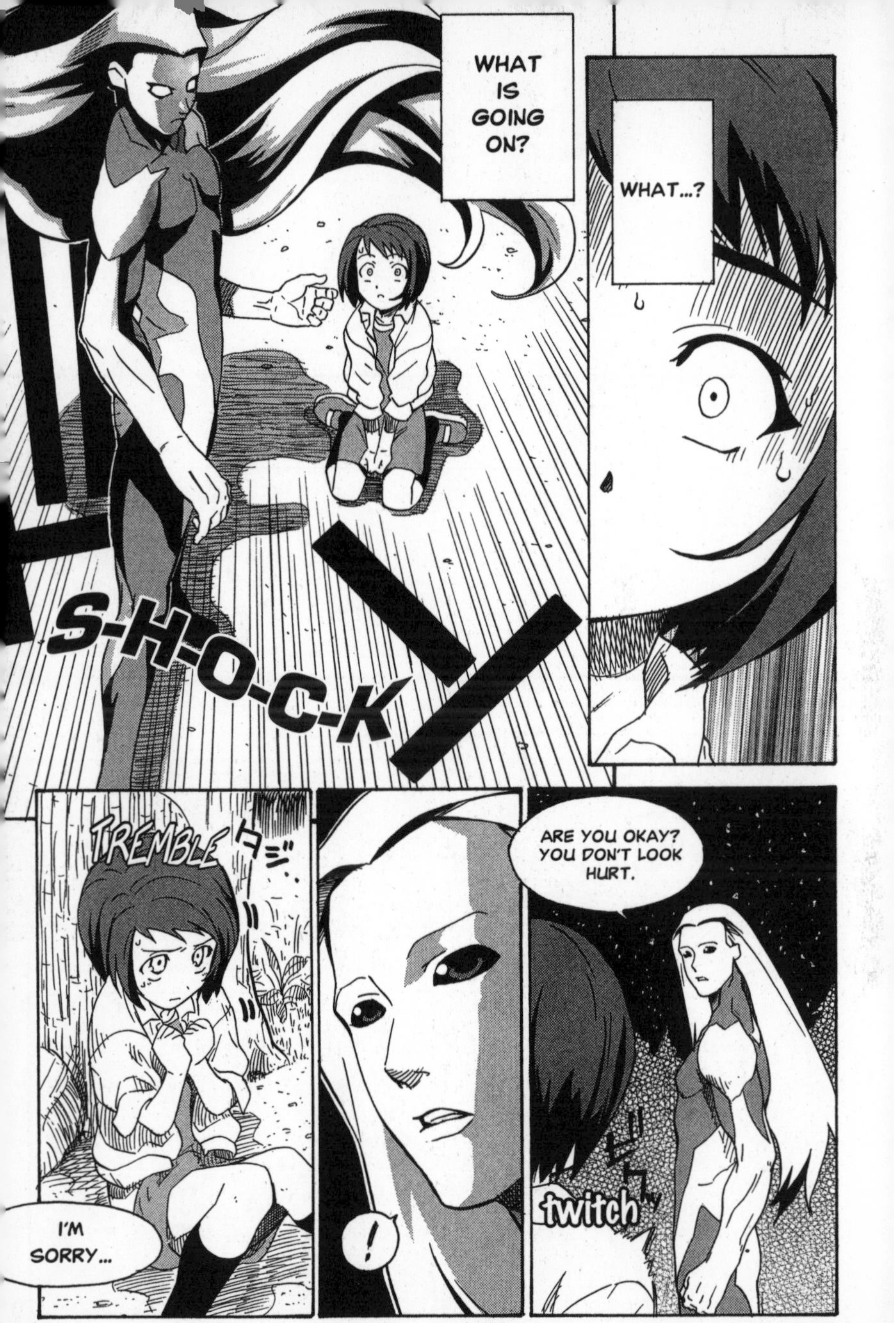
WHAT...?
WHAT IS GOING ON?
S-H-O-C-K
ARE YOU OKAY? YOU DON'T LOOK HURT.
twitch
!
TREMBLE
I'M SORRY...

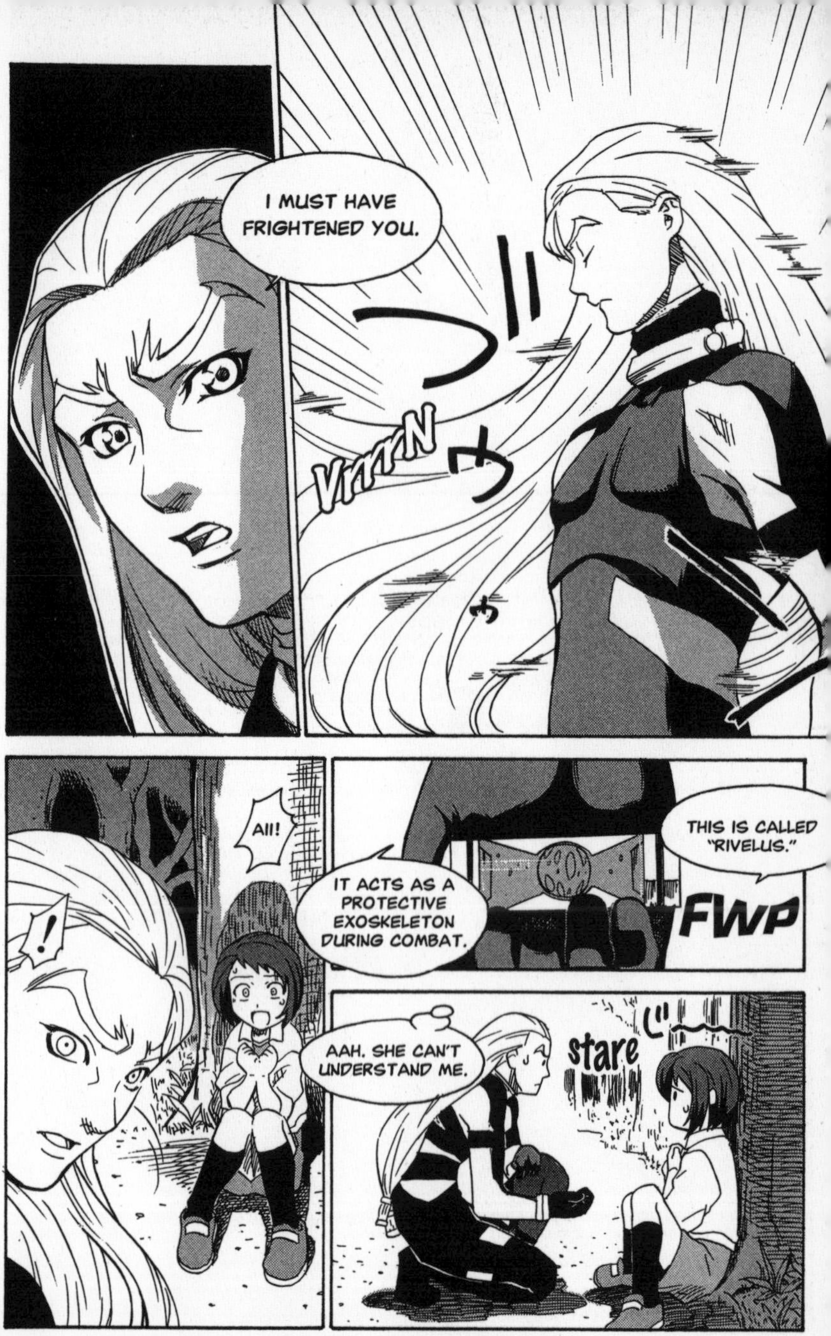
I MUST HAVE FRIGHTENED YOU.
VrrrrN
THIS IS CALLED "RIVELUS."
FWP
IT ACTS AS A PROTECTIVE EXOSKELETON DURING COMBAT.
AII!
!
stare
AAH. SHE CAN'T UNDERSTAND ME.

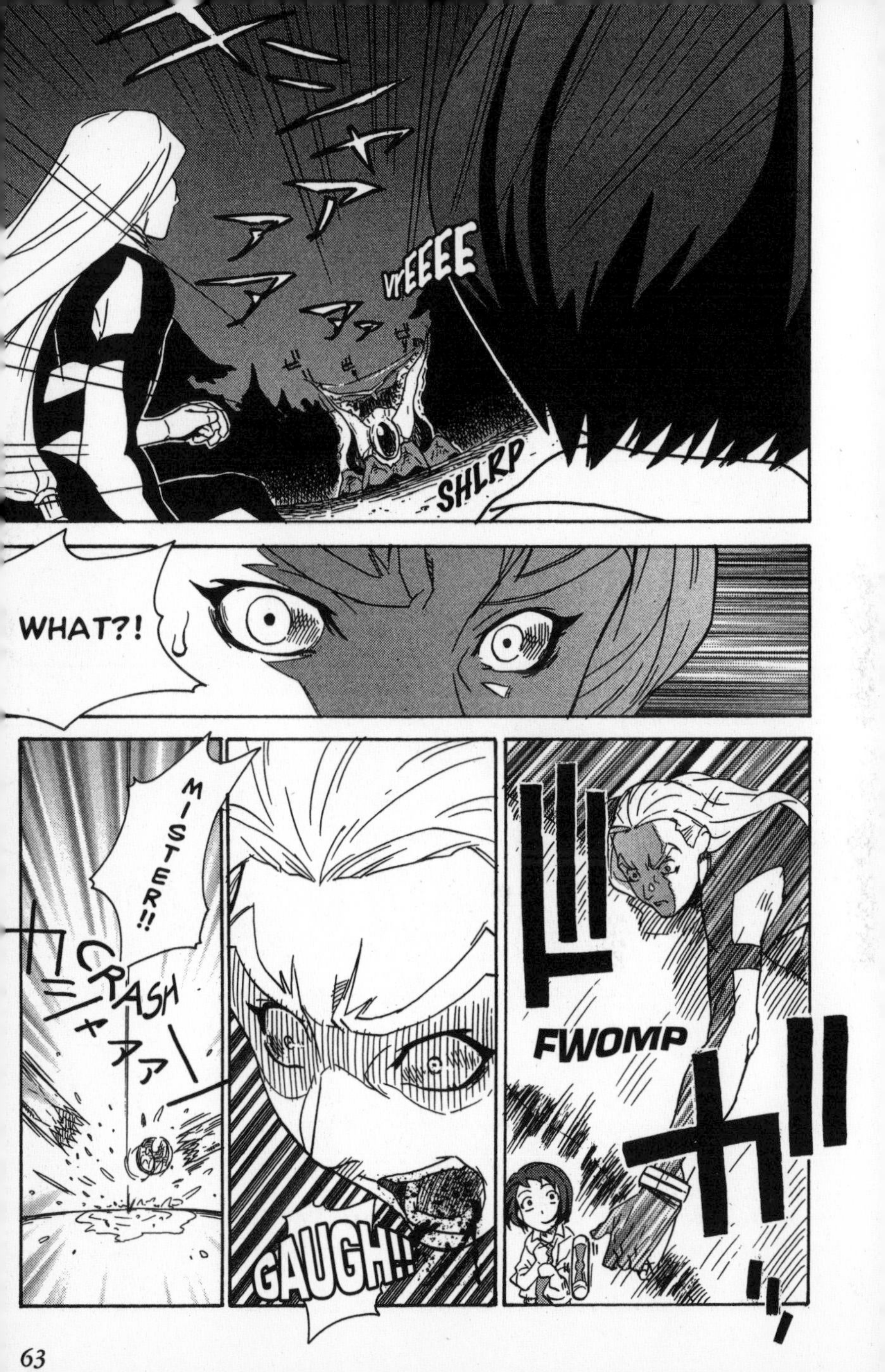
VrEEEE
SHLRP
WHAT?!
FWOMP
GAUGH!!
MISTER!!
CRASH

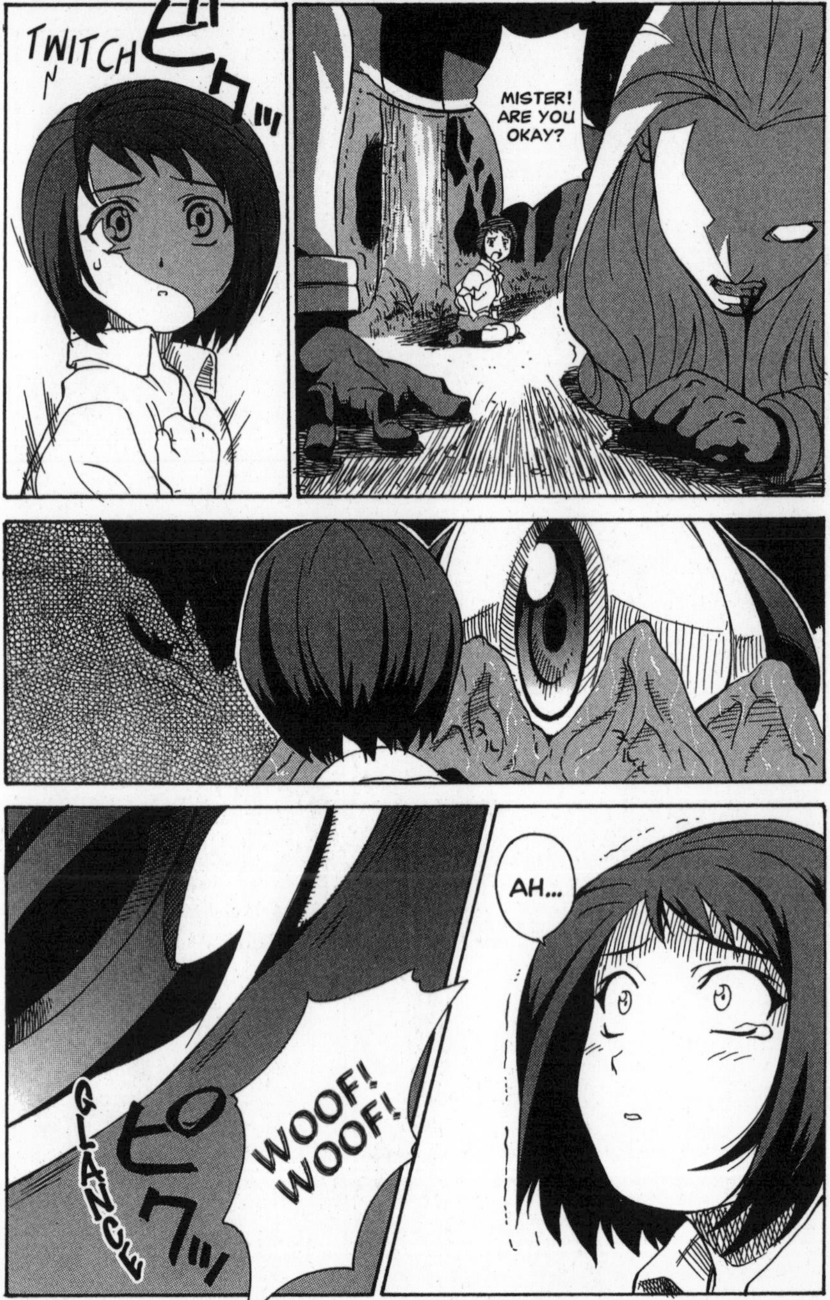
TWITCH
MISTER! ARE YOU OKAY?
AH...
WOOF! WOOF!
GLANCE

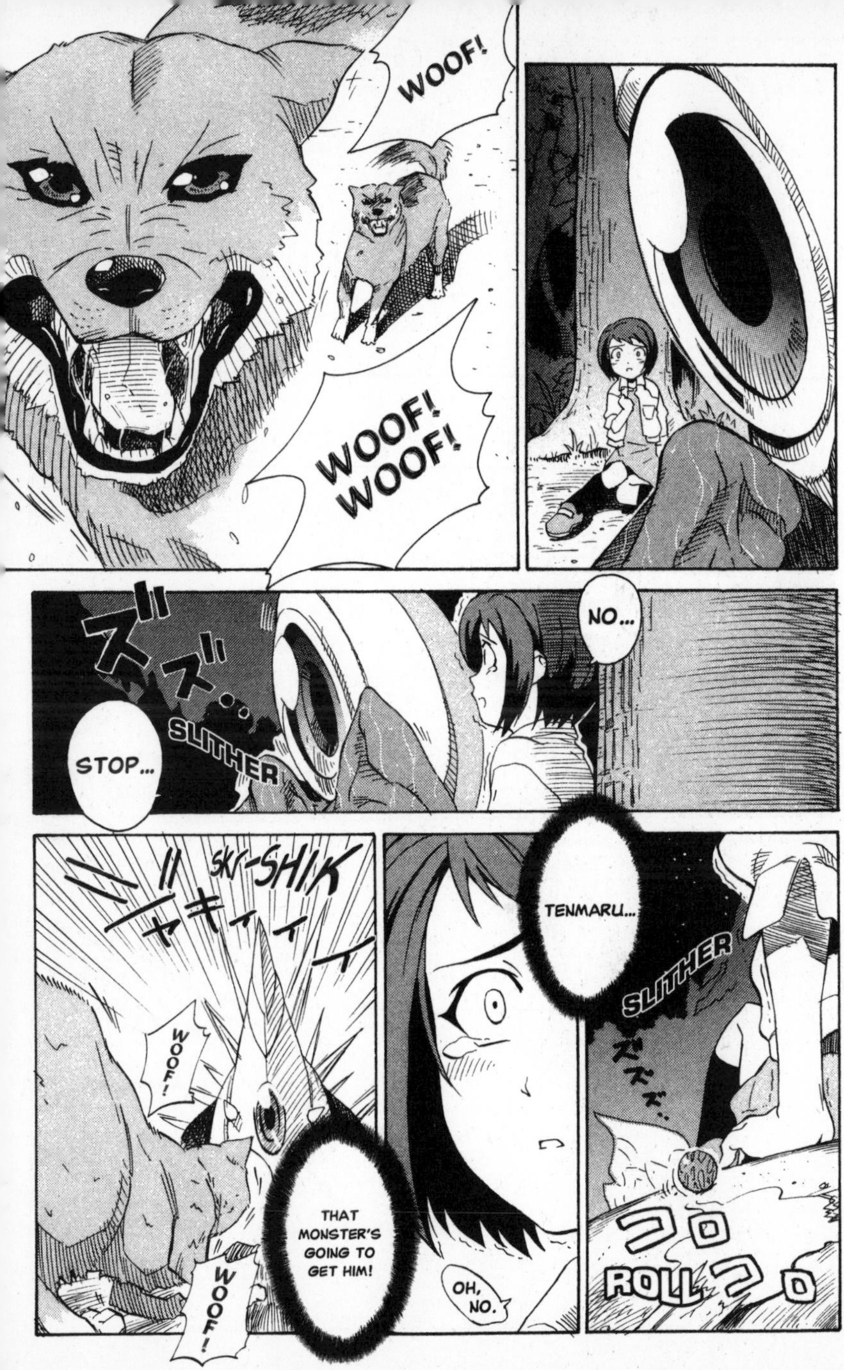
WOOF!
WOOF! WOOF!
NO...
ズズ...
SLITHER
STOP...
TENMARU...
SLITHER
ズズ...
コロ
ROLL
コロ
OH, NO.
SKI-SHIK
シャキィィー
WOOF!
THAT MONSTER'S GOING TO GET HIM!
WOOF!

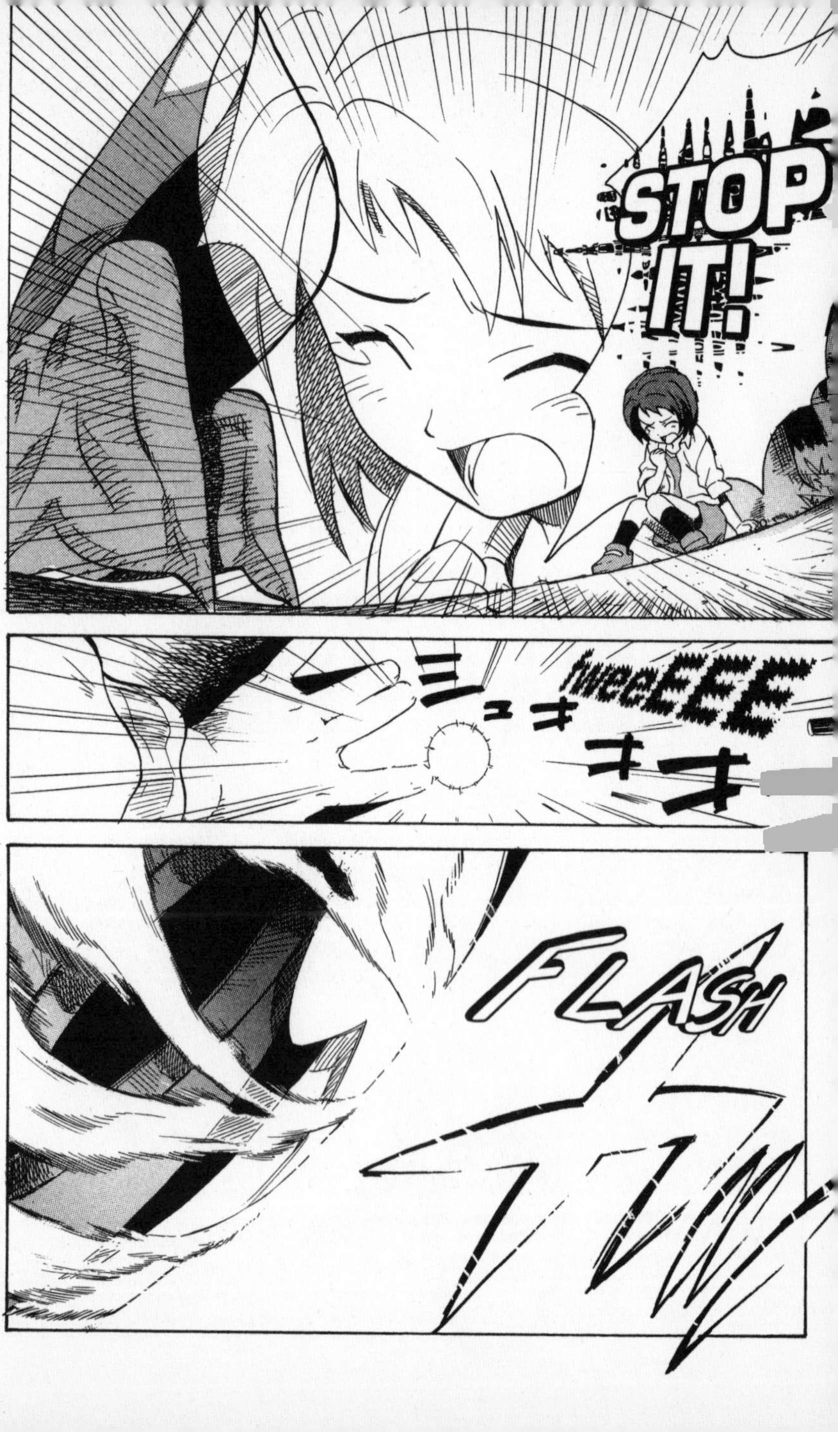
STOP IT!
tweeEEE
FLASH

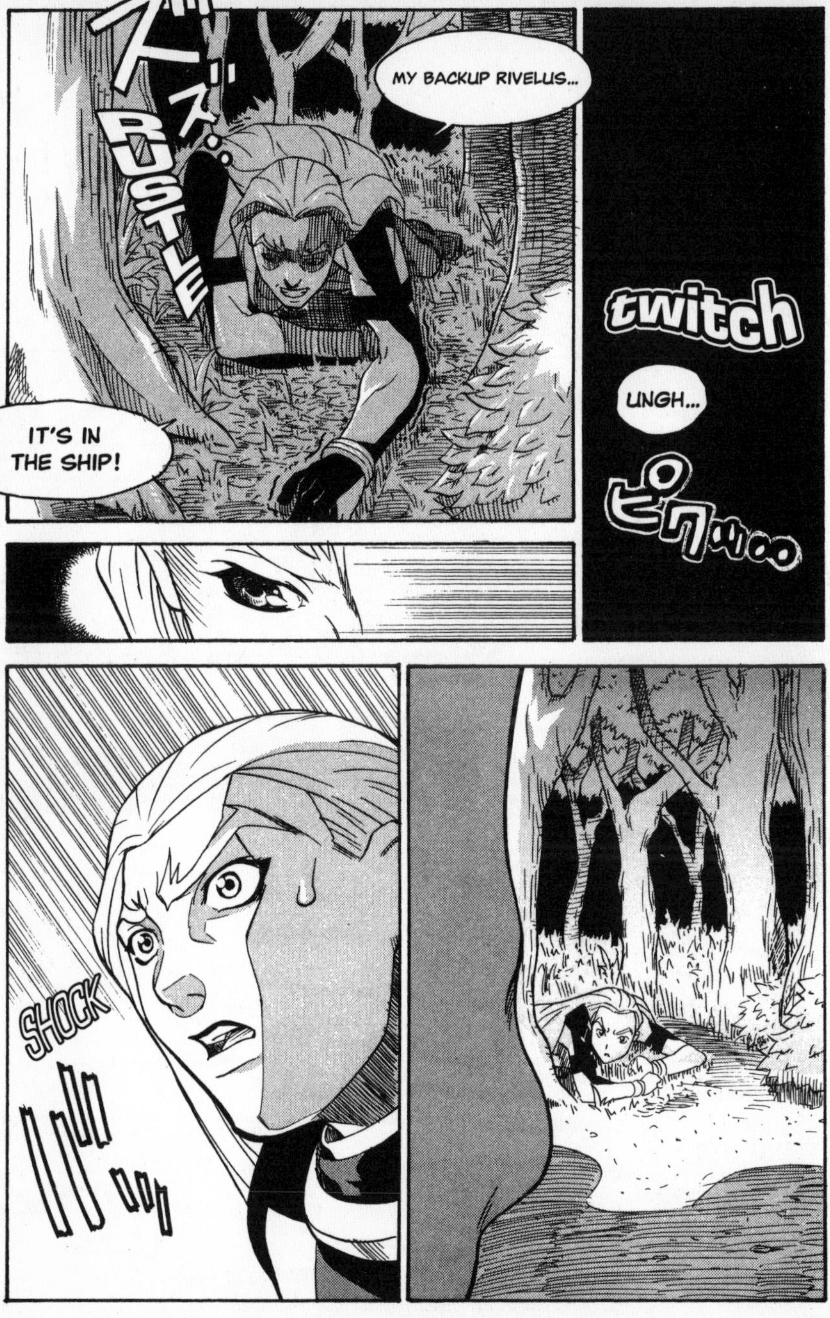

RUSTLE
MY BACKUP RIVELUS...
IT'S IN THE SHIP!
twitch
UNGH...
SHOCK

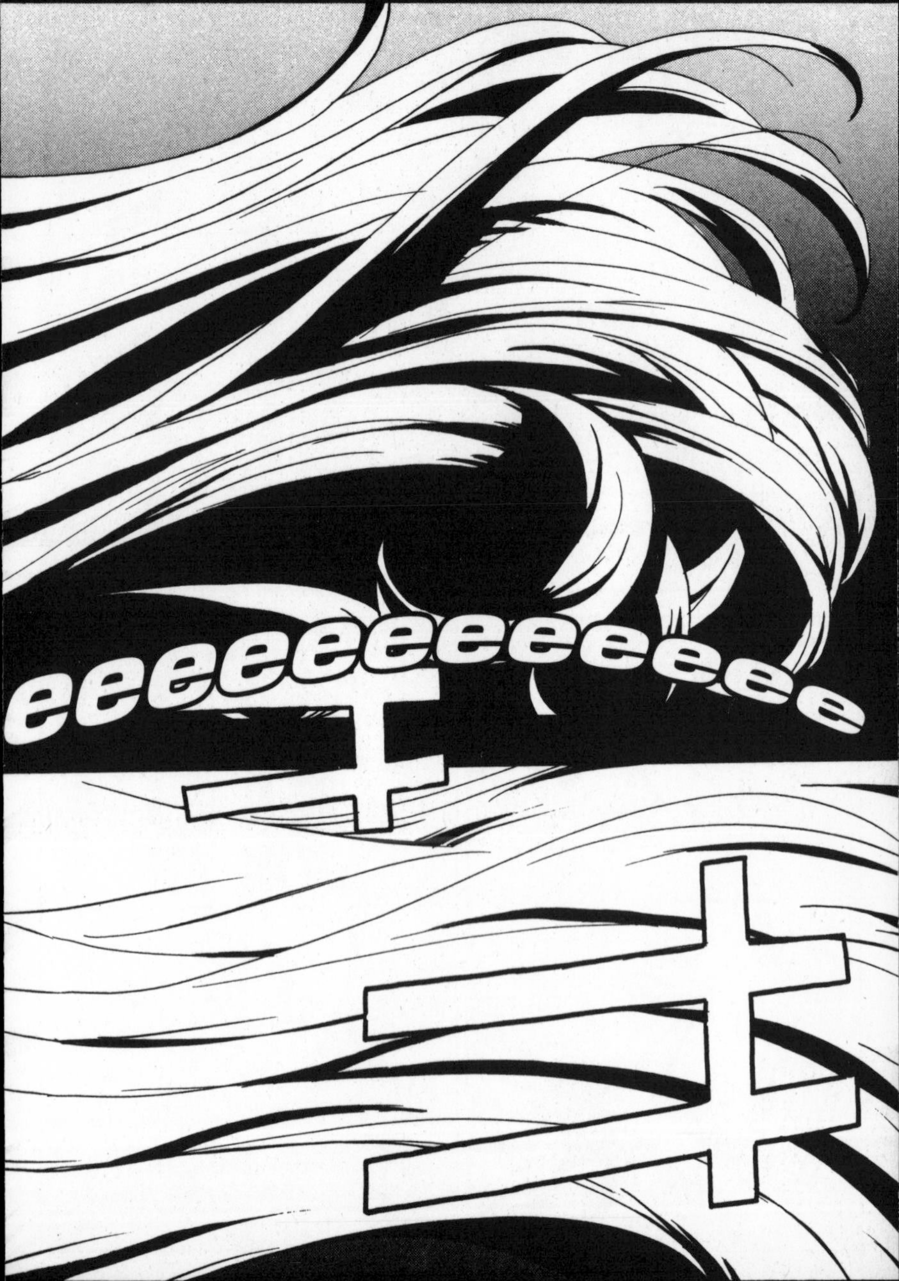
eeeeeeeeeeeeee

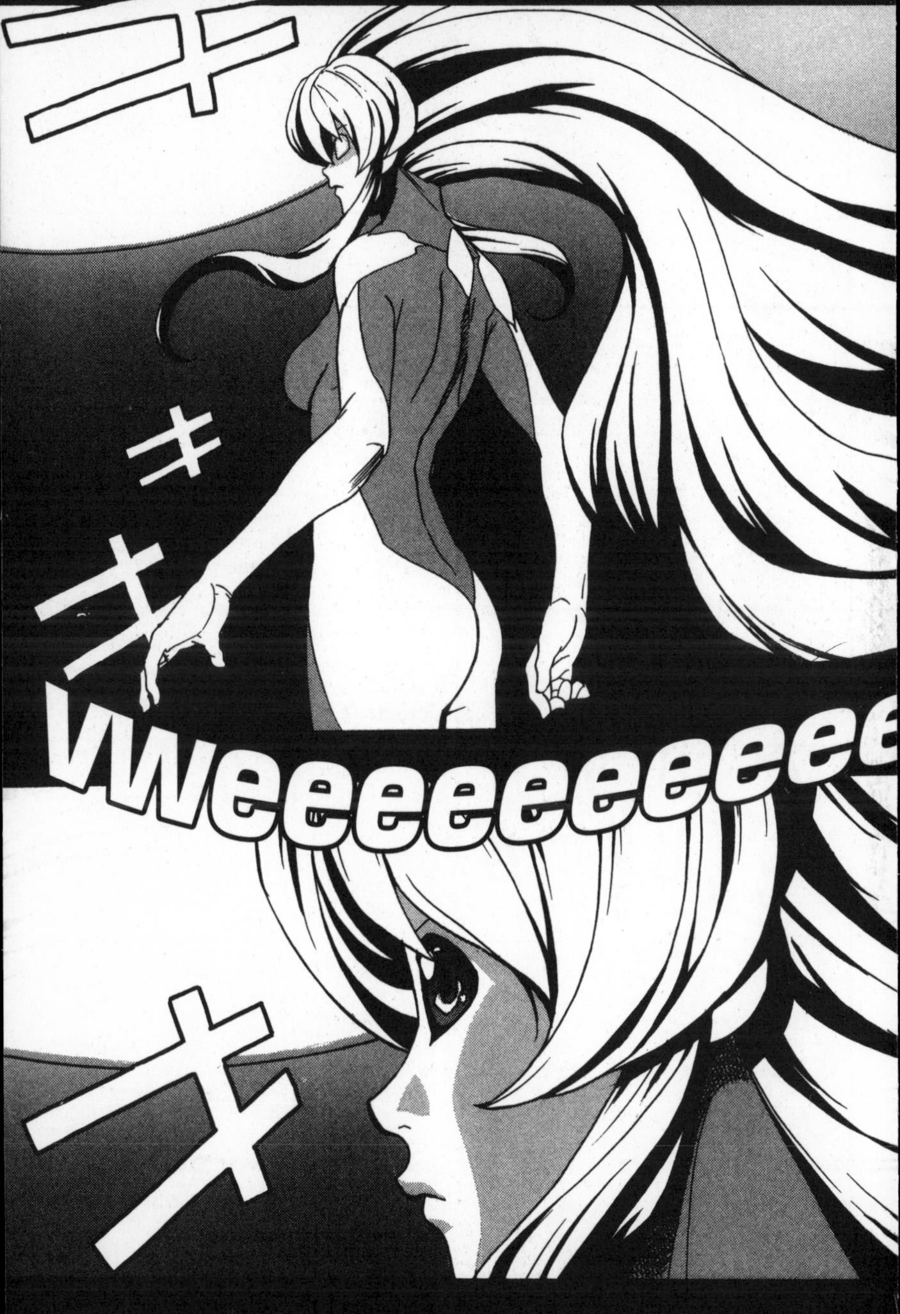
キ
キ
キ
vweeeeeeeeeee
キ

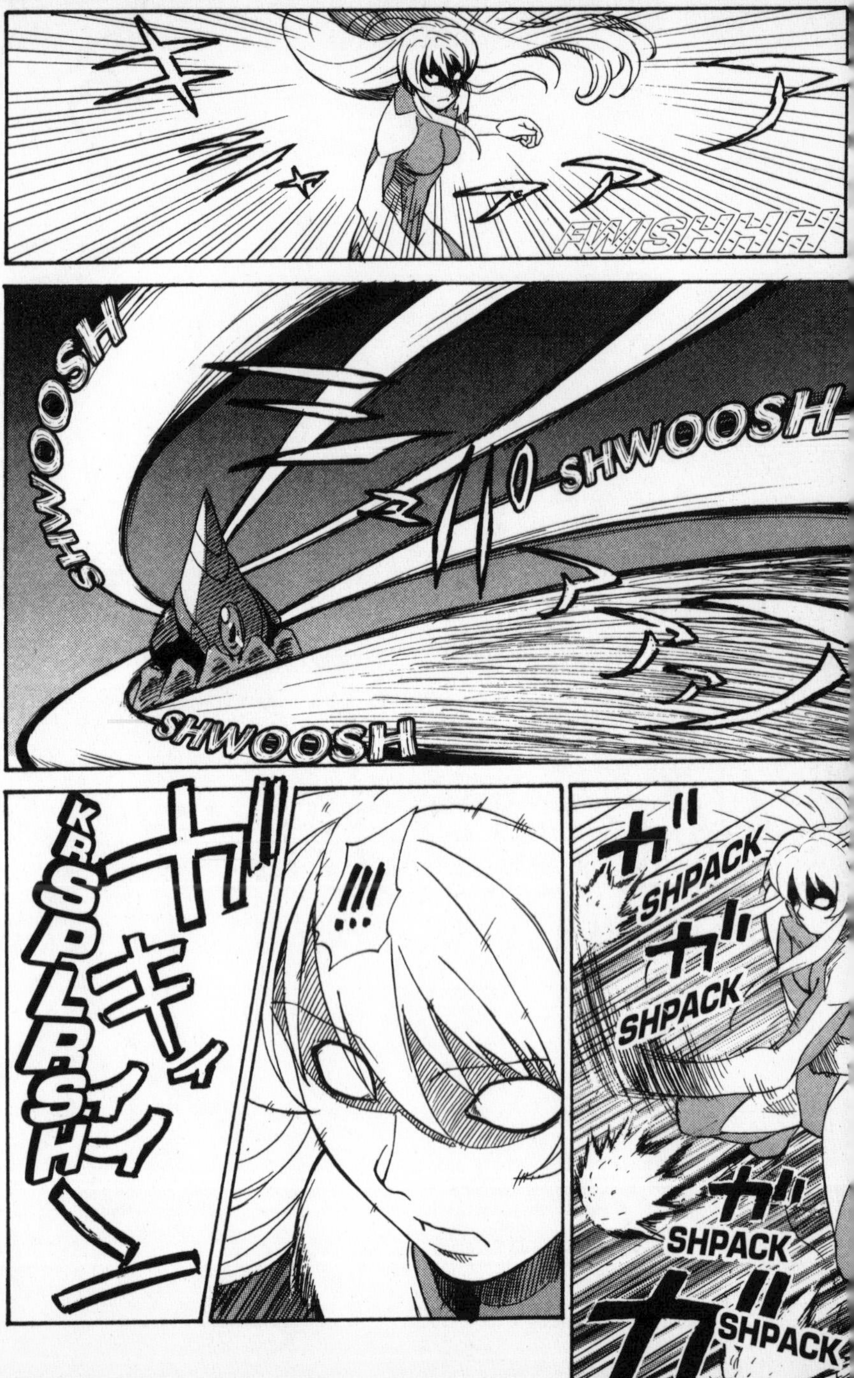
FWISHHH
SHWOOSH
SHWOOSH
SHWOOSH
SHPACK
SHPACK
SHPACK
SHPACK
!!!
KRSPLRSH

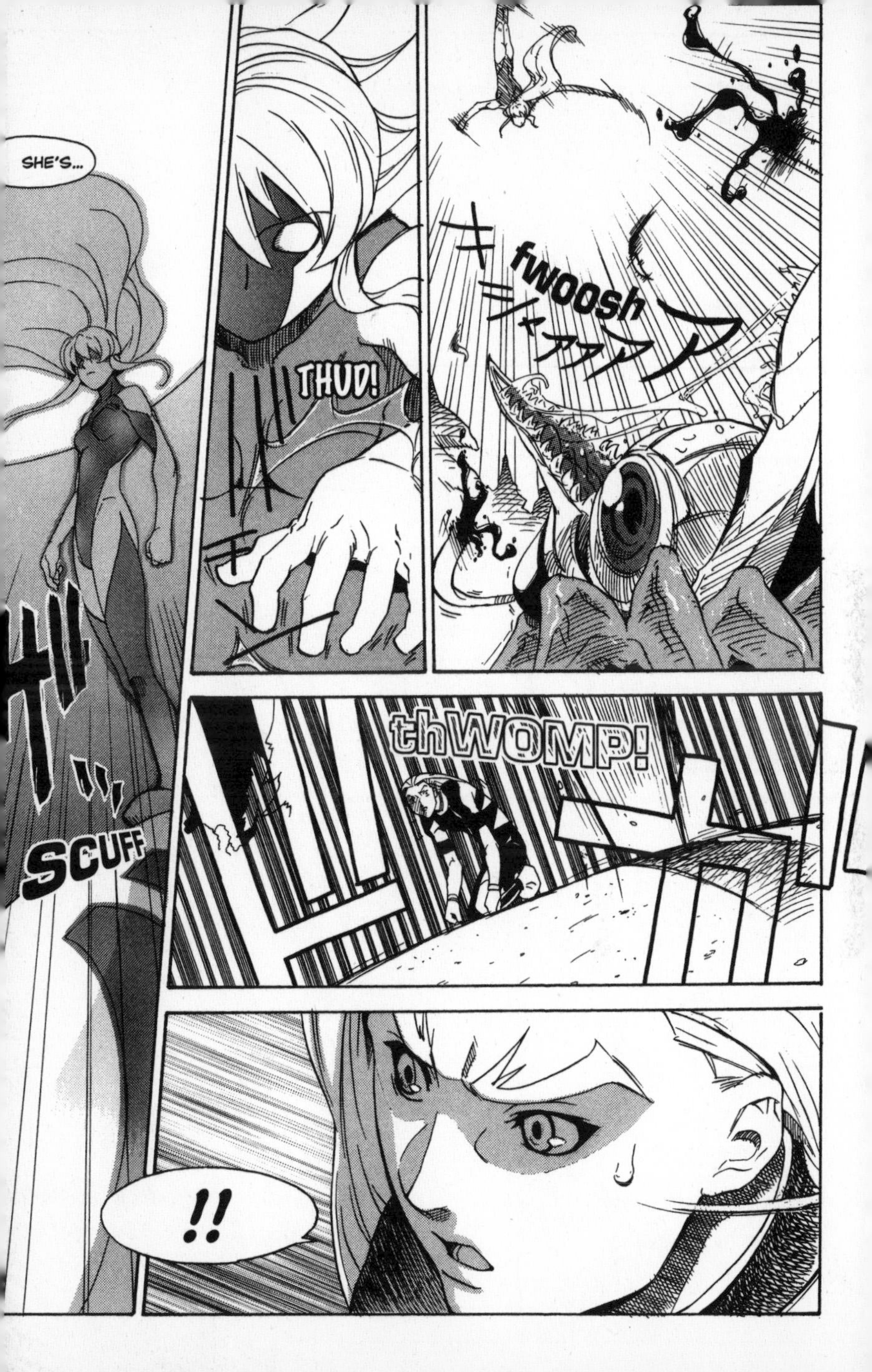
fwoosh
キシャアアアア
THUD!
SHE'S...
ザリ...
SCUFF
thWOMP!
!!

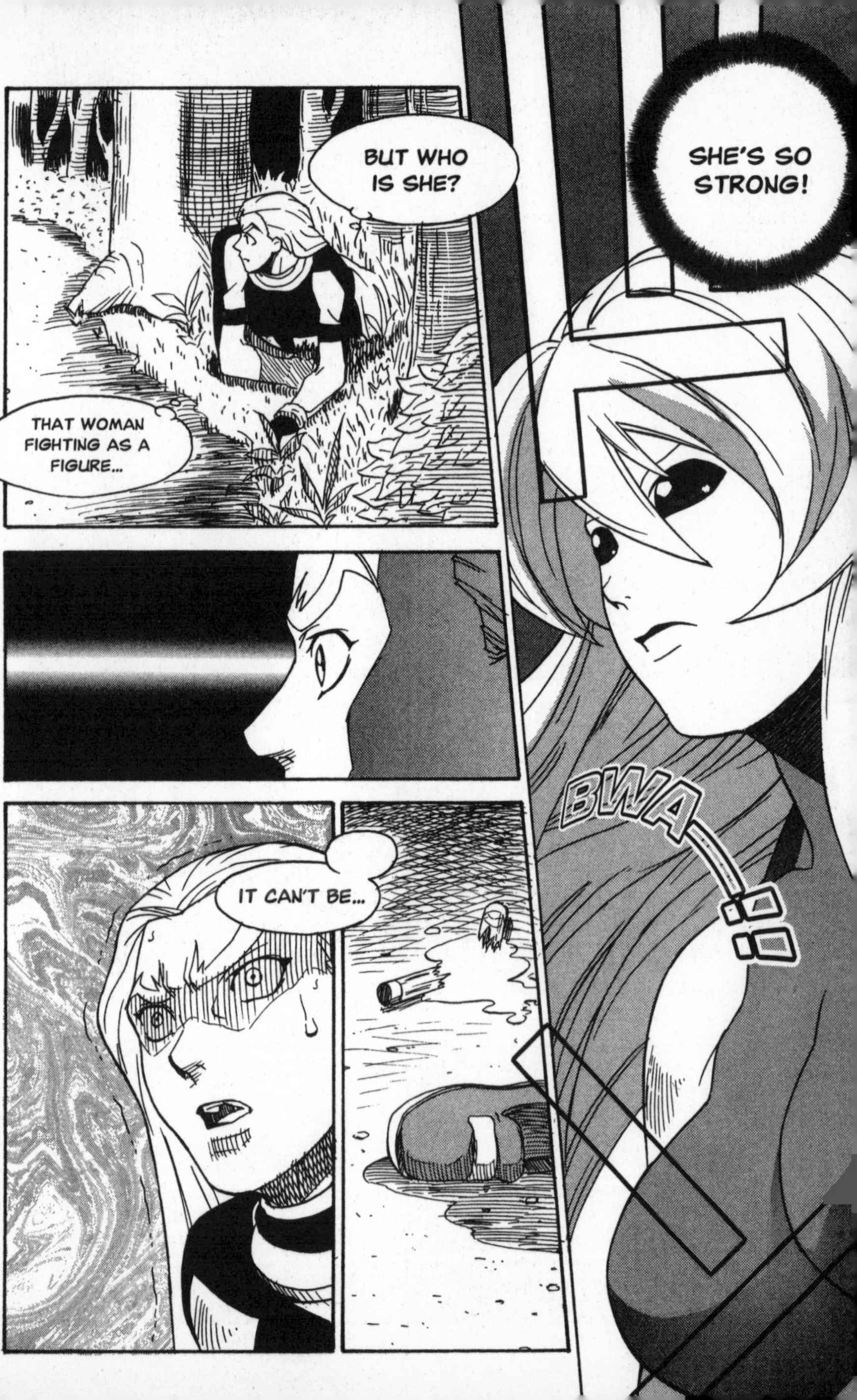
BUT WHO IS SHE?
THAT WOMAN FIGHTING AS A FIGURE...
SHE'S SO STRONG!
IT CAN'T BE...
BWA
!!

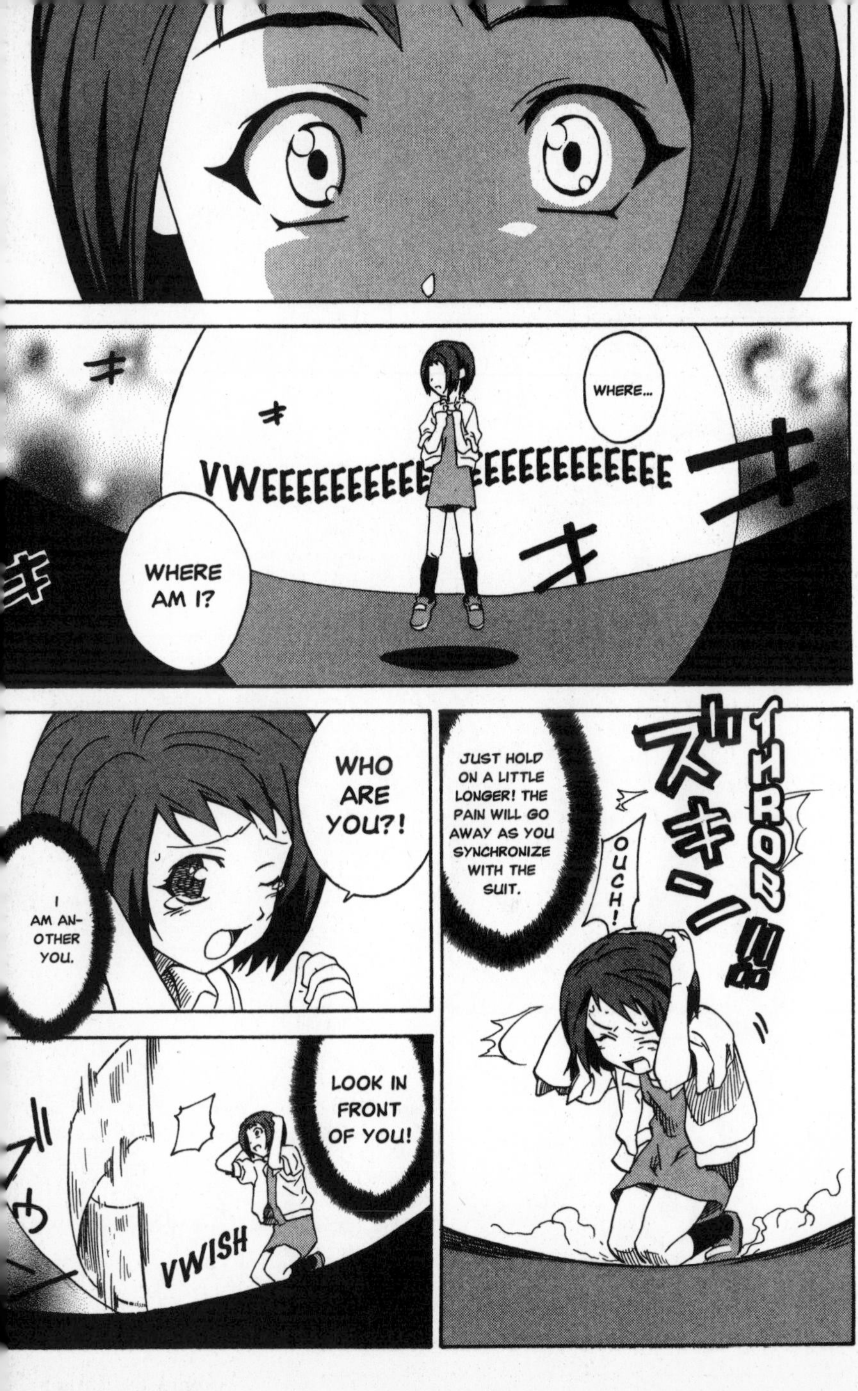
WHERE...
VWEEEEEEEEEEEEEEEEEEEEEEE
WHERE AM I?
JUST HOLD ON A LITTLE LONGER! THE PAIN WILL GO AWAY AS YOU SYNCHRONIZE WITH THE SUIT.
THROB!!
ズキー
OUCH!
WHO ARE YOU?!
I AM ANOTHER YOU.
LOOK IN FRONT OF YOU!
VWISH

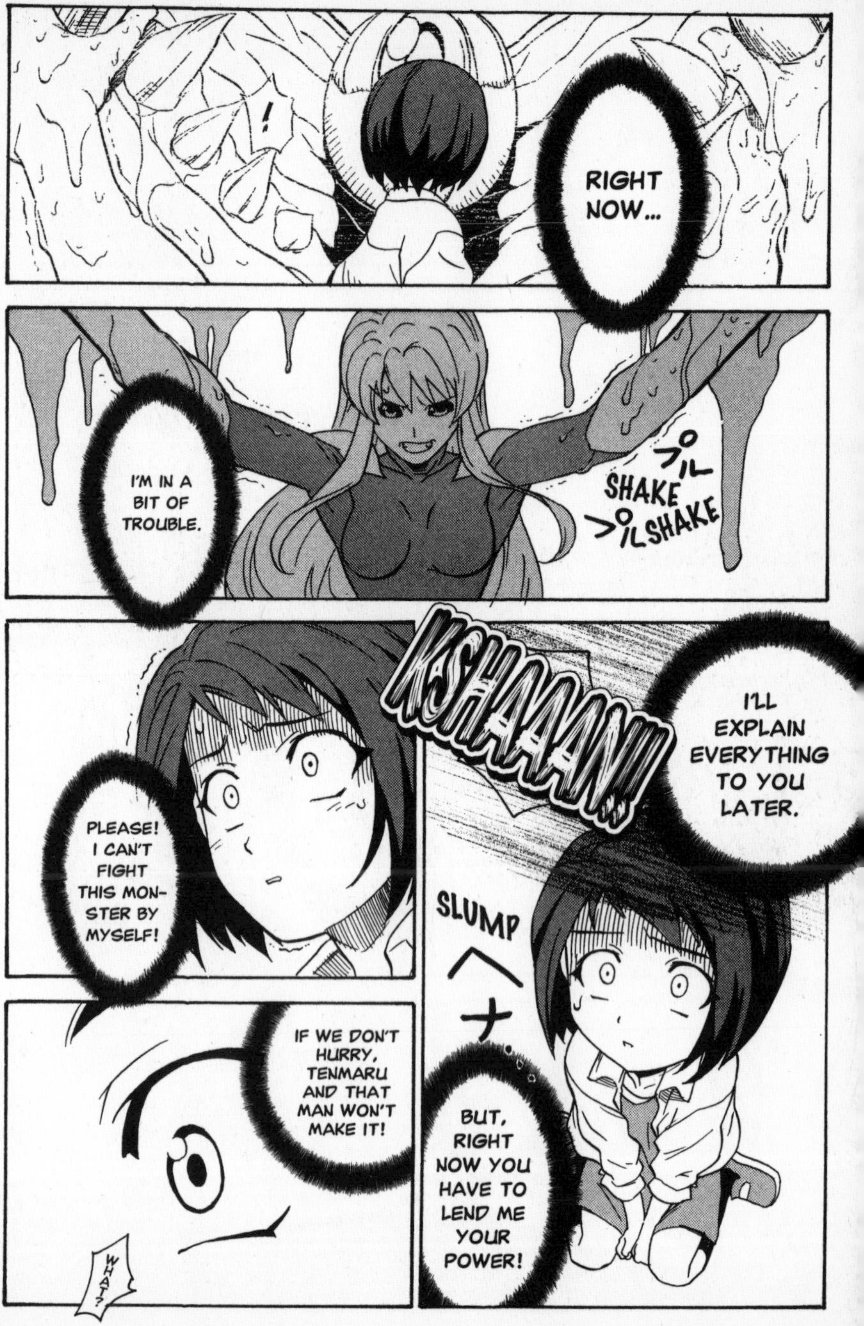
!
RIGHT NOW...
I'M IN A BIT OF TROUBLE.
SHAKE SHAKE
KSHAAAN!!
I'LL EXPLAIN EVERYTHING TO YOU LATER.
PLEASE! I CAN'T FIGHT THIS MONSTER BY MYSELF!
SLUMP
IF WE DON'T HURRY, TENMARU AND THAT MAN WON'T MAKE IT!
BUT, RIGHT NOW YOU HAVE TO LEND ME YOUR POWER!
WHAT?!

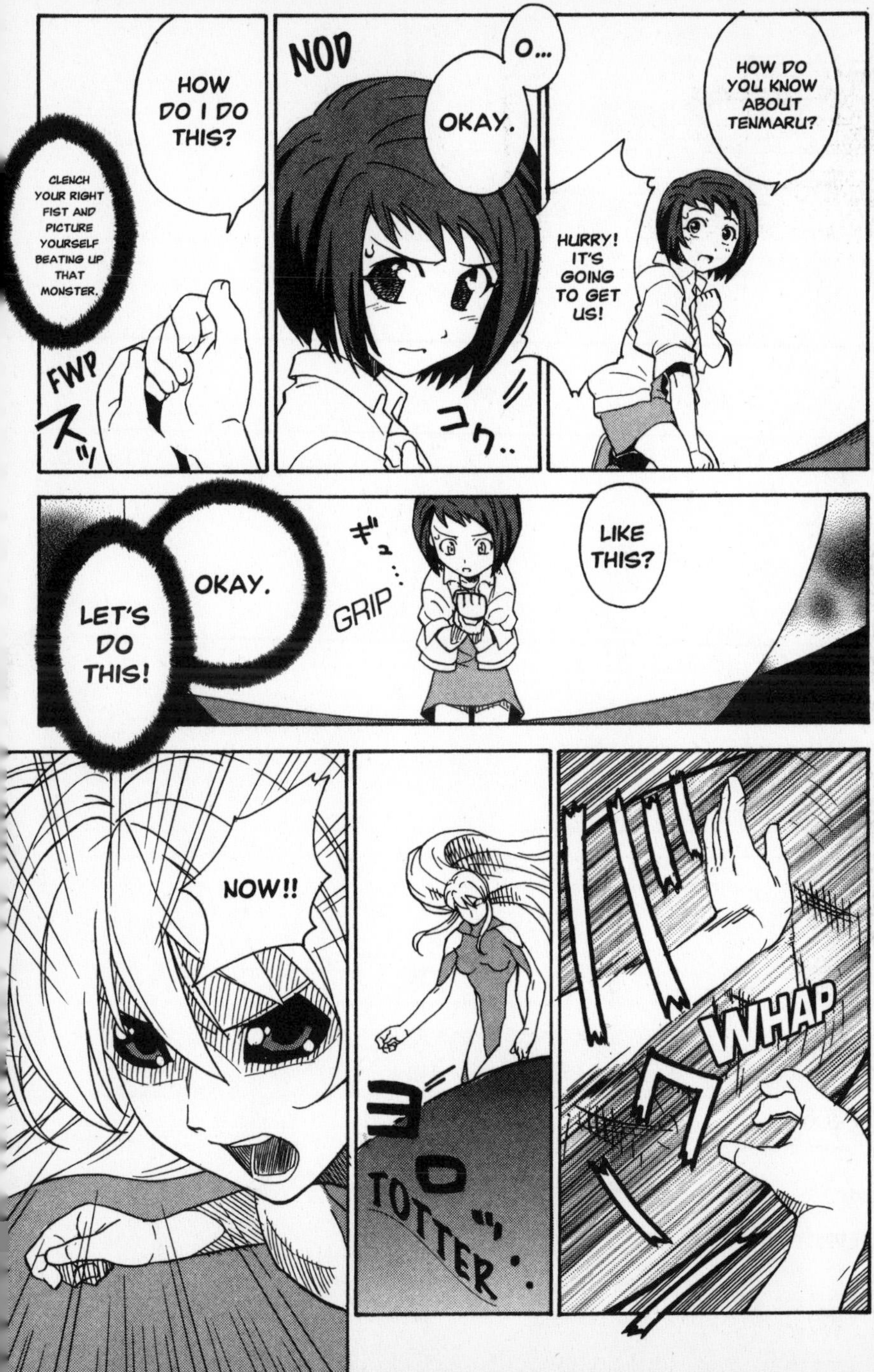
HOW DO YOU KNOW ABOUT TENMARU?
HURRY! IT'S GOING TO GET US!
NOD
O...
OKAY.
コク..
HOW DO I DO THIS?
CLENCH YOUR RIGHT FIST AND PICTURE YOURSELF BEATING UP THAT MONSTER.
FWP
スッ
LIKE THIS?
ギュ...
GRIP
OKAY.
LET'S DO THIS!
WHAP
ヨロ...
TOTTER
NOW!!

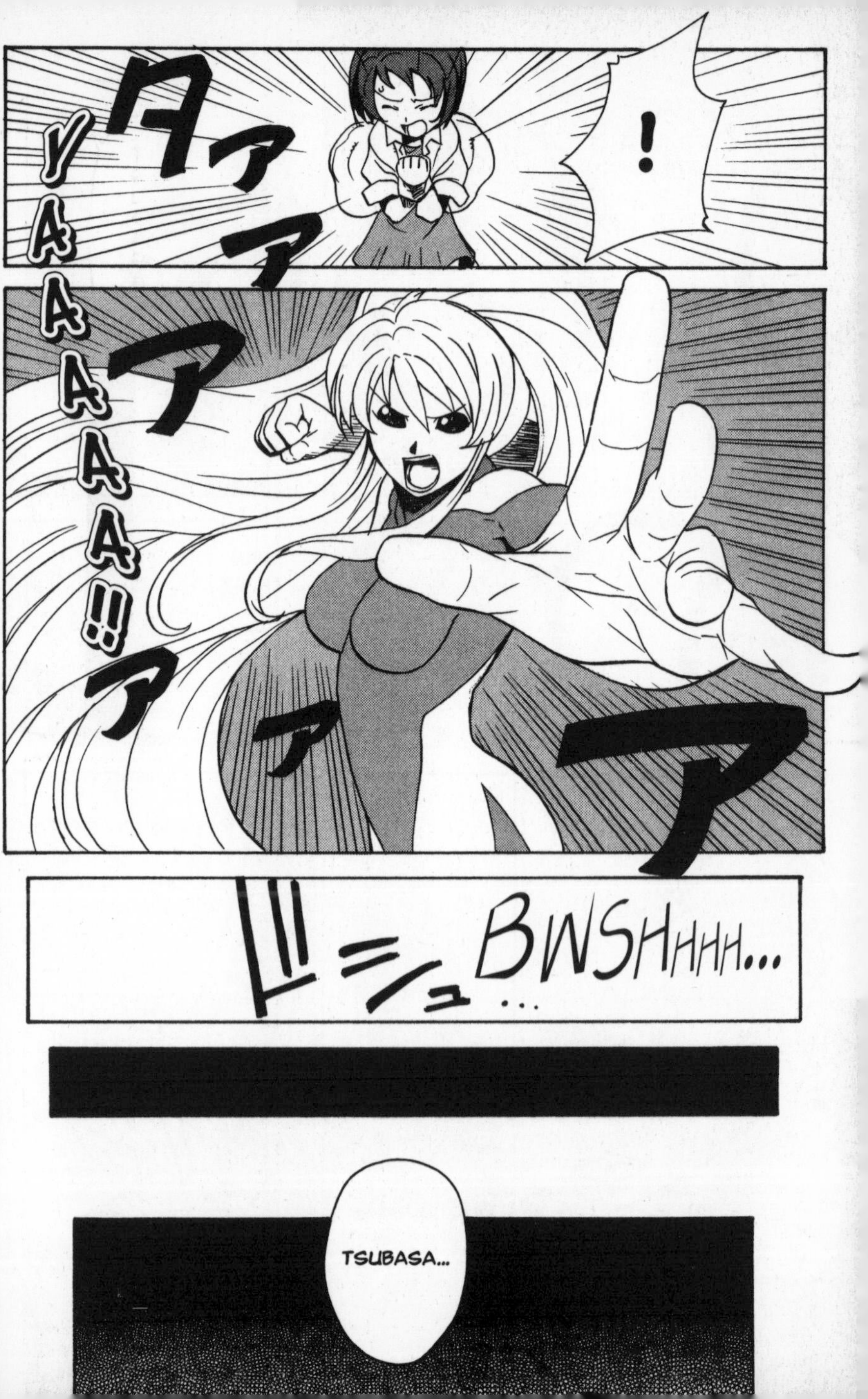
!
YAAAAAA!!
BWSHHHH...
TSUBASA...

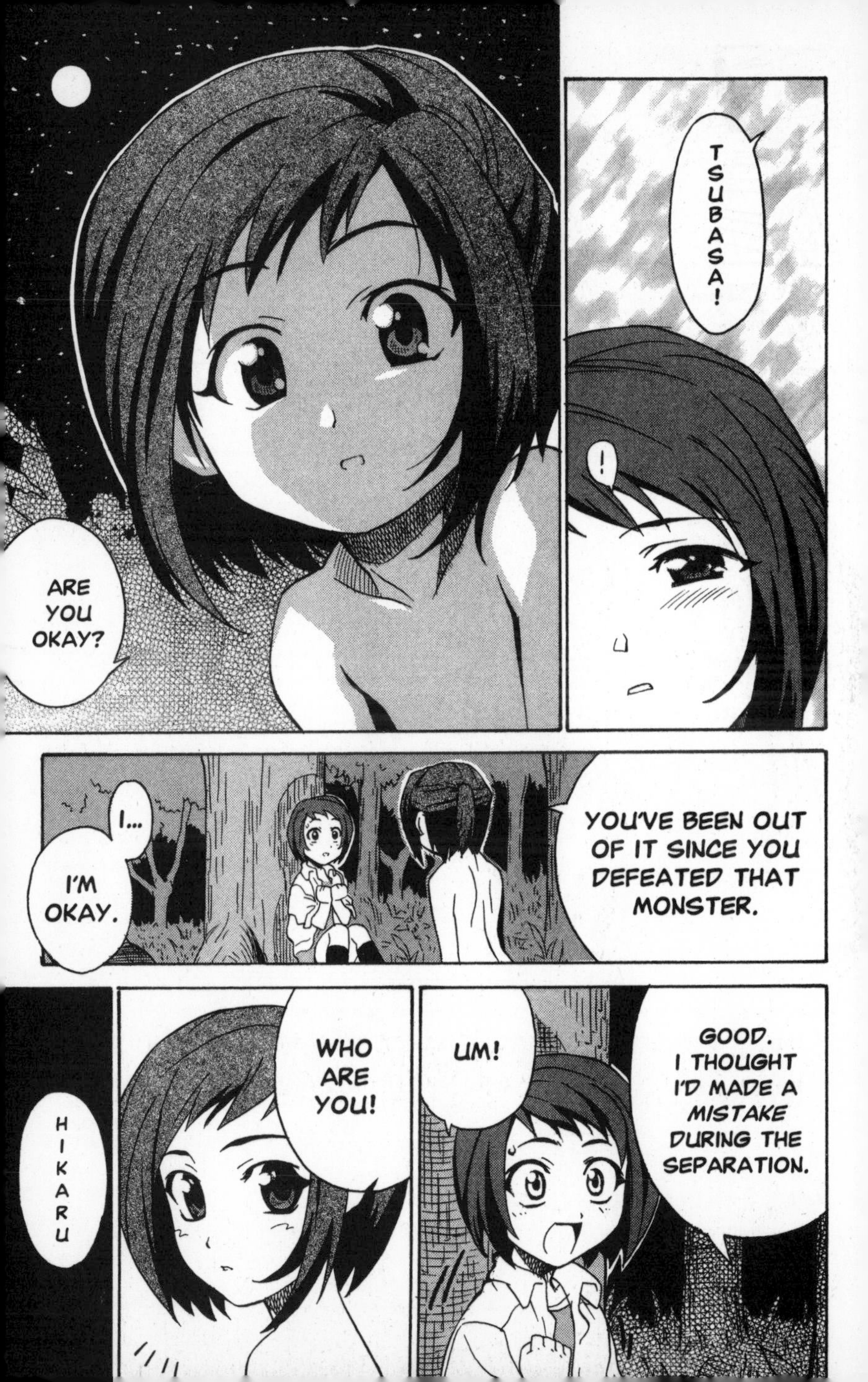
TSUBASA!
!
ARE YOU OKAY?
YOU'VE BEEN OUT OF IT SINCE YOU DEFEATED THAT MONSTER.
I...
I'M OKAY.
GOOD. I THOUGHT I'D MADE A *MISTAKE* DURING THE SEPARATION.
UM!
WHO ARE YOU!
HIKARU

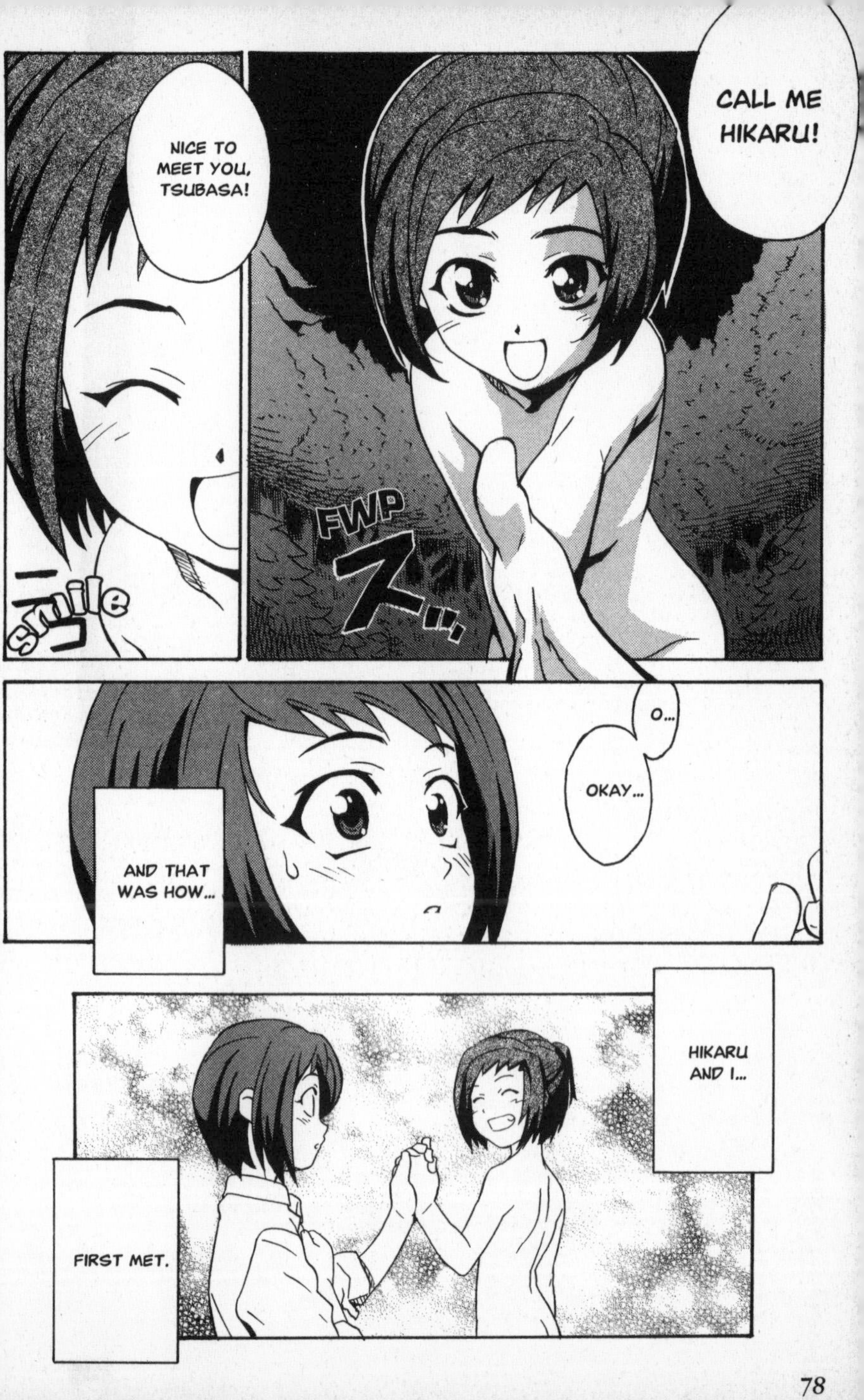
CALL ME HIKARU!
FWP
NICE TO MEET YOU, TSUBASA!
smile
O...
OKAY...
AND THAT WAS HOW...
HIKARU AND I...
FIRST MET.

F I G U R E S E V E N T E E N

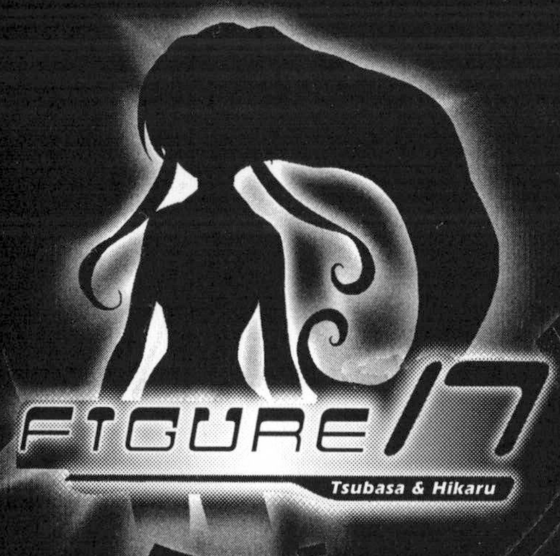
FIGURE 17
Tsubasa & Hikaru

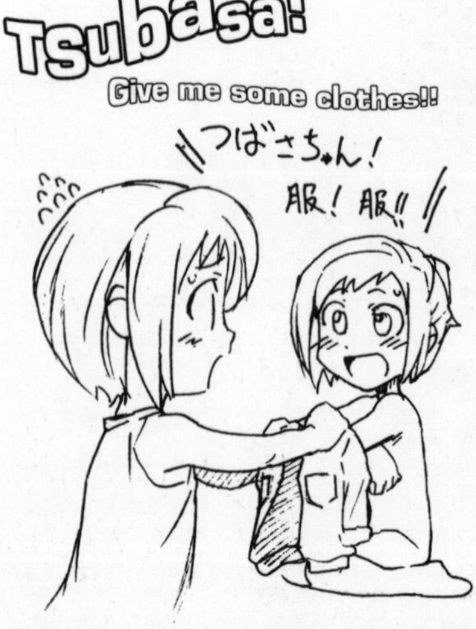
Tsubasa!
Give me some clothes!!
つばさちゃん！
服！服!!

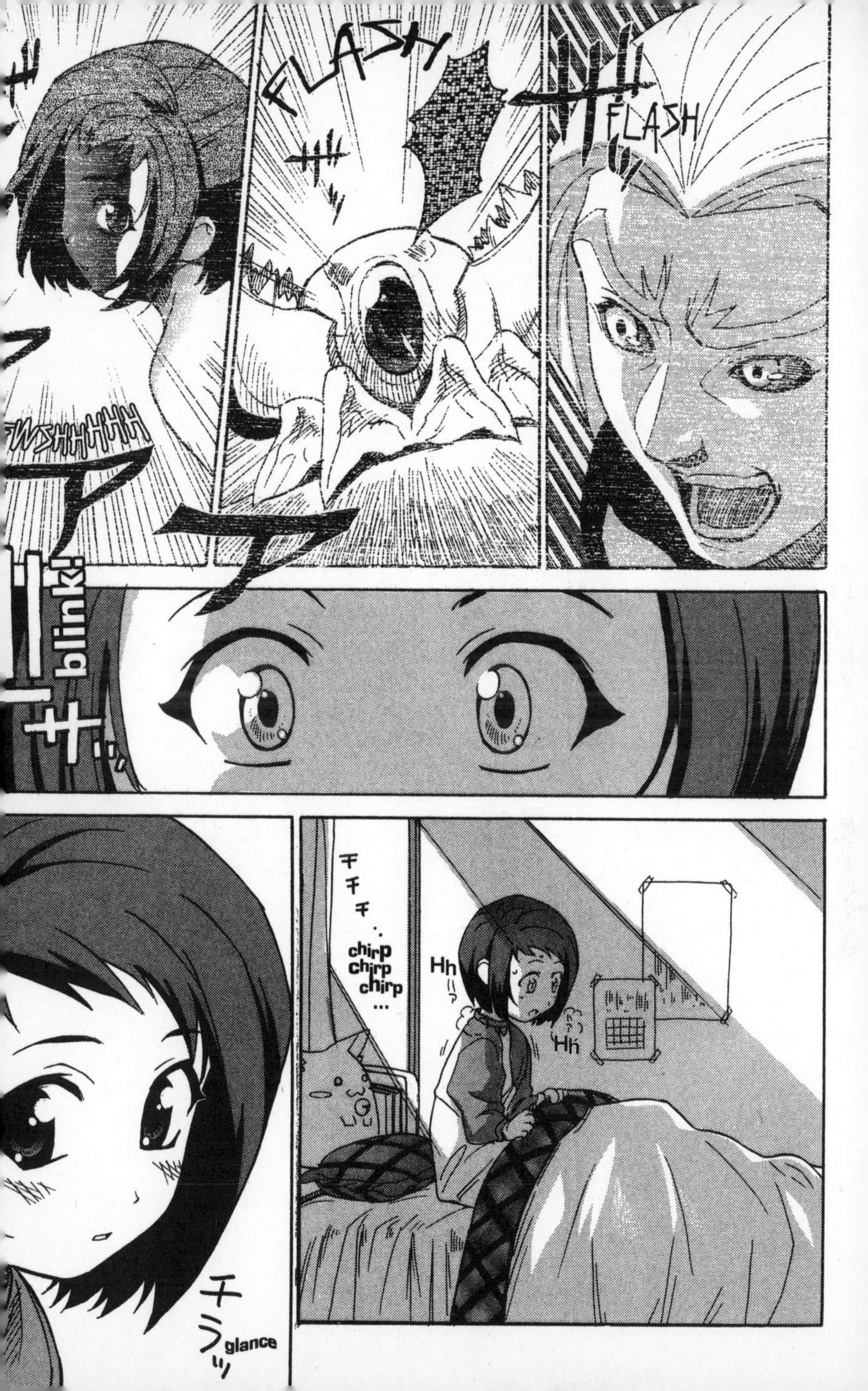
FLASH
FLASH
FWSHHHHHH
blink!
チチチ...
chirp chirp chirp ...
Hh
Hh
チラッ
glance

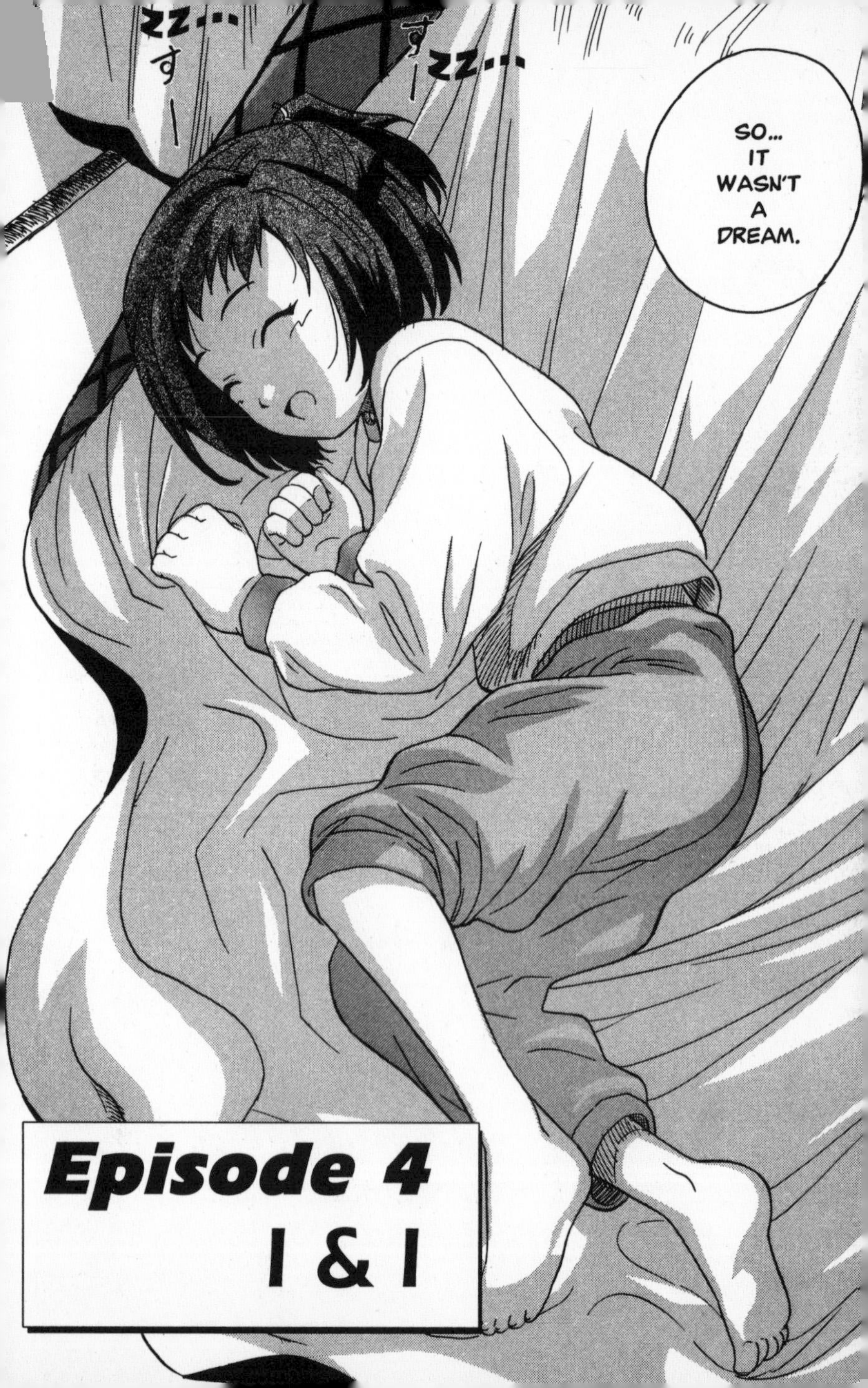
す
ZZ...
ZZ...
す
SO... IT WASN'T A DREAM.
Episode 4
I & I

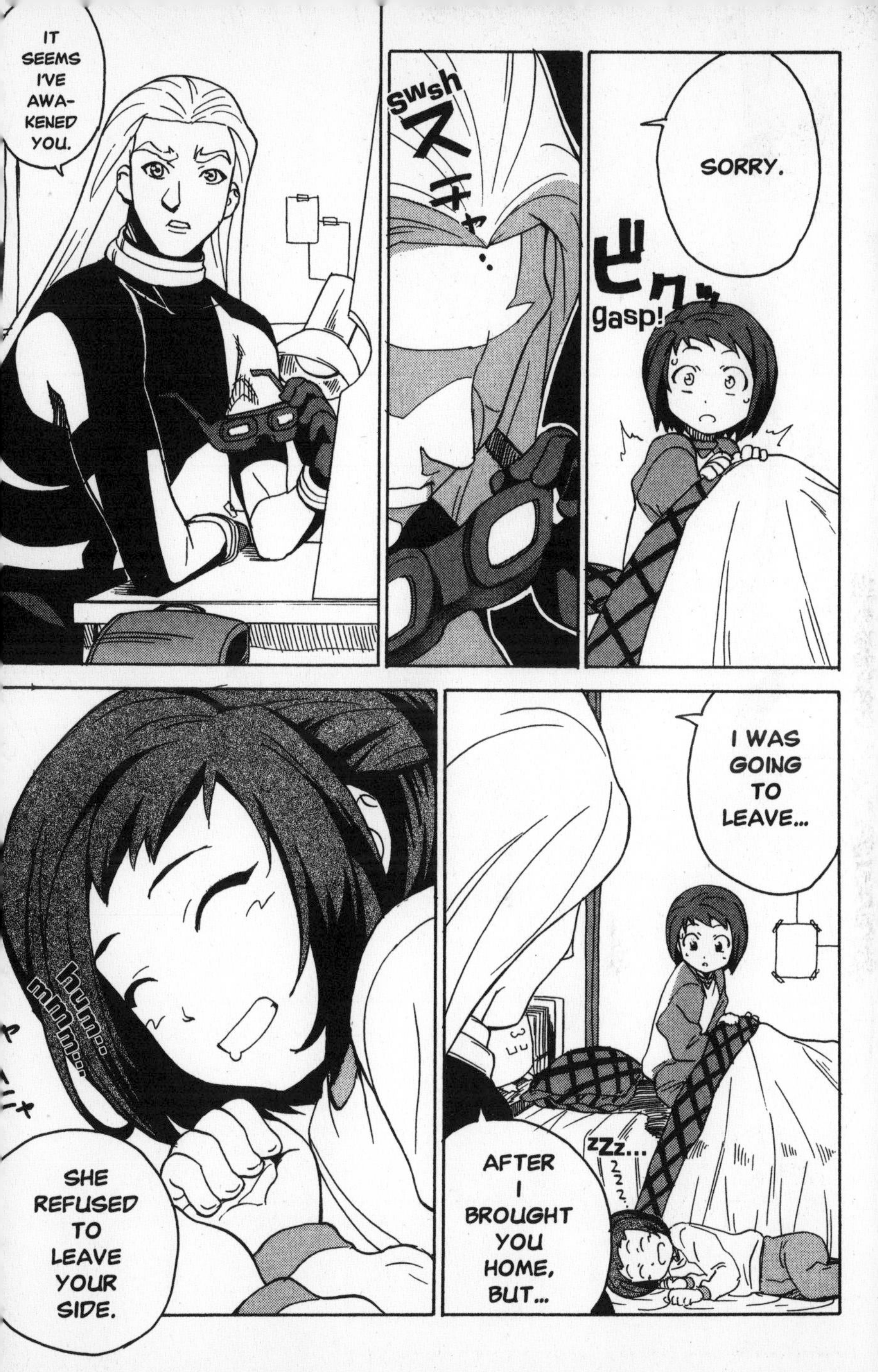
SORRY.
gasp!
swsh
IT SEEMS I'VE AWAKENED YOU.
I WAS GOING TO LEAVE...
AFTER I BROUGHT YOU HOME, BUT...
zZz...
hum... mmm...
SHE REFUSED TO LEAVE YOUR SIDE.

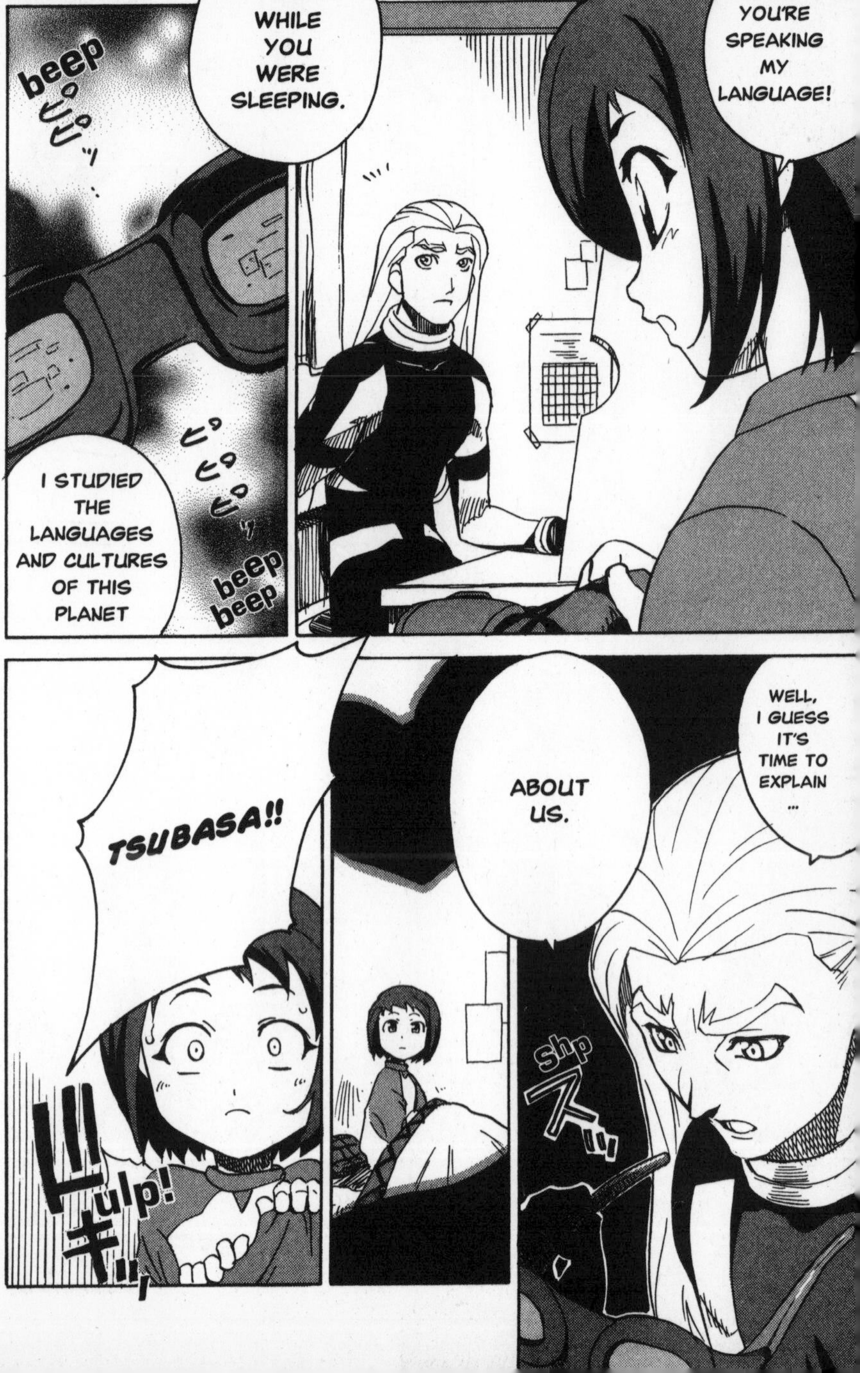
HEY, YOU'RE SPEAKING MY LANGUAGE!
WHILE YOU WERE SLEEPING.
beep
I STUDIED THE LANGUAGES AND CULTURES OF THIS PLANET
beep beep
WELL, I GUESS IT'S TIME TO EXPLAIN ...
ABOUT US.
shp
TSUBASA!!
ulp!

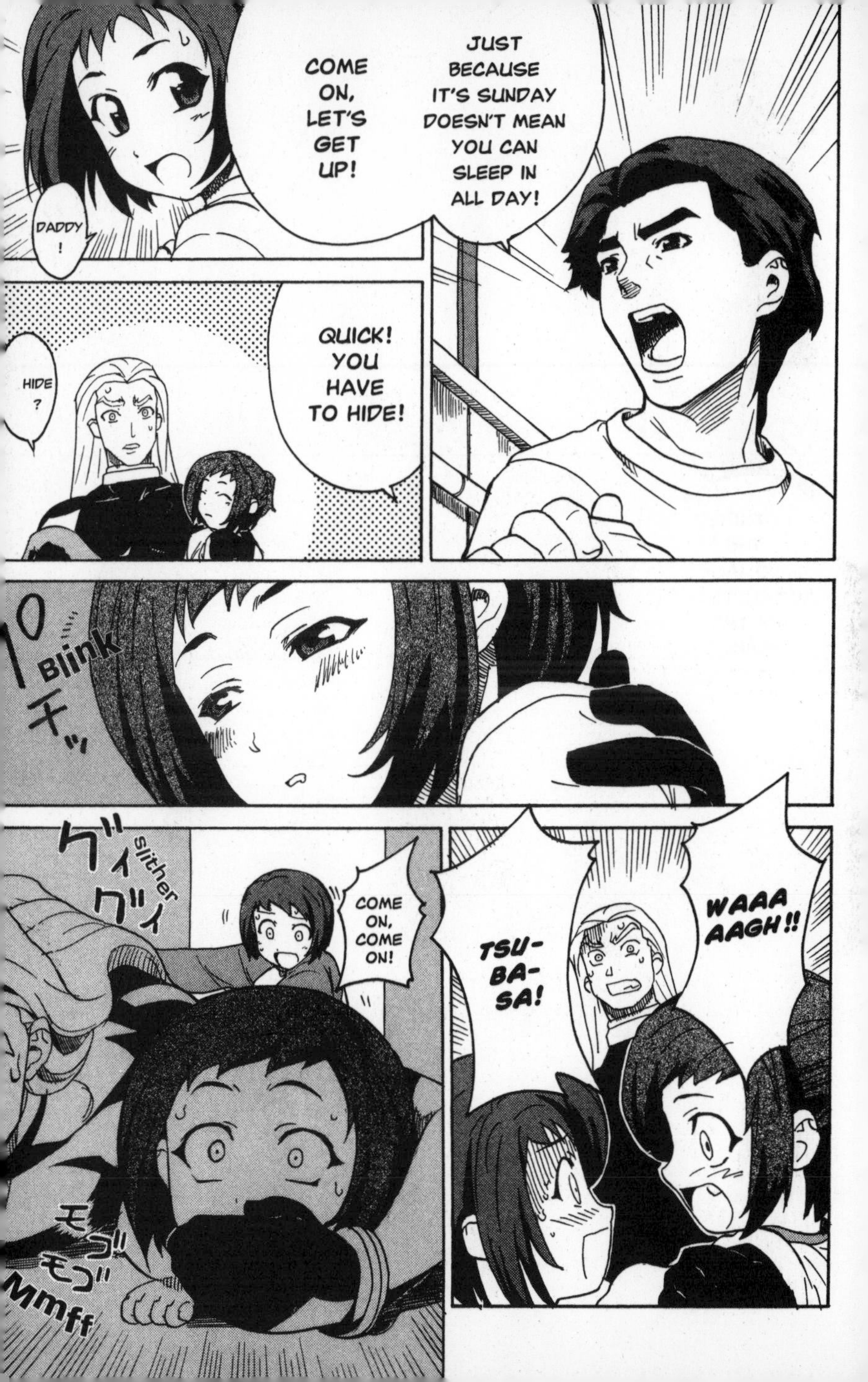
JUST BECAUSE IT'S SUNDAY DOESN'T MEAN YOU CAN SLEEP IN ALL DAY!
COME ON, LET'S GET UP!
DADDY!
QUICK! YOU HAVE TO HIDE!
HIDE?
Blink
WAAAAAGH!!
TSU-BA-SA!
COME ON, COME ON!
slither
Mmff

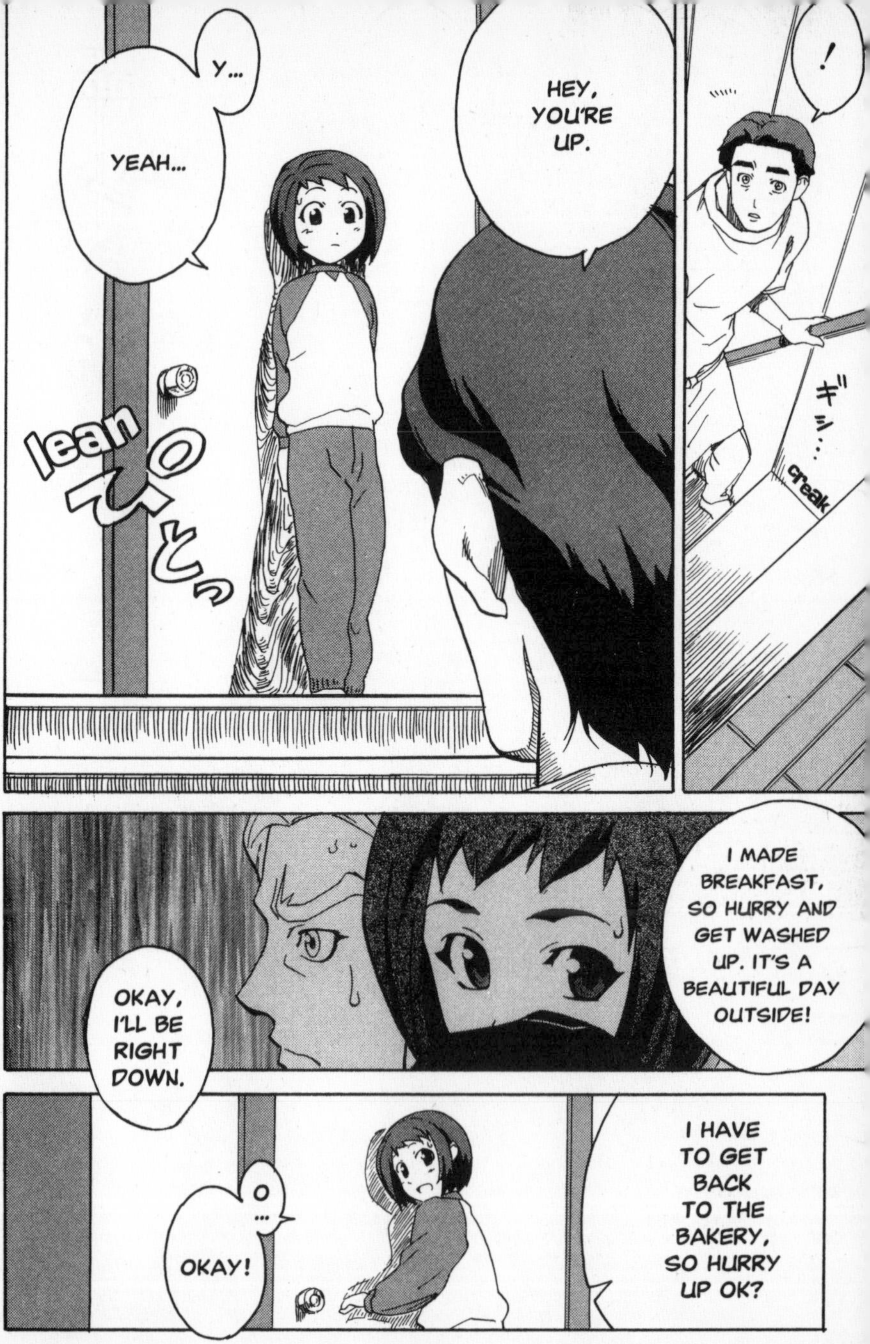
!
ギシ…
creak
HEY, YOU'RE UP.
Y... YEAH...
lean
I MADE BREAKFAST, SO HURRY AND GET WASHED UP. IT'S A BEAUTIFUL DAY OUTSIDE!
OKAY, I'LL BE RIGHT DOWN.
I HAVE TO GET BACK TO THE BAKERY, SO HURRY UP OK?
O... OKAY!

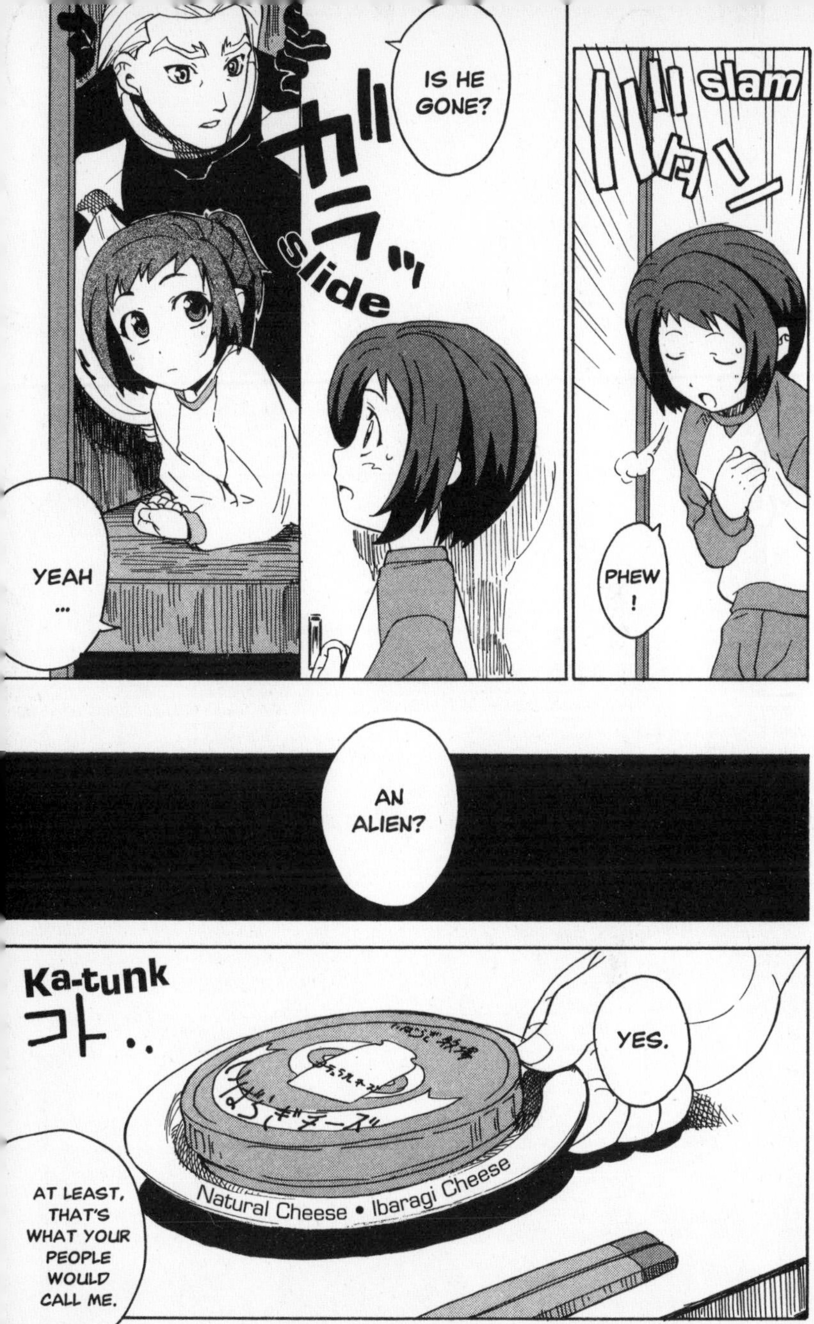
slam
PHEW!
slide
IS HE GONE?
YEAH...
AN ALIEN?
Ka-tunk
YES.
AT LEAST, THAT'S WHAT YOUR PEOPLE WOULD CALL ME.
Natural Cheese • Ibaragi Cheese

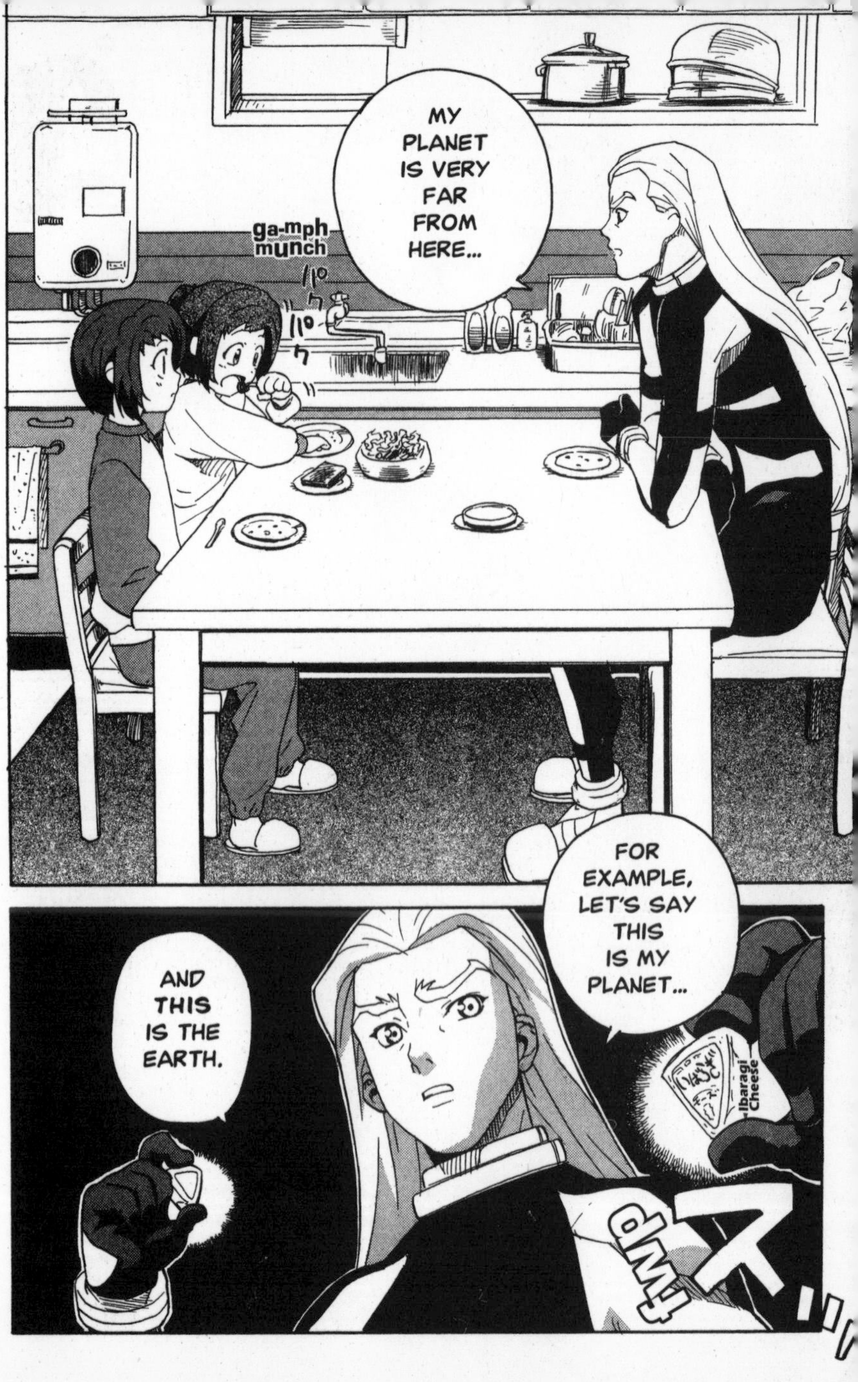
MY PLANET IS VERY FAR FROM HERE...
ga-mph munch
FOR EXAMPLE, LET'S SAY THIS IS MY PLANET...
Ibaragi Cheese
AND THIS IS THE EARTH.

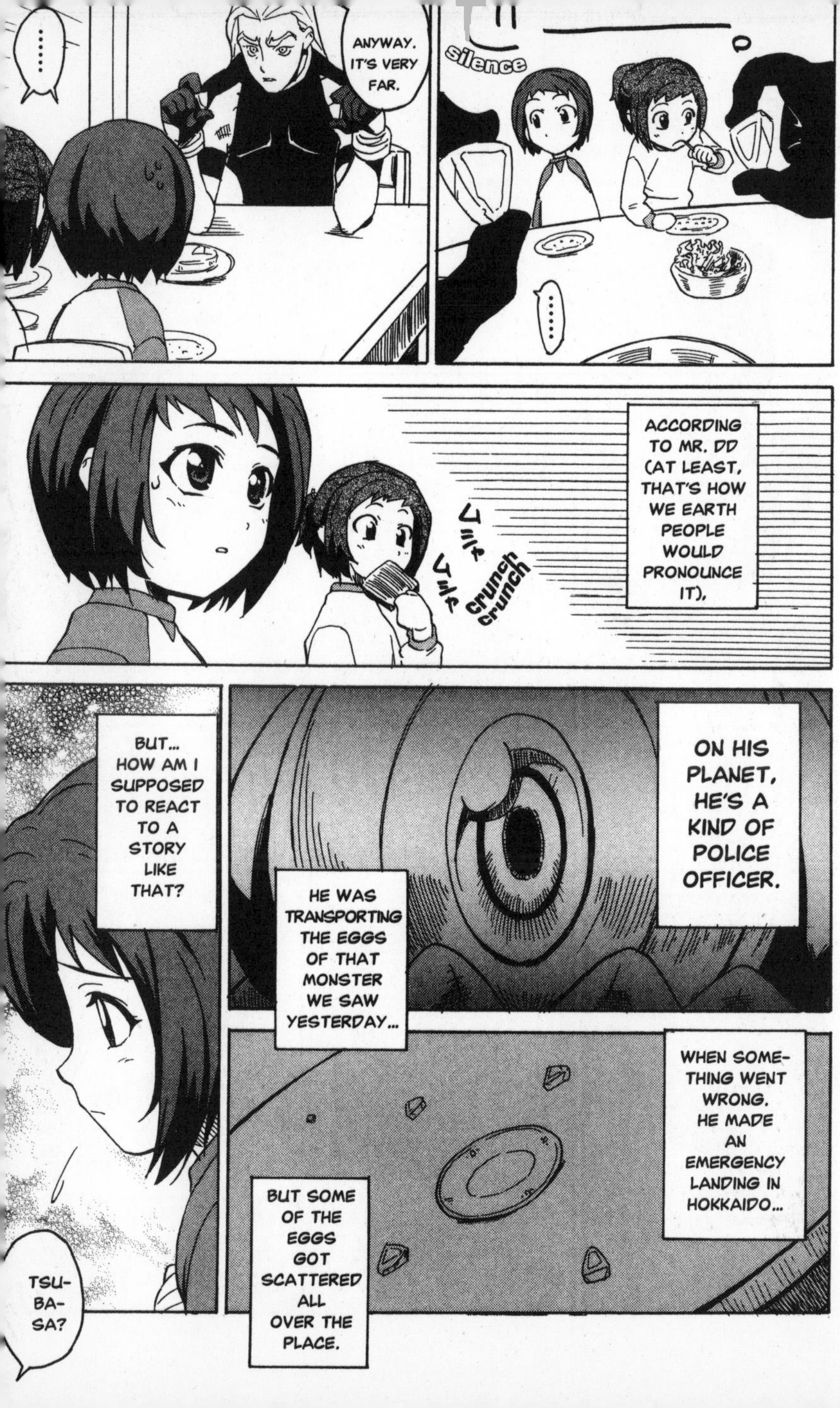
silence
......
ANYWAY. IT'S VERY FAR.
......
ACCORDING TO MR. DD (AT LEAST, THAT'S HOW WE EARTH PEOPLE WOULD PRONOUNCE IT),
crunch crunch
ON HIS PLANET, HE'S A KIND OF POLICE OFFICER.
HE WAS TRANSPORTING THE EGGS OF THAT MONSTER WE SAW YESTERDAY...
WHEN SOMETHING WENT WRONG, HE MADE AN EMERGENCY LANDING IN HOKKAIDO...
BUT SOME OF THE EGGS GOT SCATTERED ALL OVER THE PLACE.
BUT... HOW AM I SUPPOSED TO REACT TO A STORY LIKE THAT?
TSU-BA-SA?

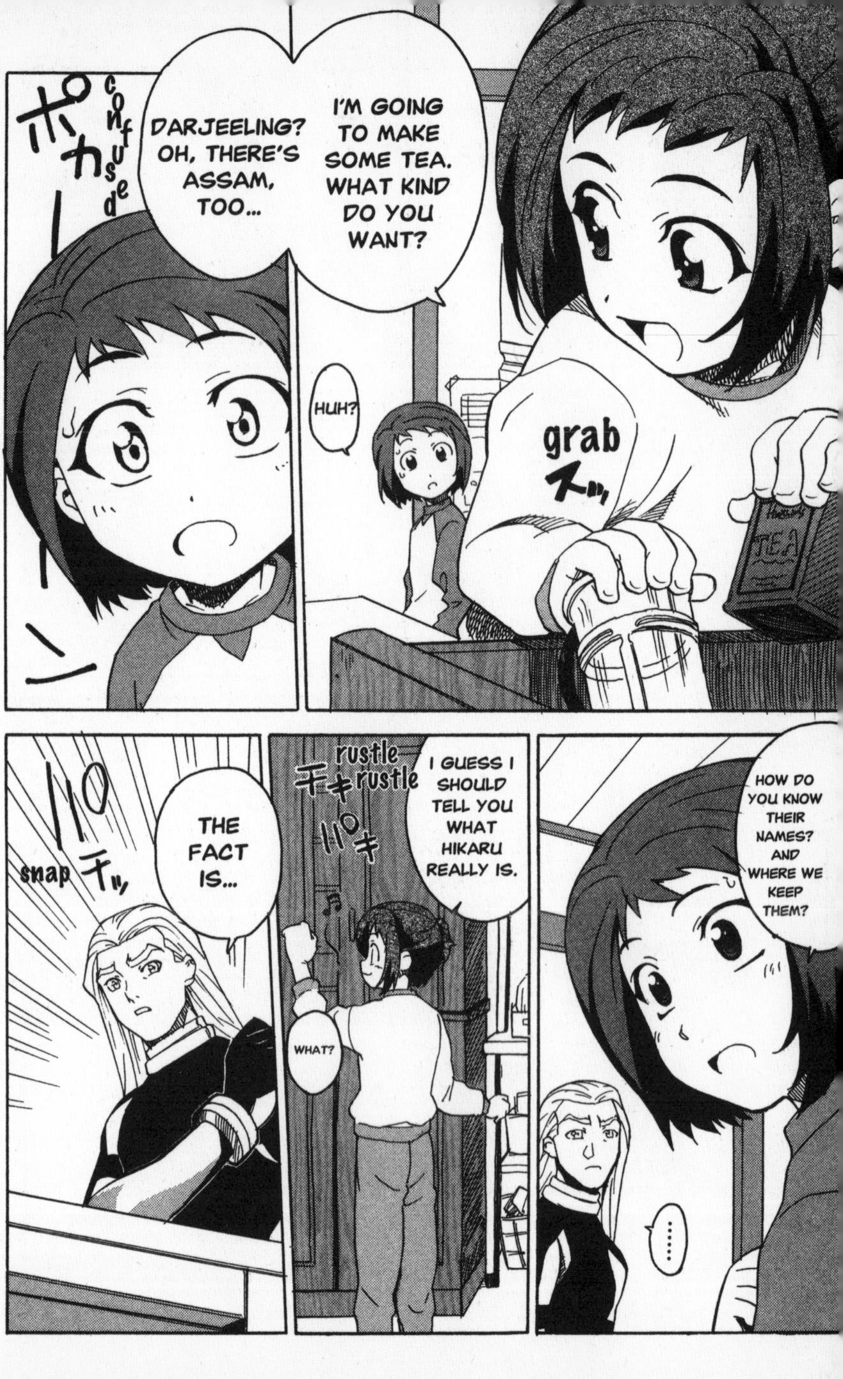

I'M GOING TO MAKE SOME TEA. WHAT KIND DO YOU WANT?
DARJEELING? OH, THERE'S ASSAM, TOO...
confused
ポカ
ーン
grab
スッ
HUH?
HOW DO YOU KNOW THEIR NAMES? AND WHERE WE KEEP THEM?
......
I GUESS I SHOULD TELL YOU WHAT HIKARU REALLY IS.
rustle rustle
ゴキ パキ
WHAT?
THE FACT IS...
snap
パチッ

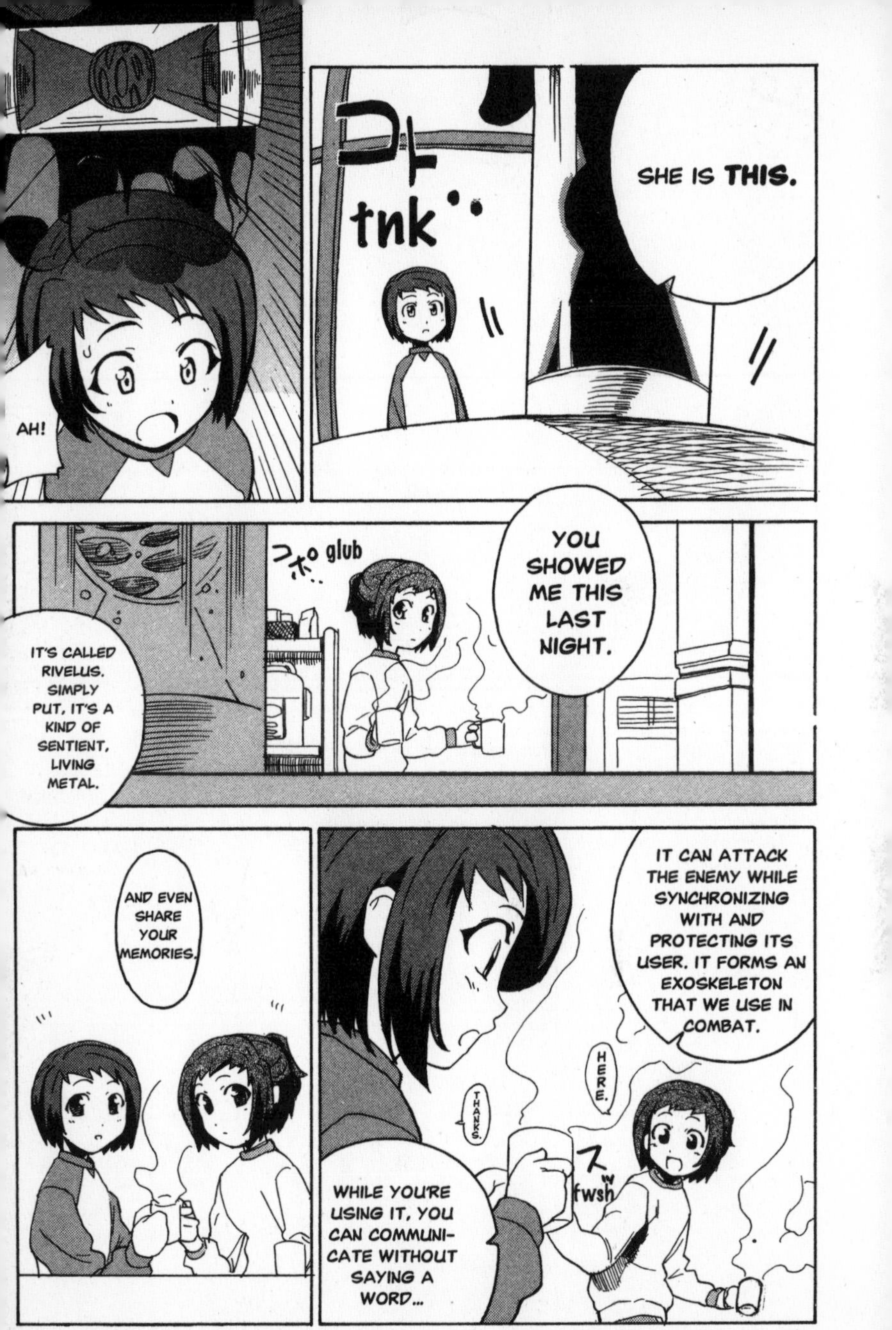
SHE IS THIS.
tnk
AH!
YOU SHOWED ME THIS LAST NIGHT.
glub
IT'S CALLED RIVELUS. SIMPLY PUT, IT'S A KIND OF SENTIENT, LIVING METAL.
IT CAN ATTACK THE ENEMY WHILE SYNCHRONIZING WITH AND PROTECTING ITS USER. IT FORMS AN EXOSKELETON THAT WE USE IN COMBAT.
HERE.
THANKS.
fwsh
WHILE YOU'RE USING IT, YOU CAN COMMUNICATE WITHOUT SAYING A WORD...
AND EVEN SHARE YOUR MEMORIES.

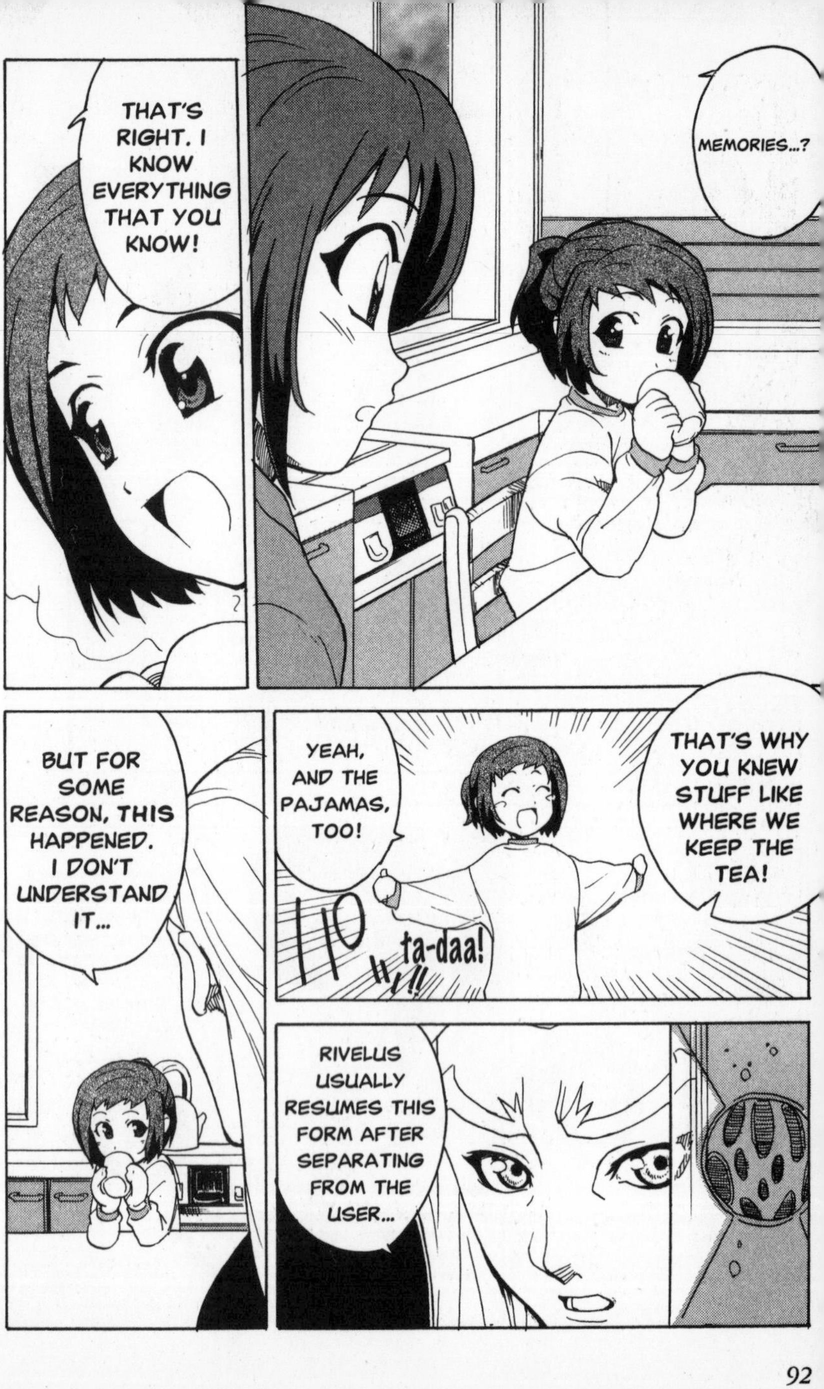
MEMORIES...?
THAT'S RIGHT. I KNOW EVERYTHING THAT YOU KNOW!
THAT'S WHY YOU KNEW STUFF LIKE WHERE WE KEEP THE TEA!
YEAH, AND THE PAJAMAS, TOO!
ta-daa!
BUT FOR SOME REASON, THIS HAPPENED. I DON'T UNDERSTAND IT...
RIVELUS USUALLY RESUMES THIS FORM AFTER SEPARATING FROM THE USER...

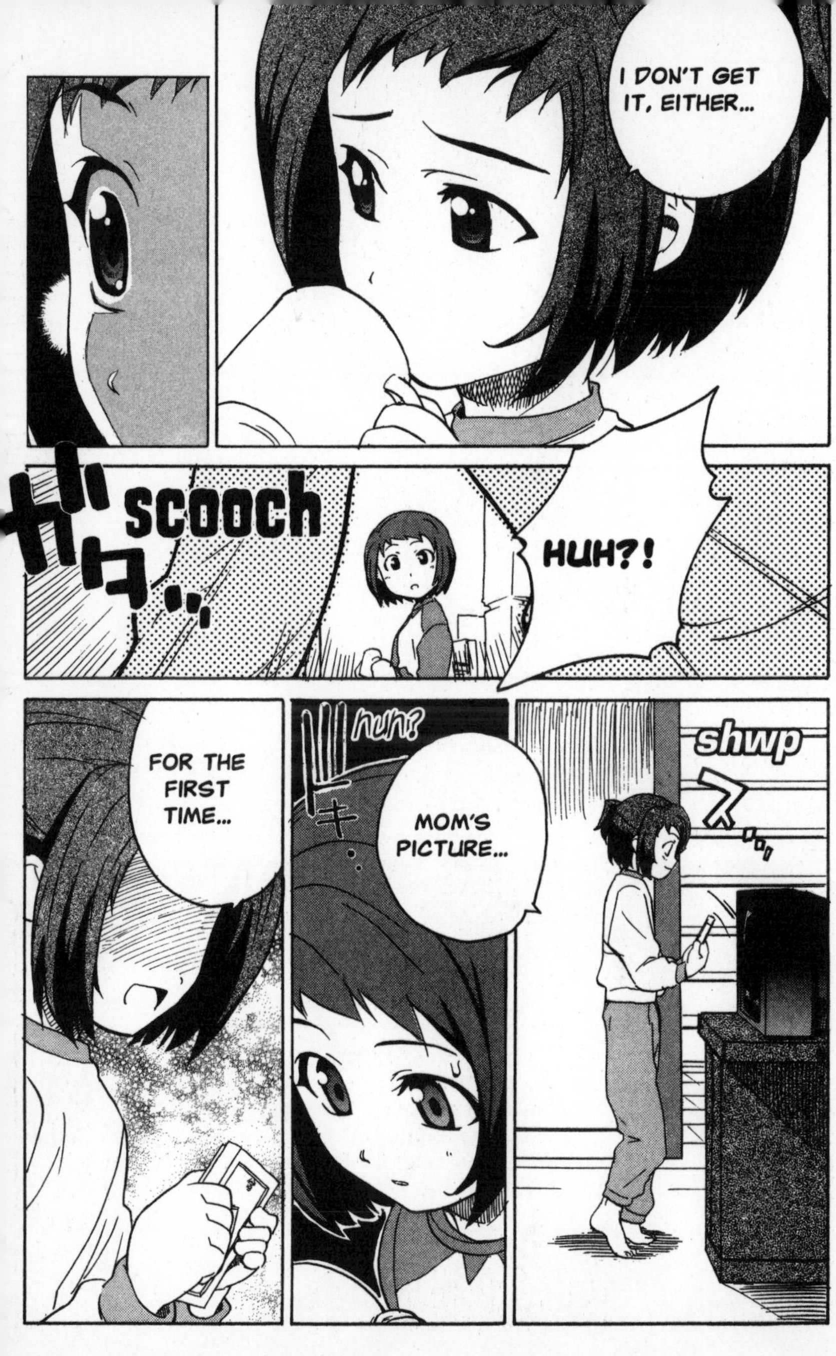
I DON'T GET IT, EITHER...
HUH?!
ガタ
scooch
ス
shwp
nun?
ドキ
MOM'S PICTURE...
FOR THE FIRST TIME...

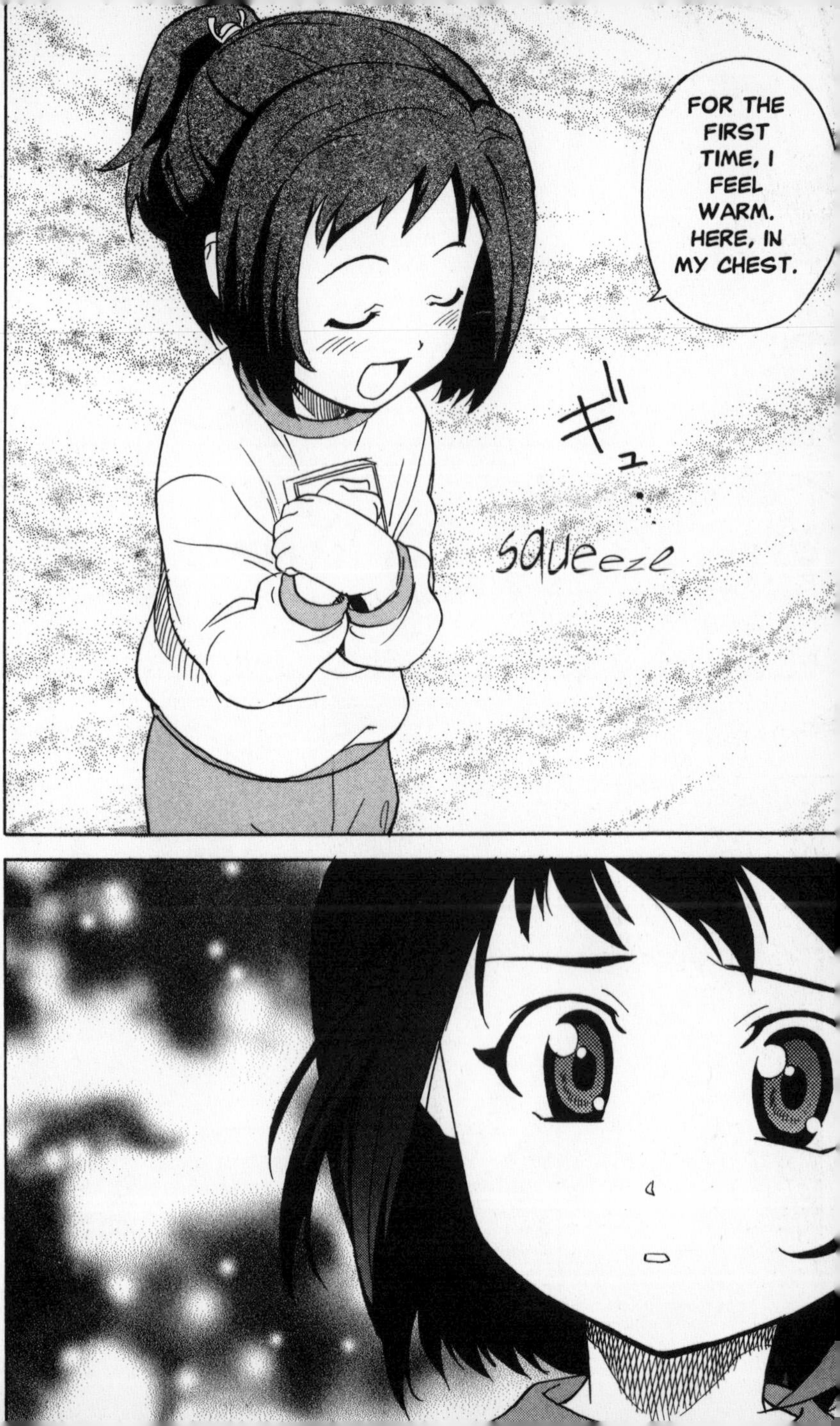
FOR THE FIRST TIME, I FEEL WARM. HERE, IN MY CHEST.
ギュ…
squeeze

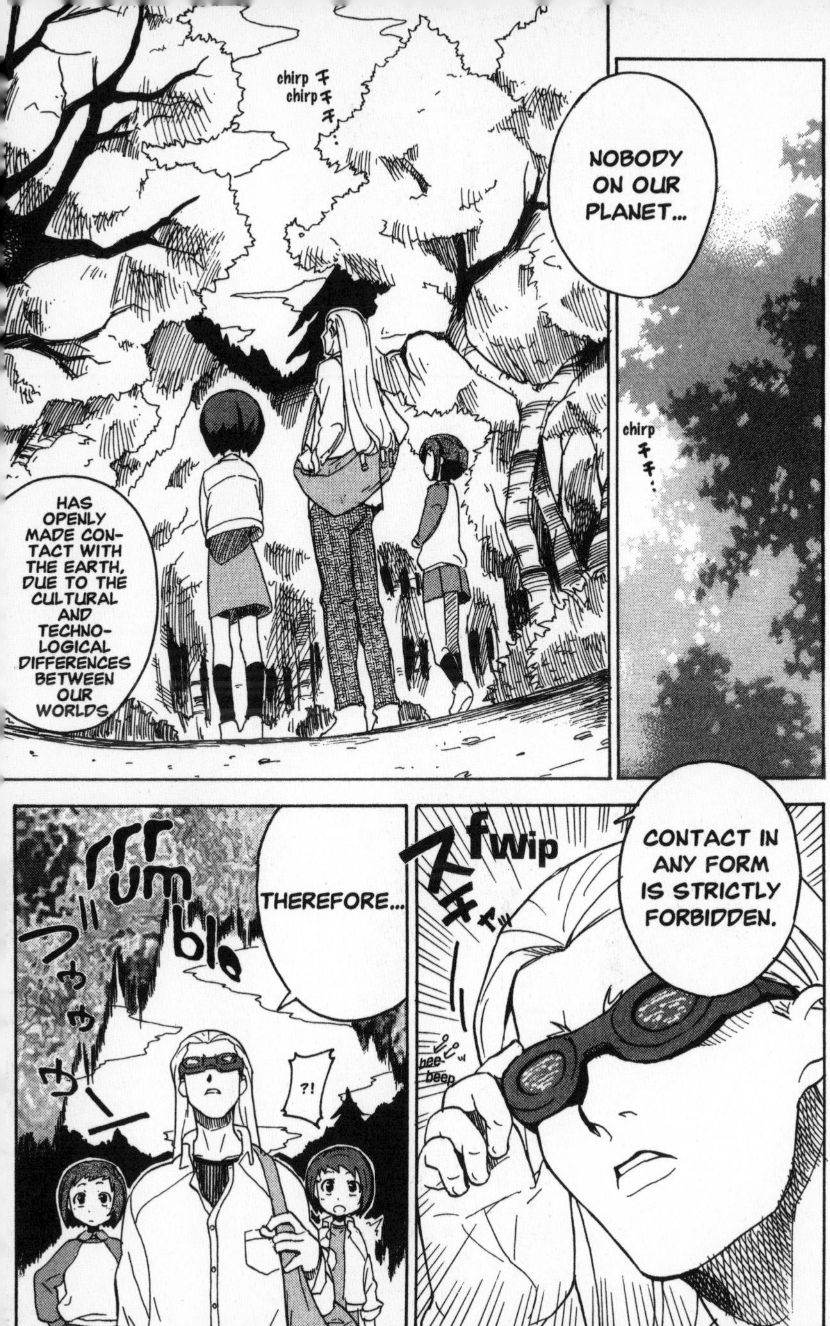
chirp チチ
chirp チチ…
NOBODY ON OUR PLANET...
chirp チチ…
HAS OPENLY MADE CONTACT WITH THE EARTH, DUE TO THE CULTURAL AND TECHNOLOGICAL DIFFERENCES BETWEEN OUR WORLDS.
CONTACT IN ANY FORM IS STRICTLY FORBIDDEN.
fwip
bee-beep
THEREFORE...
rrrumble
?!

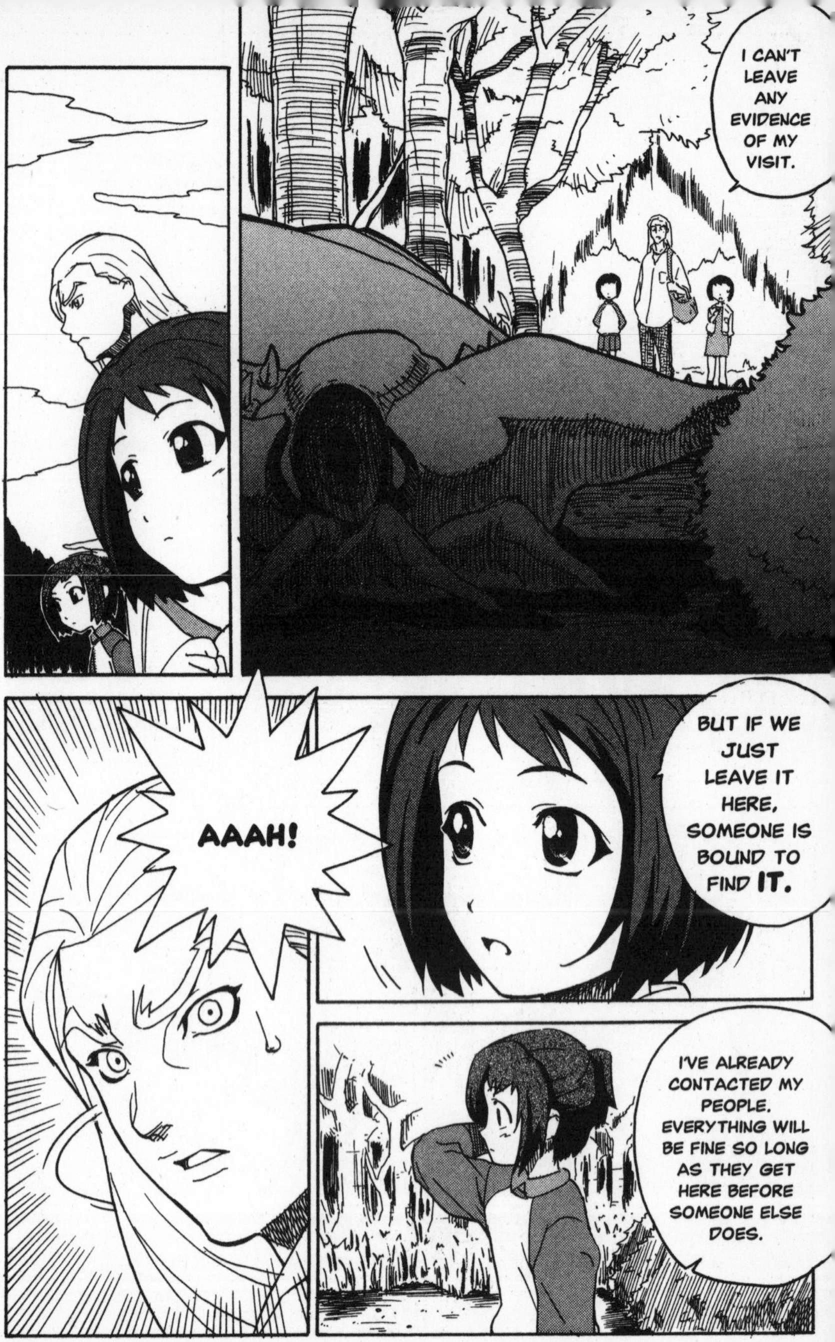
I CAN'T LEAVE ANY EVIDENCE OF MY VISIT.
BUT IF WE JUST LEAVE IT HERE, SOMEONE IS BOUND TO FIND IT.
AAAH!
I'VE ALREADY CONTACTED MY PEOPLE. EVERYTHING WILL BE FINE SO LONG AS THEY GET HERE BEFORE SOMEONE ELSE DOES.

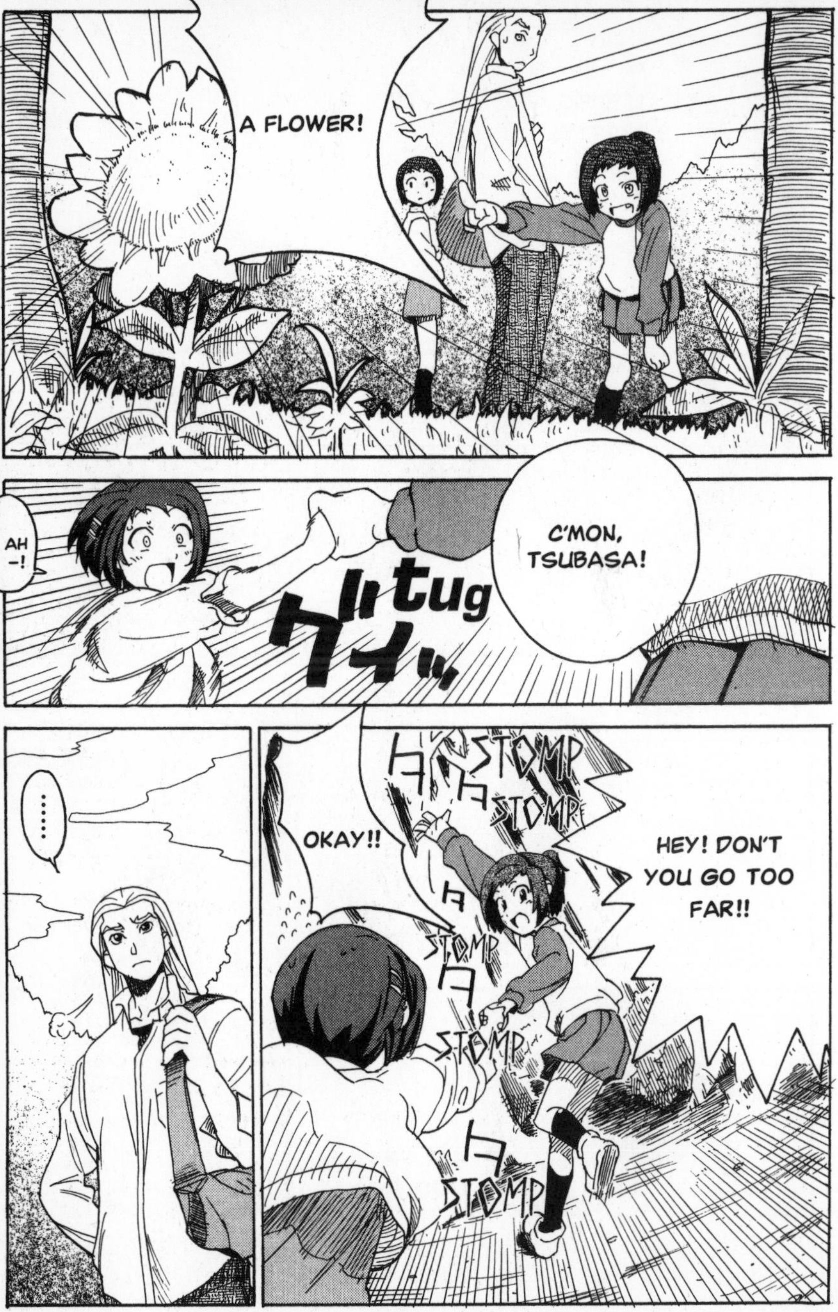
A FLOWER!
C'MON, TSUBASA!
AH -!
tug
HEY! DON'T YOU GO TOO FAR!!
STOMP
STOMP
OKAY!!
......
STOMP
STOMP
STOMP

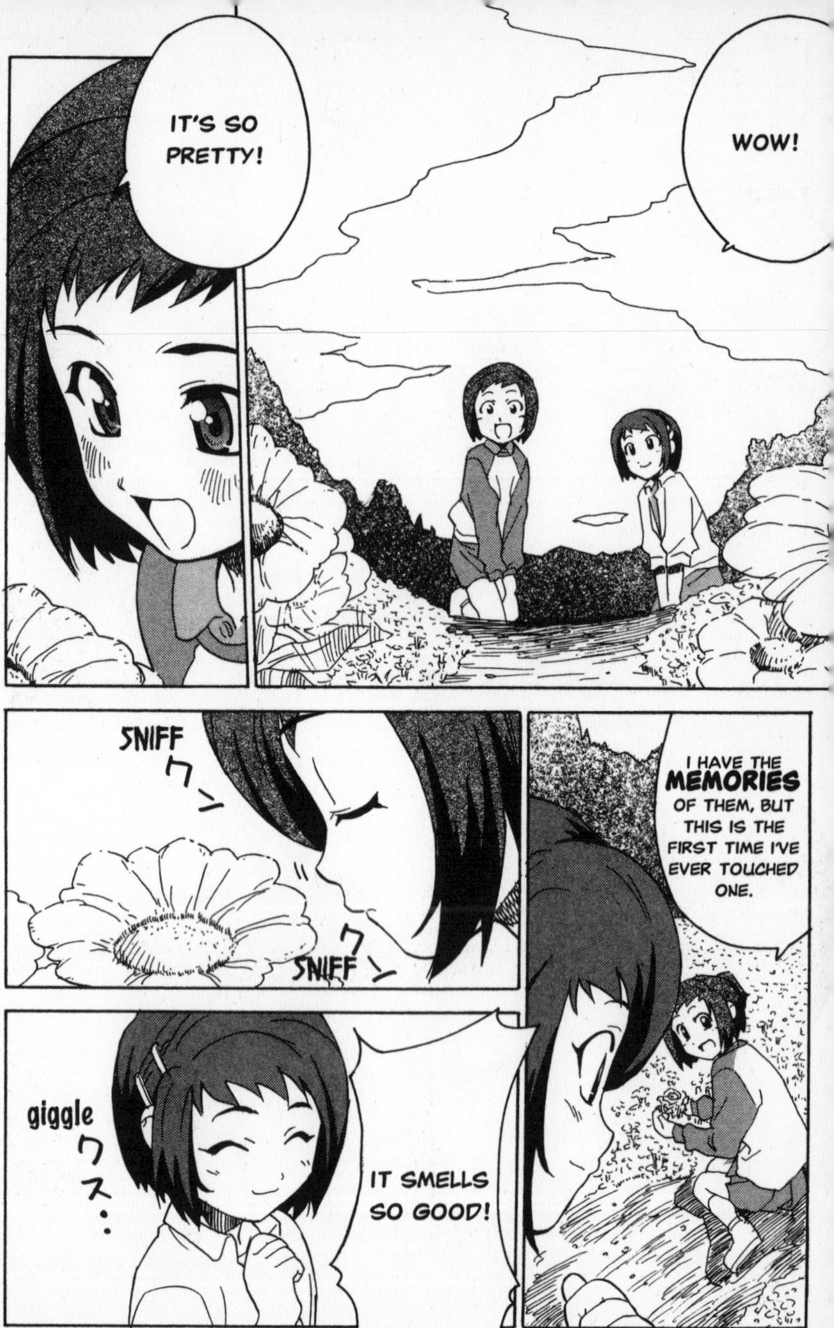
WOW!
IT'S SO PRETTY!
I HAVE THE **MEMORIES** OF THEM, BUT THIS IS THE FIRST TIME I'VE EVER TOUCHED ONE.
SNIFF クン
SNIFF クン
IT SMELLS SO GOOD!
giggle ワス・・

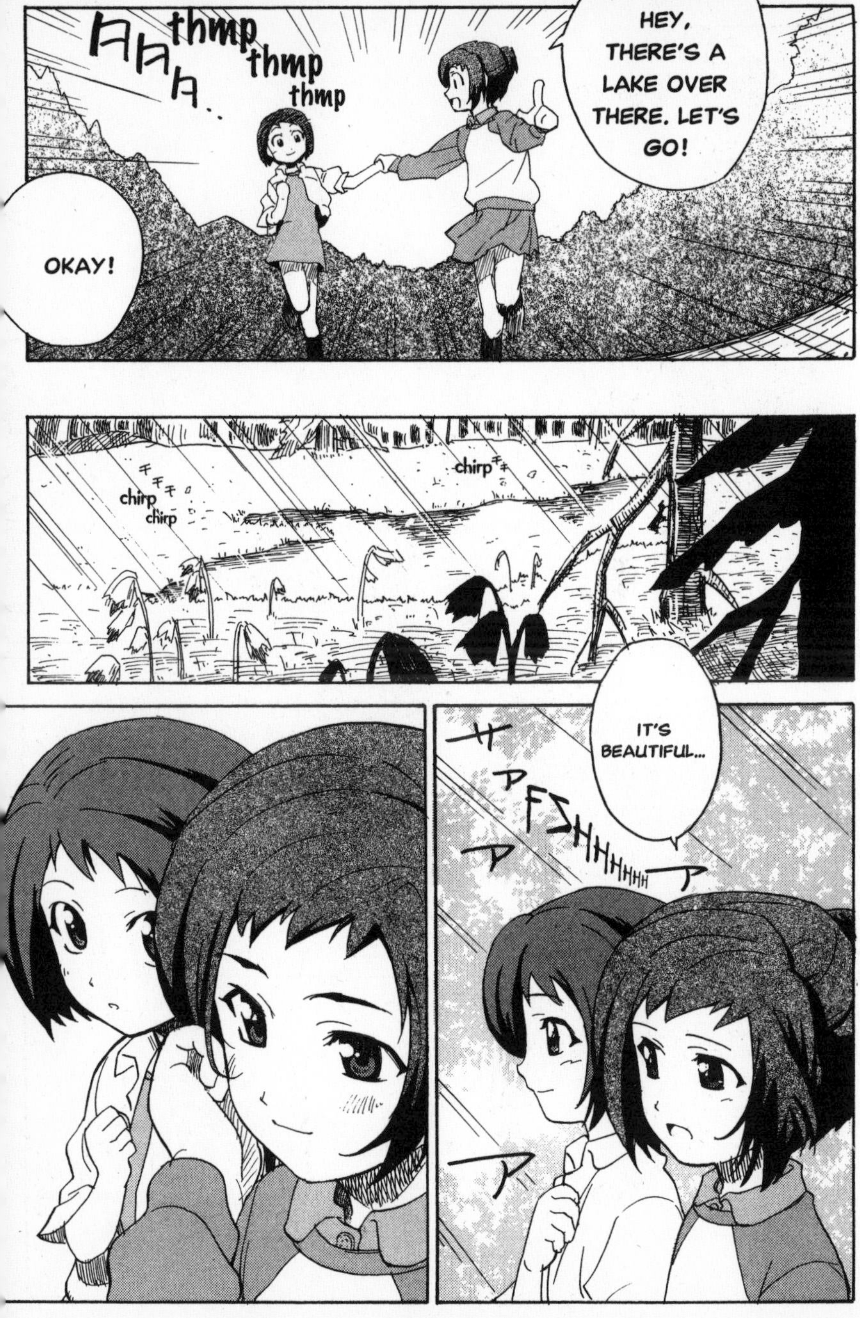
HEY, THERE'S A LAKE OVER THERE. LET'S GO!
thmp thmp thmp
OKAY!
chirp
chirp
chirp
IT'S BEAUTIFUL...
FSHHHHHHH

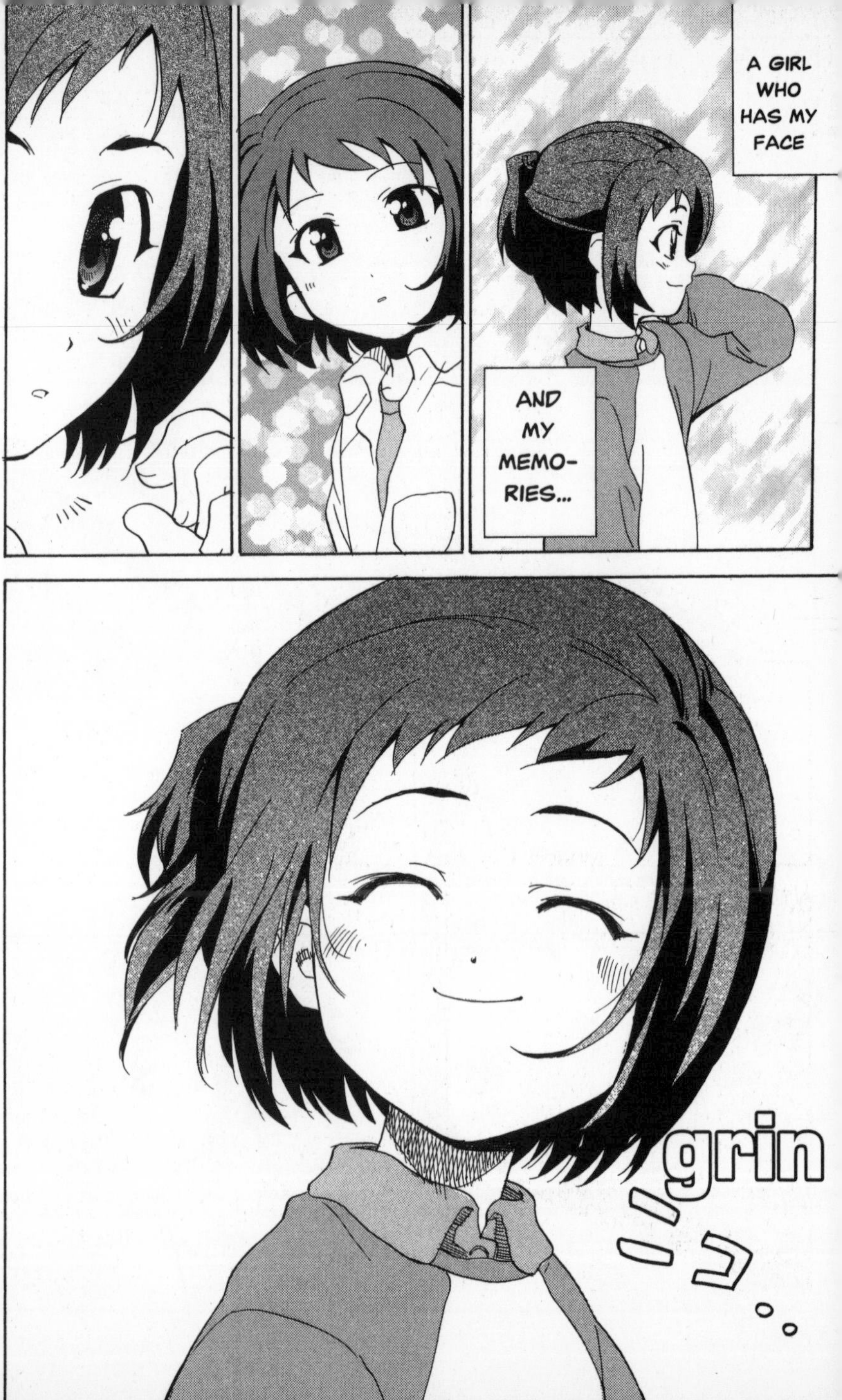
A GIRL WHO HAS MY FACE
AND MY MEMO-RIES...
grin

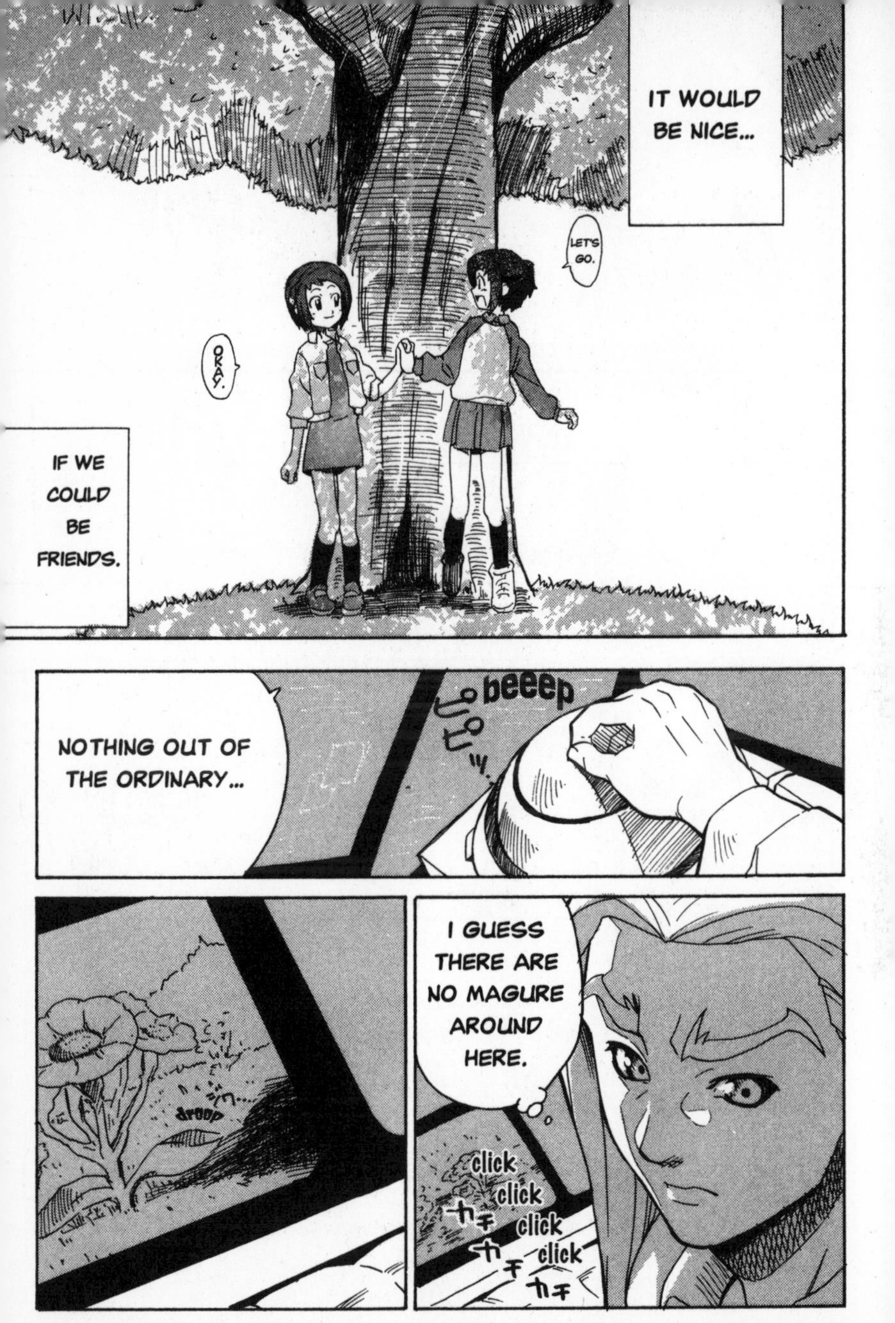

IT WOULD BE NICE...
LET'S GO.
OKAY.
IF WE COULD BE FRIENDS.
beeep
NOTHING OUT OF THE ORDINARY...
I GUESS THERE ARE NO MAGURE AROUND HERE.
click click click click
droop

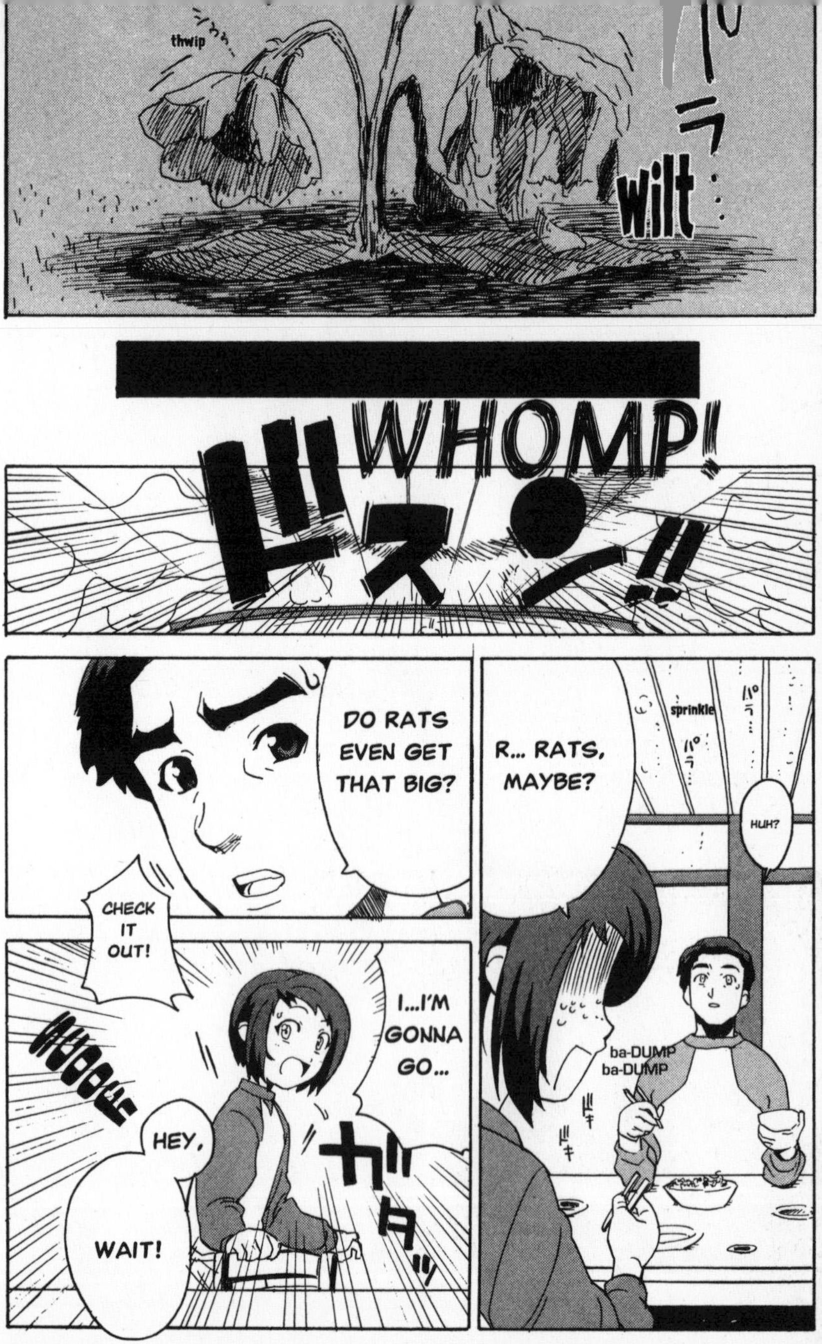
wilt
thwip
WHOMP!
sprinkle
HUH?
R... RATS, MAYBE?
ba-DUMP ba-DUMP
DO RATS EVEN GET THAT BIG?
CHECK IT OUT!
I...I'M GONNA GO...
HEY, WAIT!

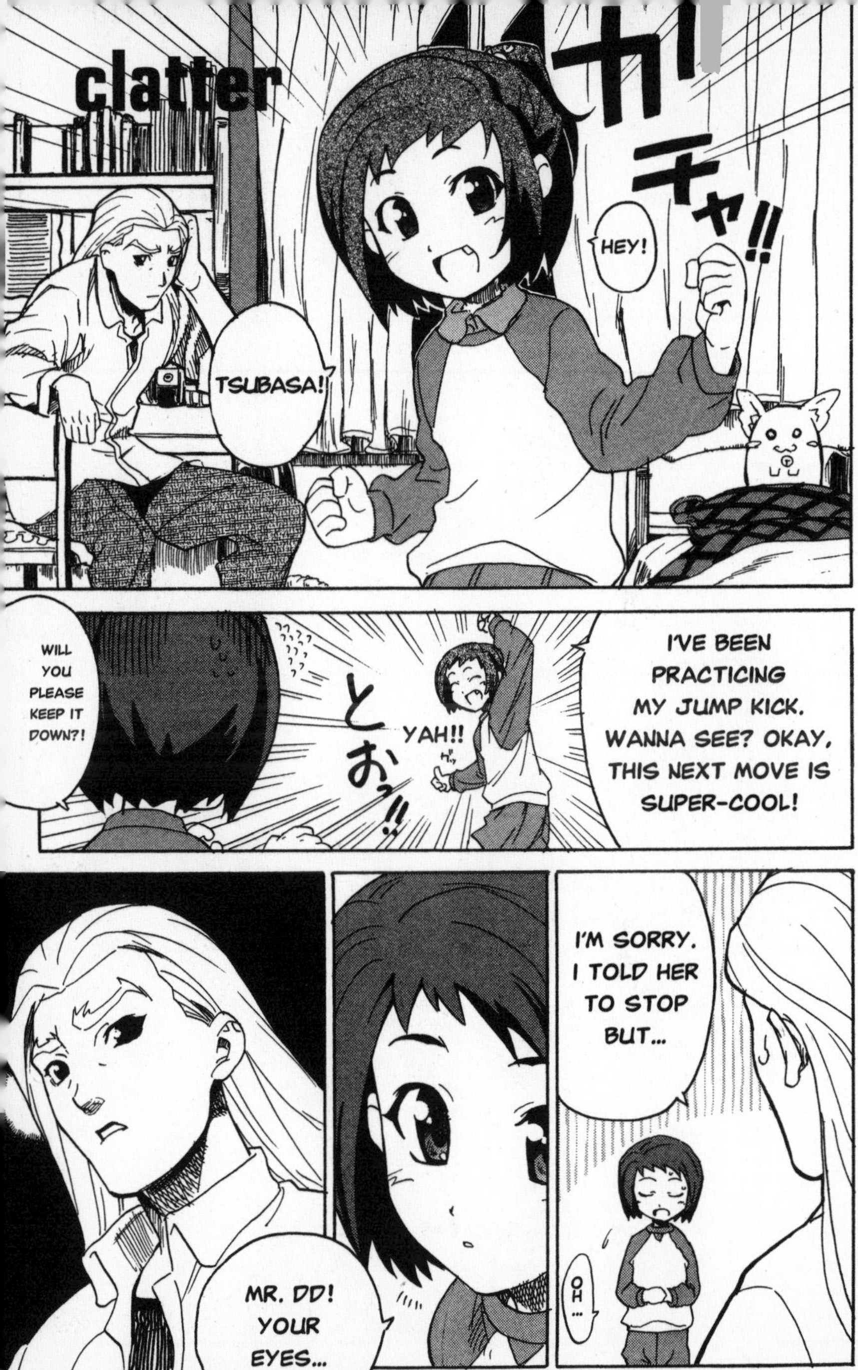
clatter
カチャ!!
HEY!
TSUBASA!
I'VE BEEN PRACTICING MY JUMP KICK. WANNA SEE? OKAY, THIS NEXT MOVE IS SUPER-COOL!
YAH!!
とおっ!!
WILL YOU PLEASE KEEP IT DOWN?!
I'M SORRY. I TOLD HER TO STOP BUT...
OH...
MR. DD! YOUR EYES...

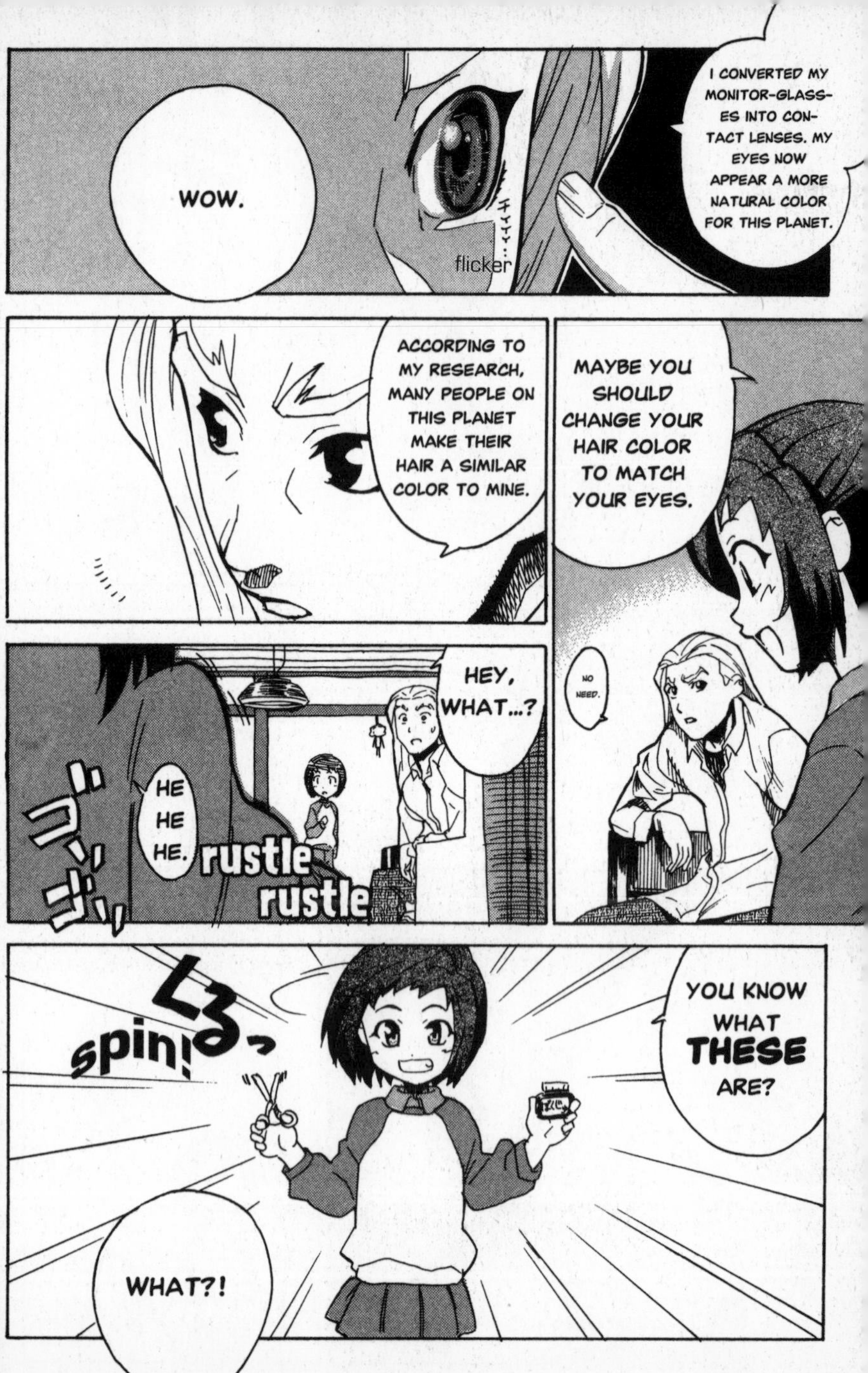

I CONVERTED MY MONITOR-GLASSES INTO CONTACT LENSES. MY EYES NOW APPEAR A MORE NATURAL COLOR FOR THIS PLANET.
チイイイ…
flicker
WOW.
MAYBE YOU SHOULD CHANGE YOUR HAIR COLOR TO MATCH YOUR EYES.
NO NEED.
ACCORDING TO MY RESEARCH, MANY PEOPLE ON THIS PLANET MAKE THEIR HAIR A SIMILAR COLOR TO MINE.
HEY, WHAT...?
HE HE HE.
rustle rustle
YOU KNOW WHAT THESE ARE?
spin!
WHAT?!

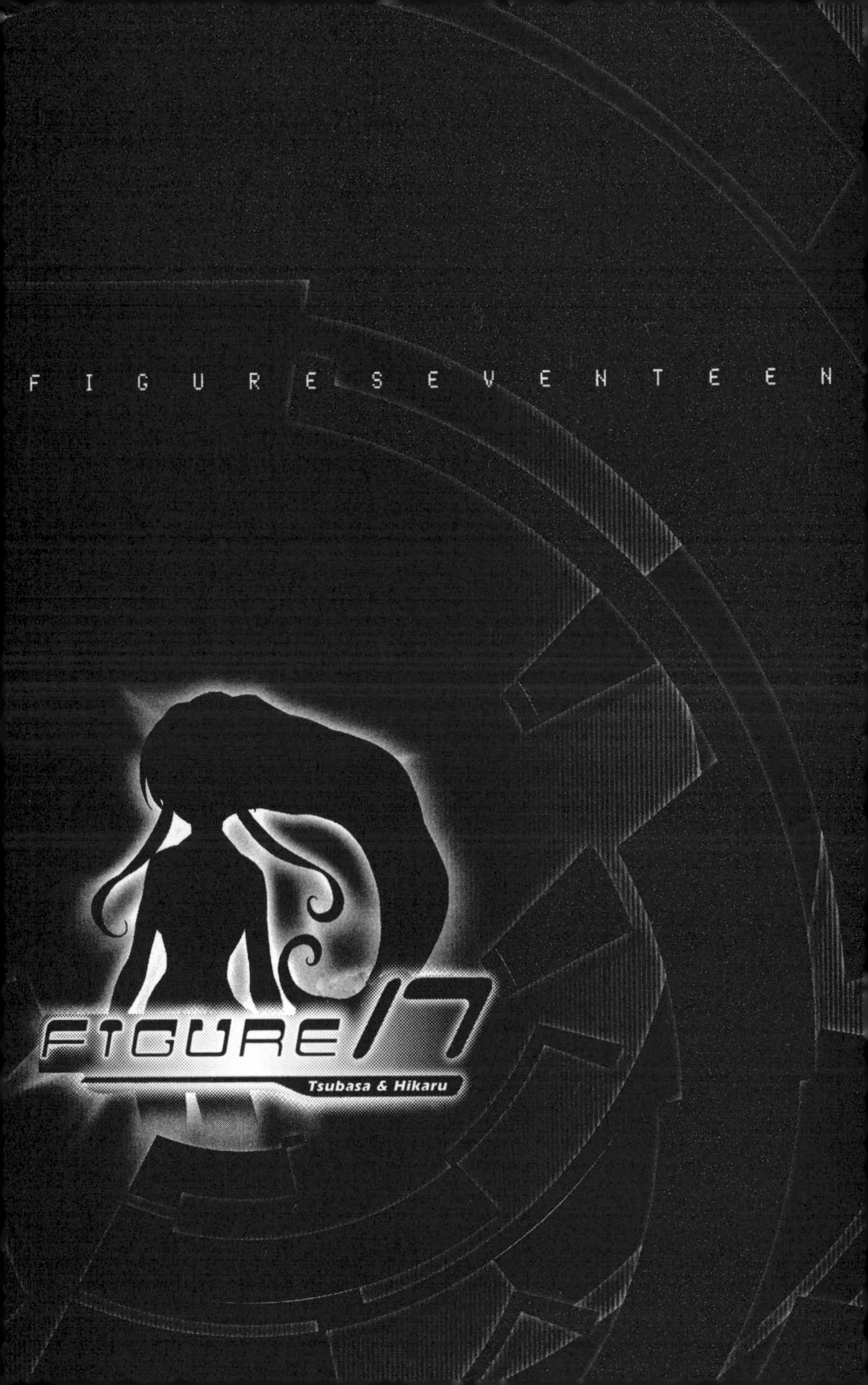
FIGURE SEVENTEEN
FIGURE 17
Tsubasa & Hikaru

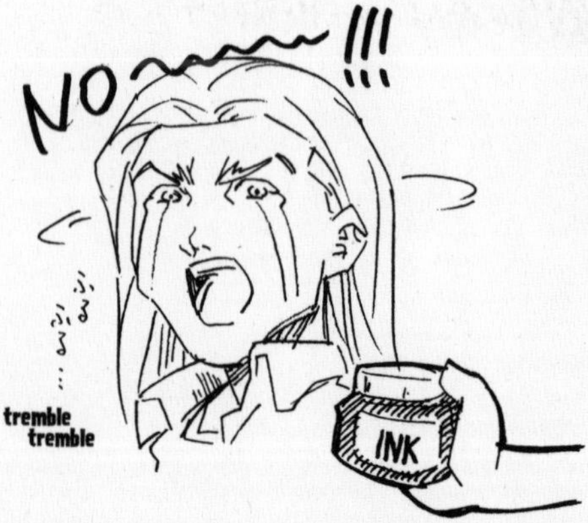
NO~~~!!!
tremble
tremble
INK

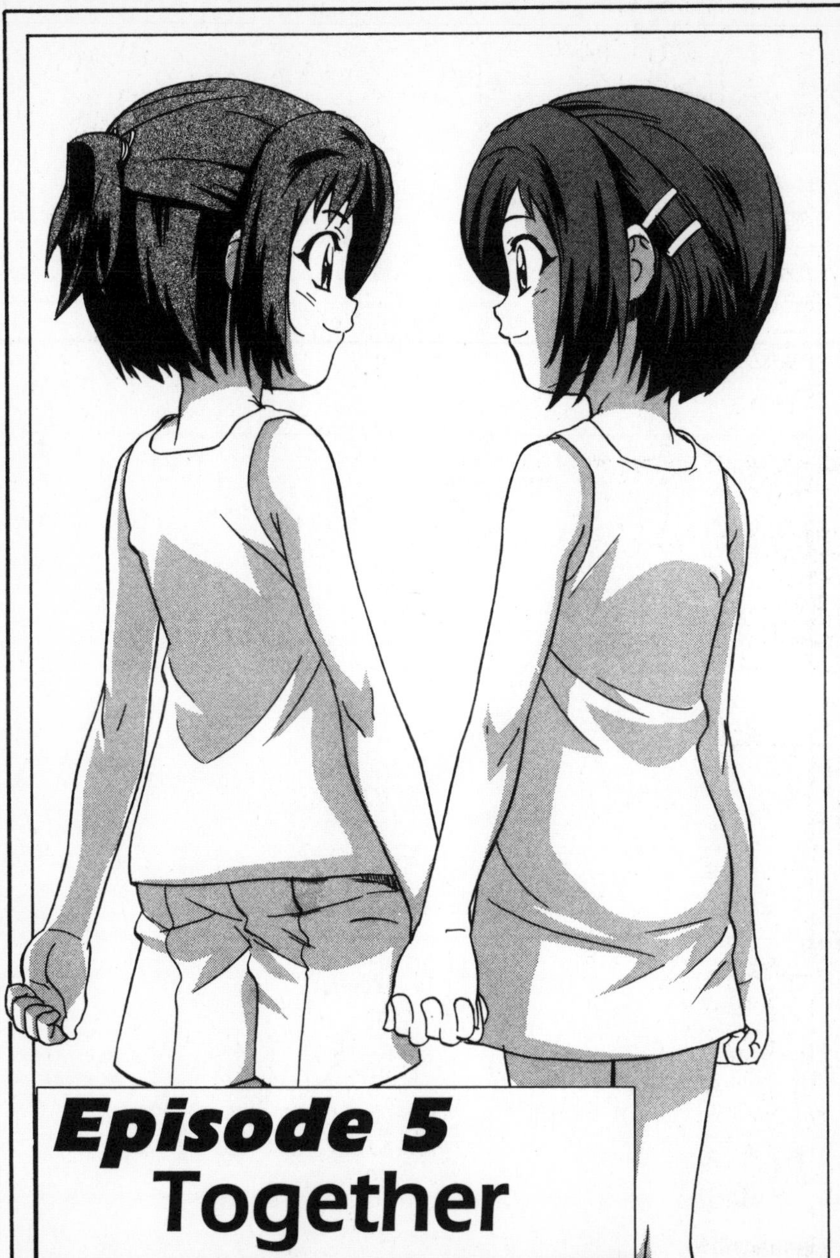
Episode 5
Together

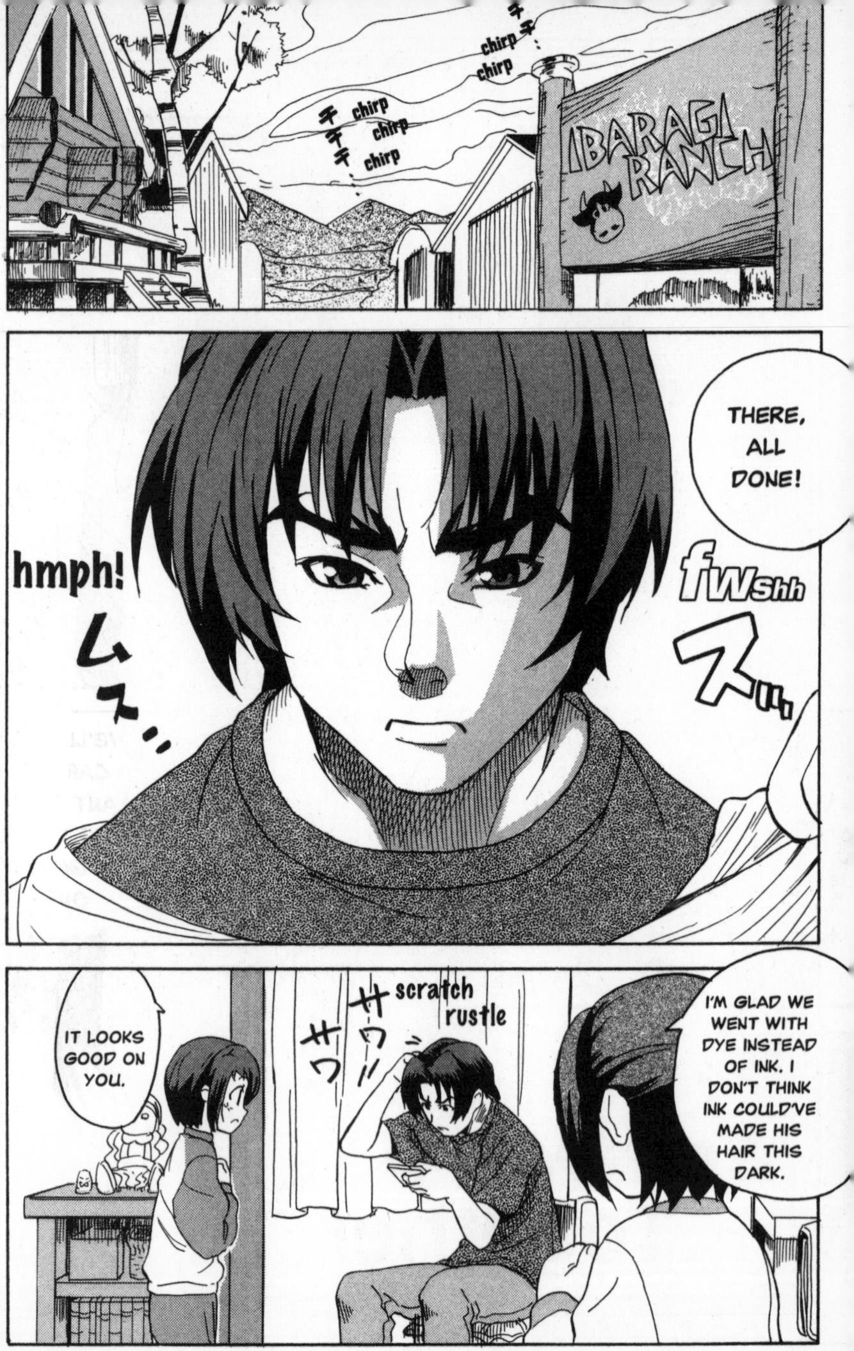
IBARAGI RANCH
チチ chirp chirp
チチチ chirp chirp chirp
THERE, ALL DONE!
fwshh
ス
hmph!
ムス
I'M GLAD WE WENT WITH DYE INSTEAD OF INK. I DON'T THINK INK COULD'VE MADE HIS HAIR THIS DARK.
サワサワ scratch rustle
IT LOOKS GOOD ON YOU.

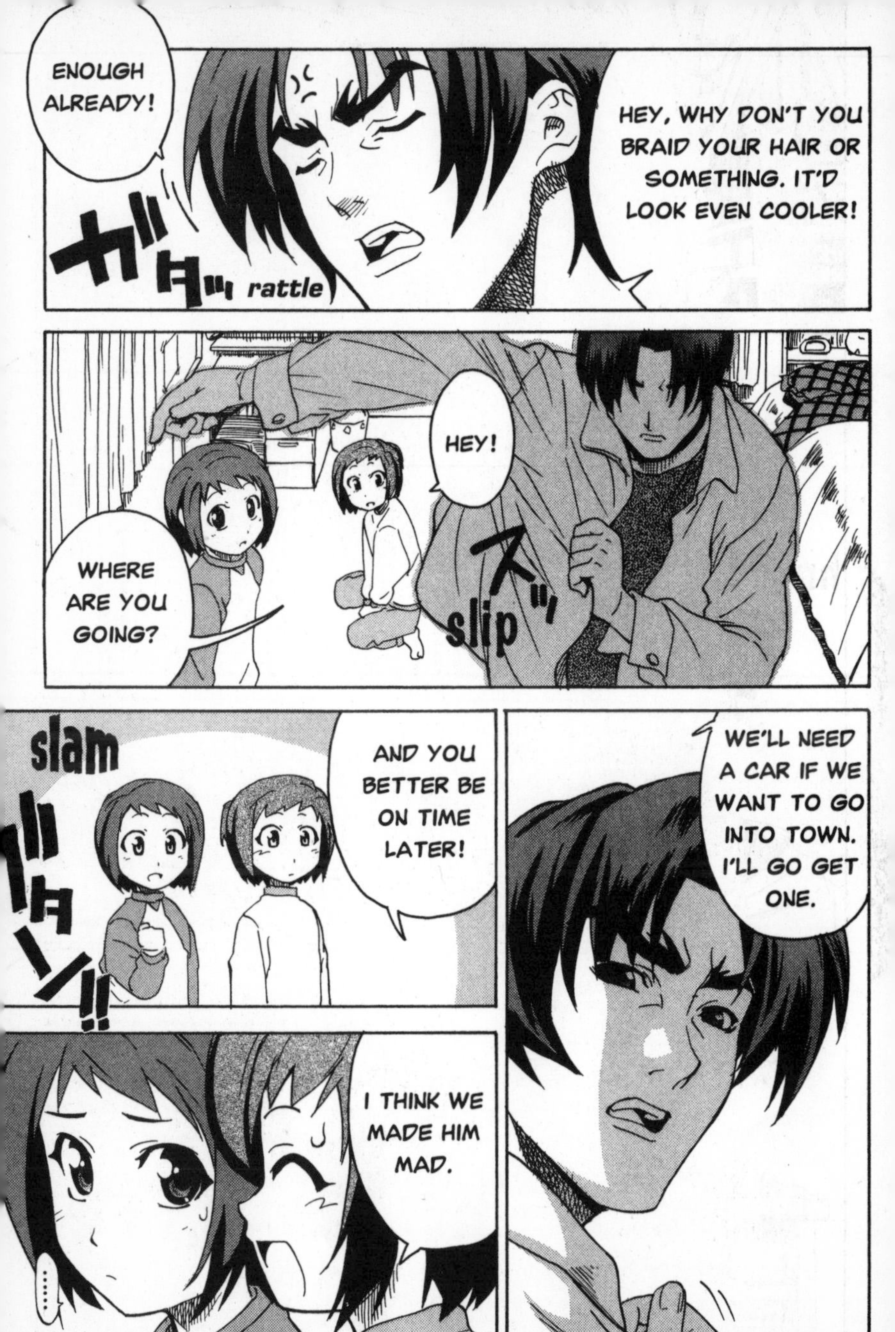
HEY, WHY DON'T YOU BRAID YOUR HAIR OR SOMETHING. IT'D LOOK EVEN COOLER!
ENOUGH ALREADY!
ガタッ rattle
HEY!
スッ slip
WHERE ARE YOU GOING?
WE'LL NEED A CAR IF WE WANT TO GO INTO TOWN. I'LL GO GET ONE.
AND YOU BETTER BE ON TIME LATER!
slam
バタン!!
I THINK WE MADE HIM MAD.
......

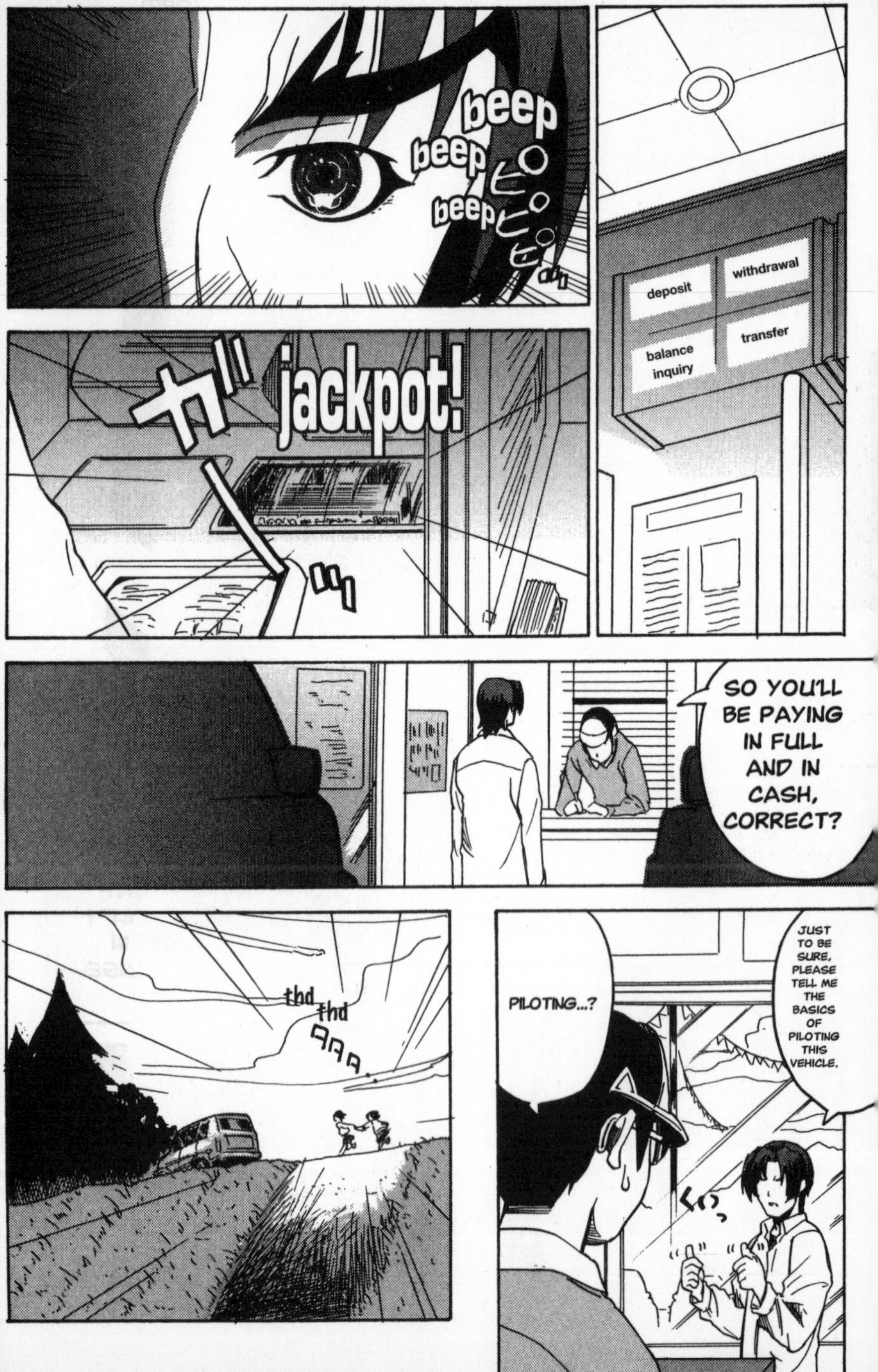
deposit
withdrawal
balance inquiry
transfer
beep
beep
beep
jackpot!
SO YOU'LL BE PAYING IN FULL AND IN CASH, CORRECT?
JUST TO BE SURE, PLEASE TELL ME THE BASICS OF PILOTING THIS VEHICLE.
PILOTING...?
thd
thd

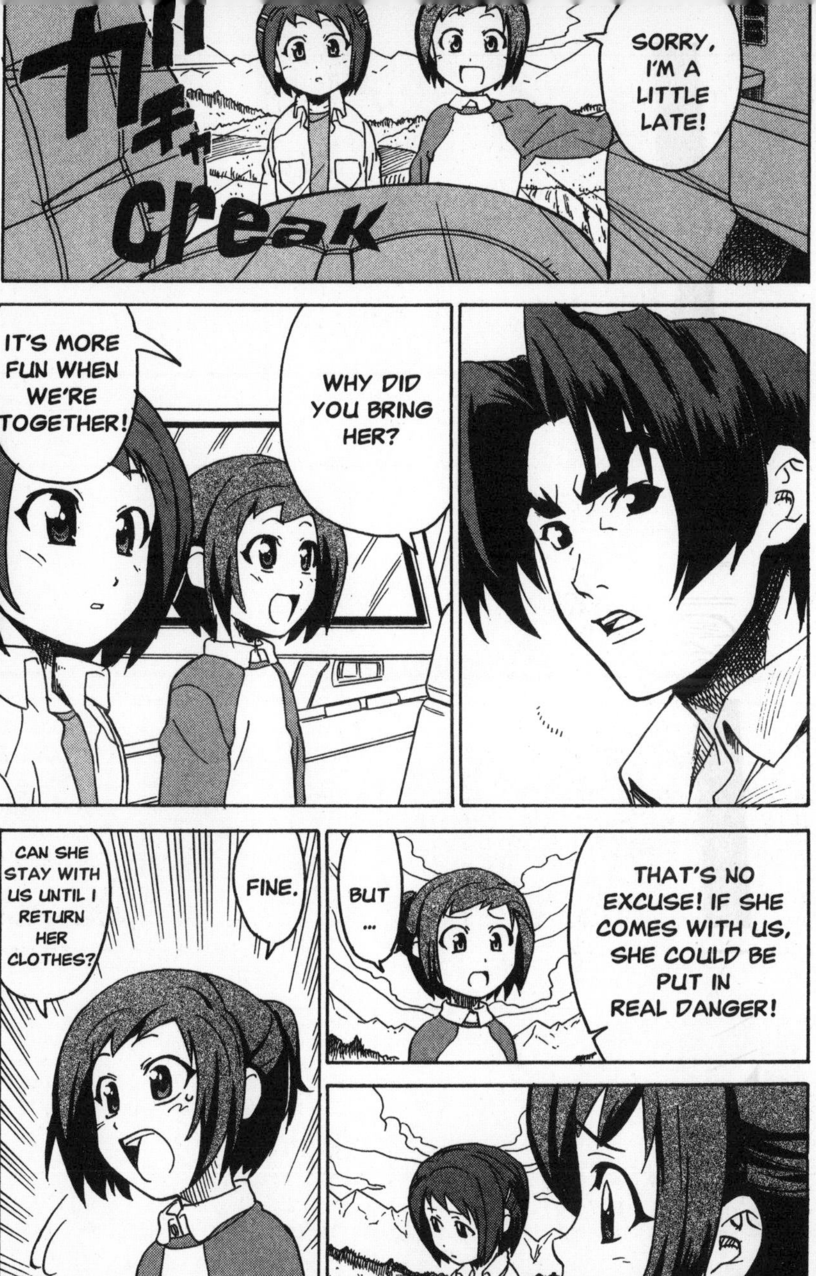
ガチャ
Creak
SORRY, I'M A LITTLE LATE!
WHY DID YOU BRING HER?
IT'S MORE FUN WHEN WE'RE TOGETHER!
THAT'S NO EXCUSE! IF SHE COMES WITH US, SHE COULD BE PUT IN REAL DANGER!
BUT ...
FINE.
CAN SHE STAY WITH US UNTIL I RETURN HER CLOTHES?

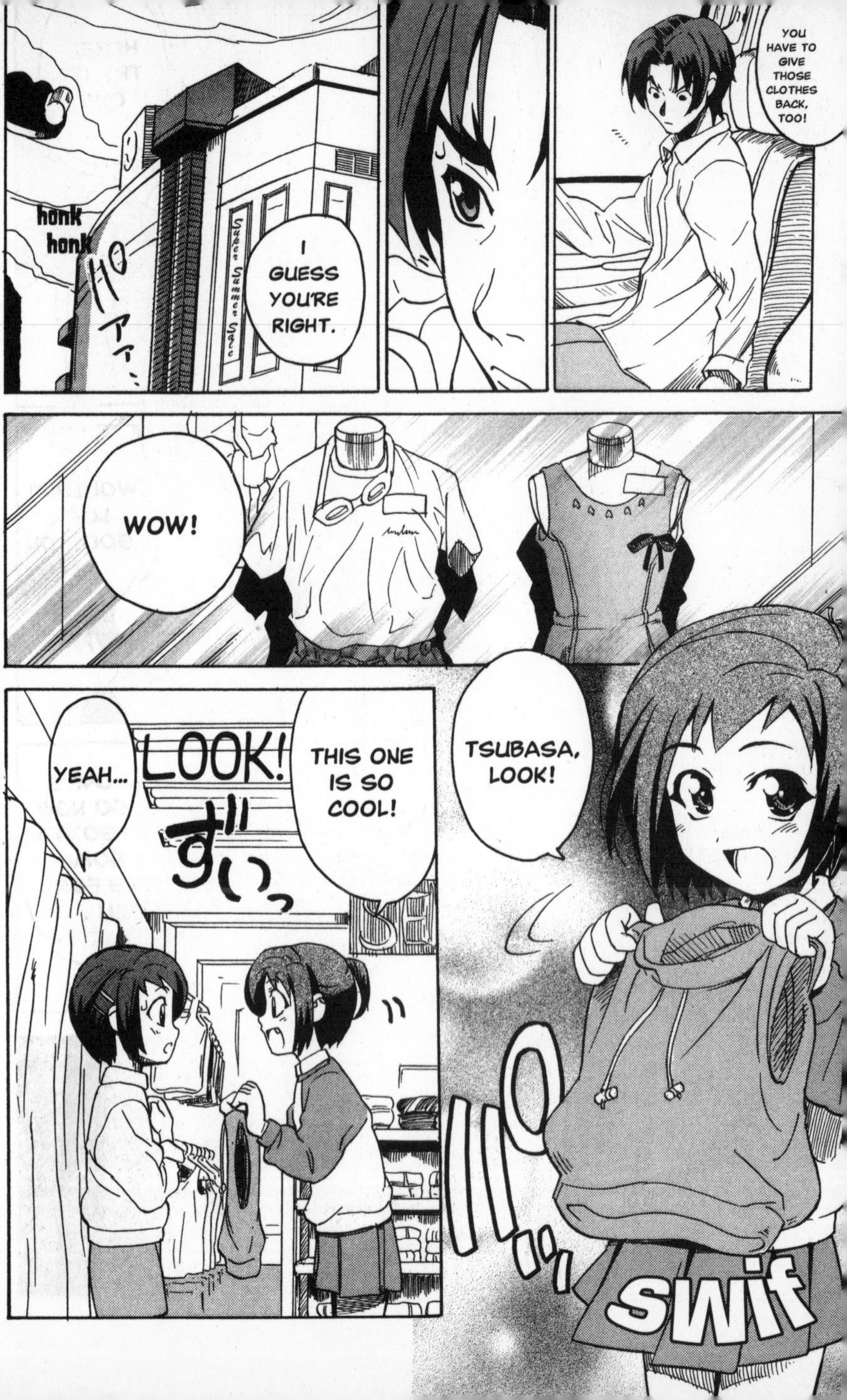

YOU HAVE TO GIVE THOSE CLOTHES BACK, TOO!
I GUESS YOU'RE RIGHT.
honk honk
Super Summer Sale
WOW!
TSUBASA, LOOK!
swif
THIS ONE IS SO COOL!
LOOK!
ずいっ
YEAH...

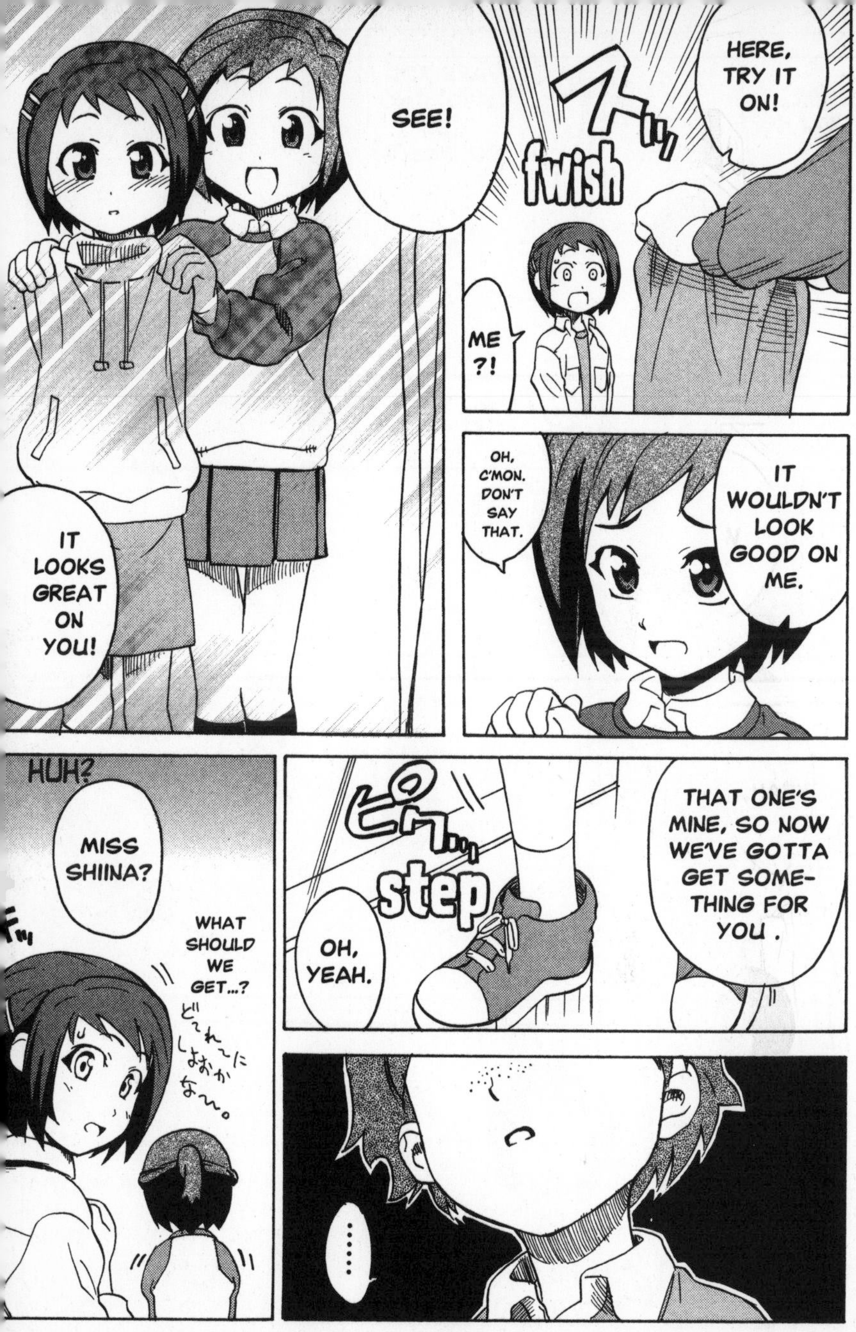
HERE, TRY IT ON!
fwish
ME ?!
SEE!
IT LOOKS GREAT ON YOU!
IT WOULDN'T LOOK GOOD ON ME.
OH, C'MON. DON'T SAY THAT.
THAT ONE'S MINE, SO NOW WE'VE GOTTA GET SOMETHING FOR YOU .
step
OH, YEAH.
HUH?
MISS SHIINA?
WHAT SHOULD WE GET...?
どれ～にしよおかな～。
......

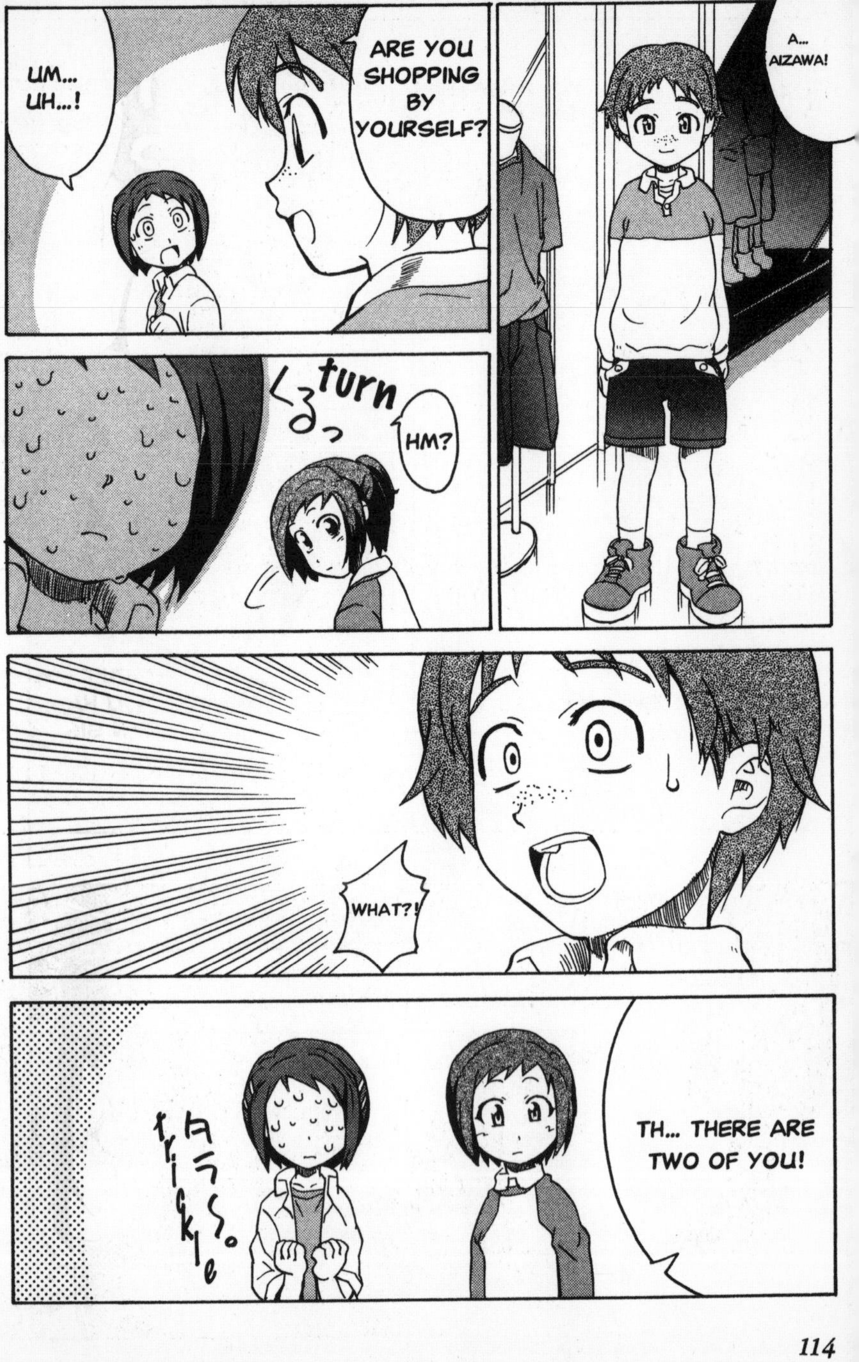
A... AIZAWA!
ARE YOU SHOPPING BY YOURSELF?
UM... UH...!
turn
HM?
WHAT?!
TH... THERE ARE TWO OF YOU!
trickle

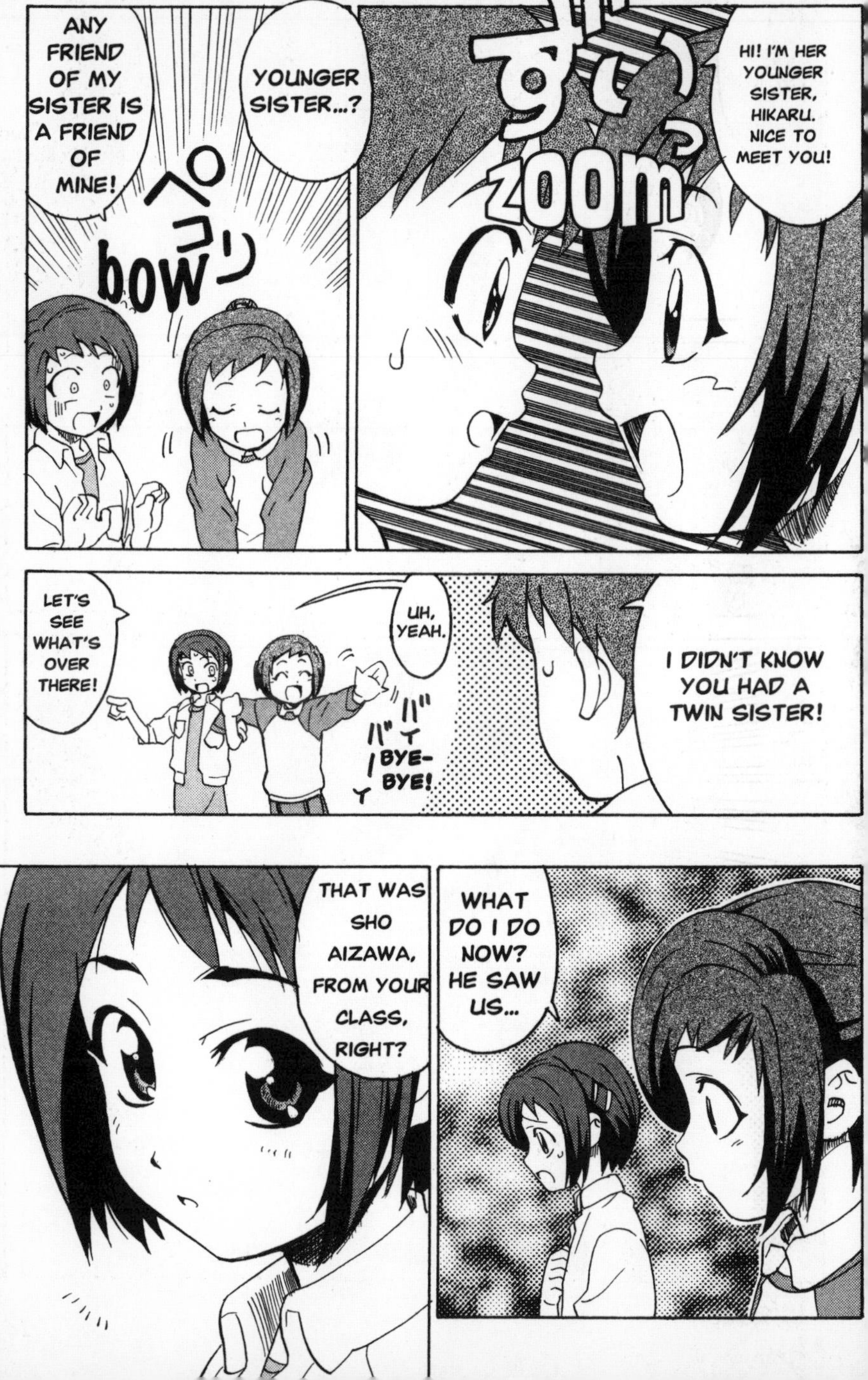
HI! I'M HER YOUNGER SISTER, HIKARU. NICE TO MEET YOU!
ずいっ
zoom
YOUNGER SISTER...?
ANY FRIEND OF MY SISTER IS A FRIEND OF MINE!
ペコリ
bow
I DIDN'T KNOW YOU HAD A TWIN SISTER!
UH, YEAH.
LET'S SEE WHAT'S OVER THERE!
バイバーイ!
BYE-BYE!
WHAT DO I DO NOW? HE SAW US...
THAT WAS SHO AIZAWA, FROM YOUR CLASS, RIGHT?

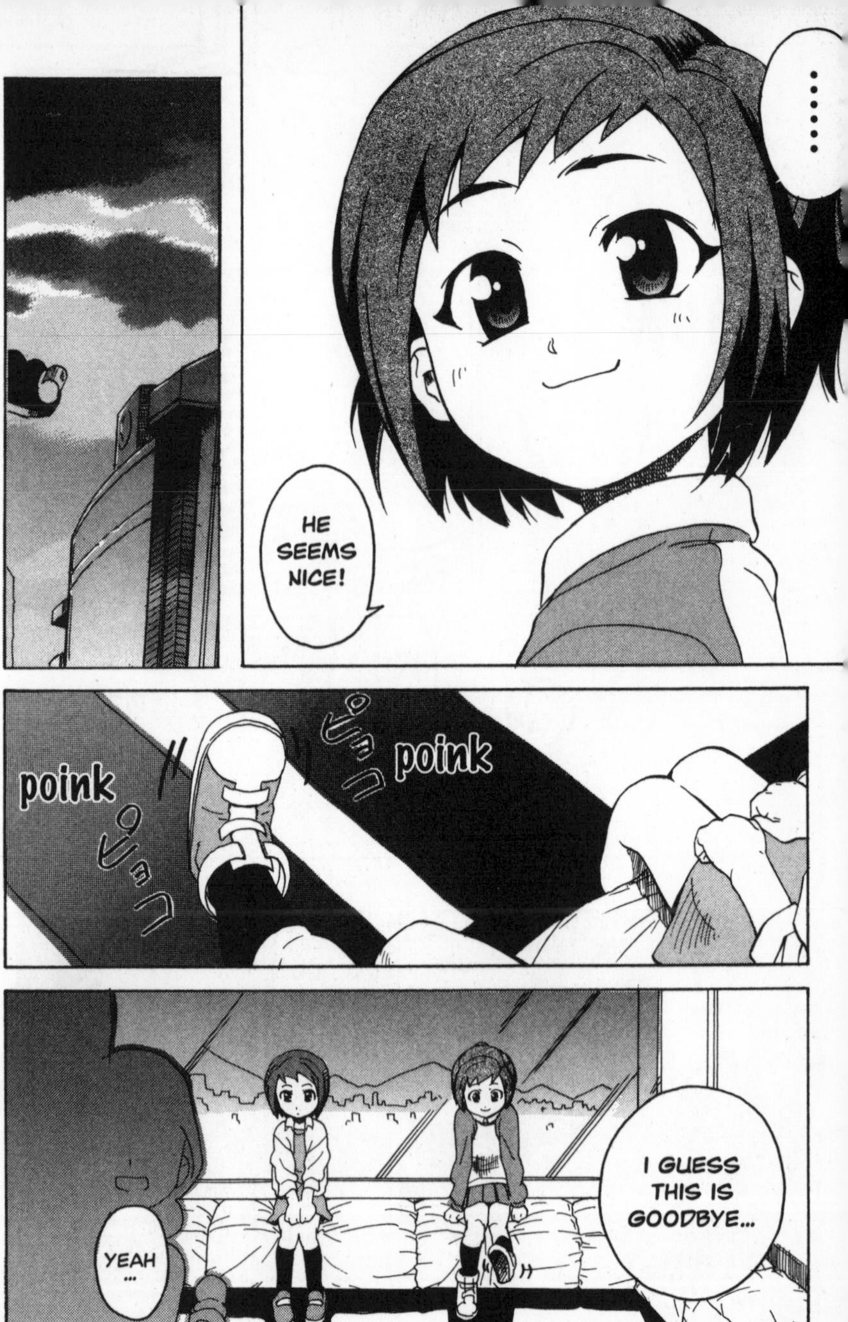
......
HE SEEMS NICE!
poink
ピョコ
poink
ピョコ
I GUESS THIS IS GOODBYE...
YEAH ...

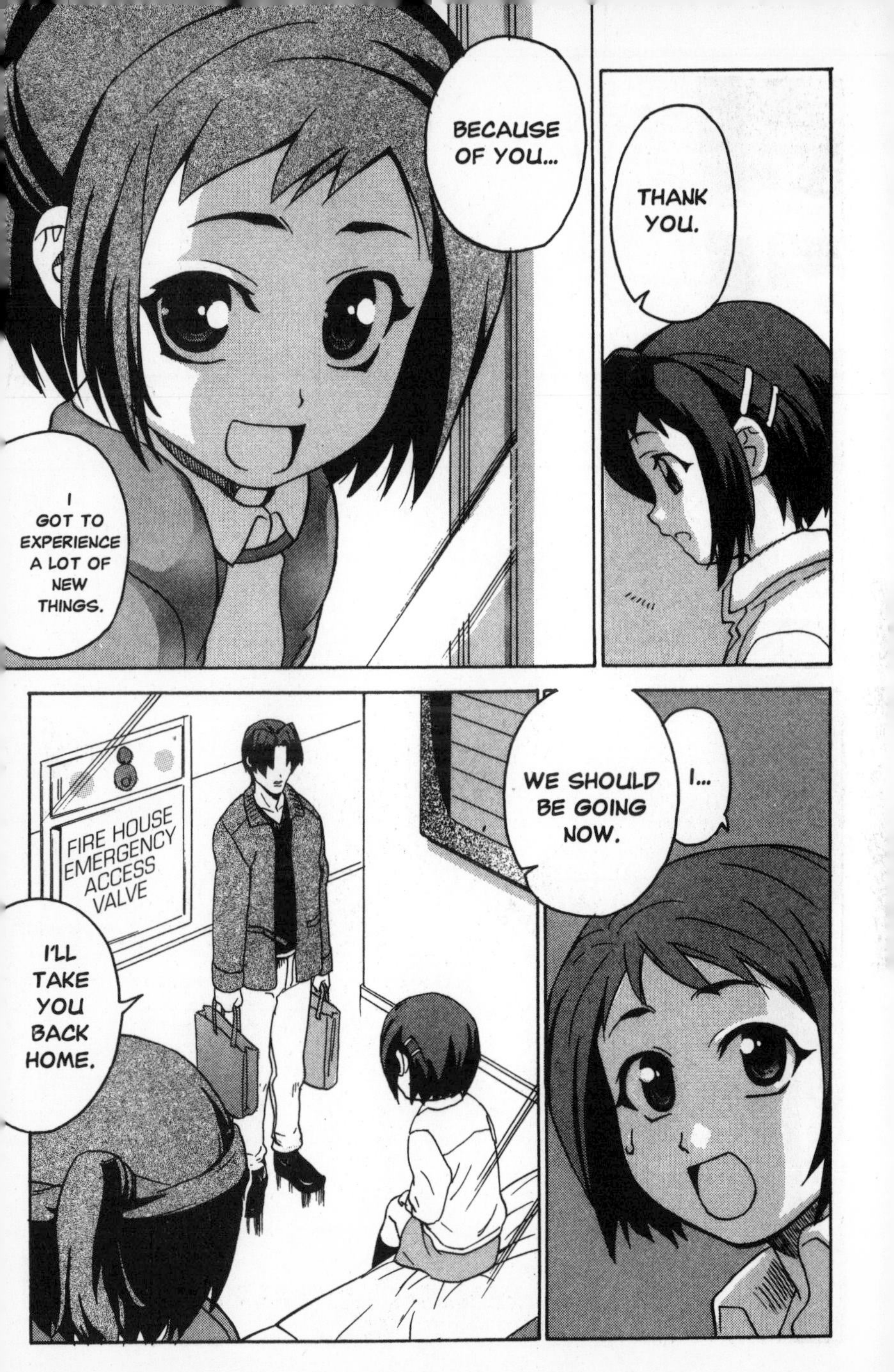
BECAUSE OF YOU...
I GOT TO EXPERIENCE A LOT OF NEW THINGS.
THANK YOU.
FIRE HOUSE EMERGENCY ACCESS VALVE
WE SHOULD BE GOING NOW.
I...
I'LL TAKE YOU BACK HOME.

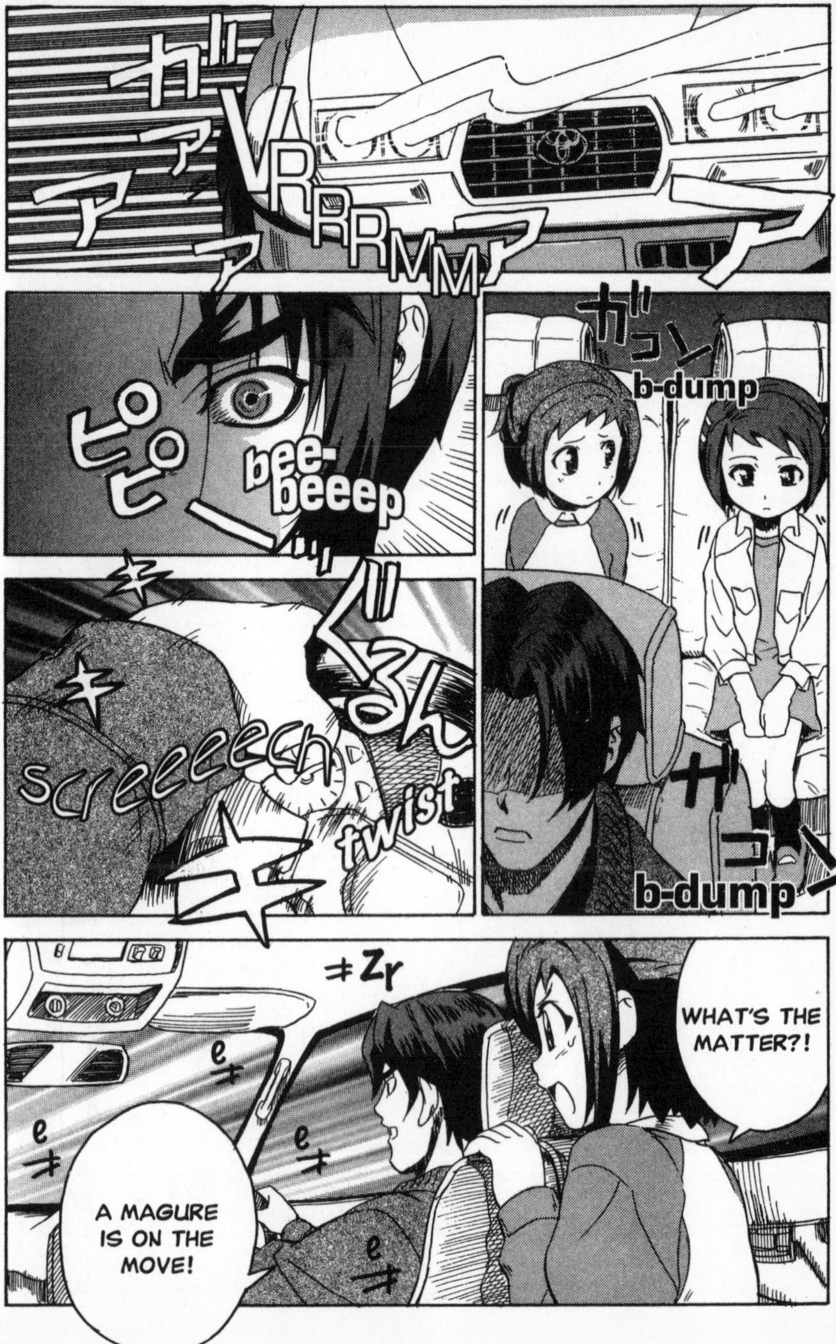
VRRRRMMM
ガコン
b-dump
ピピー
bee-beeep
ガコン
b-dump
ぐるん
twist
screeeeech
WHAT'S THE MATTER?!
A MAGURE IS ON THE MOVE!

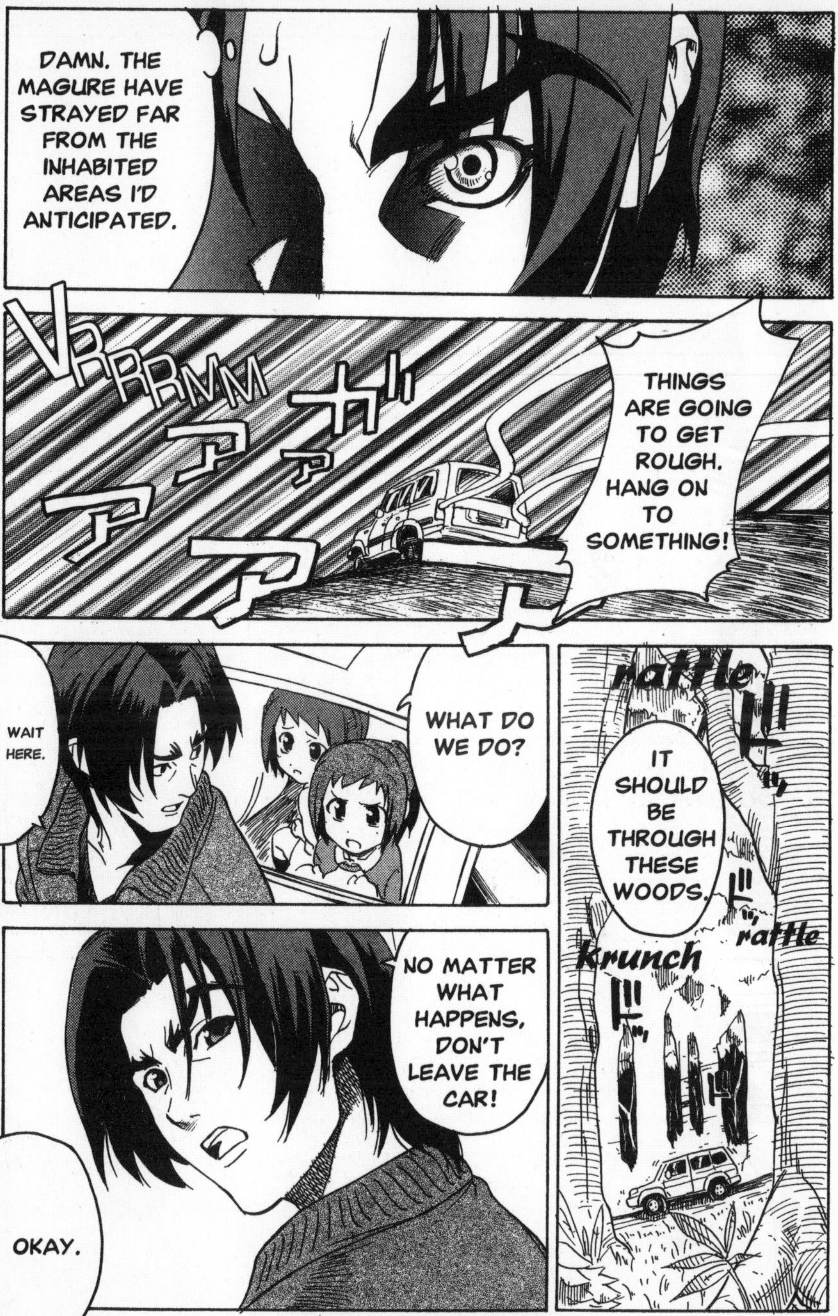
DAMN. THE MAGURE HAVE STRAYED FAR FROM THE INHABITED AREAS I'D ANTICIPATED.
VRRRMM
THINGS ARE GOING TO GET ROUGH. HANG ON TO SOMETHING!
rattle
IT SHOULD BE THROUGH THESE WOODS.
rattle
krunch
WHAT DO WE DO?
WAIT HERE.
NO MATTER WHAT HAPPENS, DON'T LEAVE THE CAR!
OKAY.

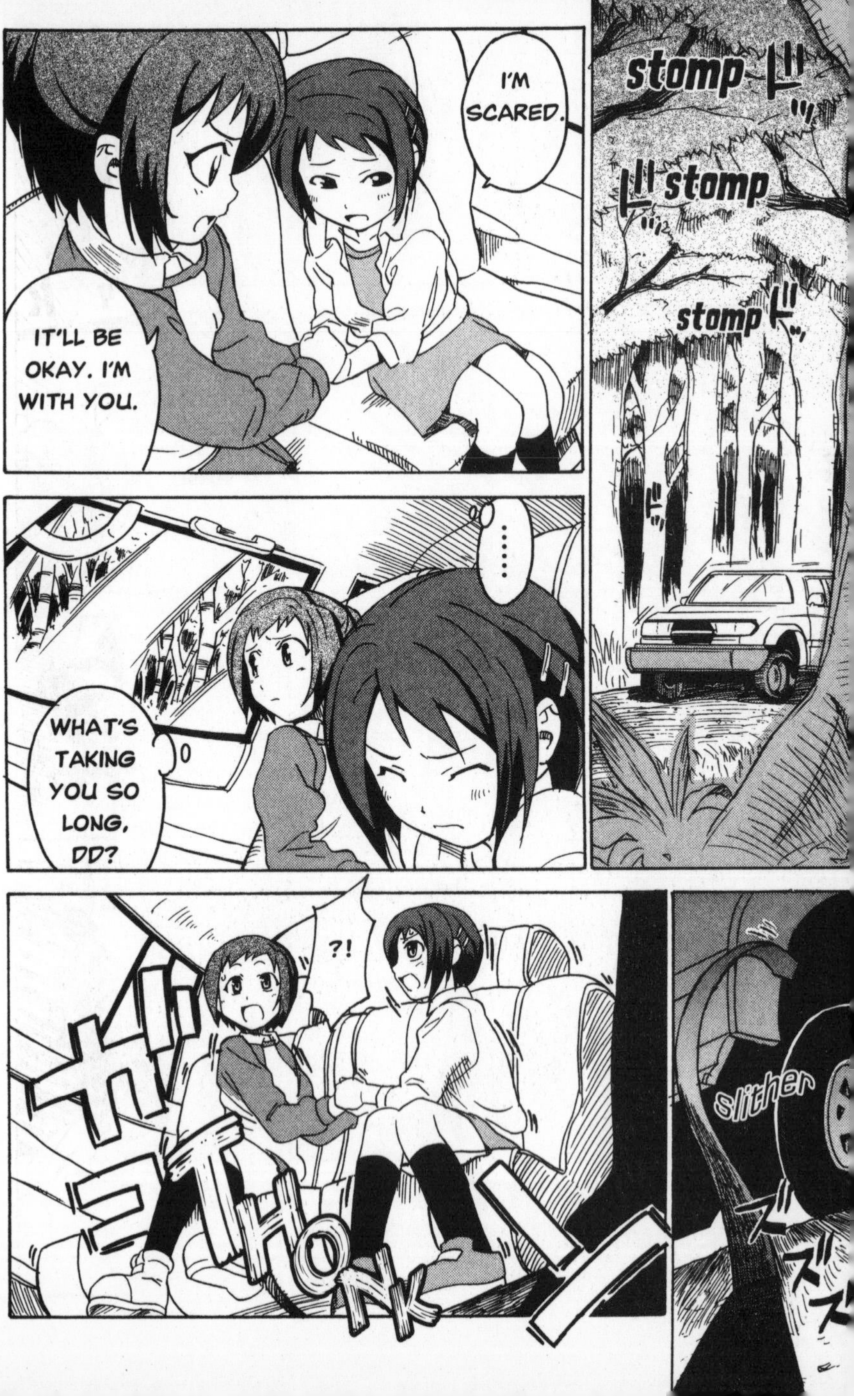
stomp
stomp
stomp
I'M SCARED.
IT'LL BE OKAY. I'M WITH YOU.
......
WHAT'S TAKING YOU SO LONG, DD?
slither
?!
HONK

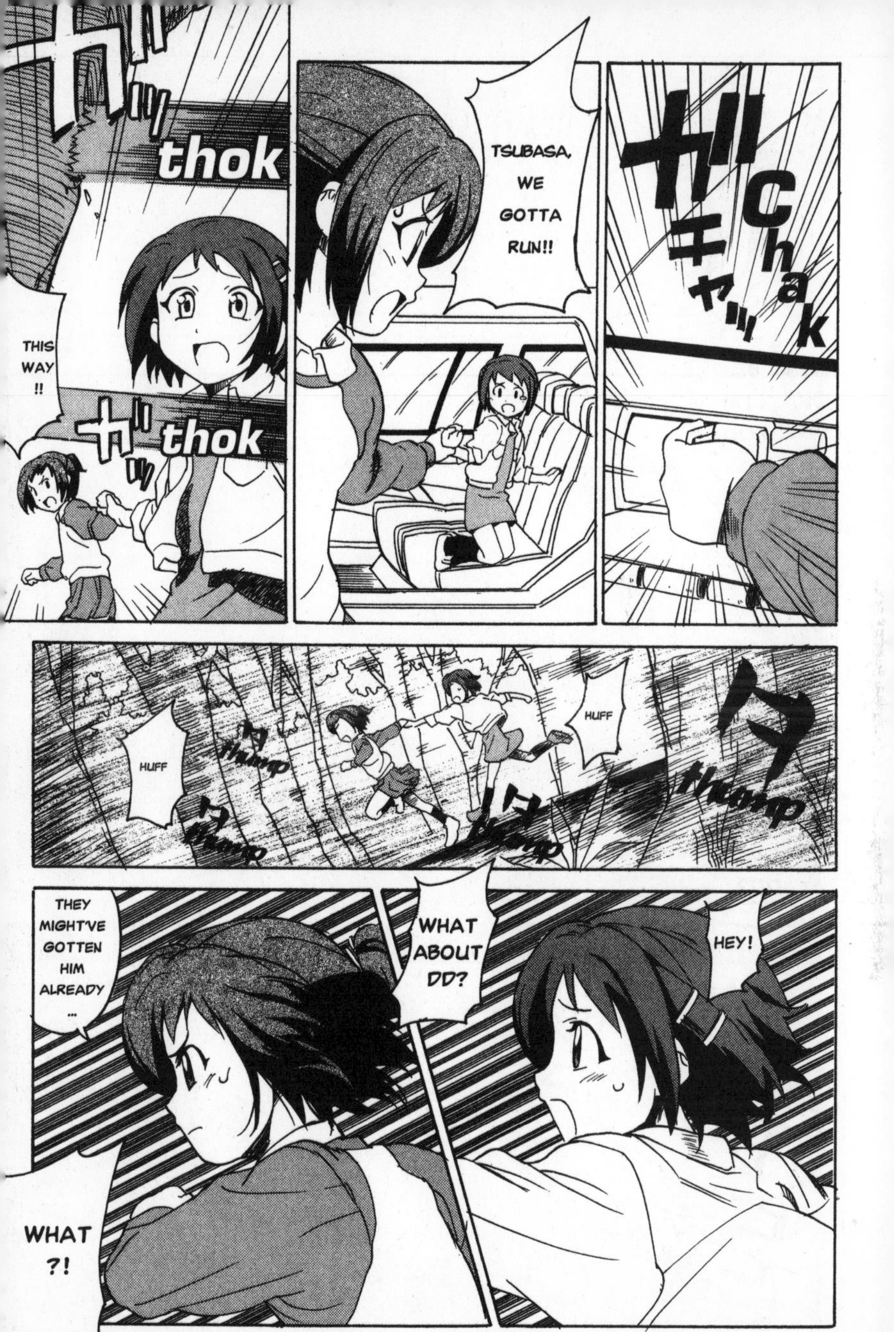
thok
THIS WAY !!
thok
TSUBASA, WE GOTTA RUN!!
chak
HUFF
thump
thump
thump
HUFF
thump
THEY MIGHT'VE GOTTEN HIM ALREADY ...
WHAT ABOUT DD?
HEY!
WHAT ?!

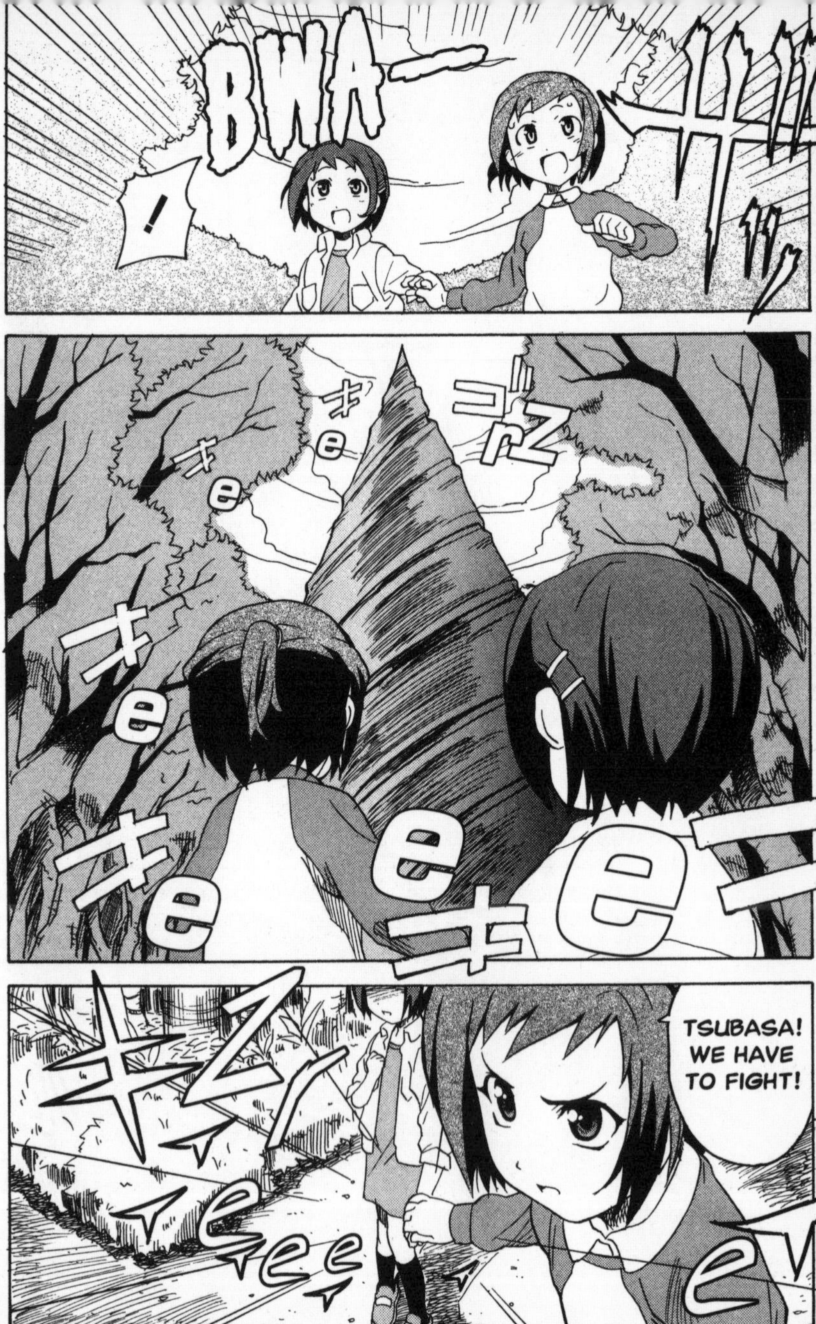
BWA—
!
TSUBASA! WE HAVE TO FIGHT!

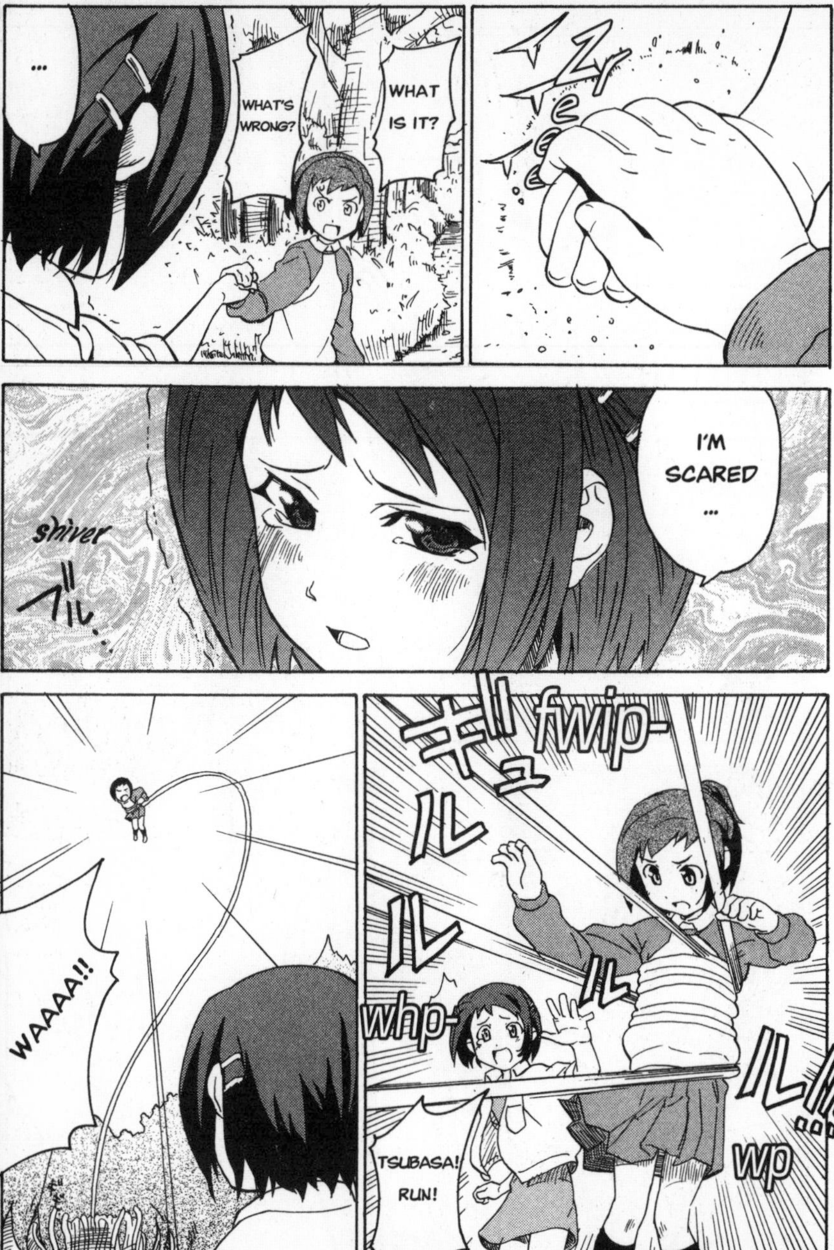
WHAT IS IT?
WHAT'S WRONG?
...
I'M SCARED ...
shiver
ブル
fwip-
キュ
whp-
wp
TSUBASA! RUN!
WAAAA!!

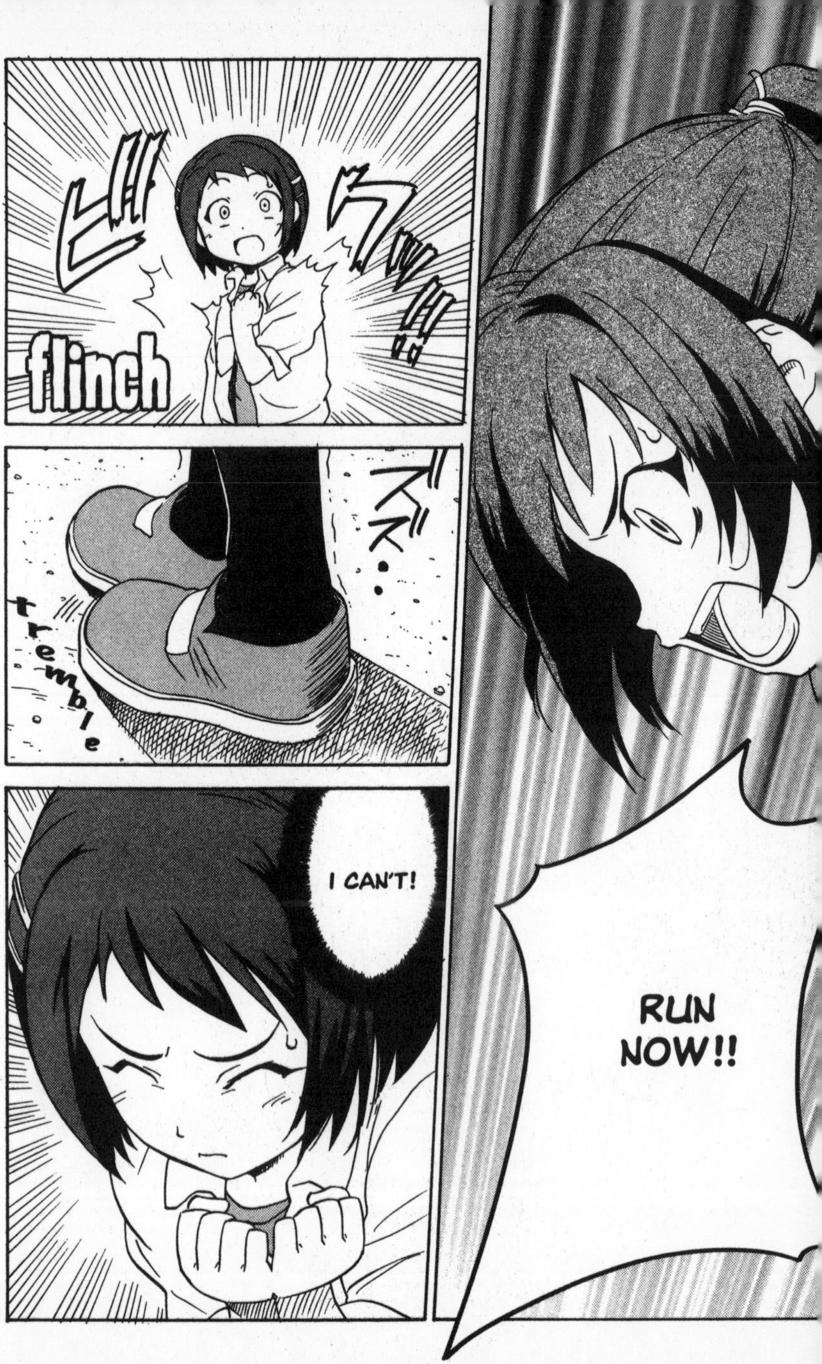
RUN NOW!!
ビクッ!!
flinch
ズズ・・
tremble
I CAN'T!

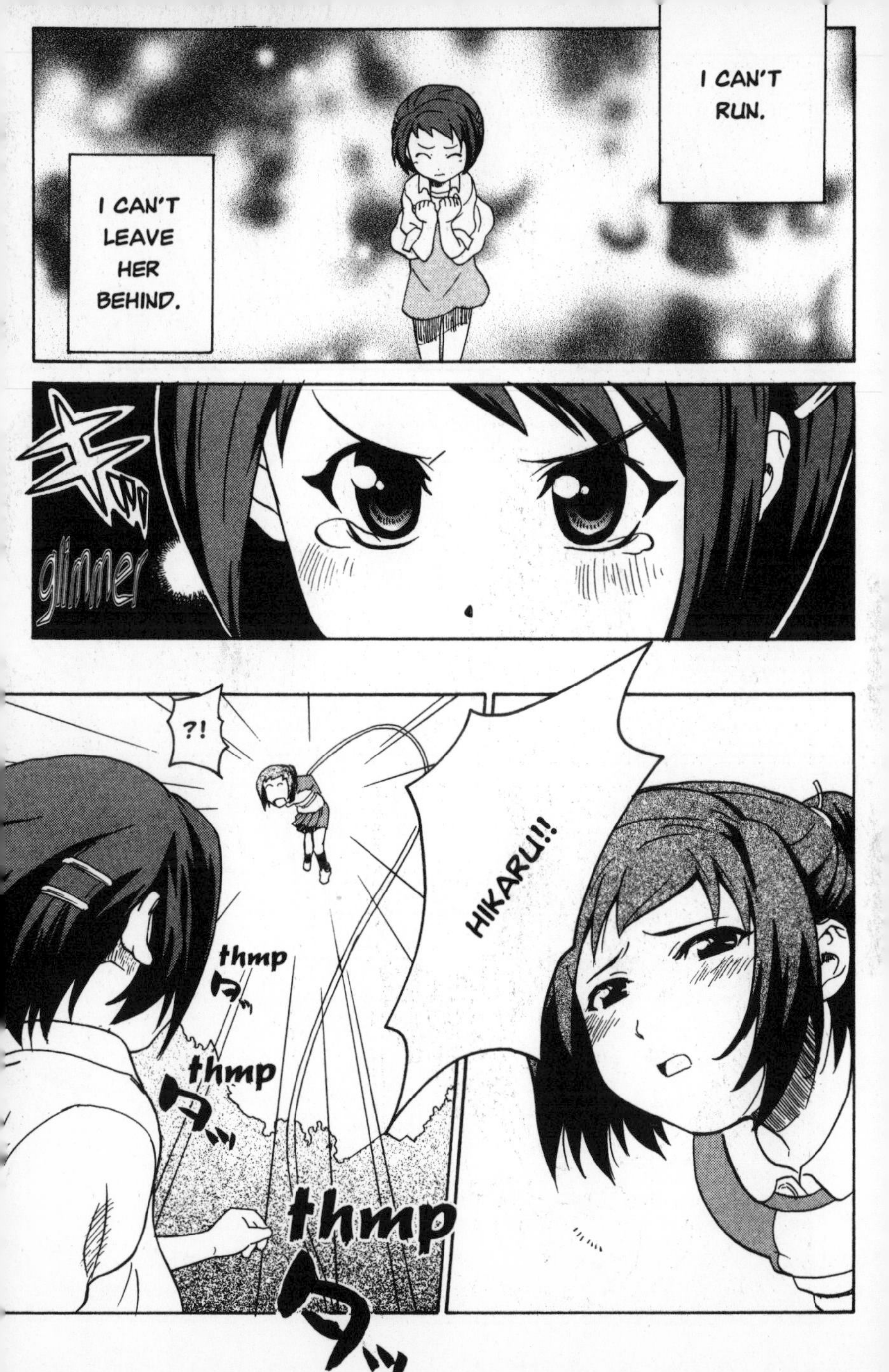
I CAN'T RUN.
I CAN'T LEAVE HER BEHIND.
glimmer
HIKARU!!
?!
thmp
thmp
thmp

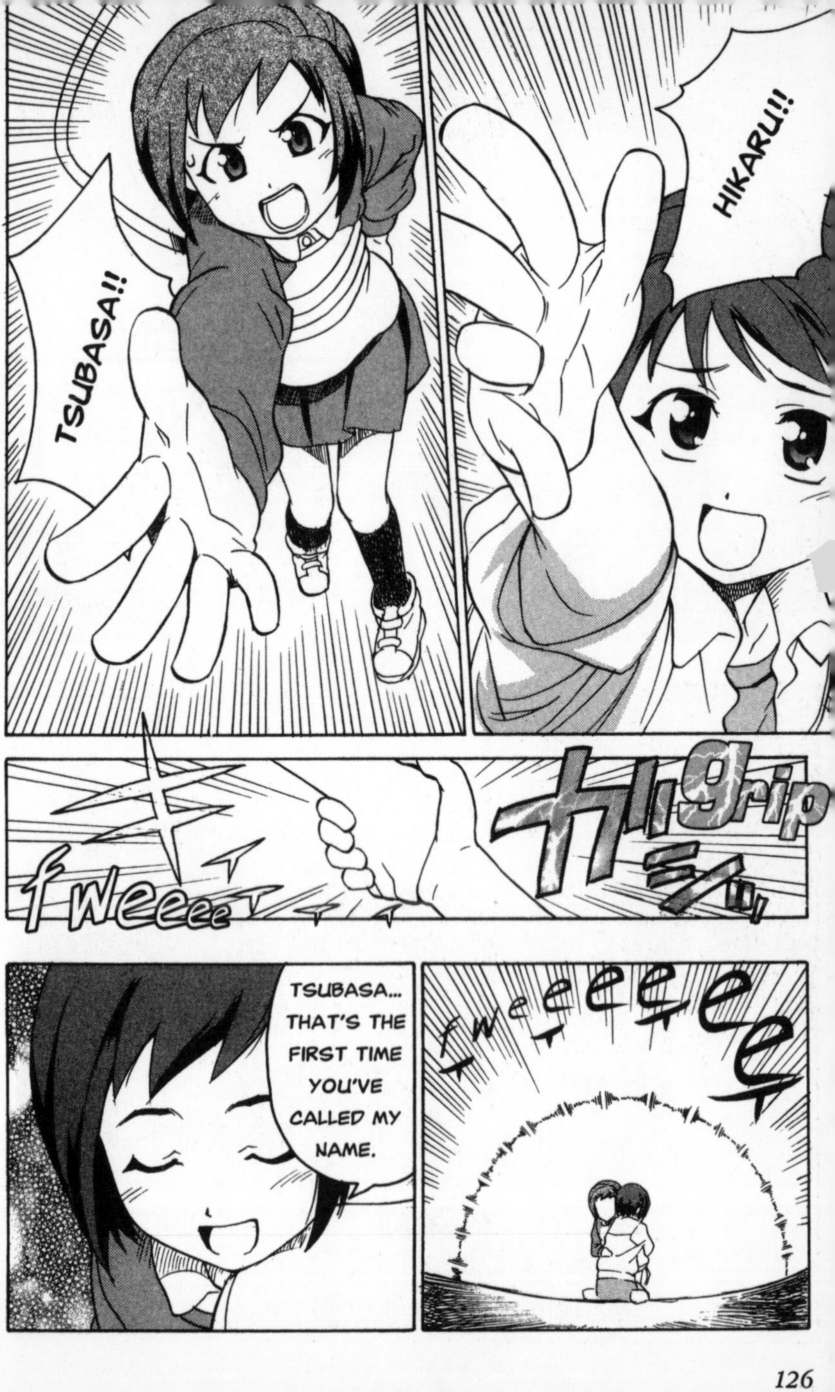
HIKARU!!
TSUBASA!!
grip
fweeee
fweeeeeeee
TSUBASA... THAT'S THE FIRST TIME YOU'VE CALLED MY NAME.

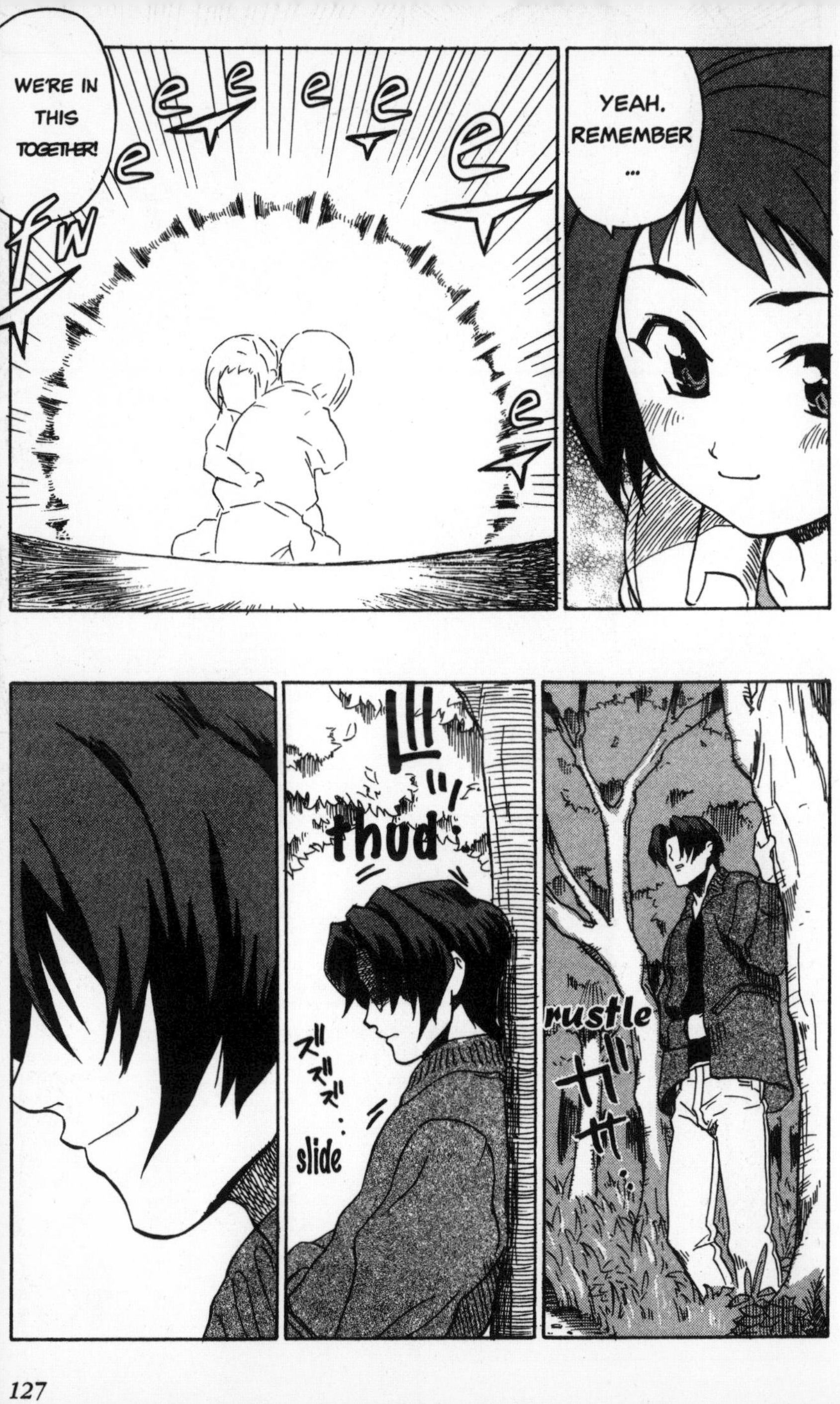
YEAH. REMEMBER ...
WE'RE IN THIS TOGETHER!
fweeeeeeeee
rustle
thud
slide

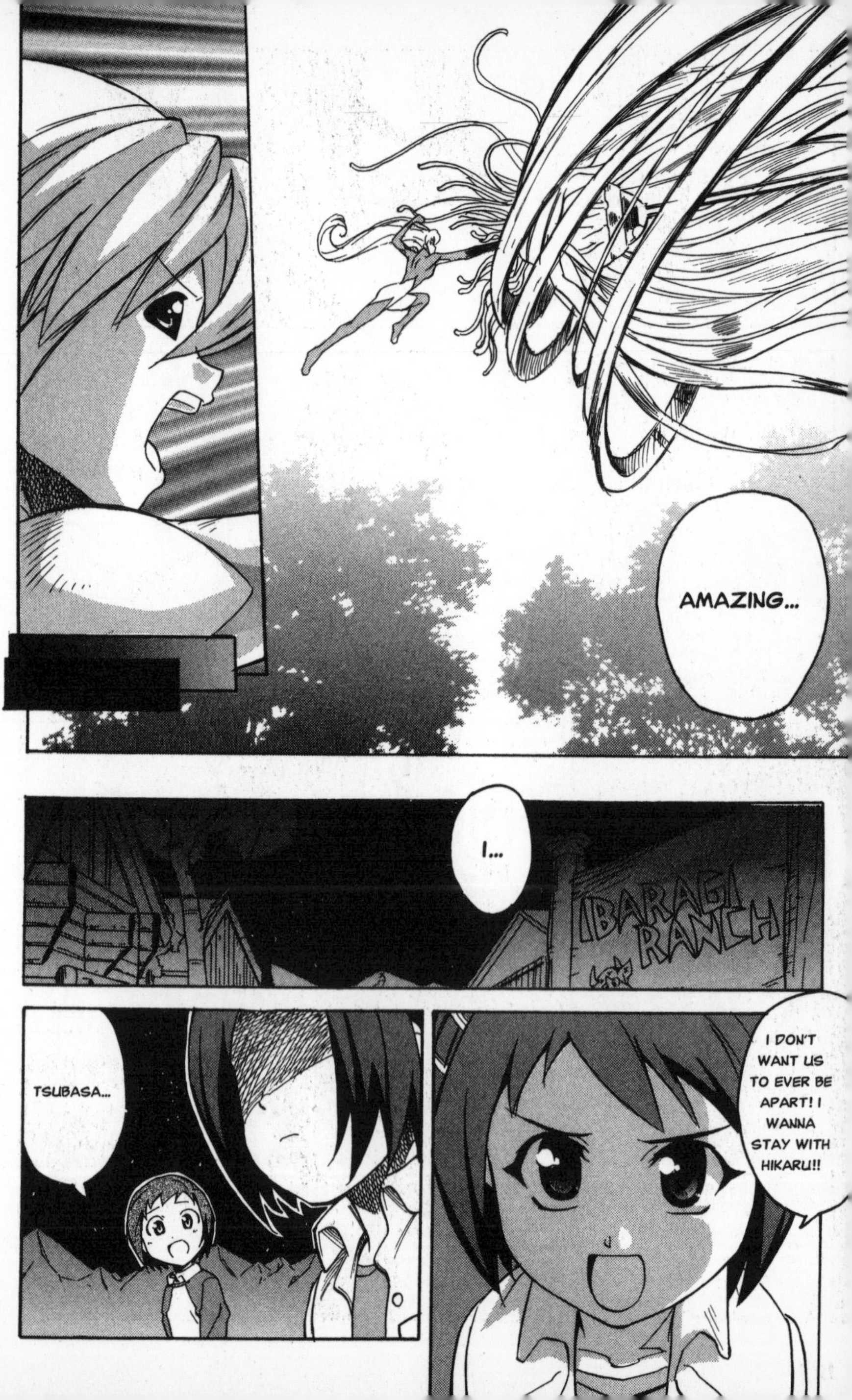
AMAZING...
[redacted]
I...
IBARAGI RANCH
I DON'T WANT US TO EVER BE APART! I WANNA STAY WITH HIKARU!!
TSUBASA...

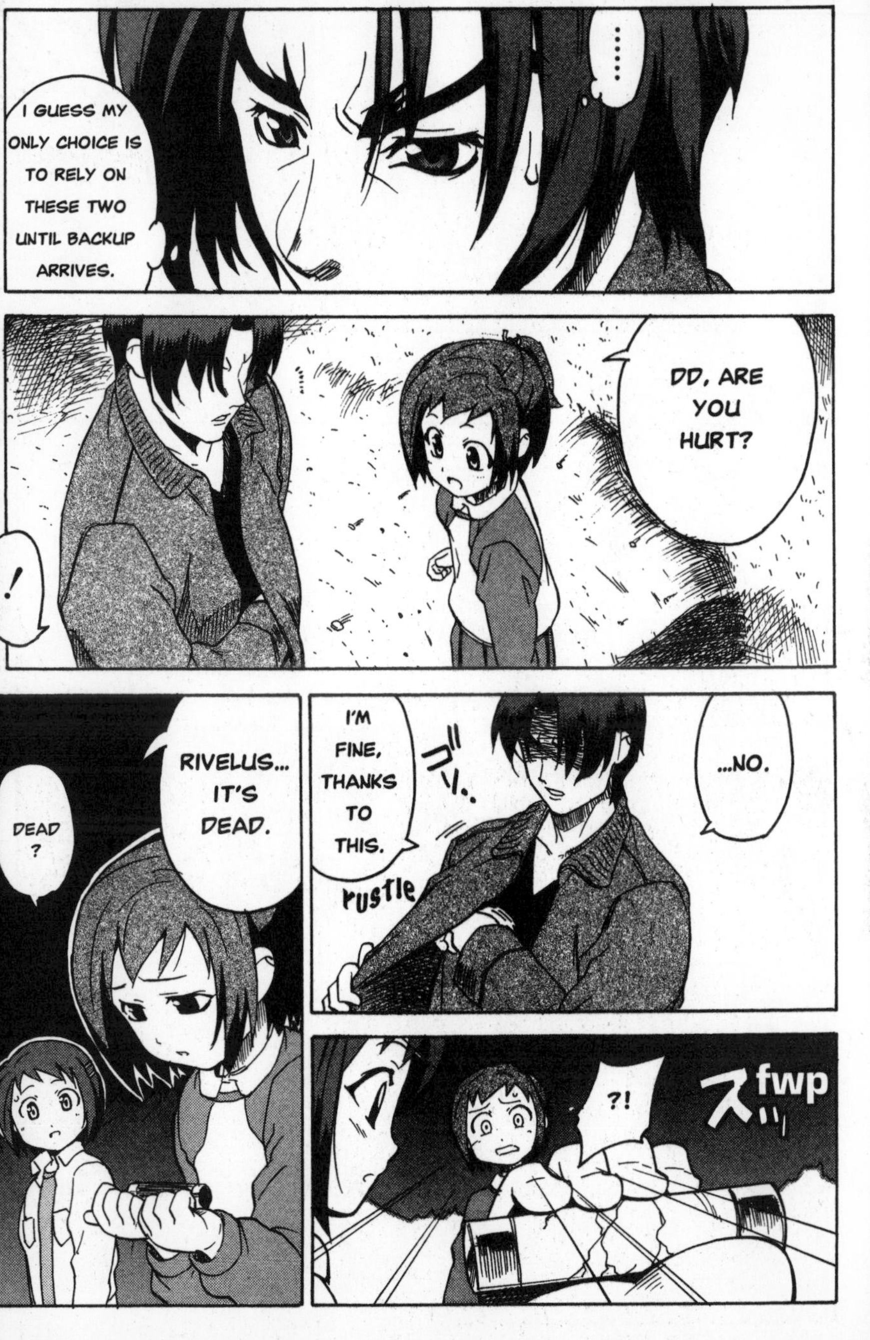
......
I GUESS MY ONLY CHOICE IS TO RELY ON THESE TWO UNTIL BACKUP ARRIVES.
DD, ARE YOU HURT?
!
...NO.
I'M FINE, THANKS TO THIS.
rustle
RIVELUS... IT'S DEAD.
DEAD?
fwp
?!

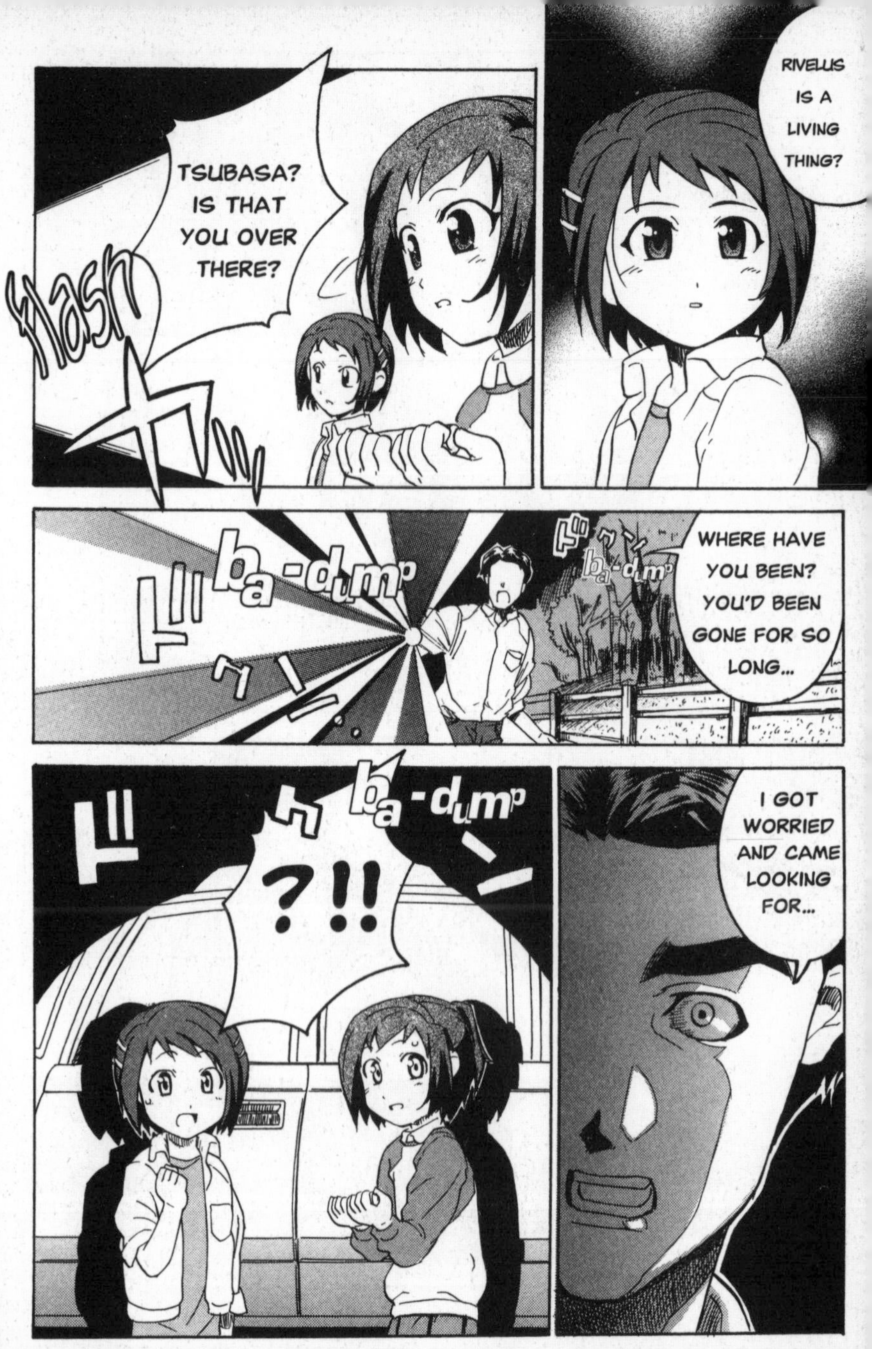
RIVELUS IS A LIVING THING?
TSUBASA? IS THAT YOU OVER THERE?
flash
WHERE HAVE YOU BEEN? YOU'D BEEN GONE FOR SO LONG...
ba-dump
ba-dump
I GOT WORRIED AND CAME LOOKING FOR...
ba-dump
?!!

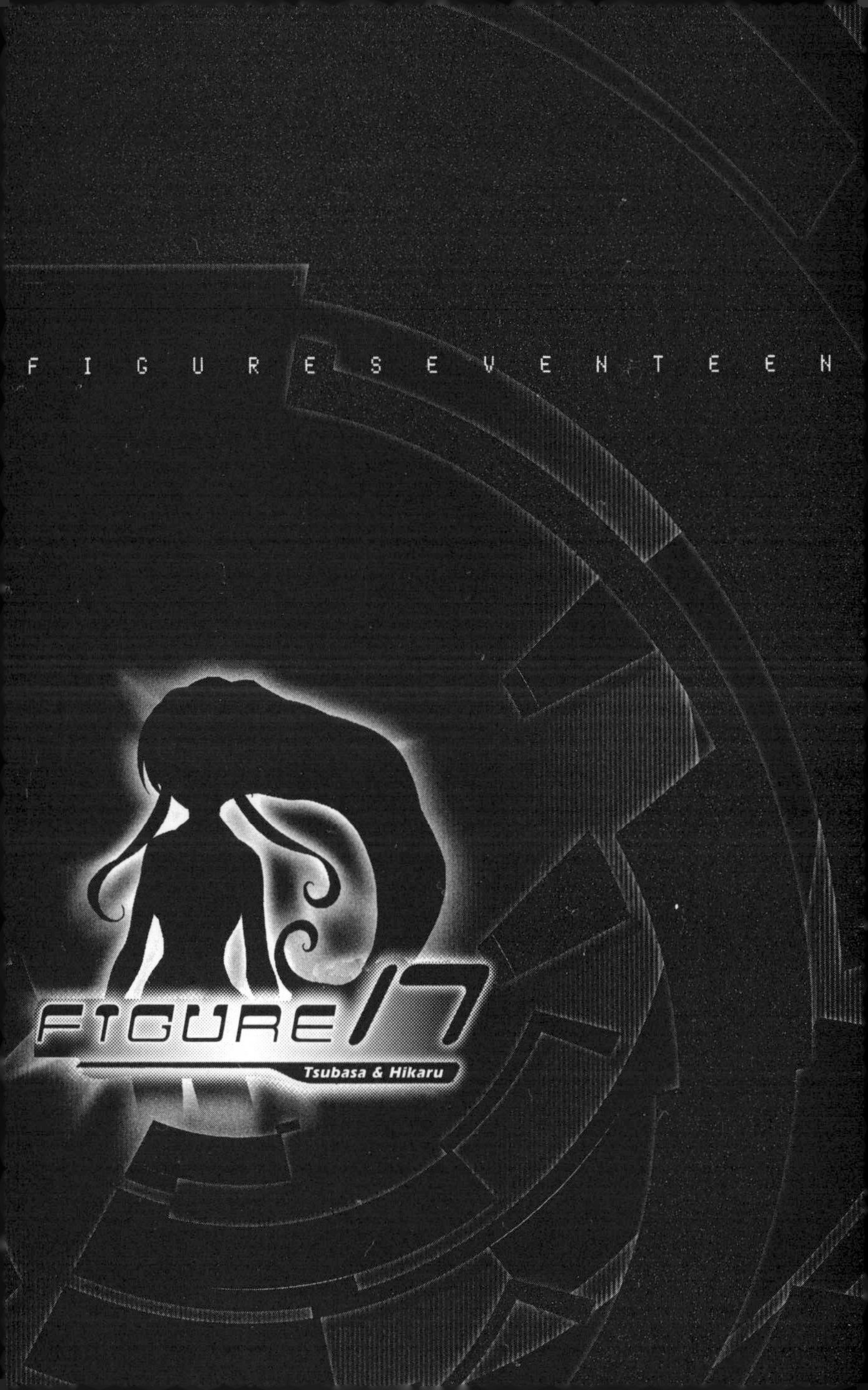
F I G U R E S E V E N T E E N
FIGURE 17
Tsubasa & Hikaru

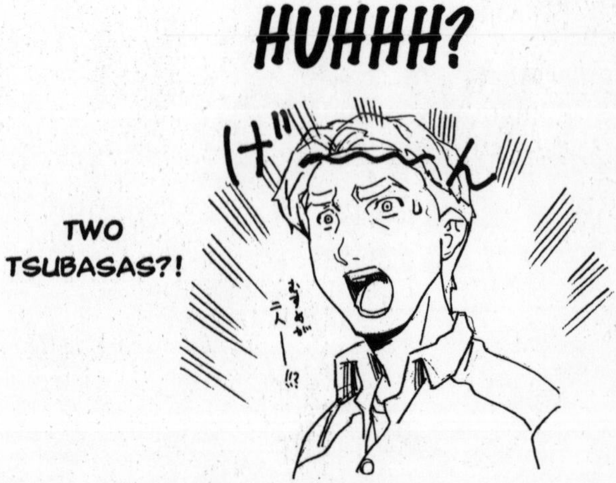
HUHHH?
TWO TSUBASAS?!
むすめが二人ーー!!?

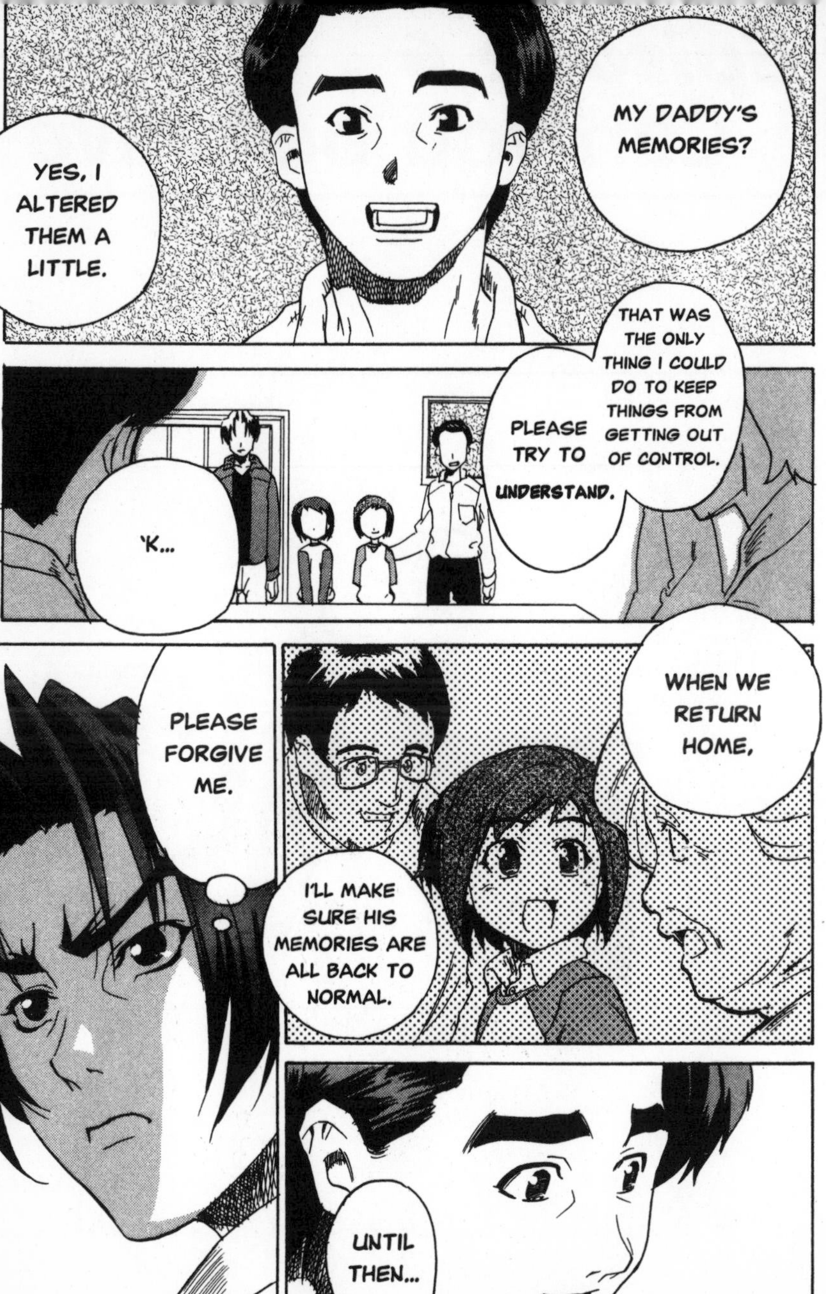
MY DADDY'S MEMORIES?
YES, I ALTERED THEM A LITTLE.
THAT WAS THE ONLY THING I COULD DO TO KEEP THINGS FROM GETTING OUT OF CONTROL.
PLEASE TRY TO UNDERSTAND.
'K...
PLEASE FORGIVE ME.
WHEN WE RETURN HOME,
I'LL MAKE SURE HIS MEMORIES ARE ALL BACK TO NORMAL.
UNTIL THEN...

Episode 6
Can you be brave?

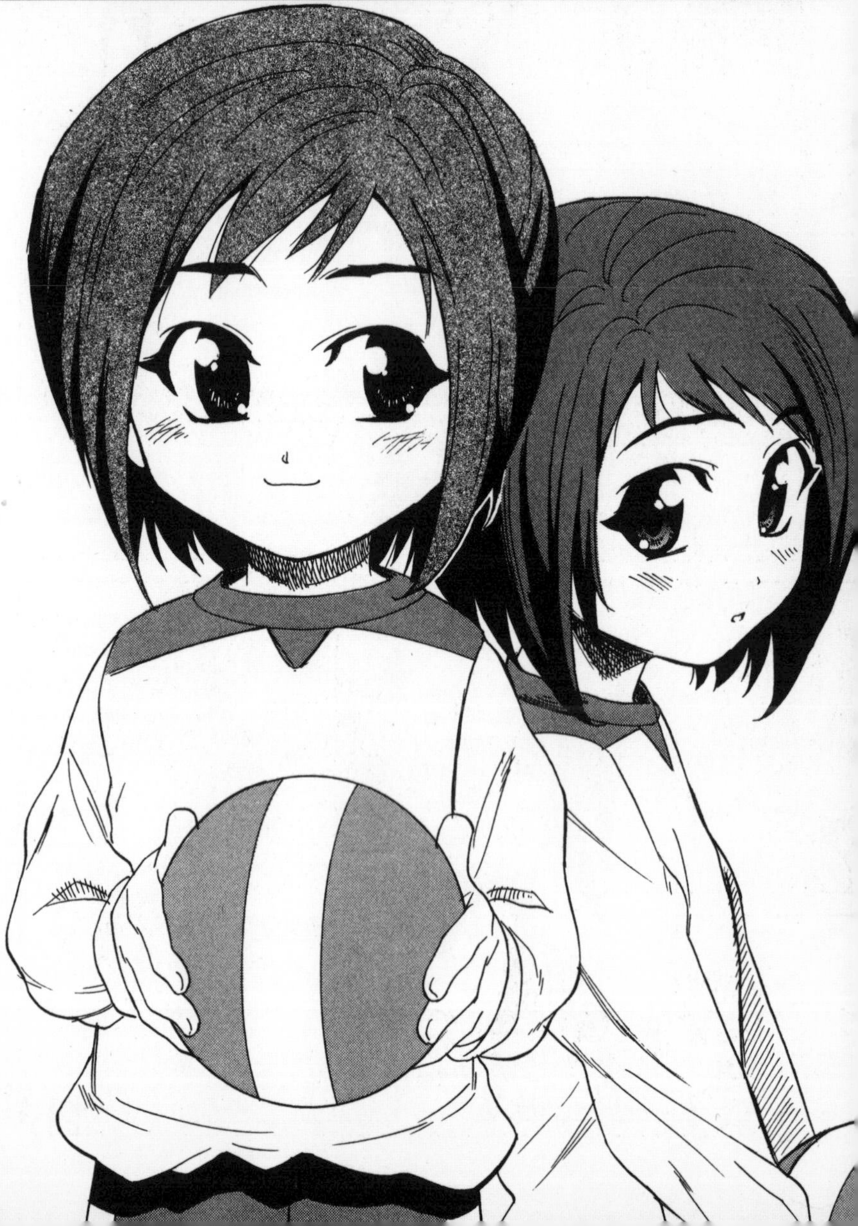

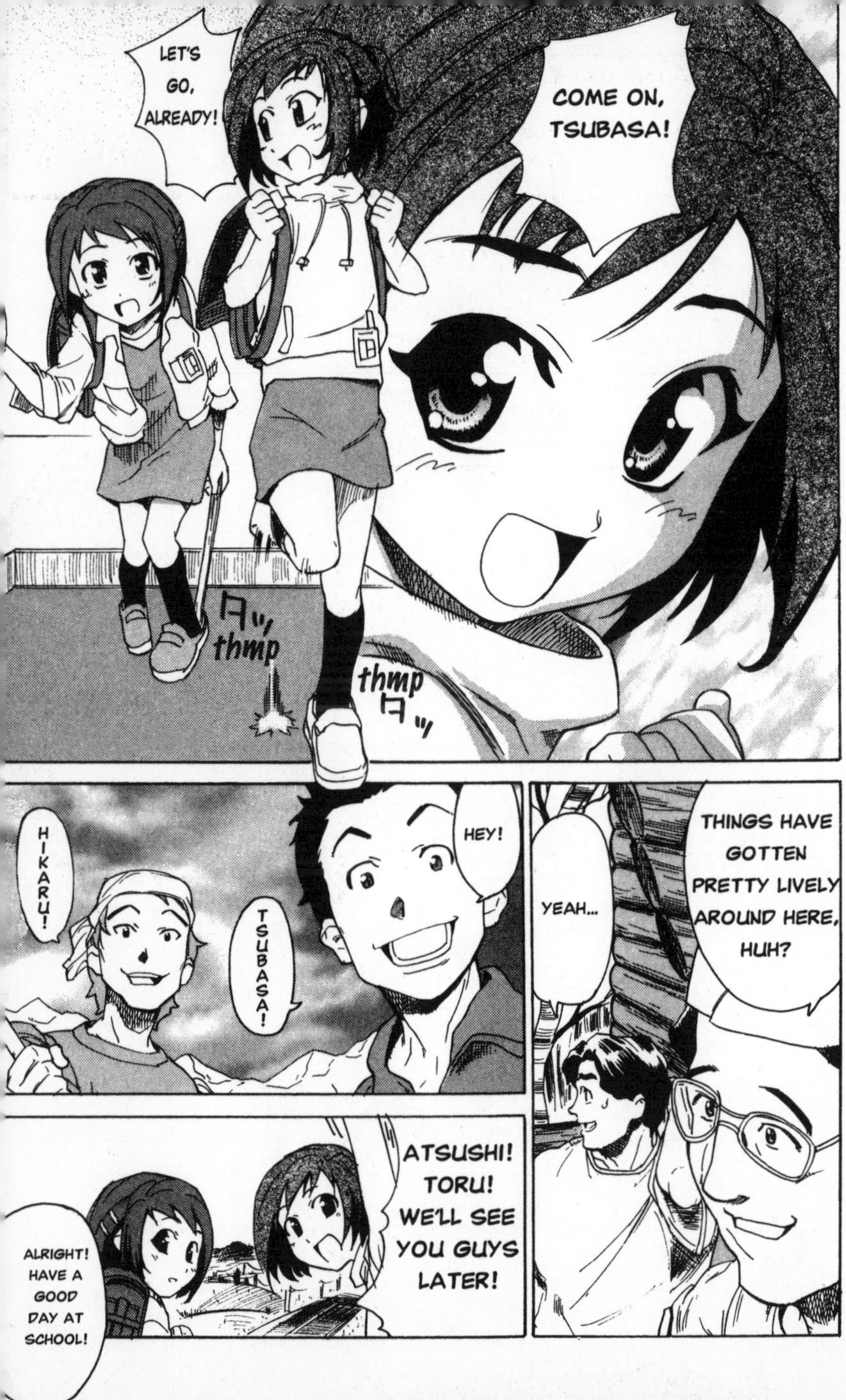
COME ON, TSUBASA!
LET'S GO, ALREADY!
タッ thmp
thmp タッ
THINGS HAVE GOTTEN PRETTY LIVELY AROUND HERE, HUH?
YEAH...
HEY!
TSUBASA!
HIKARU!
ATSUSHI! TORU! WE'LL SEE YOU GUYS LATER!
ALRIGHT! HAVE A GOOD DAY AT SCHOOL!

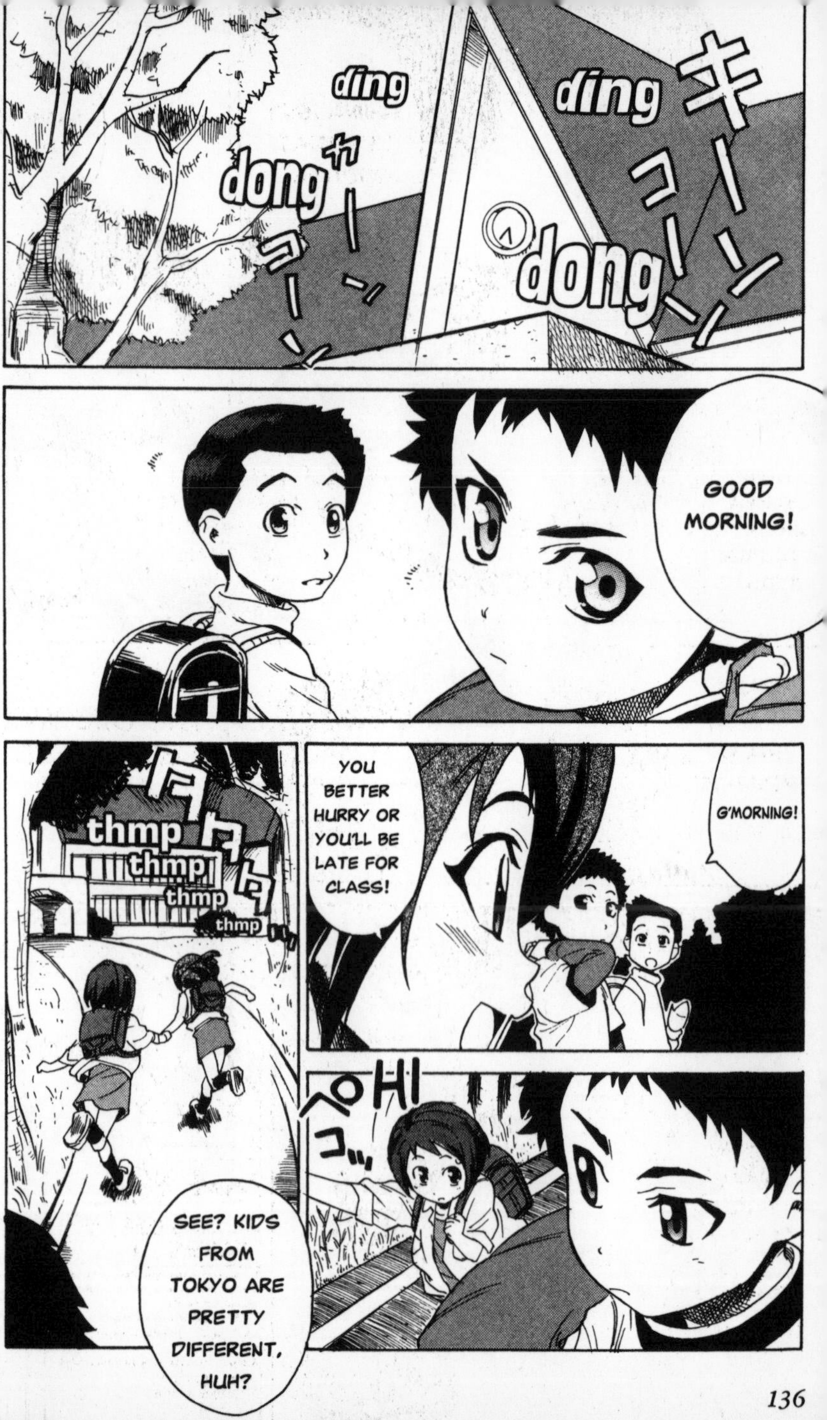

ding dong
キーンコーン
ding dong
カーンコーン
GOOD MORNING!
G'MORNING!
YOU BETTER HURRY OR YOU'LL BE LATE FOR CLASS!
thmp thmp thmp thmp
HI
SEE? KIDS FROM TOKYO ARE PRETTY DIFFERENT, HUH?

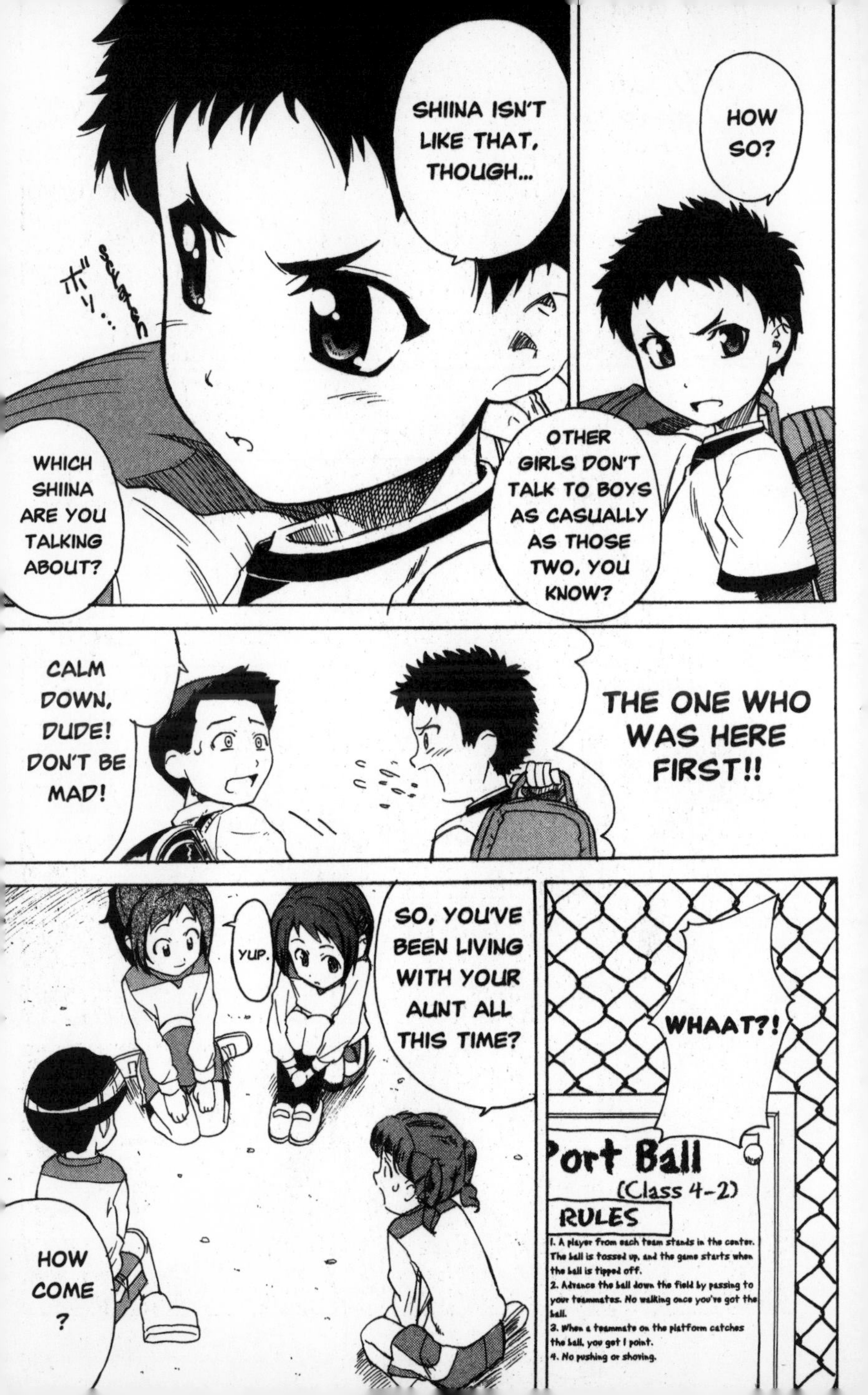
SHIINA ISN'T LIKE THAT, THOUGH...
ボリ…
scratch
HOW SO?
OTHER GIRLS DON'T TALK TO BOYS AS CASUALLY AS THOSE TWO, YOU KNOW?
WHICH SHIINA ARE YOU TALKING ABOUT?
THE ONE WHO WAS HERE FIRST!!
CALM DOWN, DUDE! DON'T BE MAD!
WHAAT?!
Port Ball
(Class 4-2)
RULES
1. A player from each team stands in the center. The ball is tossed up, and the game starts when the ball is tipped off.
2. Advance the ball down the field by passing to your teammates. No walking once you've got the ball.
3. When a teammate on the platform catches the ball, you get 1 point.
4. No pushing or shoving.
SO, YOU'VE BEEN LIVING WITH YOUR AUNT ALL THIS TIME?
YUP.
HOW COME?

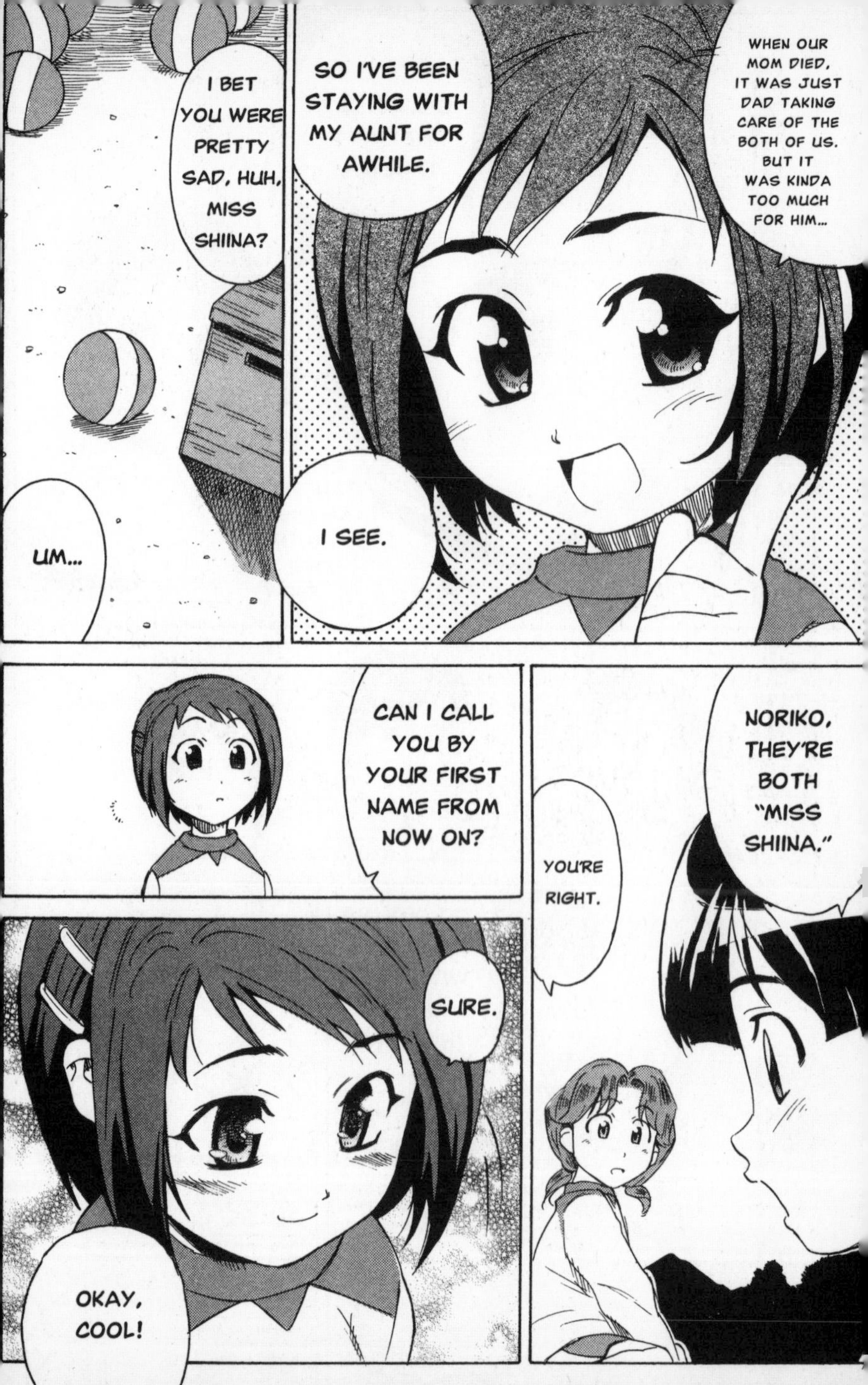
WHEN OUR MOM DIED, IT WAS JUST DAD TAKING CARE OF THE BOTH OF US. BUT IT WAS KINDA TOO MUCH FOR HIM...
SO I'VE BEEN STAYING WITH MY AUNT FOR AWHILE.
I SEE.
I BET YOU WERE PRETTY SAD, HUH, MISS SHIINA?
UM...
NORIKO, THEY'RE BOTH "MISS SHIINA."
YOU'RE RIGHT.
CAN I CALL YOU BY YOUR FIRST NAME FROM NOW ON?
SURE.
OKAY, COOL!

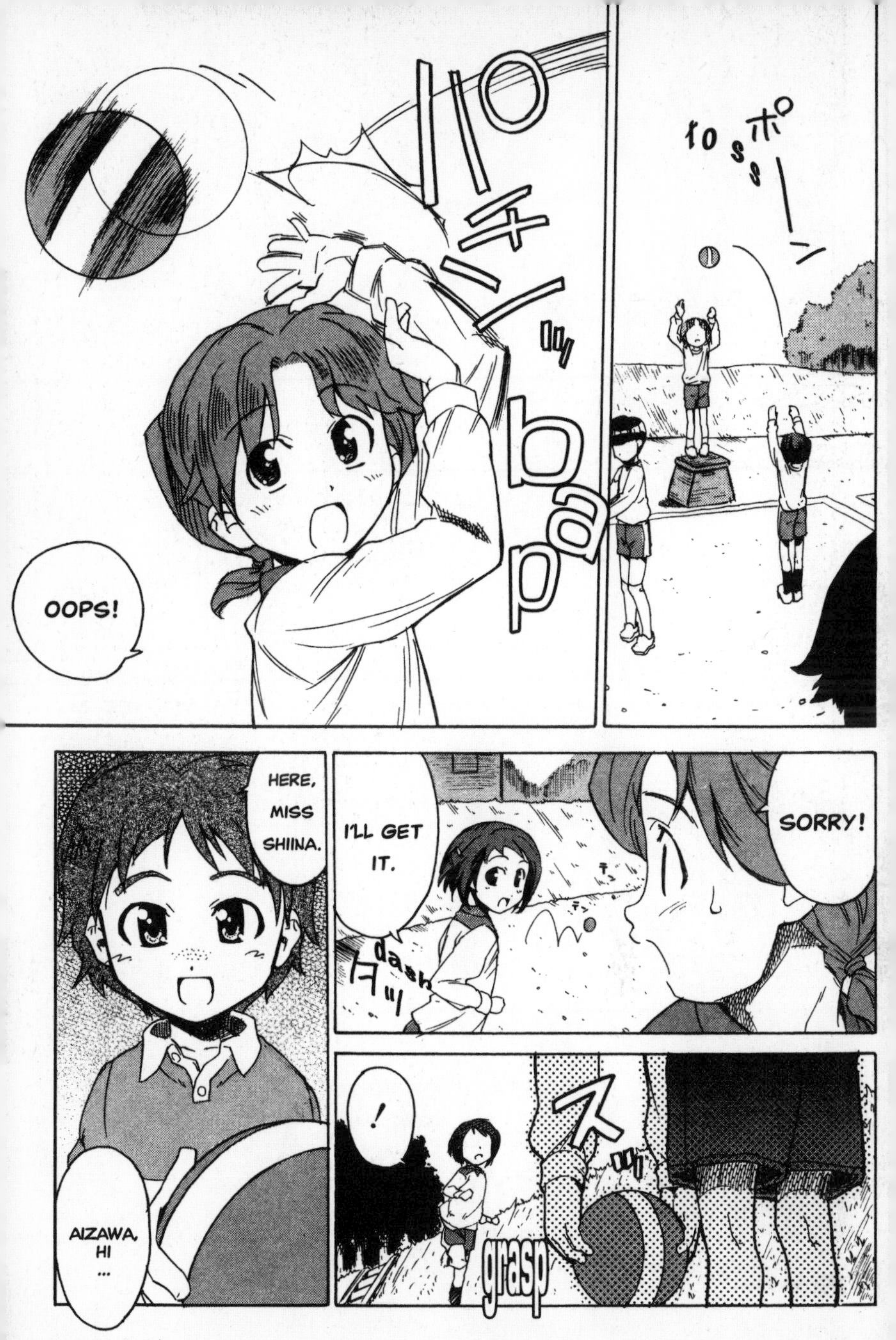

toss
ポーン
パチーンッ
bap
OOPS!
SORRY!
I'LL GET IT.
ダッ
dash
!
スッ
grasp
HERE, MISS SHIINA.
AIZAWA, HI ...

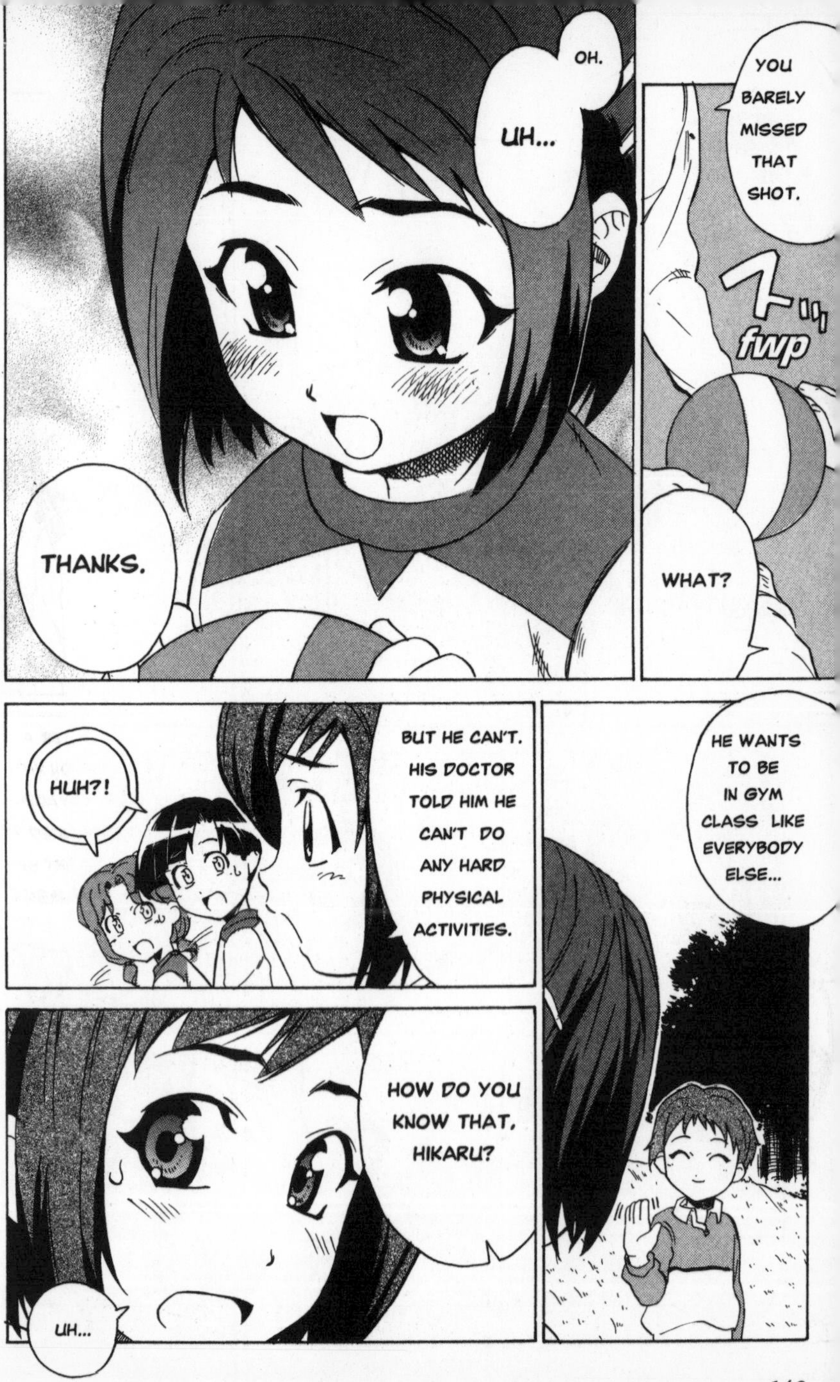
YOU BARELY MISSED THAT SHOT.
fwp
WHAT?
OH.
UH...
THANKS.
HE WANTS TO BE IN GYM CLASS LIKE EVERYBODY ELSE...
BUT HE CAN'T. HIS DOCTOR TOLD HIM HE CAN'T DO ANY HARD PHYSICAL ACTIVITIES.
HUH?!
HOW DO YOU KNOW THAT, HIKARU?
UH...

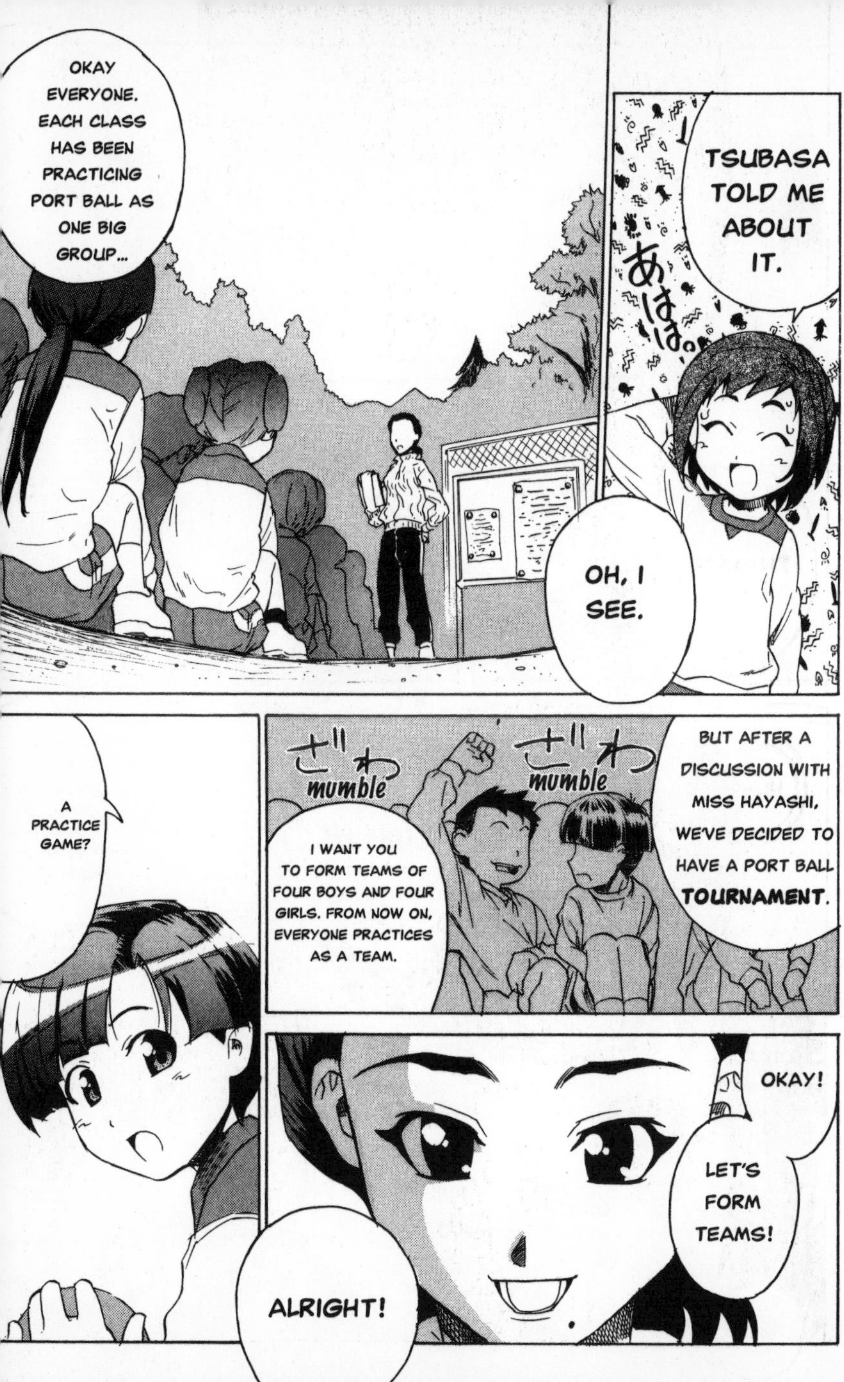

TSUBASA TOLD ME ABOUT IT.
あはは。
OH, I SEE.
OKAY EVERYONE. EACH CLASS HAS BEEN PRACTICING PORT BALL AS ONE BIG GROUP...
BUT AFTER A DISCUSSION WITH MISS HAYASHI, WE'VE DECIDED TO HAVE A PORT BALL **TOURNAMENT**.
ざわ mumble
ざわ mumble
I WANT YOU TO FORM TEAMS OF FOUR BOYS AND FOUR GIRLS. FROM NOW ON, EVERYONE PRACTICES AS A TEAM.
A PRACTICE GAME?
OKAY!
LET'S FORM TEAMS!
ALRIGHT!

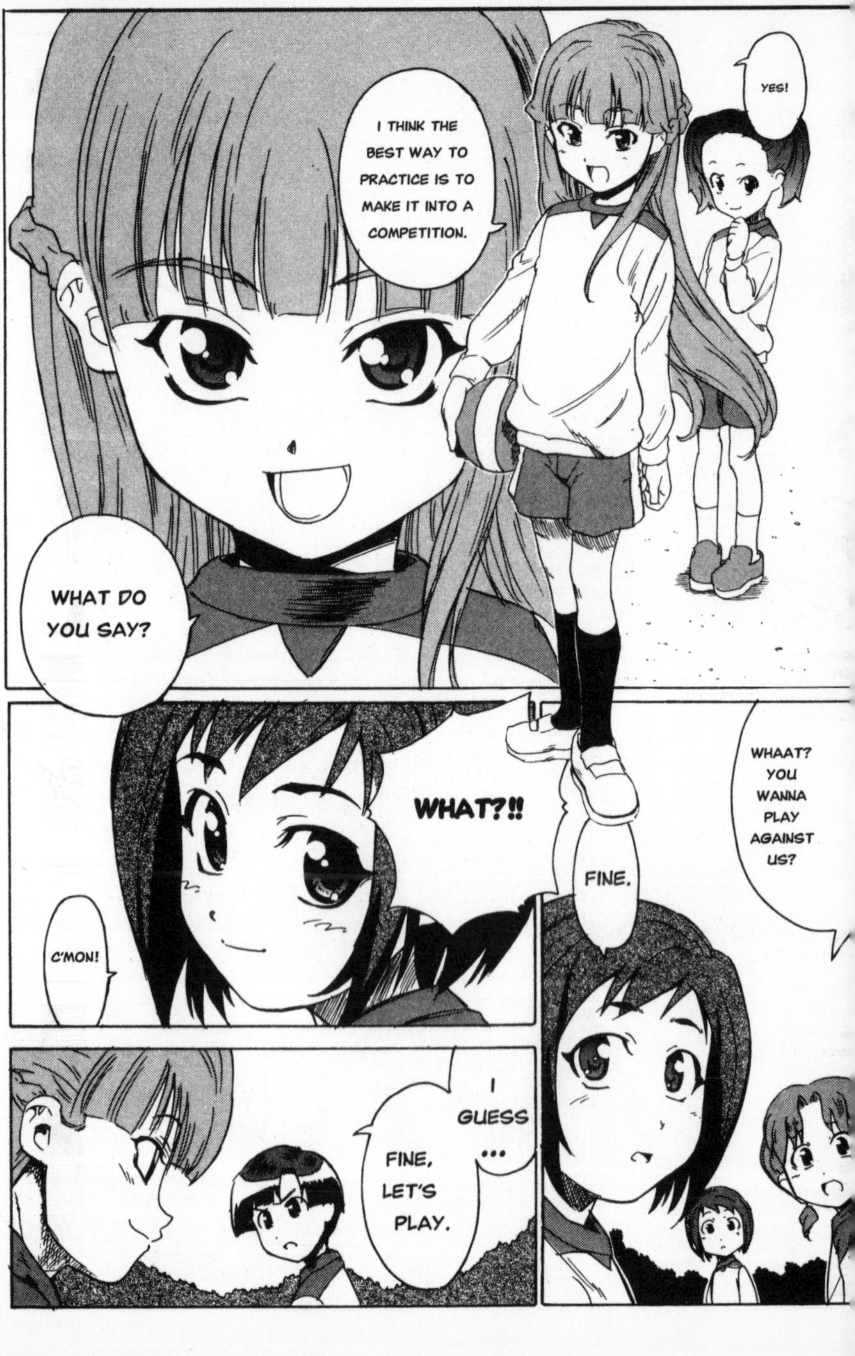
I THINK THE BEST WAY TO PRACTICE IS TO MAKE IT INTO A COMPETITION.
WHAT DO YOU SAY?
YES!
WHAAT? YOU WANNA PLAY AGAINST US?
FINE.
WHAT?!!
C'MON!
I GUESS ...
FINE, LET'S PLAY.

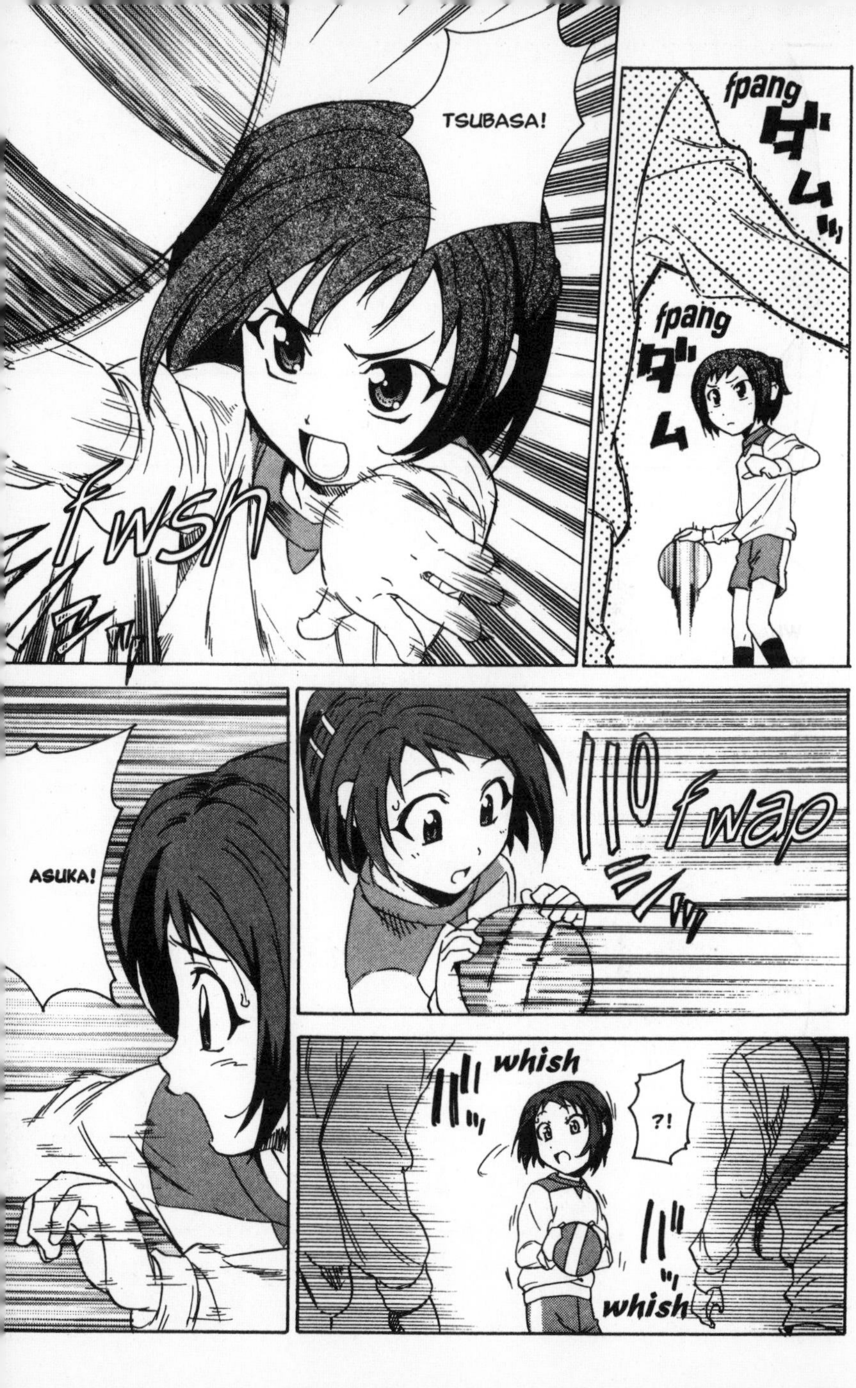
fpang
ダムッ
fpang
ダム
TSUBASA!
fwsh
fwap
whish
?!
whish
ASUKA!

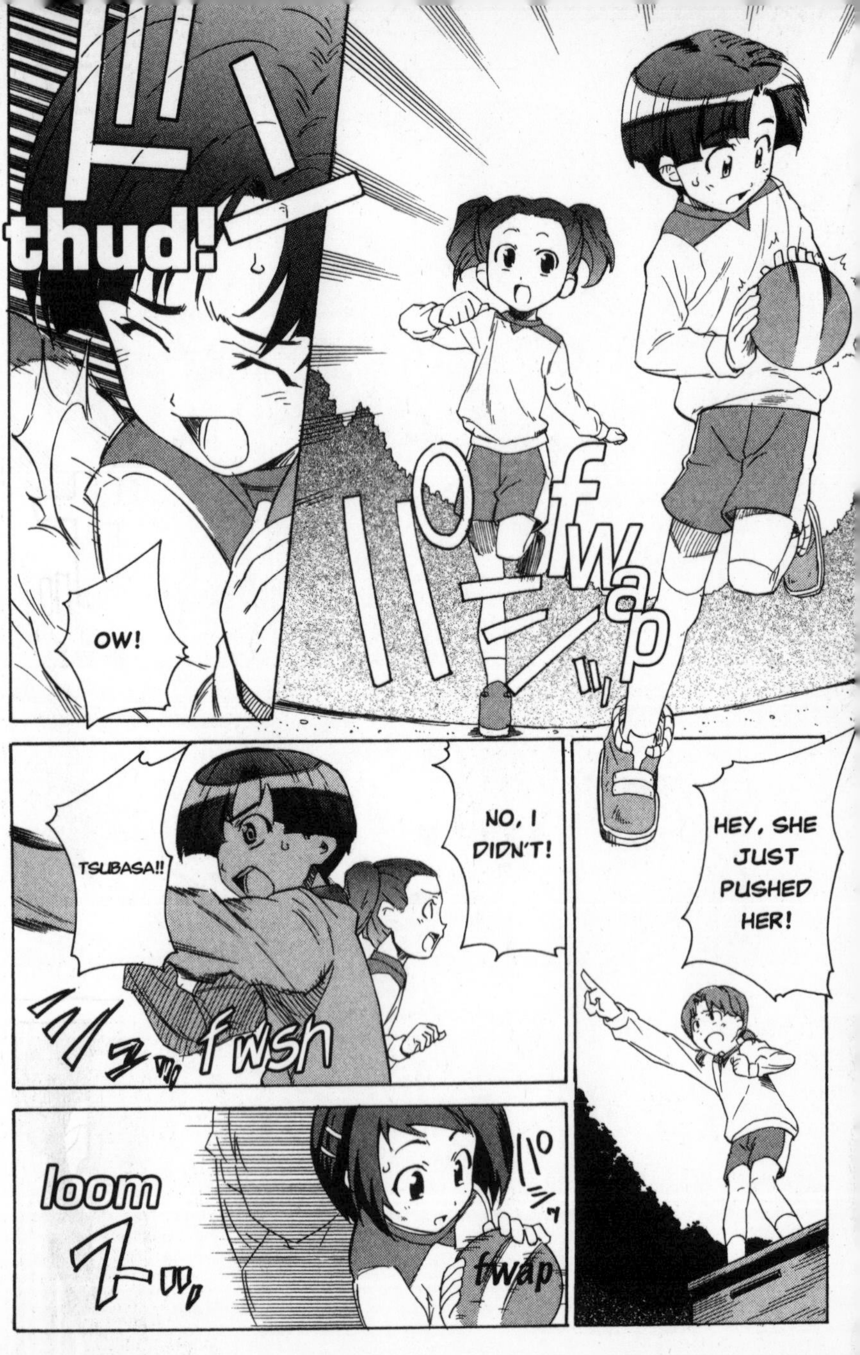
thud!
fwap
OW!
HEY, SHE JUST PUSHED HER!
NO, I DIDN'T!
TSUBASA!!
fwsh
fwap
loom

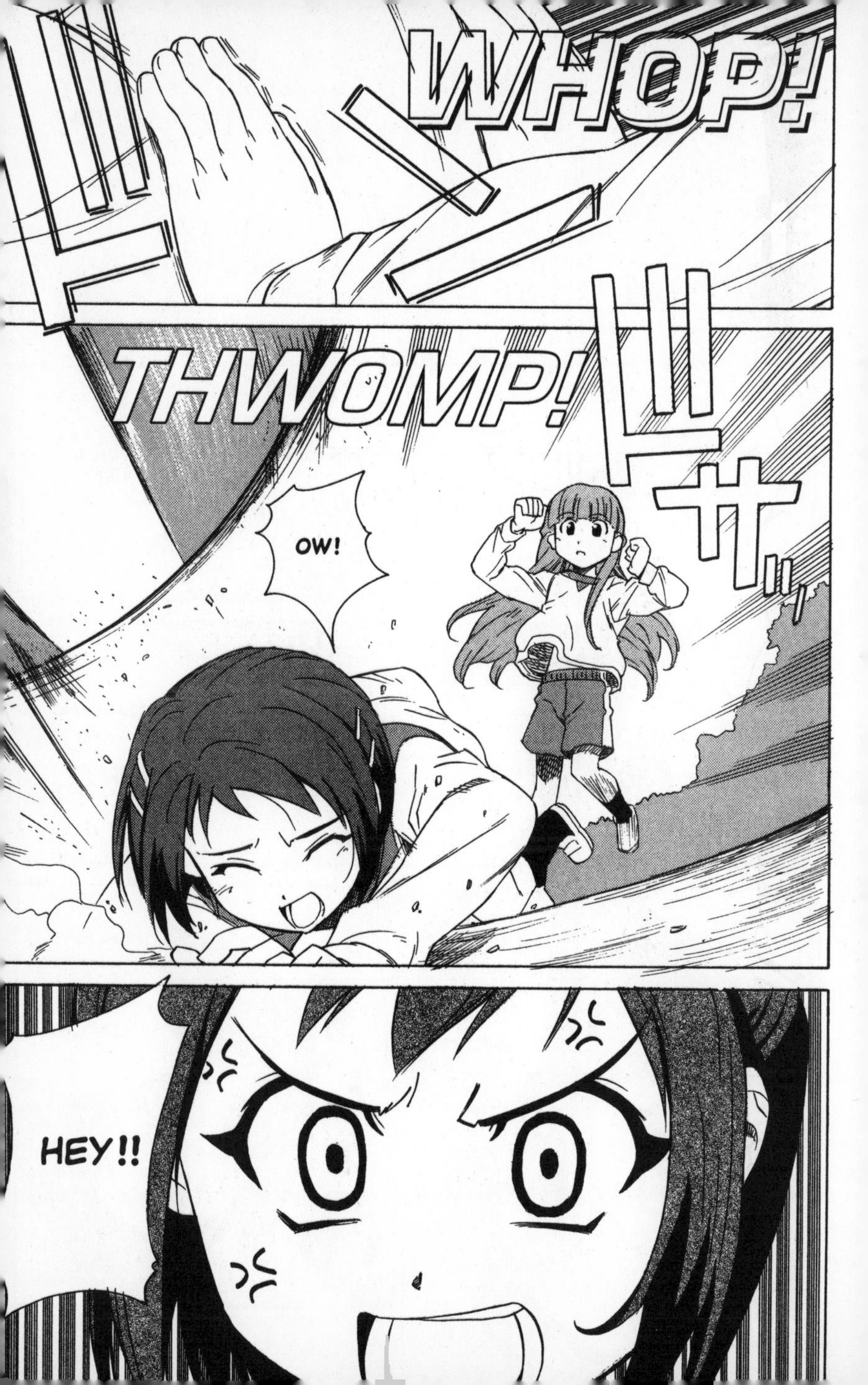
WHOP!
THWOMP!
OW!
HEY!!

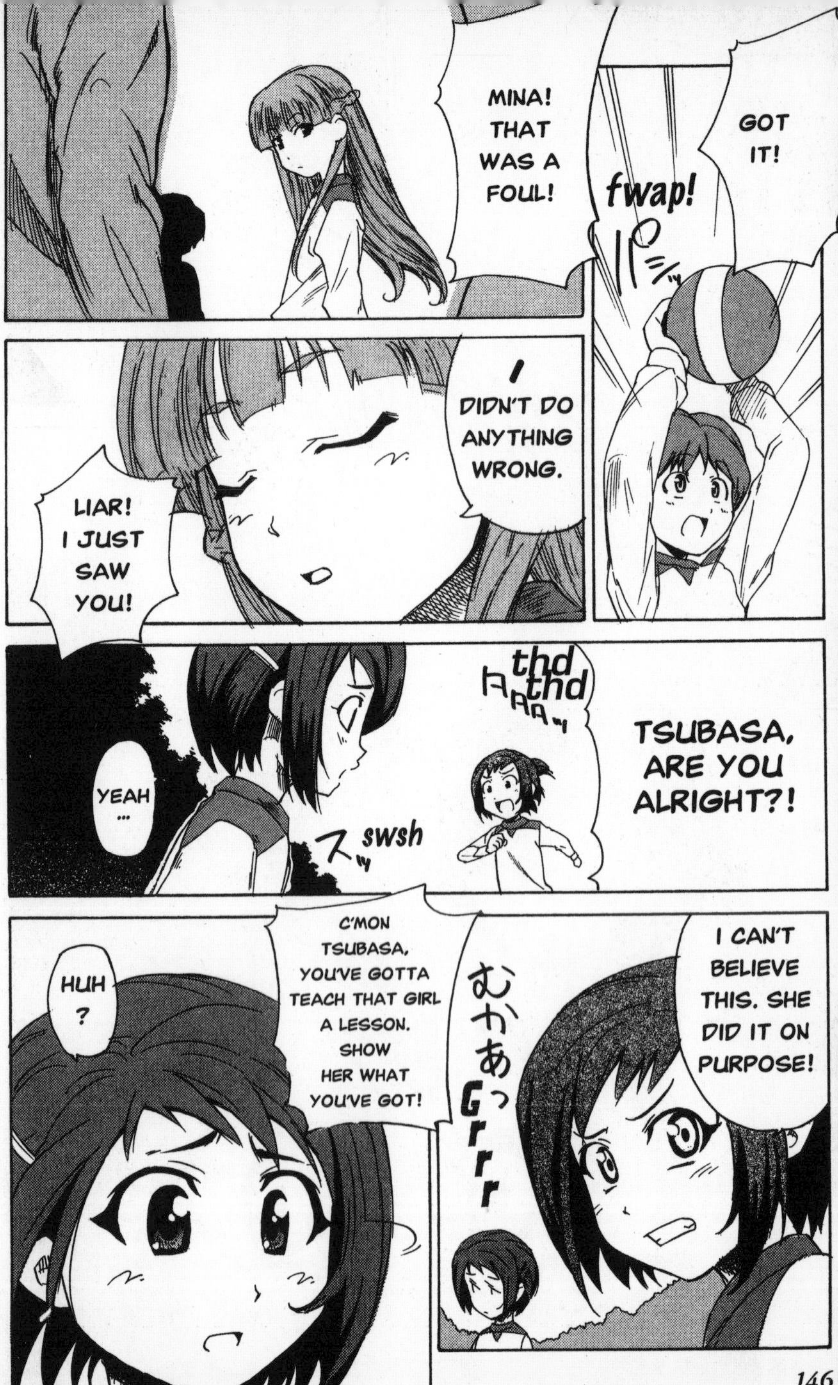

GOT IT!
fwap!
パシッ
MINA! THAT WAS A FOUL!
I DIDN'T DO ANYTHING WRONG.
LIAR! I JUST SAW YOU!
TSUBASA, ARE YOU ALRIGHT?!
thd thd
タタタッ
スッ
swsh
YEAH...
I CAN'T BELIEVE THIS. SHE DID IT ON PURPOSE!
むかあっ
Grrr
C'MON TSUBASA, YOU'VE GOTTA TEACH THAT GIRL A LESSON. SHOW HER WHAT YOU'VE GOT!
HUH?

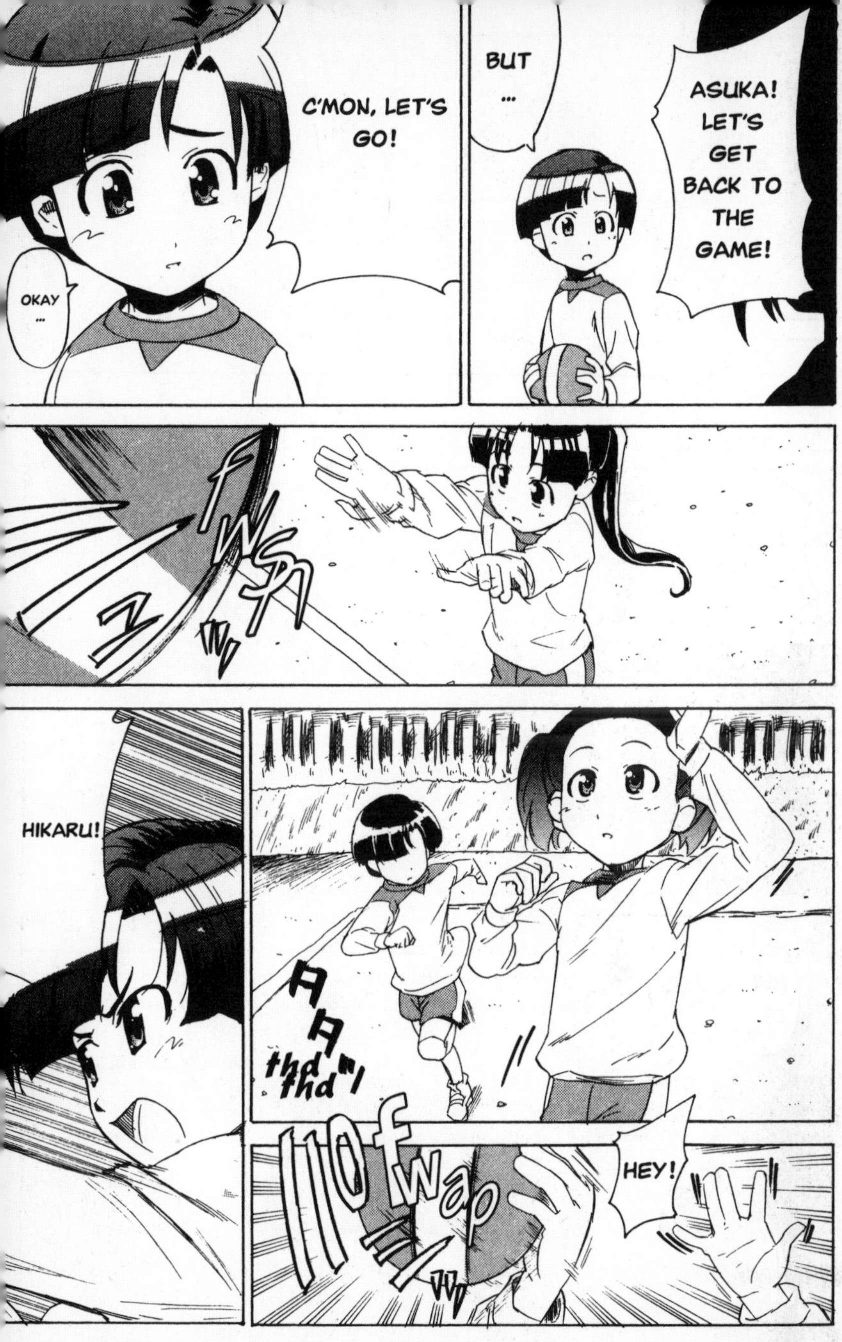
ASUKA! LET'S GET BACK TO THE GAME!
BUT ...
C'MON, LET'S GO!
OKAY ...
fwsh
thd thd
HIKARU!
HEY!
fwap

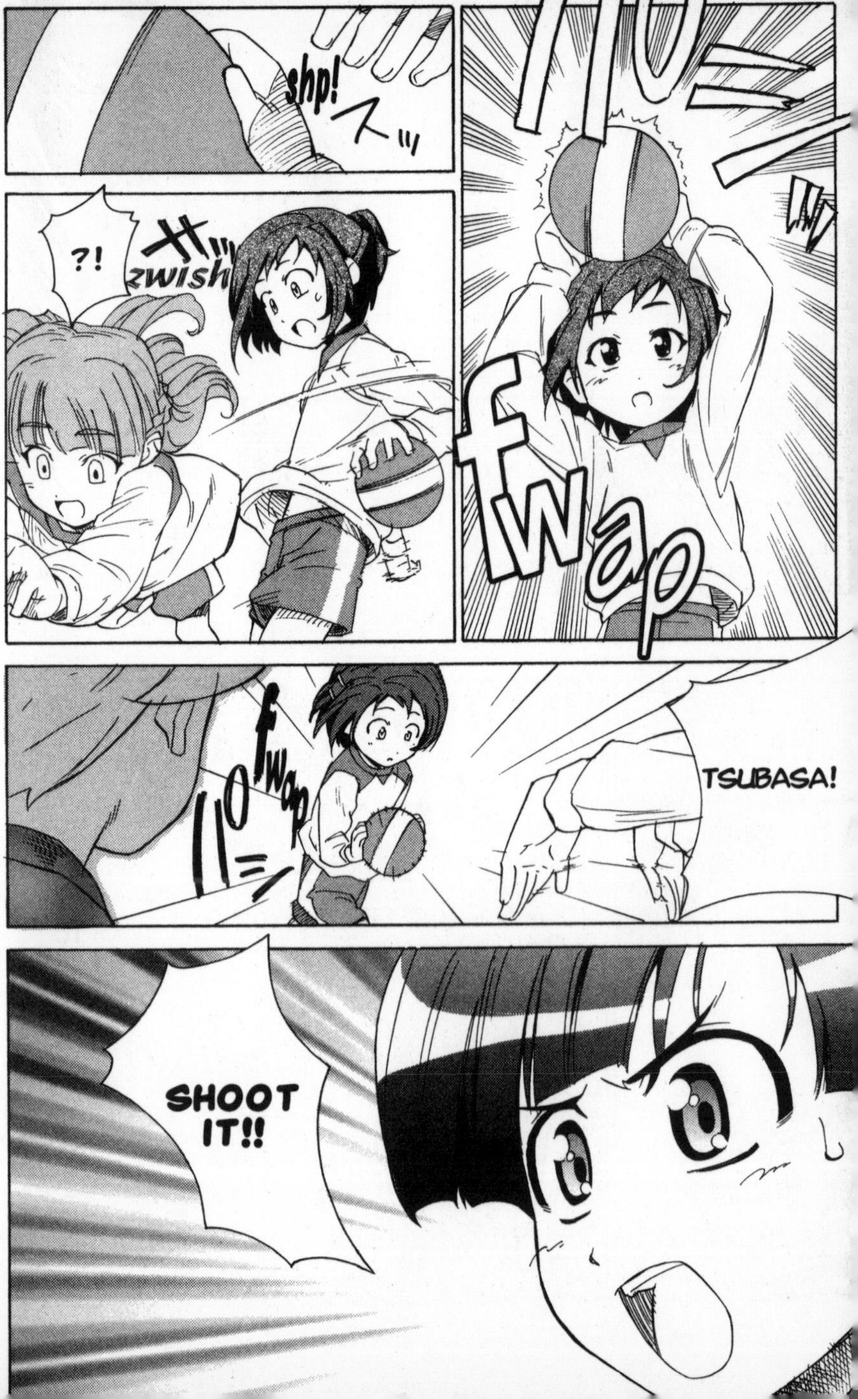

shp!
スッ
?!
zwish
fwap
fwap
TSUBASA!
SHOOT IT!!

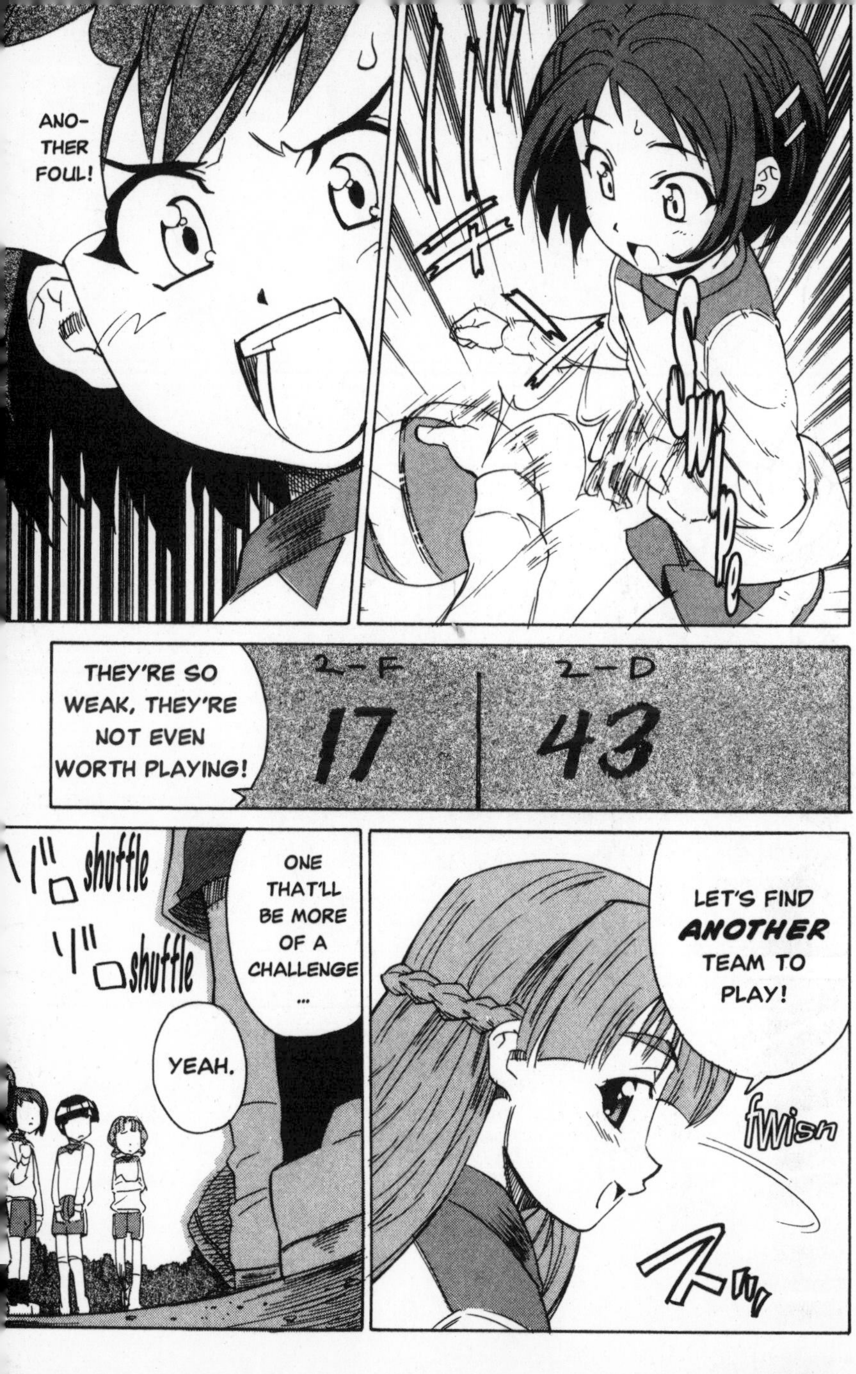

ANO-THER FOUL!
THEY'RE SO WEAK, THEY'RE NOT EVEN WORTH PLAYING!
2-F
17
2-D
43
LET'S FIND ANOTHER TEAM TO PLAY!
fwish
ONE THAT'LL BE MORE OF A CHALLENGE ...
YEAH.
shuffle
shuffle

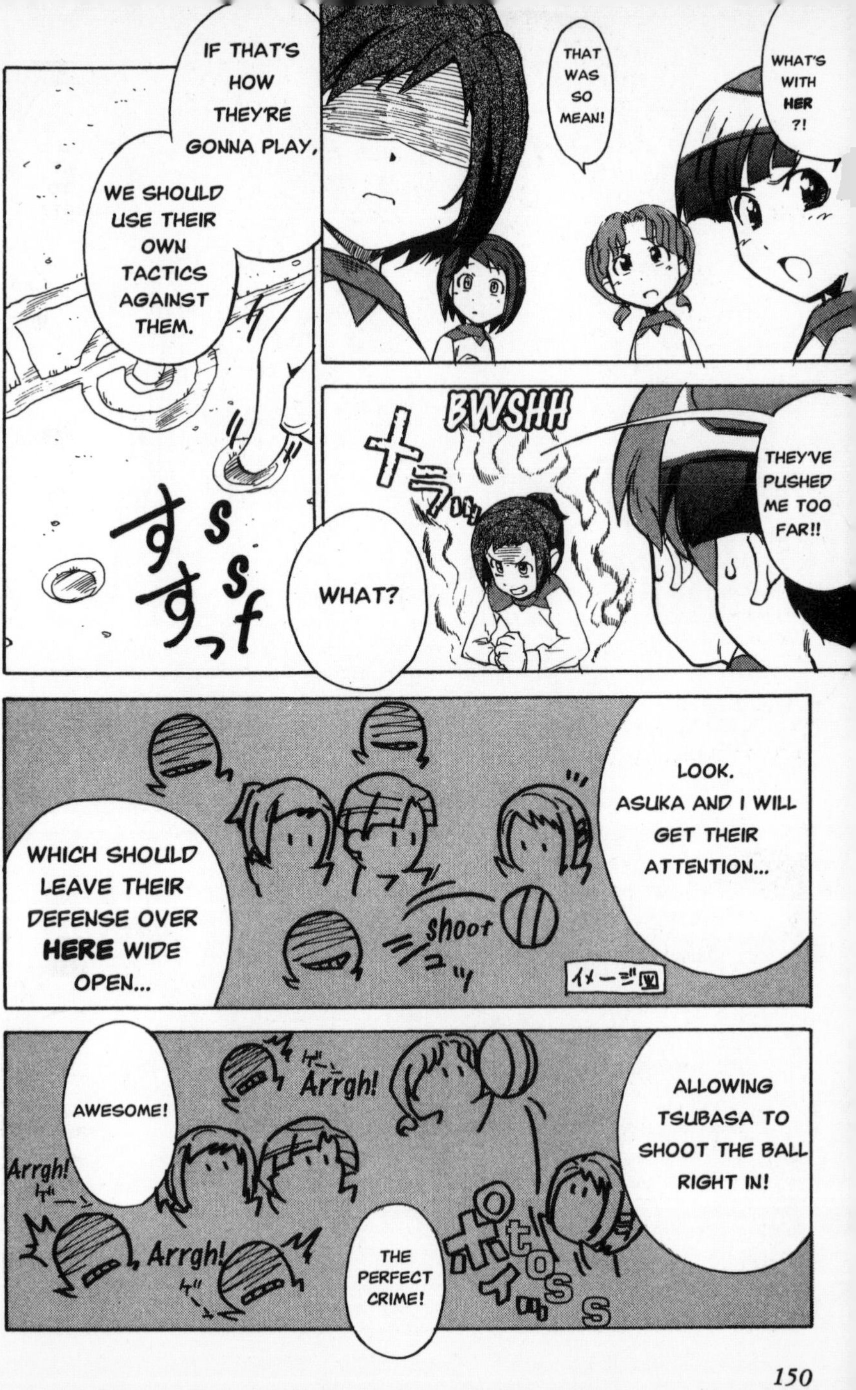
WHAT'S WITH HER?!
THAT WAS SO MEAN!
IF THAT'S HOW THEY'RE GONNA PLAY,
WE SHOULD USE THEIR OWN TACTICS AGAINST THEM.
BWSHH
THEY'VE PUSHED ME TOO FAR!!
WHAT?
s s f
LOOK. ASUKA AND I WILL GET THEIR ATTENTION...
WHICH SHOULD LEAVE THEIR DEFENSE OVER HERE WIDE OPEN...
shoot
イメージ図
ALLOWING TSUBASA TO SHOOT THE BALL RIGHT IN!
toss
THE PERFECT CRIME!
Arrgh!
AWESOME!
Arrgh!
Arrgh!

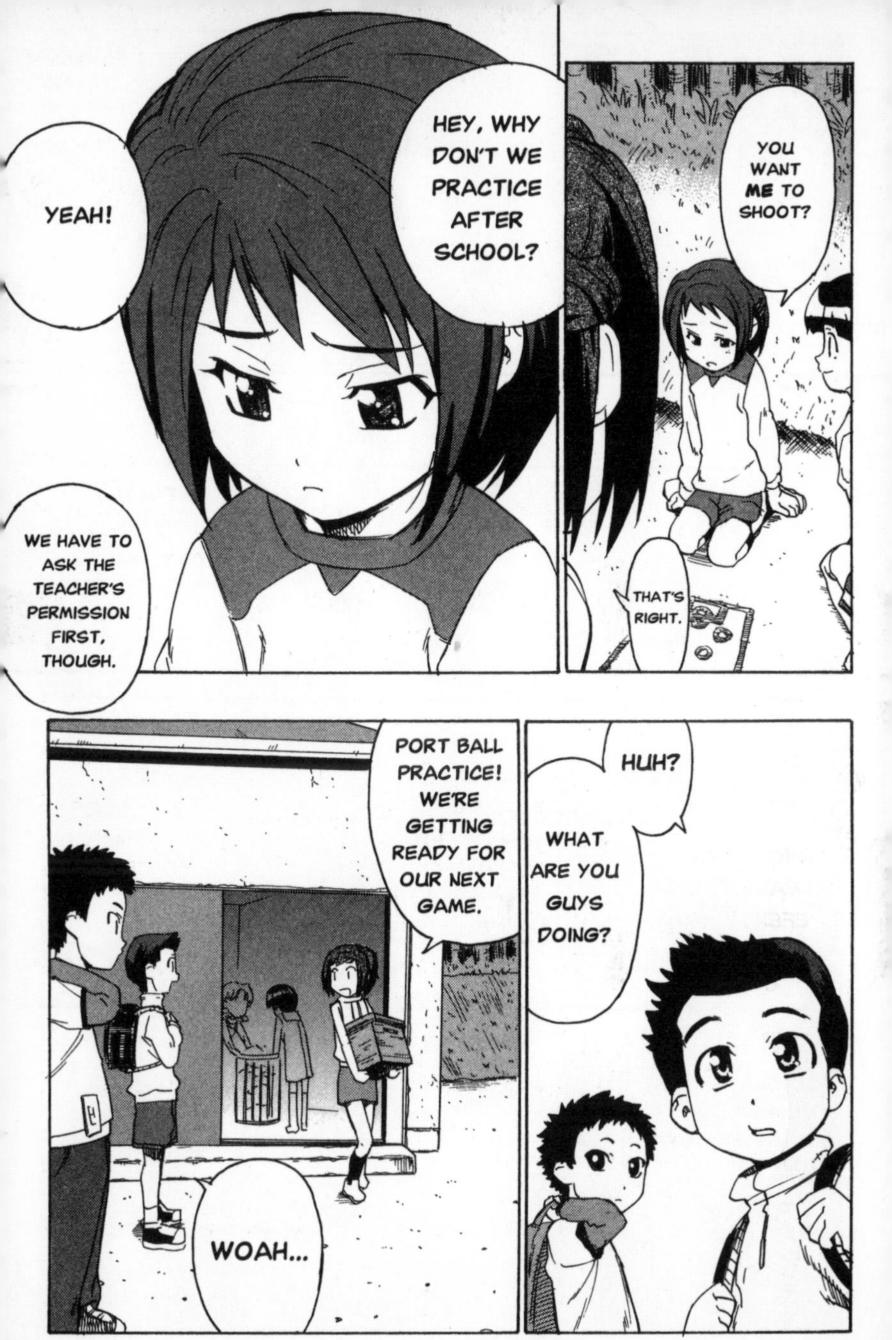

YOU WANT ME TO SHOOT?
THAT'S RIGHT.
HEY, WHY DON'T WE PRACTICE AFTER SCHOOL?
YEAH!
WE HAVE TO ASK THE TEACHER'S PERMISSION FIRST, THOUGH.
HUH?
WHAT ARE YOU GUYS DOING?
PORT BALL PRACTICE! WE'RE GETTING READY FOR OUR NEXT GAME.
WOAH...

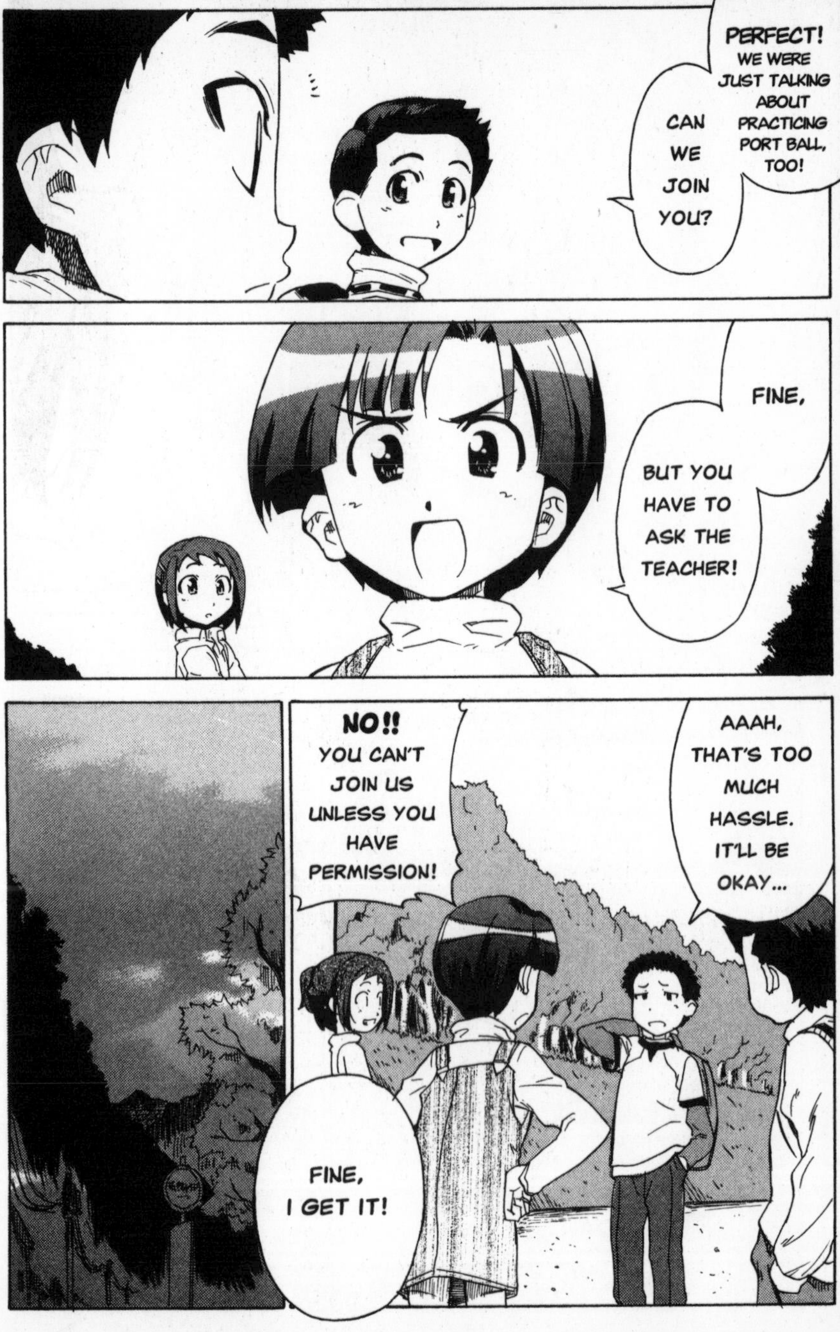
PERFECT! WE WERE JUST TALKING ABOUT PRACTICING PORT BALL, TOO!
CAN WE JOIN YOU?
FINE,
BUT YOU HAVE TO ASK THE TEACHER!
AAAH, THAT'S TOO MUCH HASSLE. IT'LL BE OKAY...
NO!! YOU CAN'T JOIN US UNLESS YOU HAVE PERMISSION!
FINE, I GET IT!

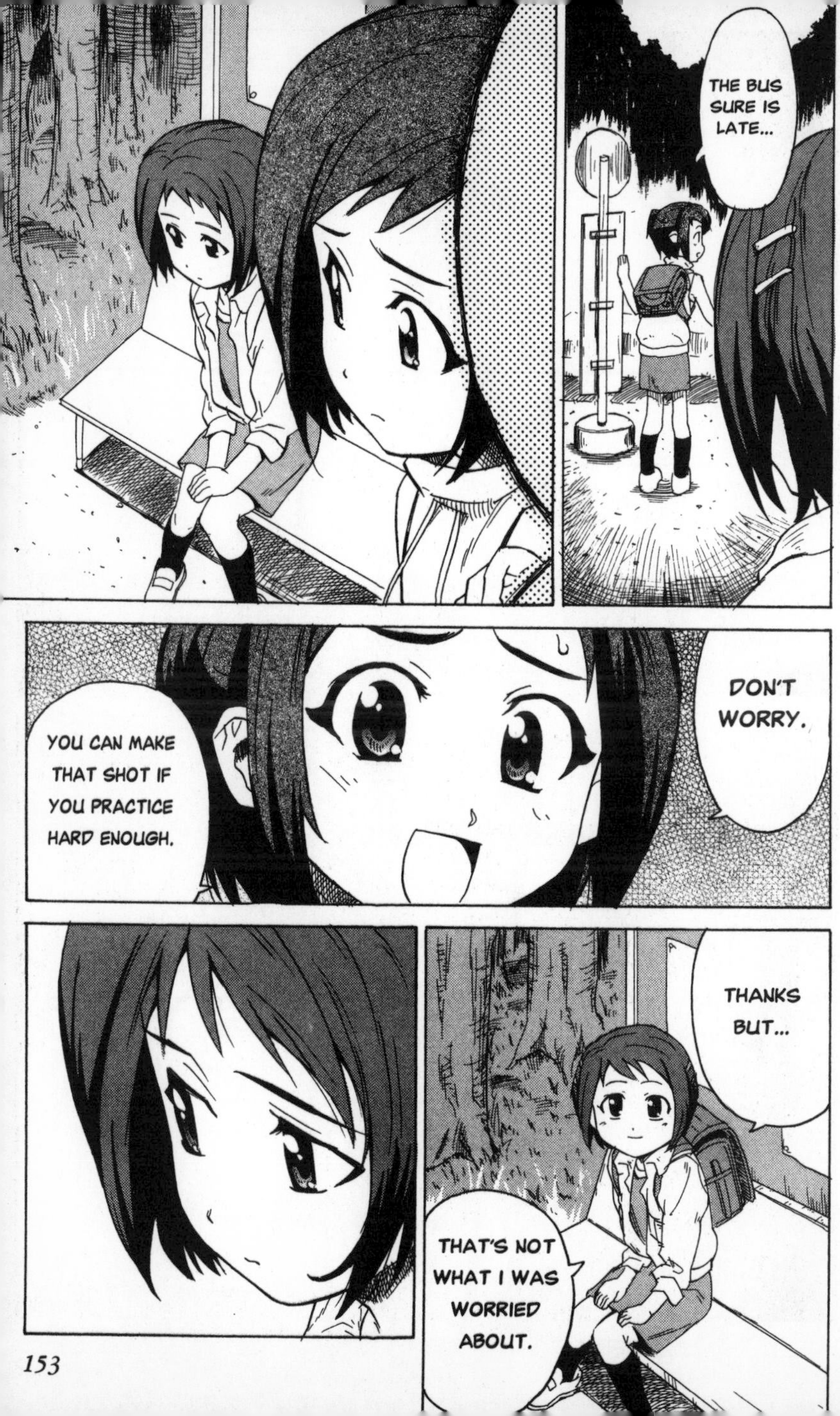
THE BUS SURE IS LATE...
DON'T WORRY.
YOU CAN MAKE THAT SHOT IF YOU PRACTICE HARD ENOUGH.
THANKS BUT...
THAT'S NOT WHAT I WAS WORRIED ABOUT.

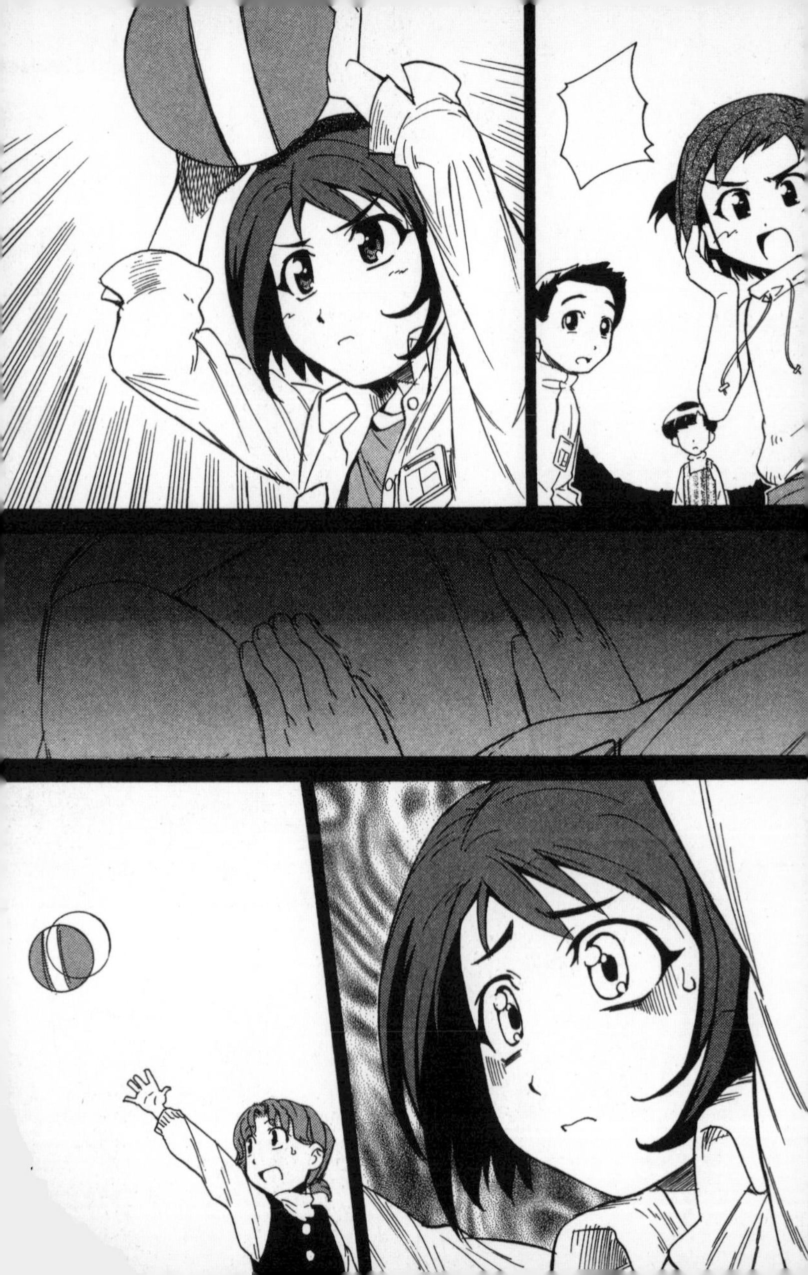

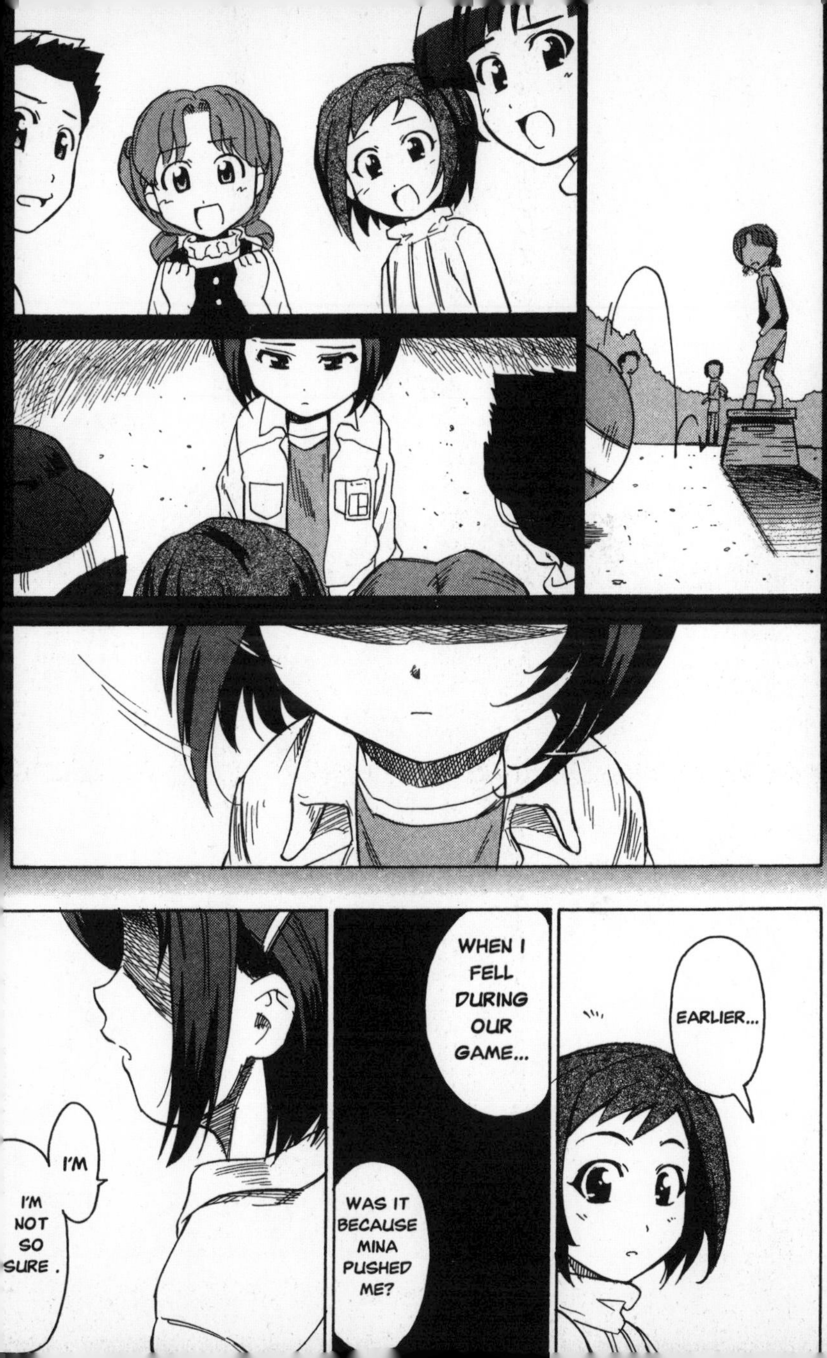
EARLIER...
WHEN I FELL DURING OUR GAME...
WAS IT BECAUSE MINA PUSHED ME?
I'M
I'M NOT SO SURE.

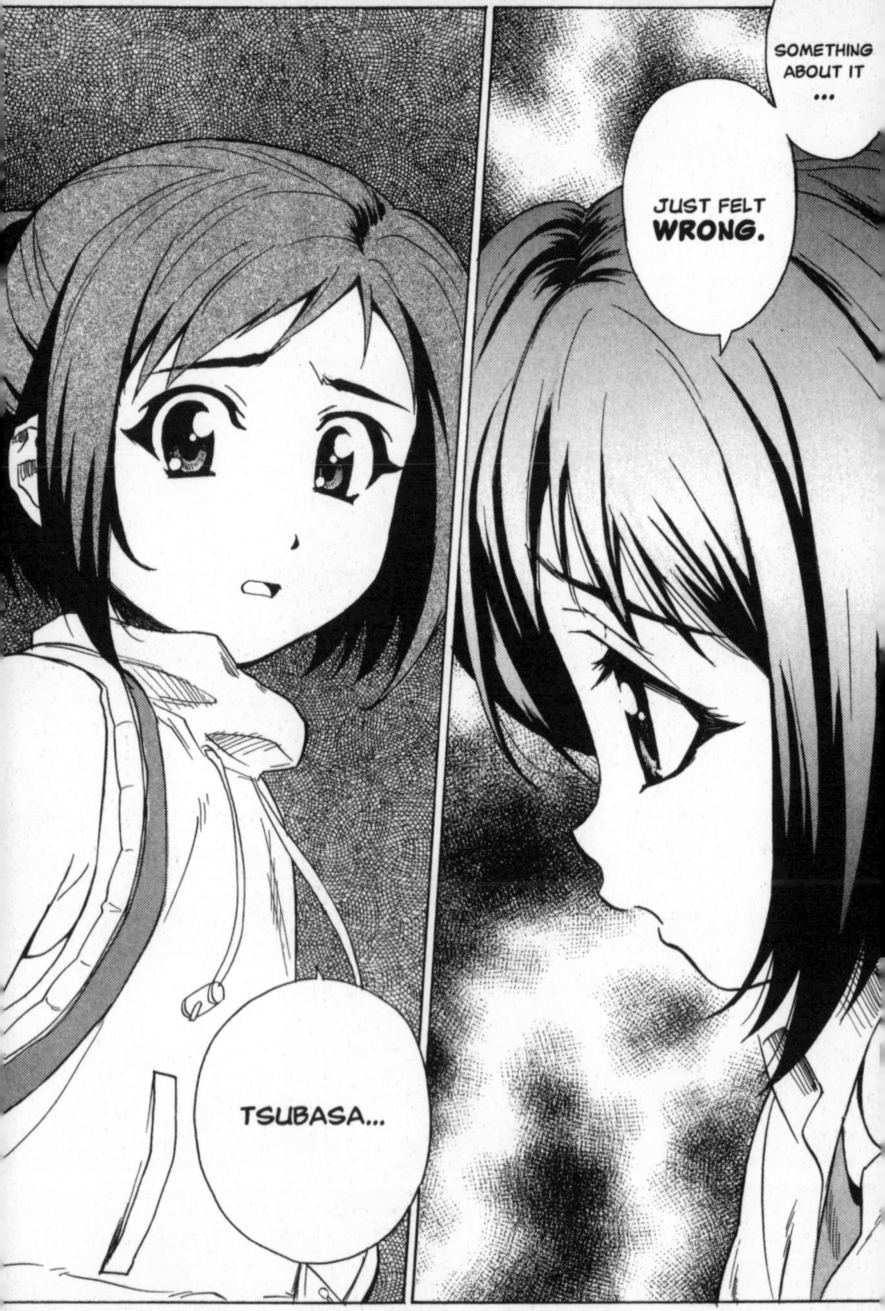
SOMETHING ABOUT IT ...
JUST FELT WRONG.
TSUBASA...

F I G U R E S E V E N T E E N

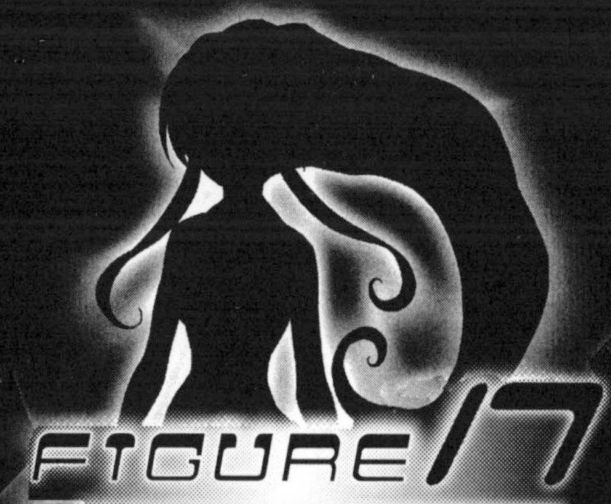
FIGURE 17
Tsubasa & Hikaru

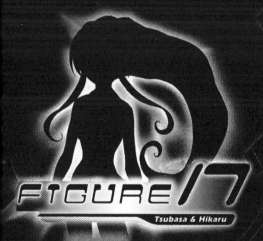

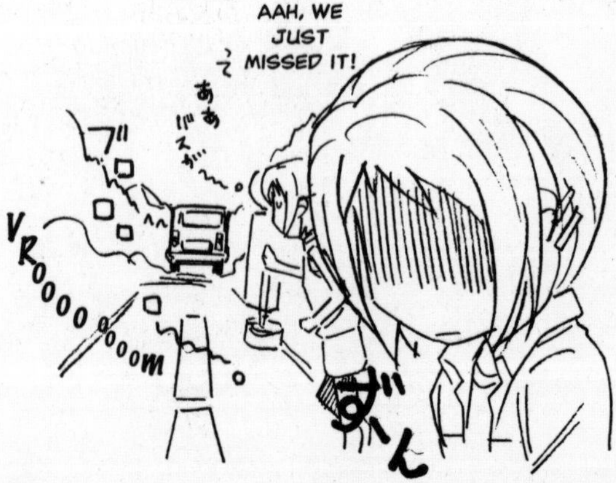
AAH, WE JUST MISSED IT!
VROOOO OOOOM
SIGH

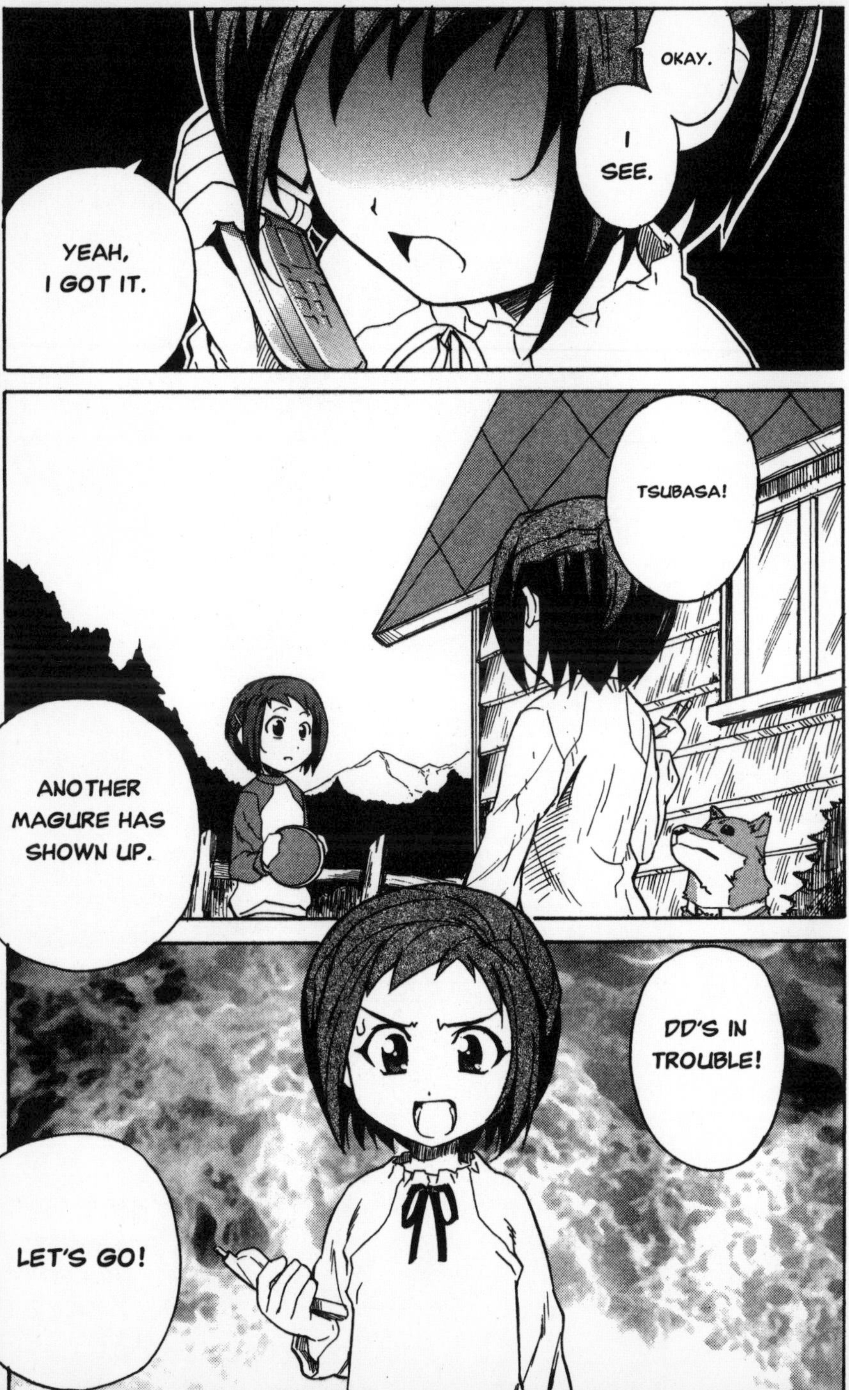
OKAY.
I SEE.
YEAH, I GOT IT.
TSUBASA!
ANOTHER MAGURE HAS SHOWN UP.
DD'S IN TROUBLE!
LET'S GO!

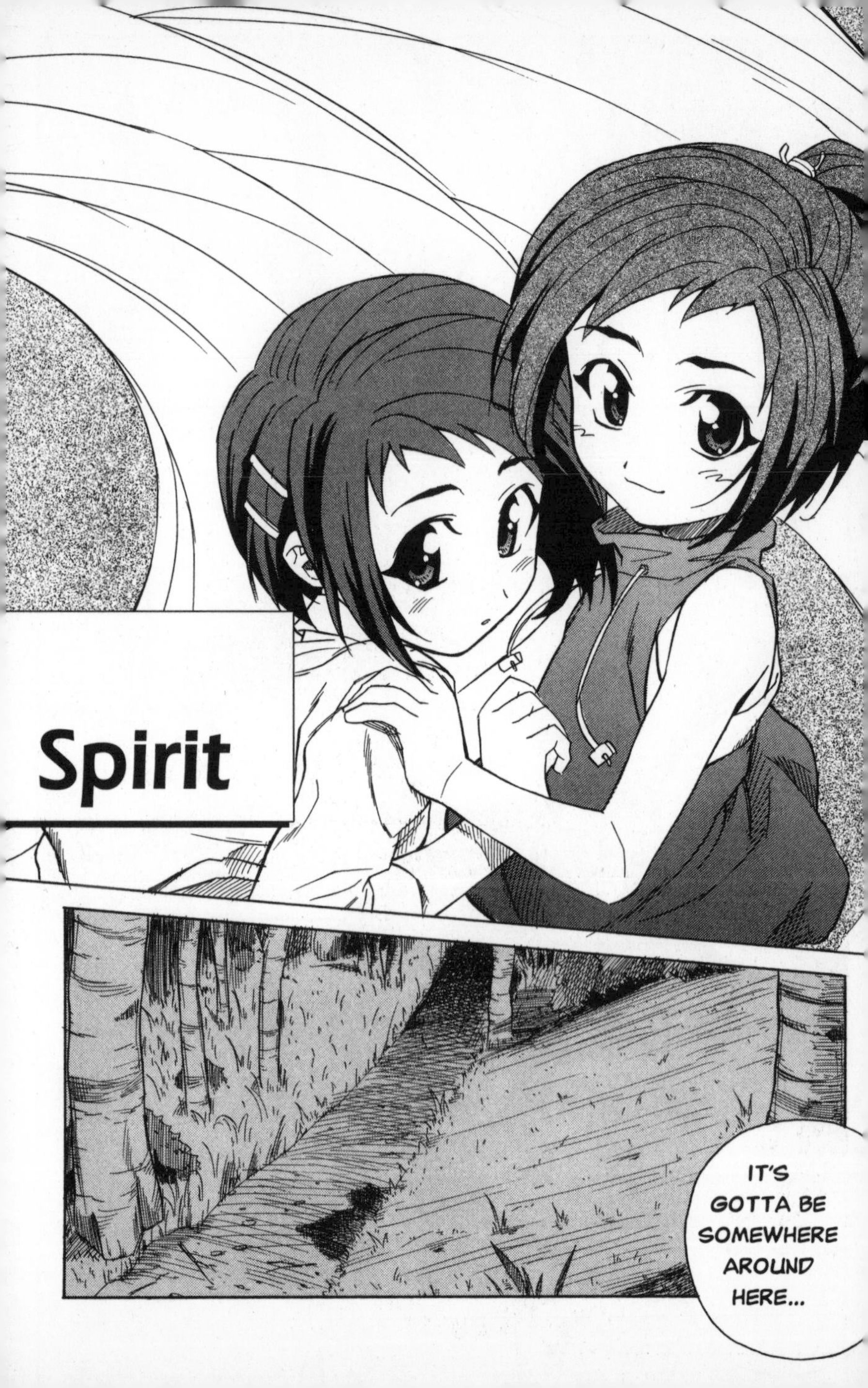
Spirit
IT'S GOTTA BE SOMEWHERE AROUND HERE...

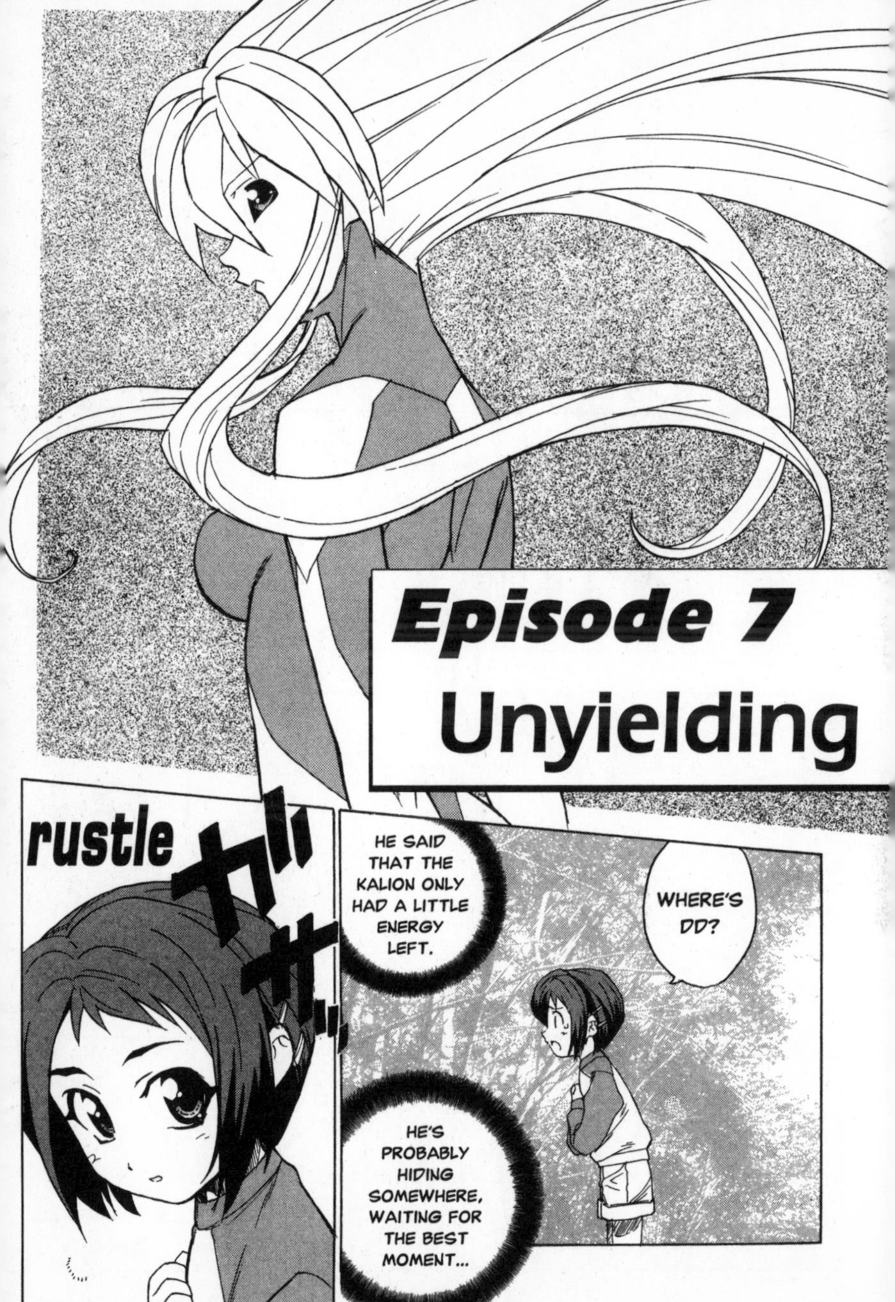
Episode 7
Unyielding
rustle
HE SAID THAT THE KALION ONLY HAD A LITTLE ENERGY LEFT.
WHERE'S DD?
HE'S PROBABLY HIDING SOMEWHERE, WAITING FOR THE BEST MOMENT...

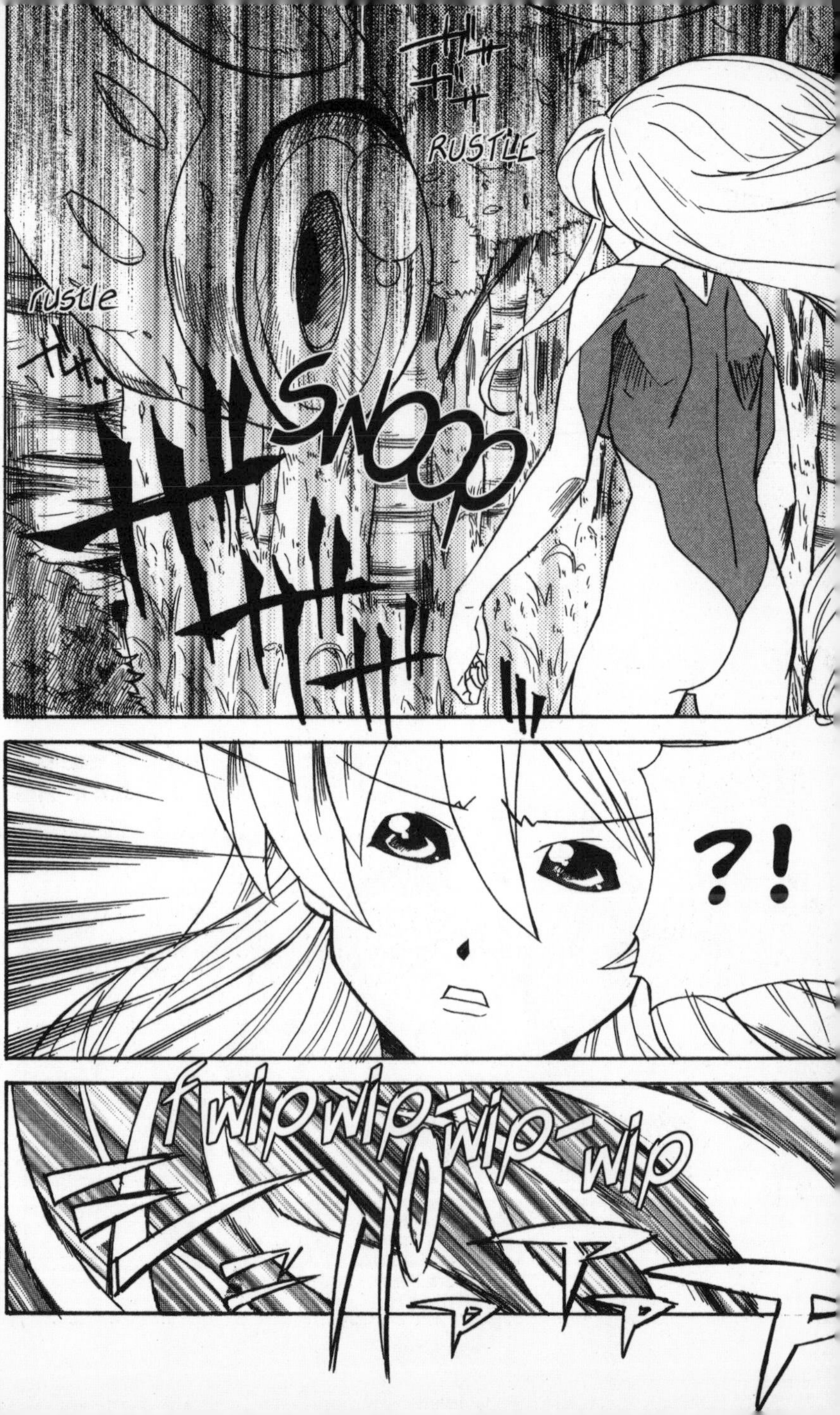
RUSTLE
rustle
SWOOP
?!
fwipwip-wip-wip

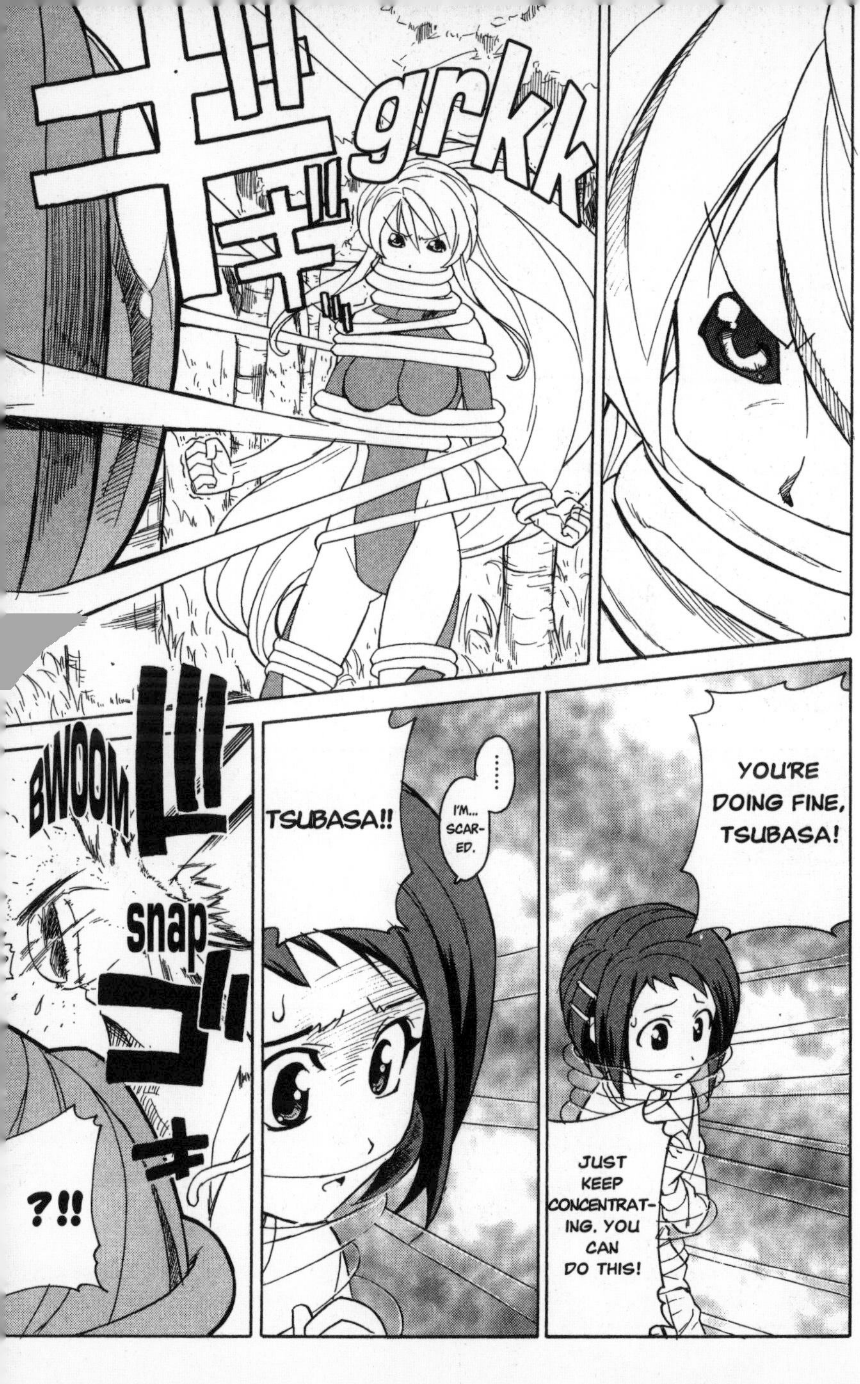
grkk
YOU'RE DOING FINE, TSUBASA!
JUST KEEP CONCENTRAT-ING. YOU CAN DO THIS!
......
I'M... SCAR-ED.
TSUBASA!!
BWOOM!!
snap
?!!

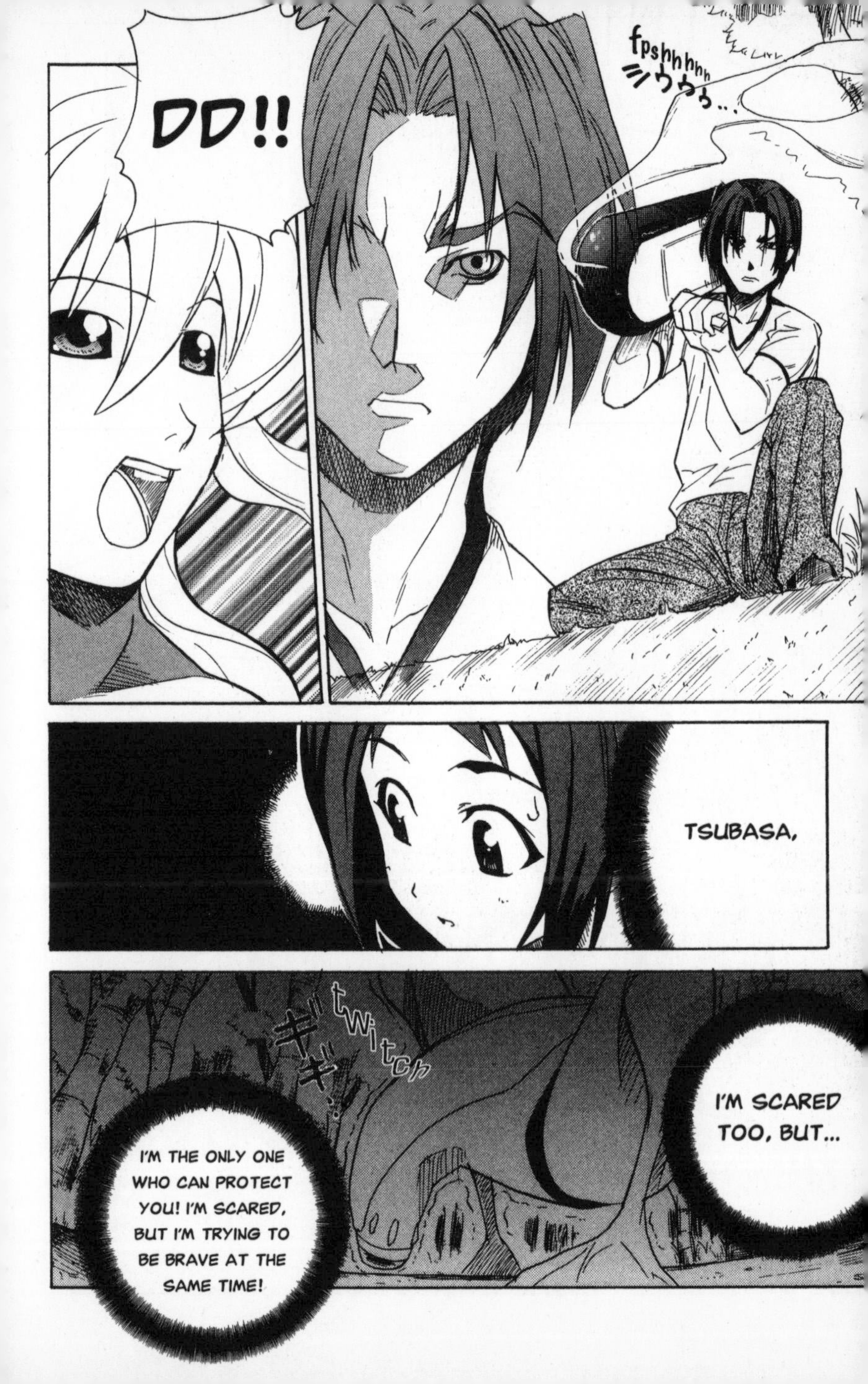
fpshhhhh
DD!!
TSUBASA,
twitch
I'M SCARED TOO, BUT...
I'M THE ONLY ONE WHO CAN PROTECT YOU! I'M SCARED, BUT I'M TRYING TO BE BRAVE AT THE SAME TIME!

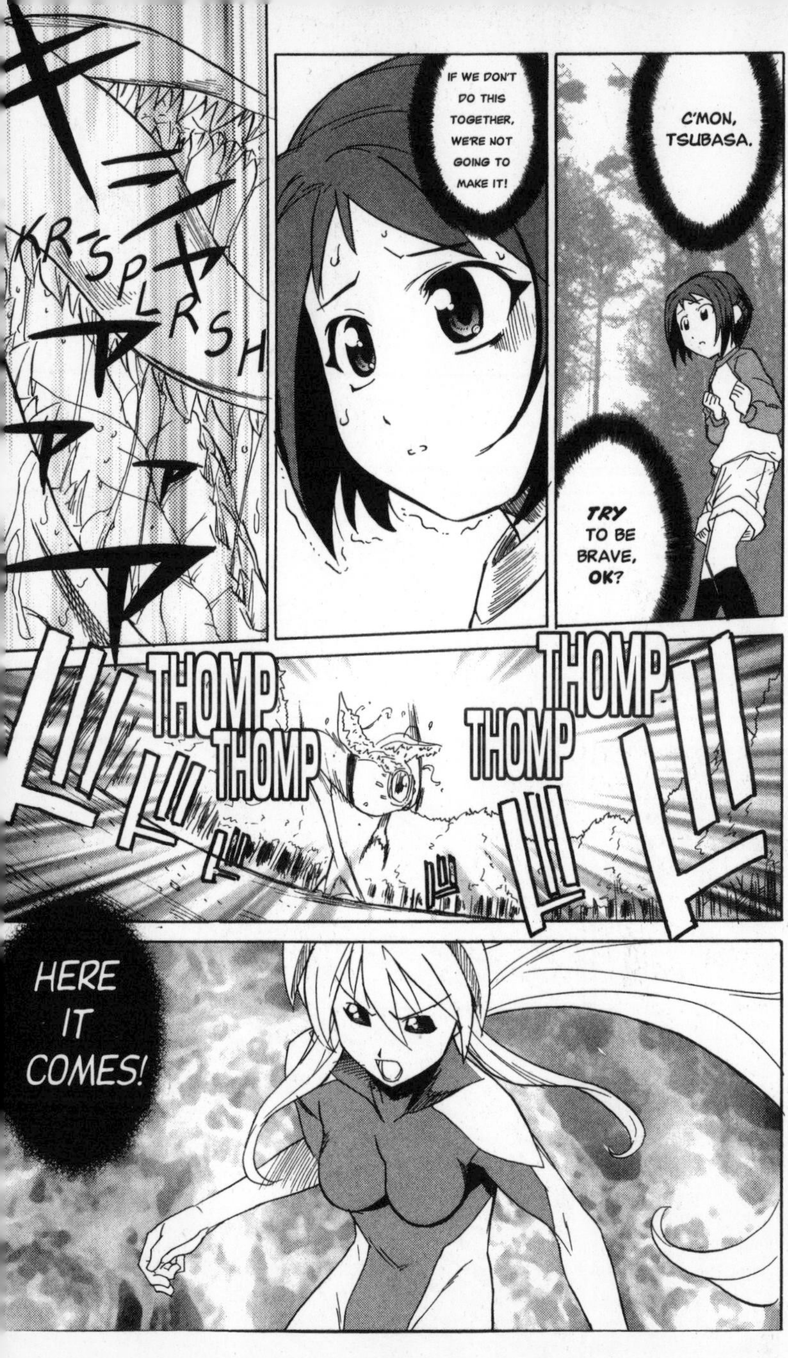
C'MON, TSUBASA.
TRY TO BE BRAVE, OK?
IF WE DON'T DO THIS TOGETHER, WE'RE NOT GOING TO MAKE IT!
KR-SPLRSH
THOMP
THOMP
THOMP
THOMP
HERE IT COMES!

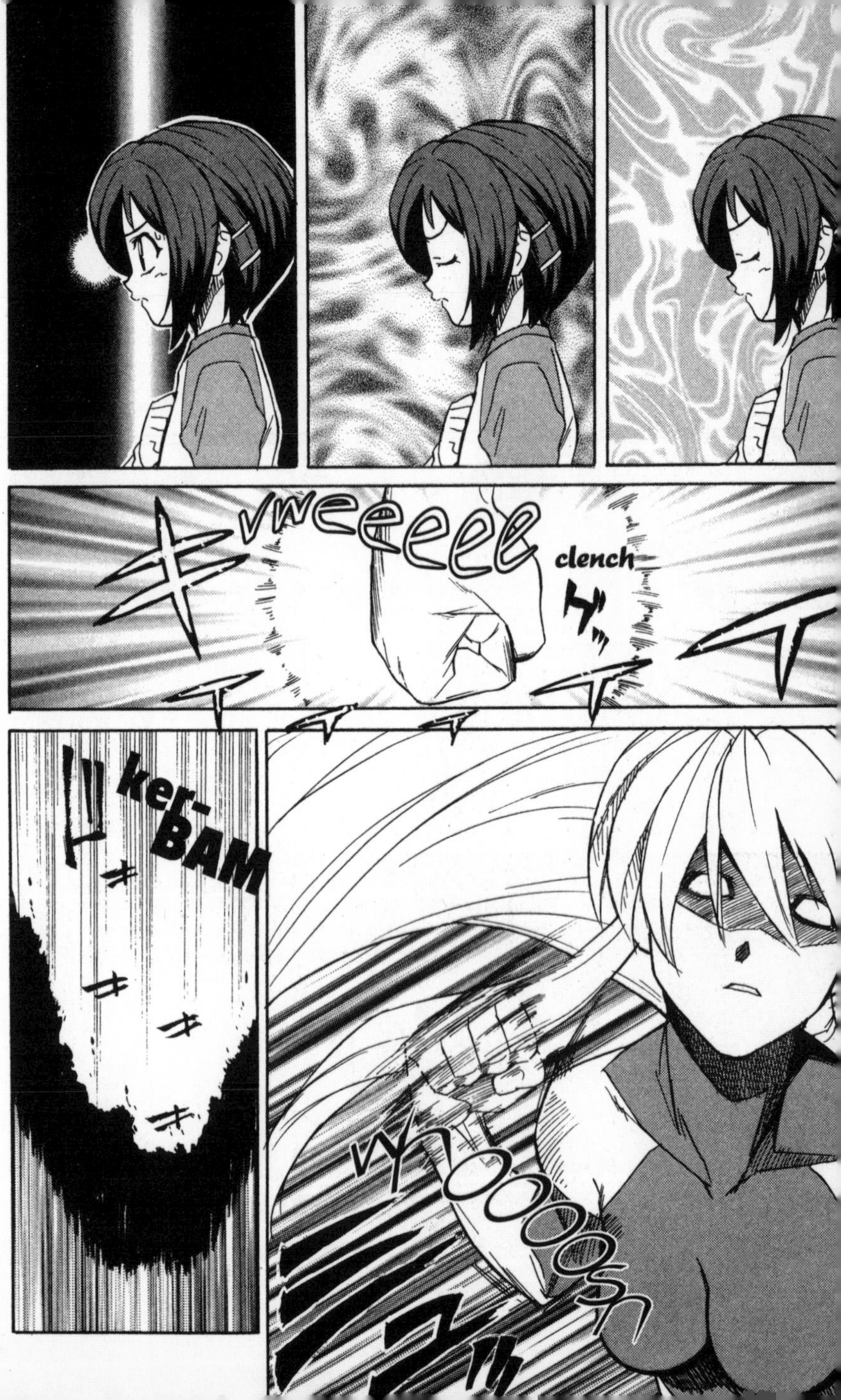
vweeeee
clench
ker-BAM
vwoooosh

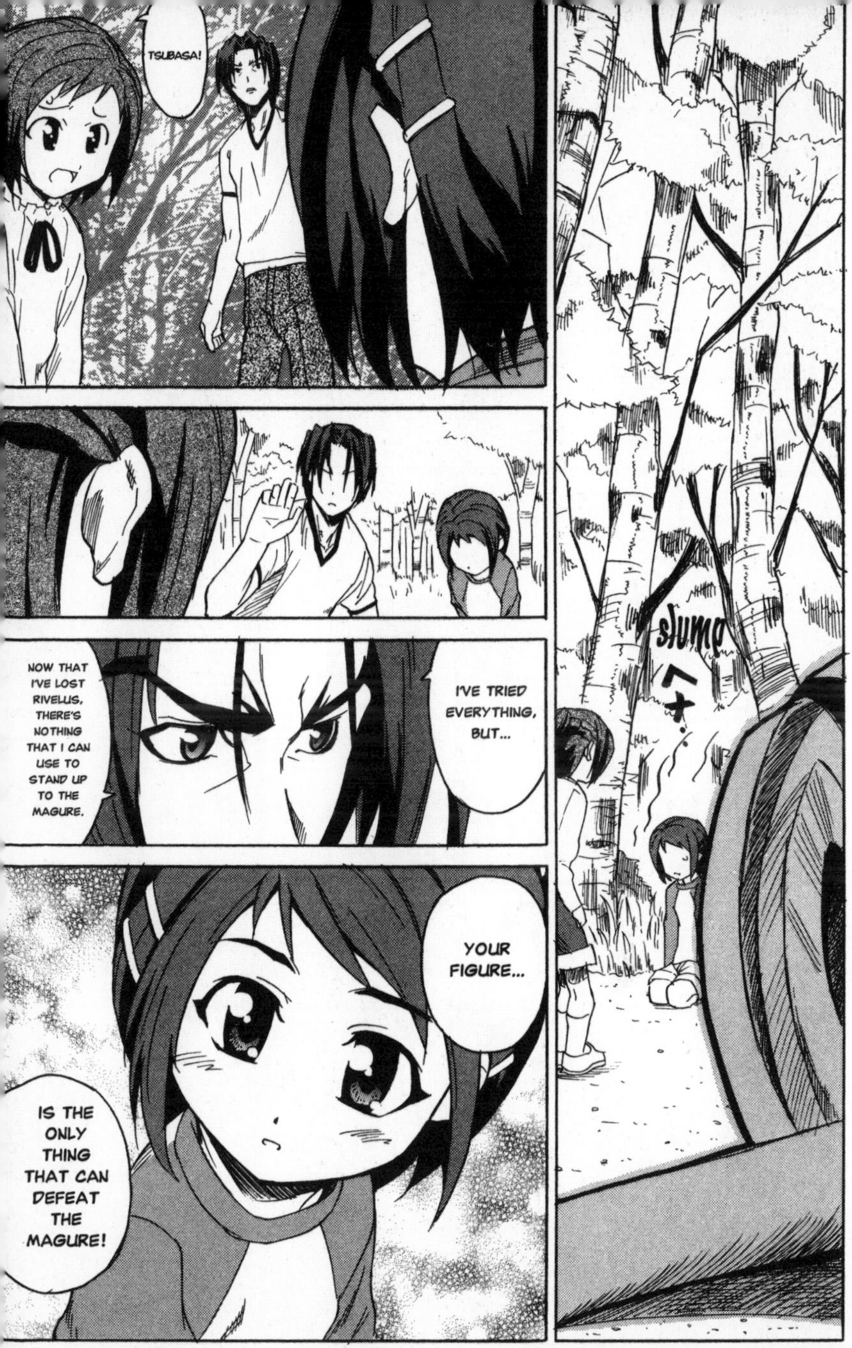
TSUBASA!
I'VE TRIED EVERYTHING, BUT...
NOW THAT I'VE LOST RIVELUS, THERE'S NOTHING THAT I CAN USE TO STAND UP TO THE MAGURE.
YOUR FIGURE...
IS THE ONLY THING THAT CAN DEFEAT THE MAGURE!
slump

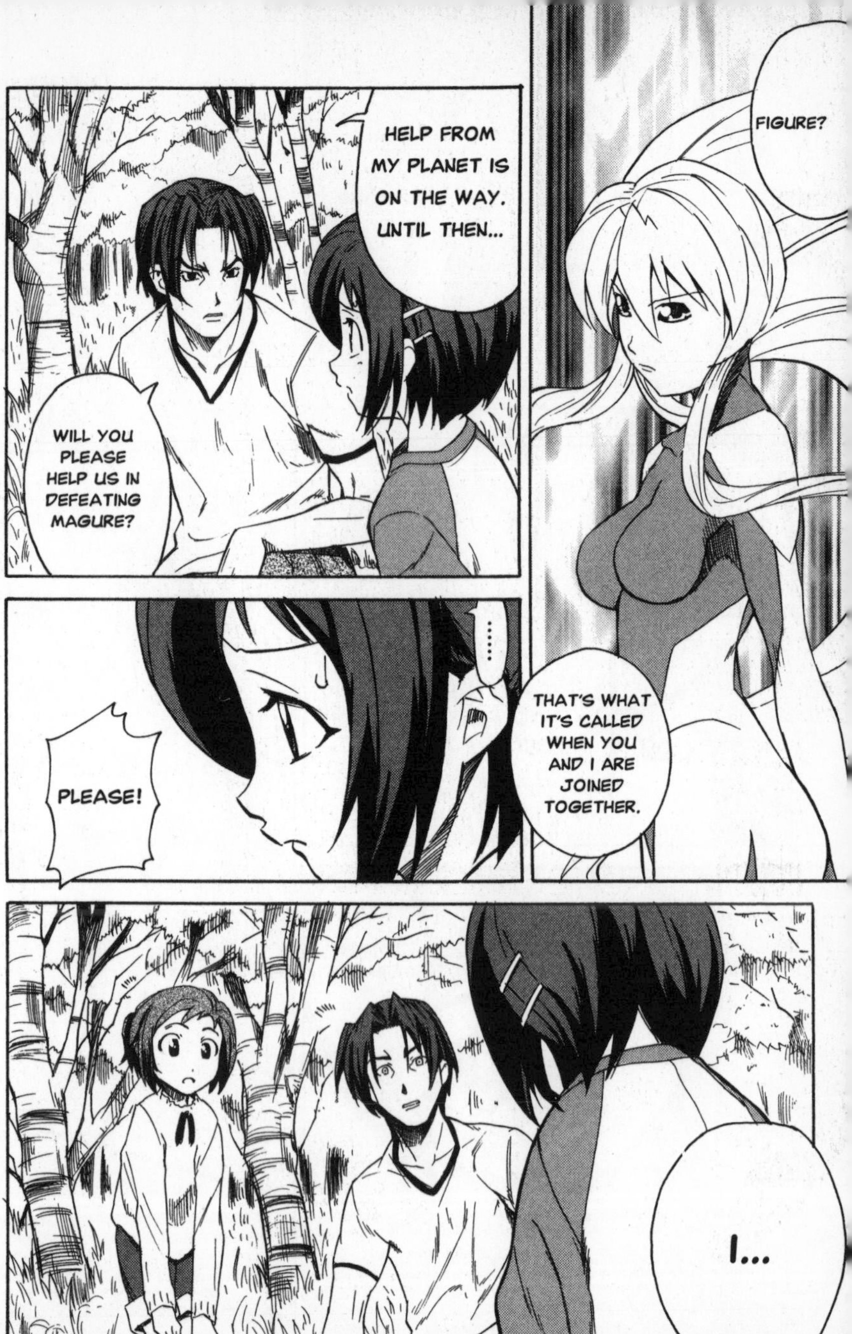
FIGURE?
THAT'S WHAT IT'S CALLED WHEN YOU AND I ARE JOINED TOGETHER.
HELP FROM MY PLANET IS ON THE WAY. UNTIL THEN...
WILL YOU PLEASE HELP US IN DEFEATING MAGURE?
......
PLEASE!
I...

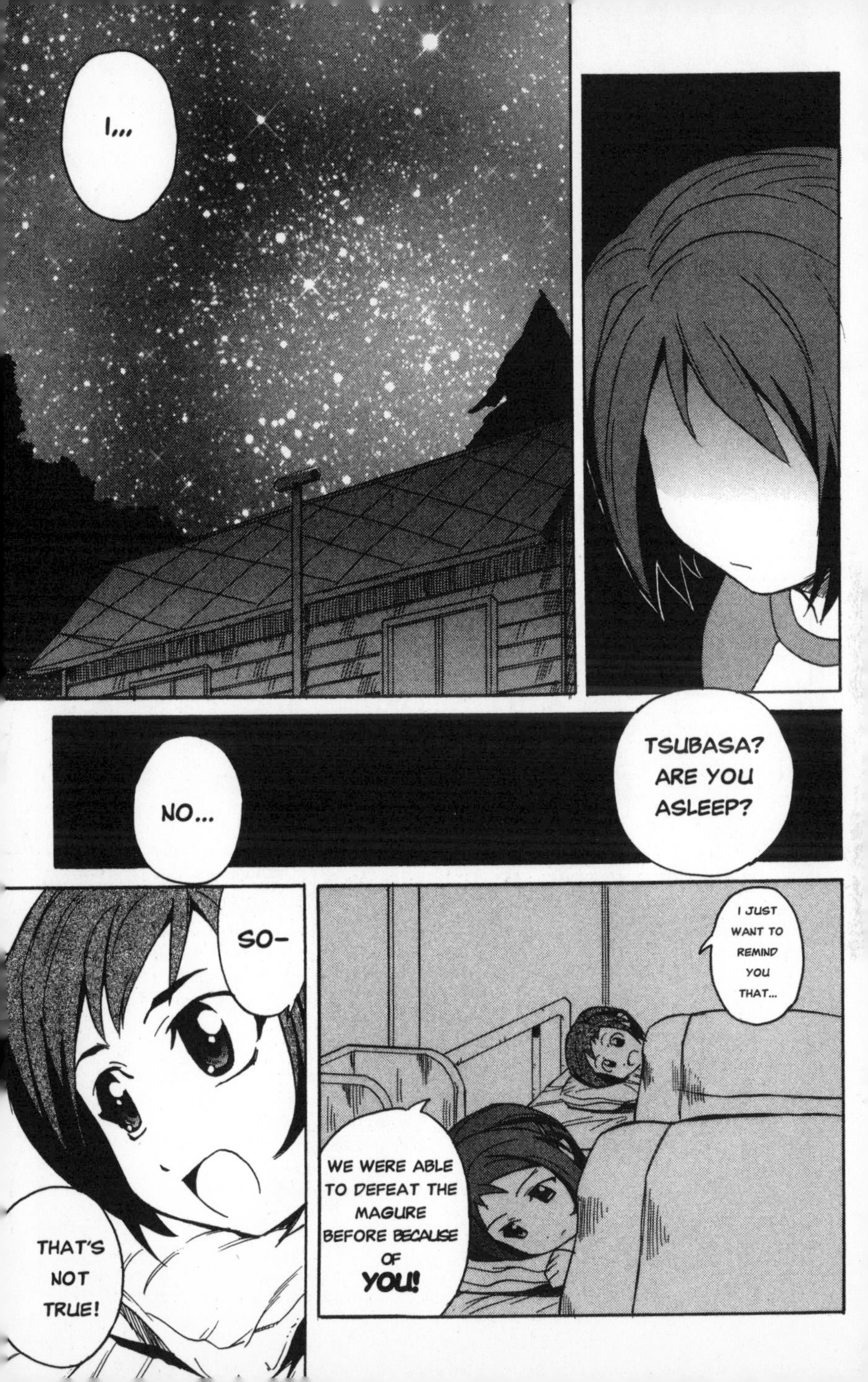
I...
TSUBASA? ARE YOU ASLEEP?
NO...
I JUST WANT TO REMIND YOU THAT...
WE WERE ABLE TO DEFEAT THE MAGURE BEFORE BECAUSE OF YOU!
SO-
THAT'S NOT TRUE!

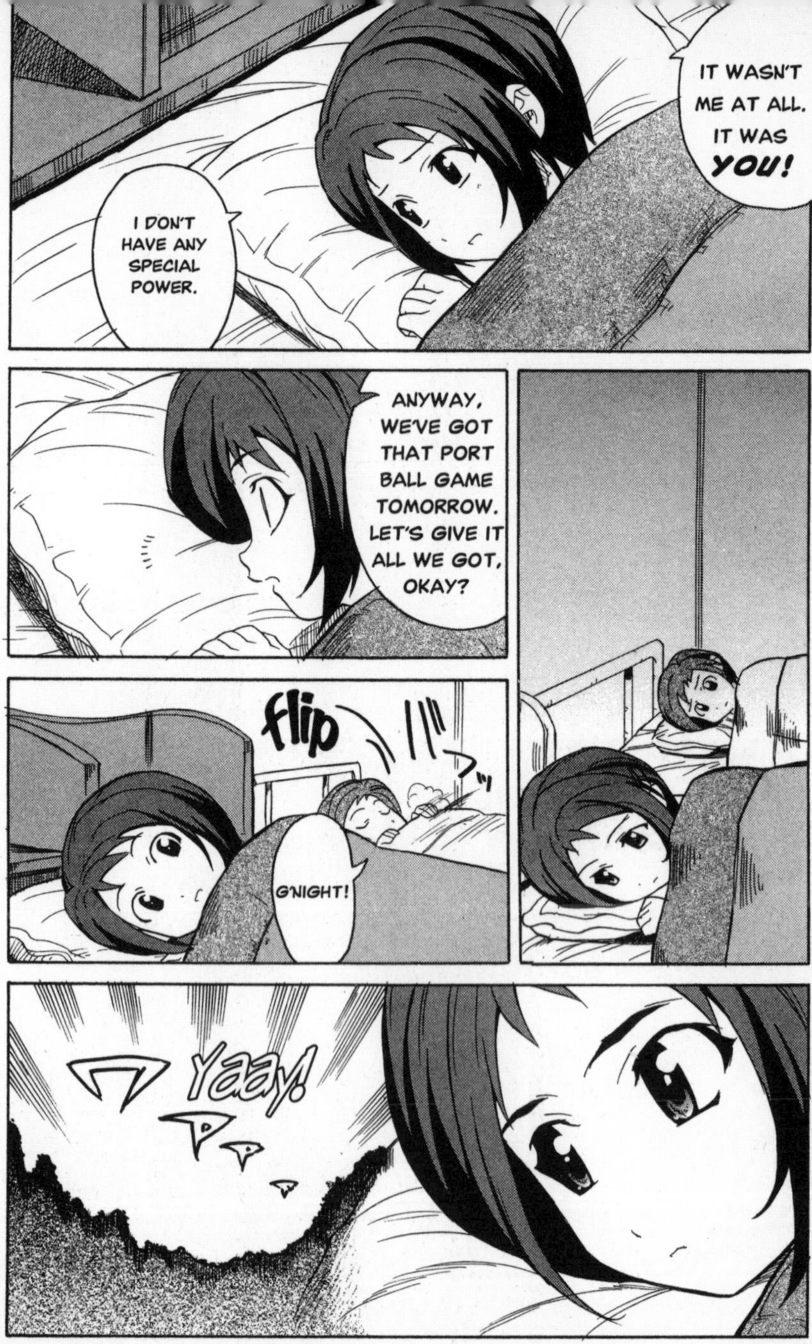
IT WASN'T ME AT ALL. IT WAS YOU!
I DON'T HAVE ANY SPECIAL POWER.
ANYWAY, WE'VE GOT THAT PORT BALL GAME TOMORROW. LET'S GIVE IT ALL WE GOT, OKAY?
flip
G'NIGHT!
Yaay!

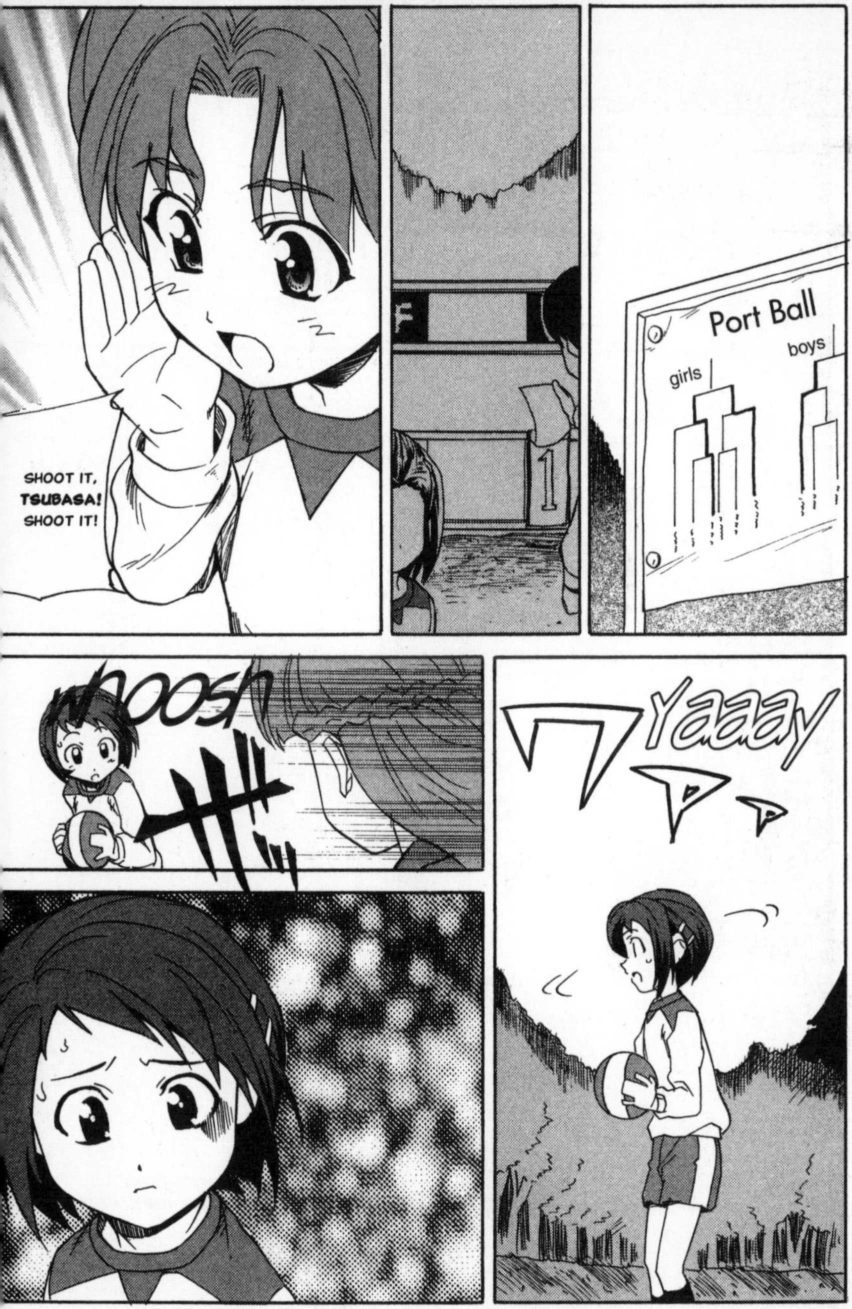
SHOOT IT, TSUBASA! SHOOT IT!
Port Ball
girls
boys
whoosh
Yaaay

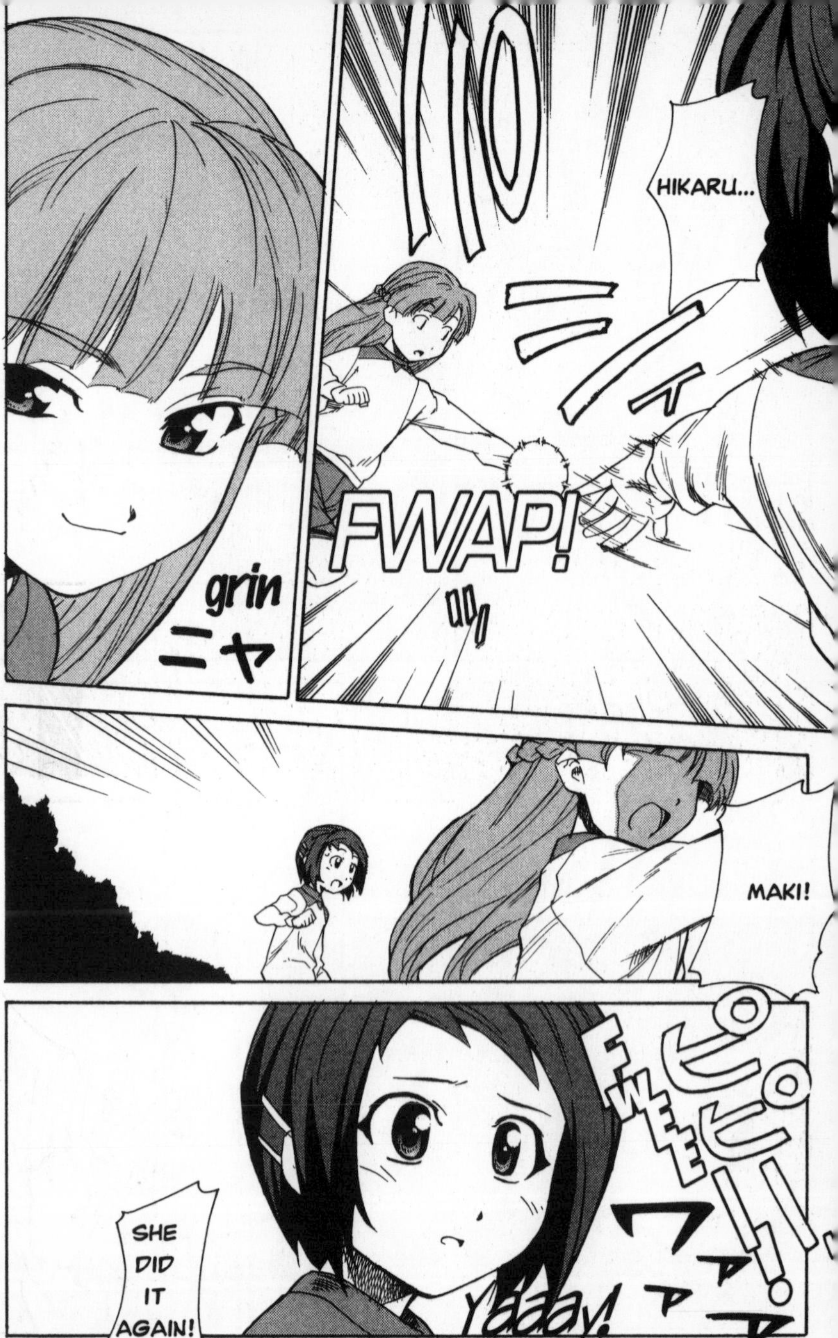
HIKARU...
FWAP!
grin
ニヤ
MAKI!
FWEEE
Yaaay!
SHE DID IT AGAIN!

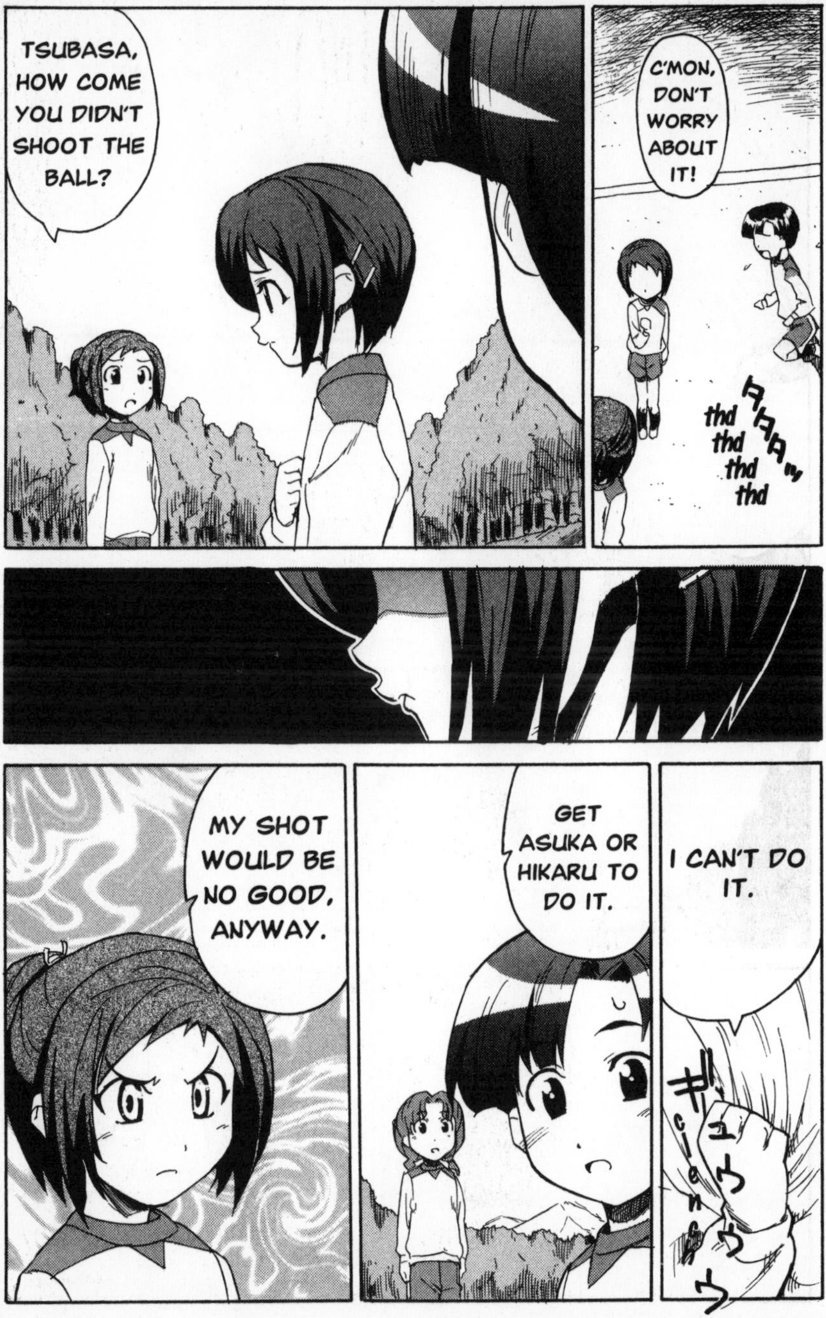
C'MON, DON'T WORRY ABOUT IT!
タタタッ thd thd thd thd
TSUBASA, HOW COME YOU DIDN'T SHOOT THE BALL?
I CAN'T DO IT.
ギュウウウ clench
GET ASUKA OR HIKARU TO DO IT.
MY SHOT WOULD BE NO GOOD, ANYWAY.

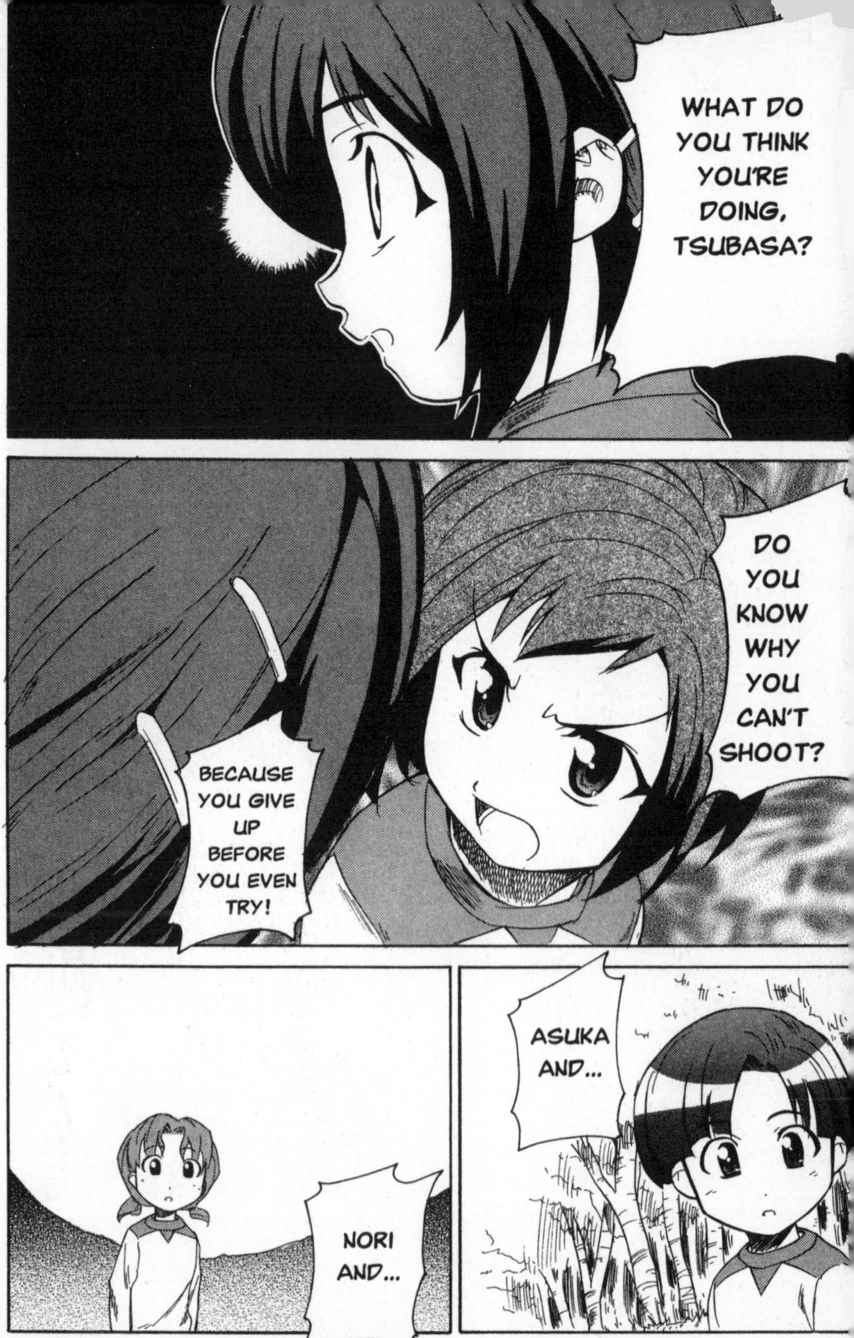
WHAT DO YOU THINK YOU'RE DOING, TSUBASA?
DO YOU KNOW WHY YOU CAN'T SHOOT?
BECAUSE YOU GIVE UP BEFORE YOU EVEN TRY!
ASUKA AND...
NORI AND...

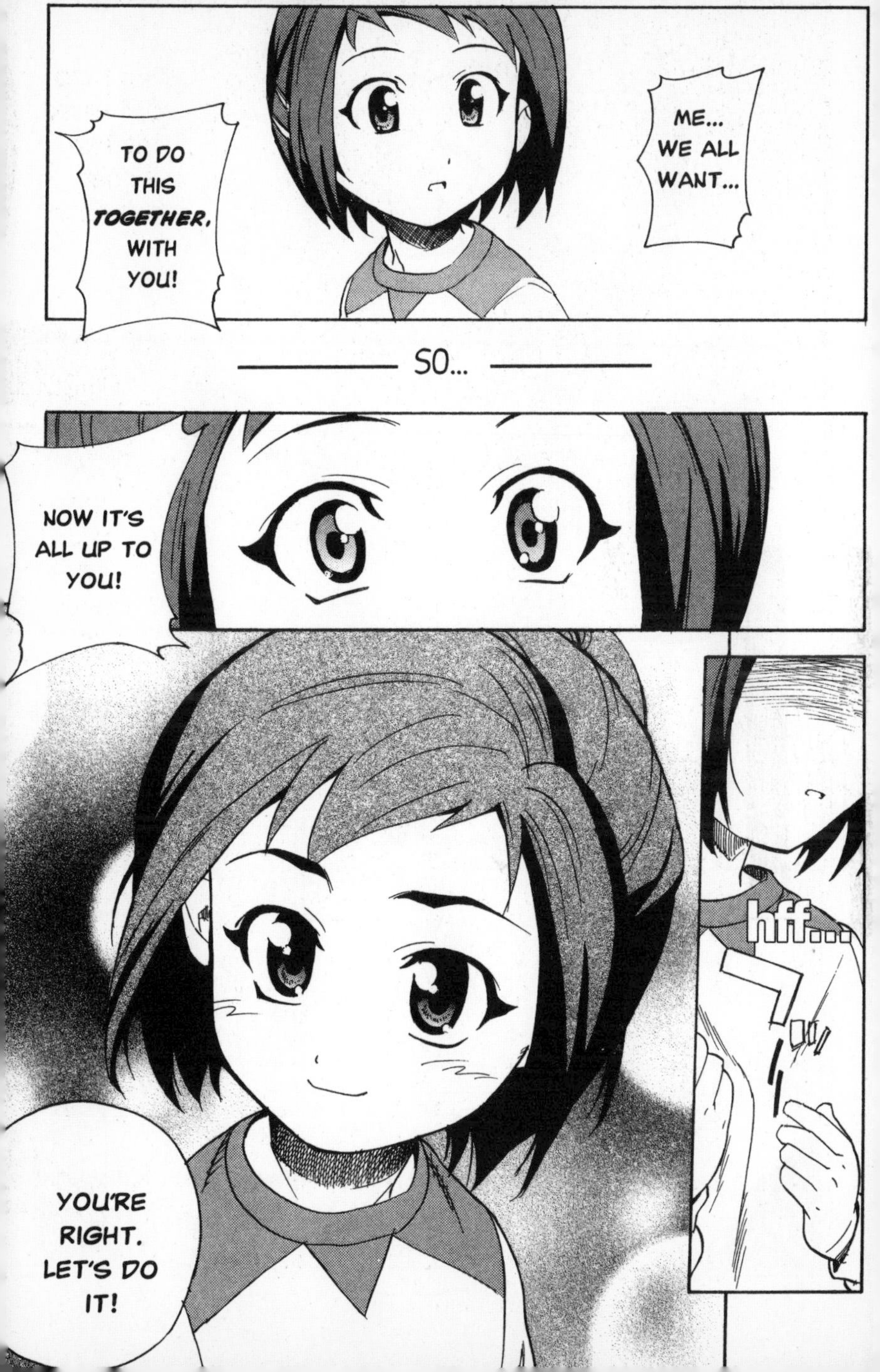
ME... WE ALL WANT...
TO DO THIS *TOGETHER*, WITH YOU!
SO...
NOW IT'S ALL UP TO YOU!
hff...
YOU'RE RIGHT. LET'S DO IT!

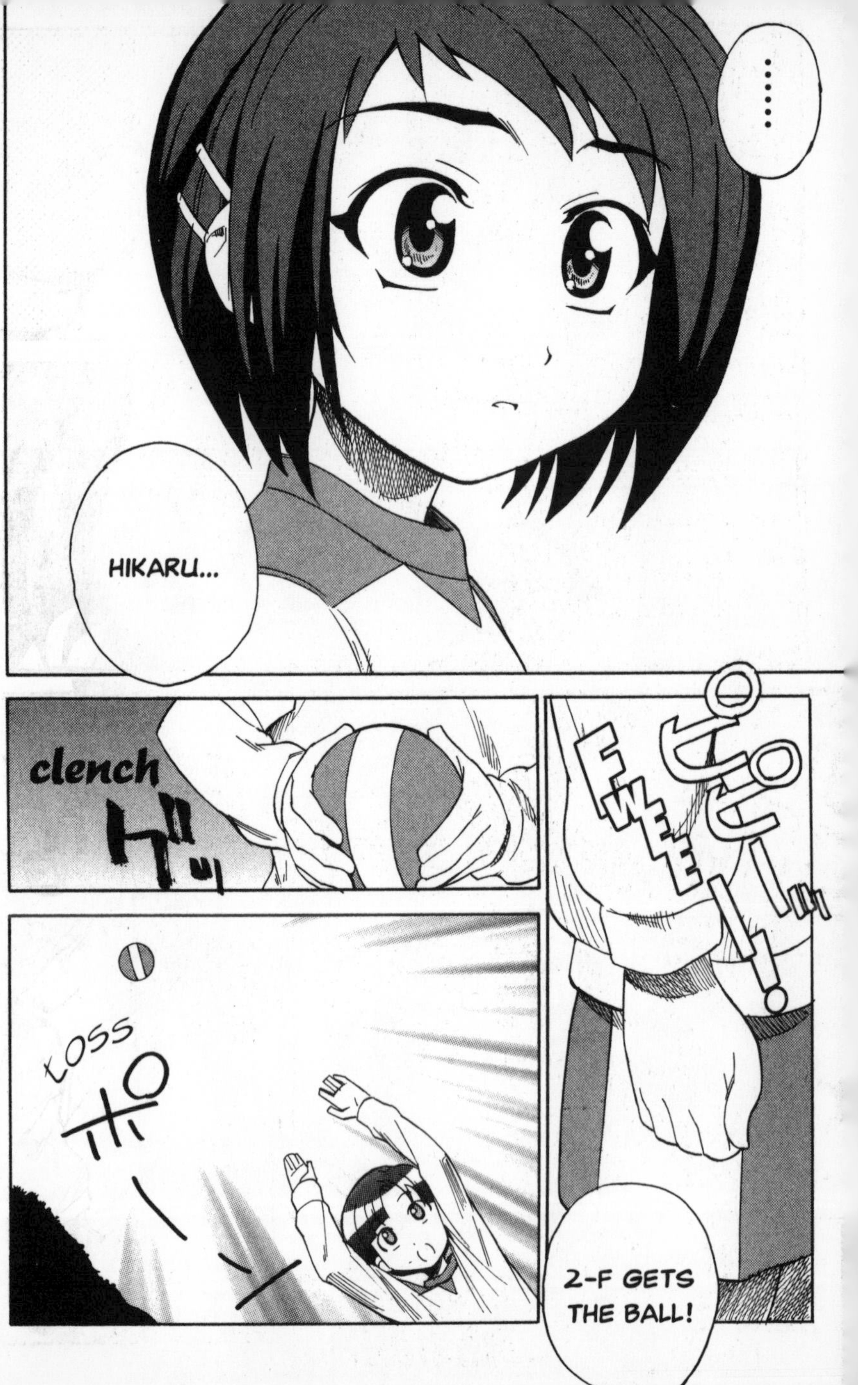
......
HIKARU...
FWEE
clench
2-F GETS THE BALL!
toss

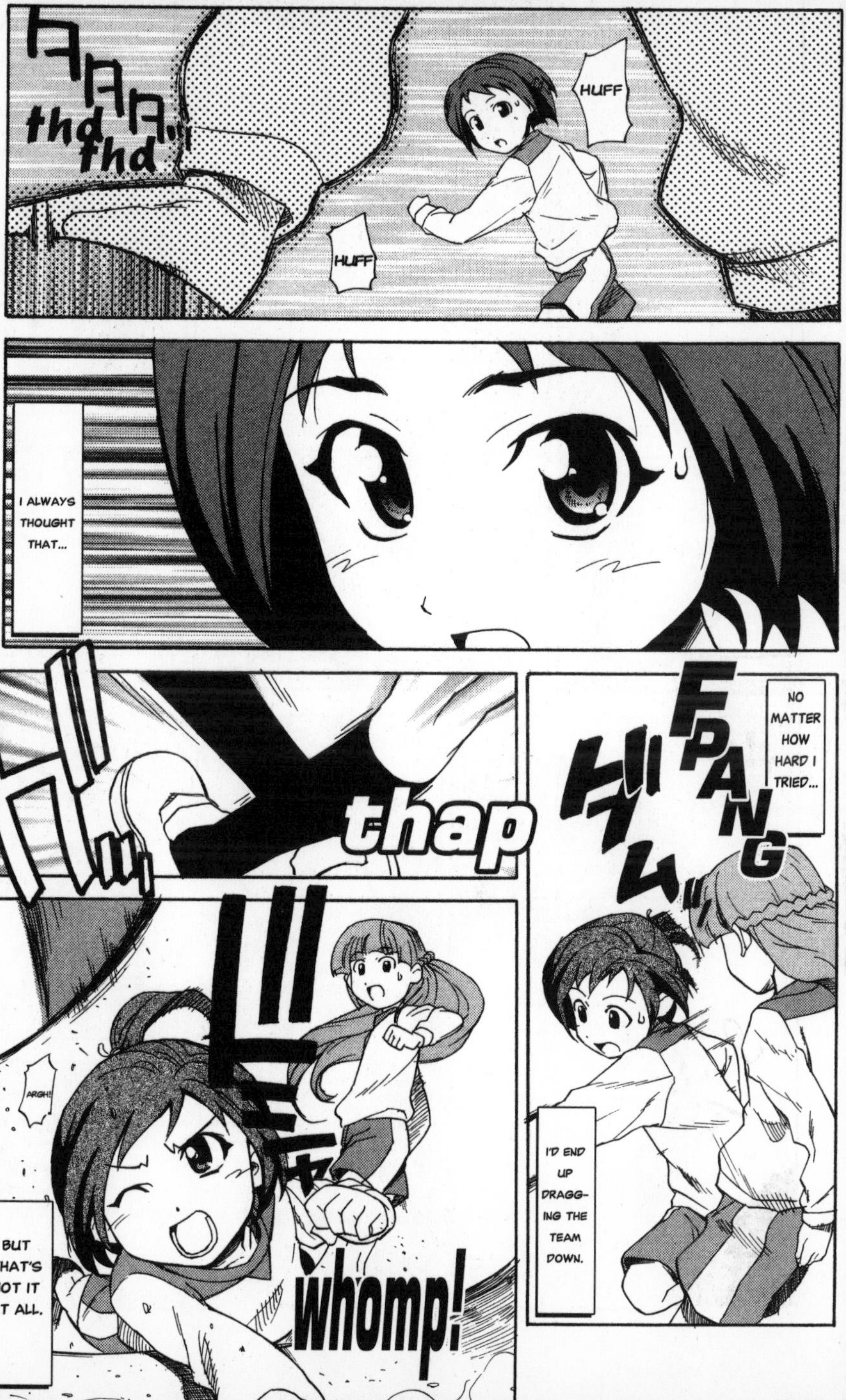
HUFF
HUFF
thd
thd
I ALWAYS THOUGHT THAT...
NO MATTER HOW HARD I TRIED...
FPANG
thap
I'D END UP DRAGGING THE TEAM DOWN.
ARGH!
BUT THAT'S NOT IT AT ALL.
whomp!

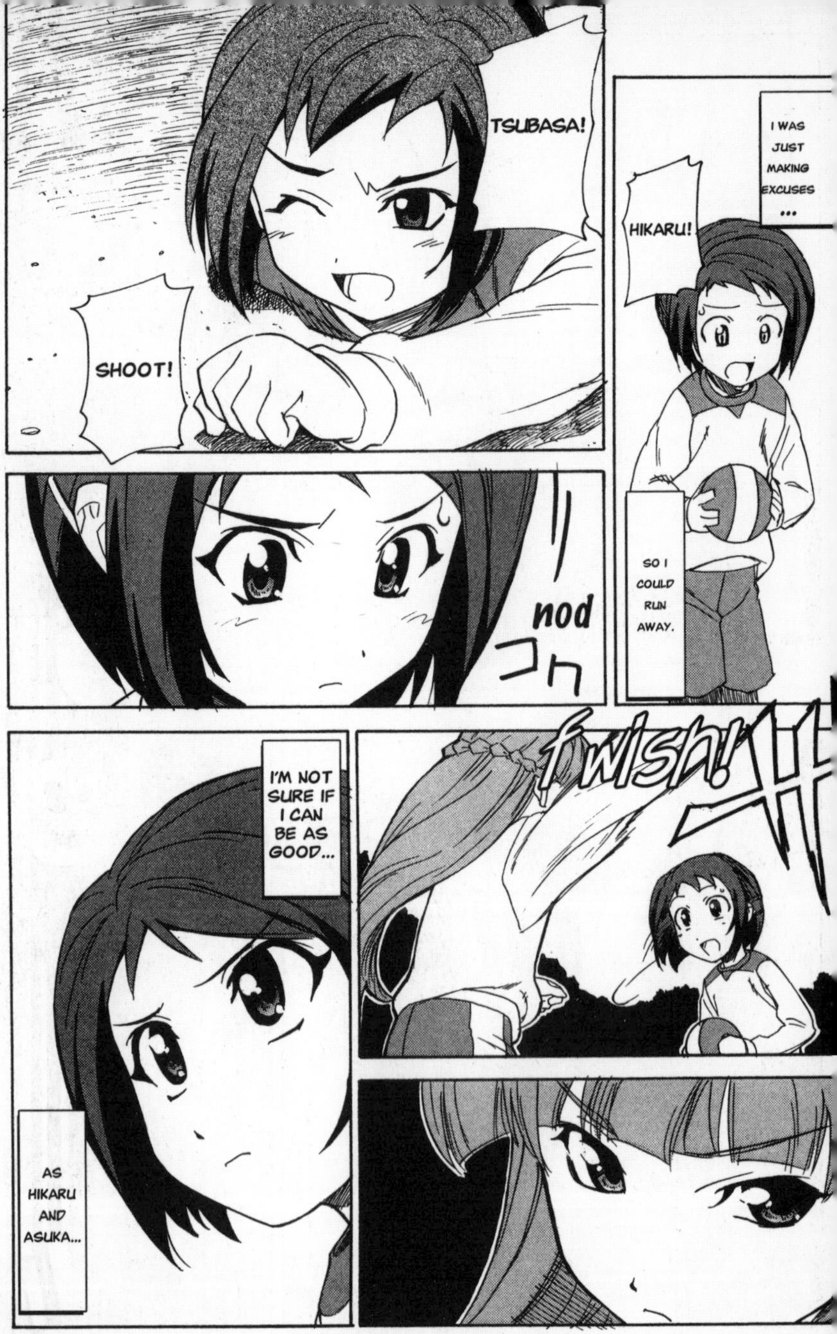
I WAS JUST MAKING EXCUSES ...
HIKARU!
SO I COULD RUN AWAY.
TSUBASA!
SHOOT!
nod
コク
fwish!
I'M NOT SURE IF I CAN BE AS GOOD...
AS HIKARU AND ASUKA...

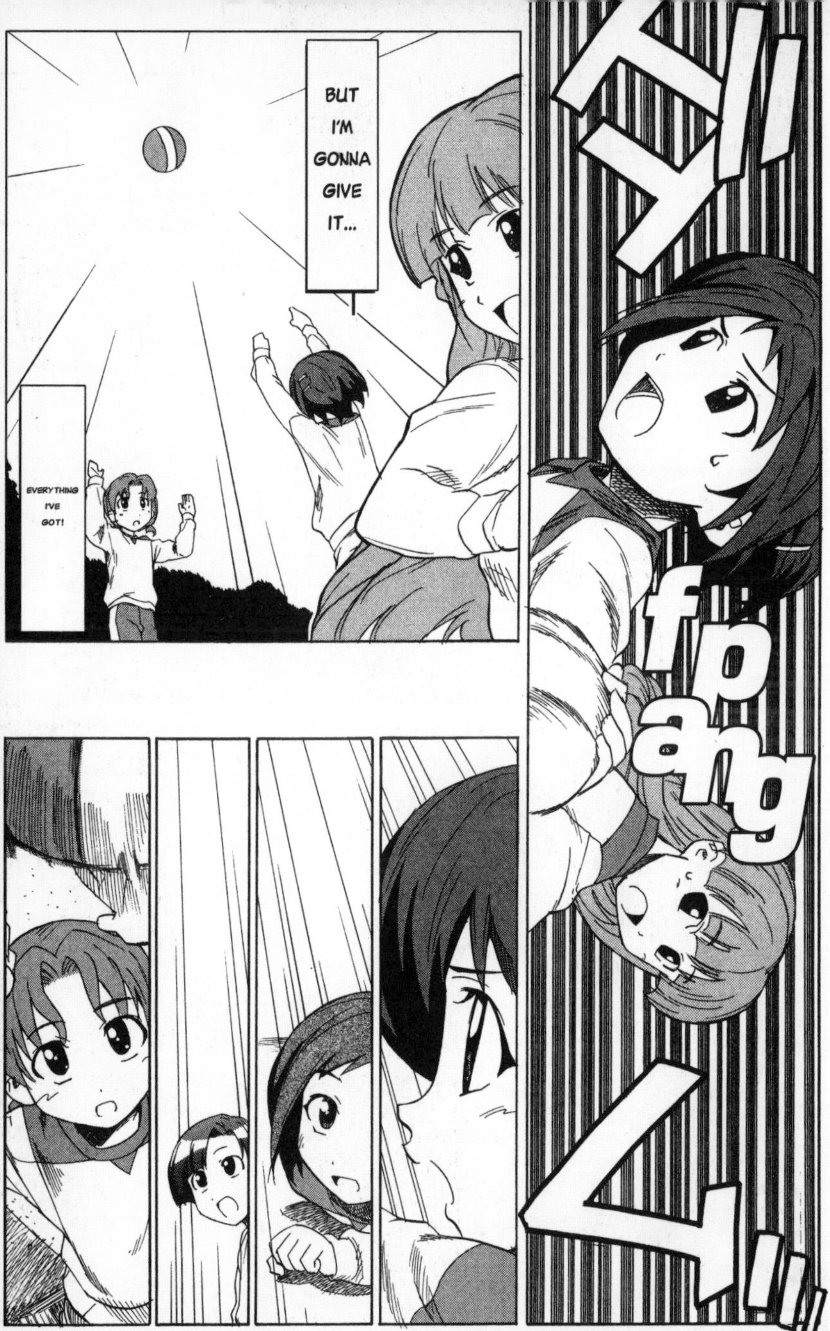
BUT I'M GONNA GIVE IT...
EVERYTHING I'VE GOT!
fpang

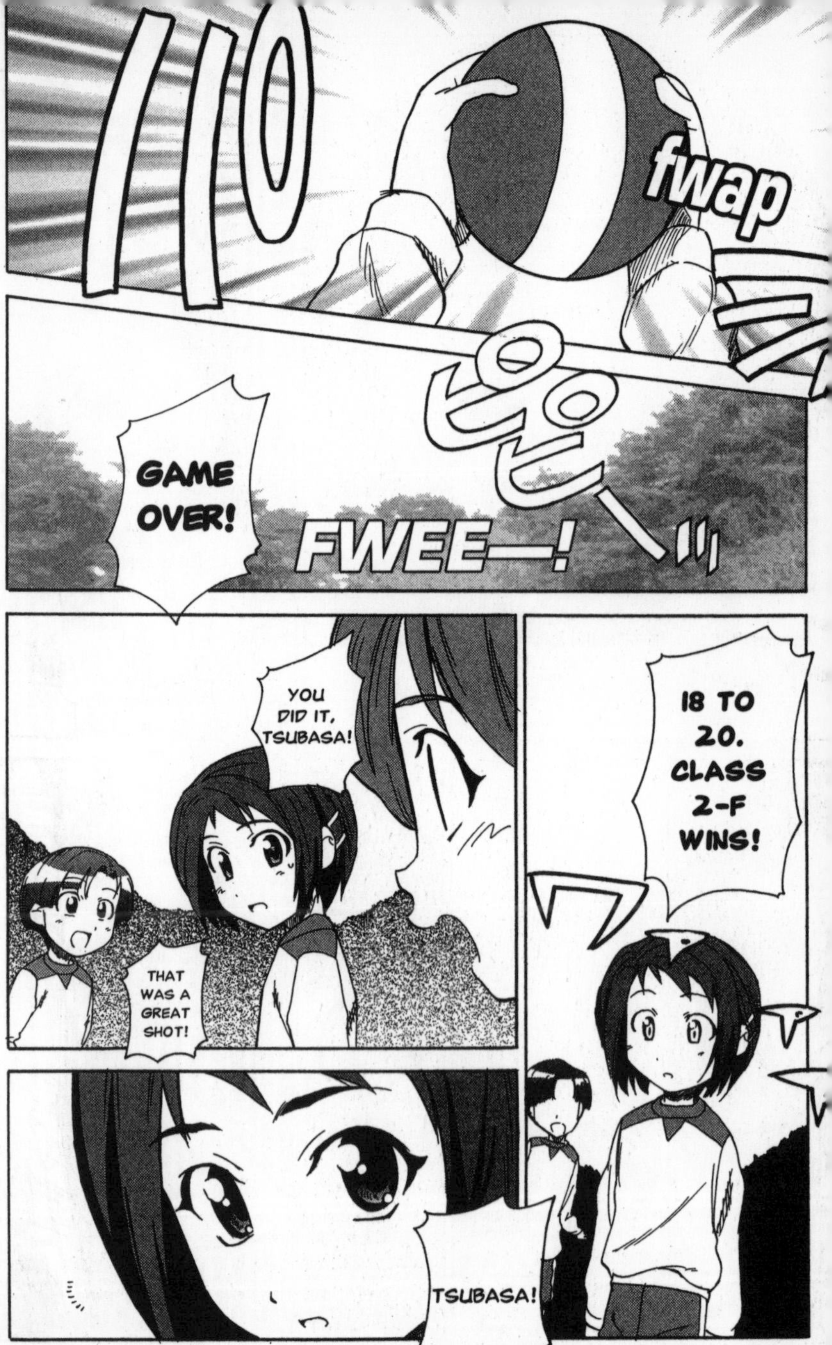
fwap
FWEE—!
GAME OVER!
18 TO 20. CLASS 2-F WINS!
YOU DID IT, TSUBASA!
THAT WAS A GREAT SHOT!
TSUBASA!

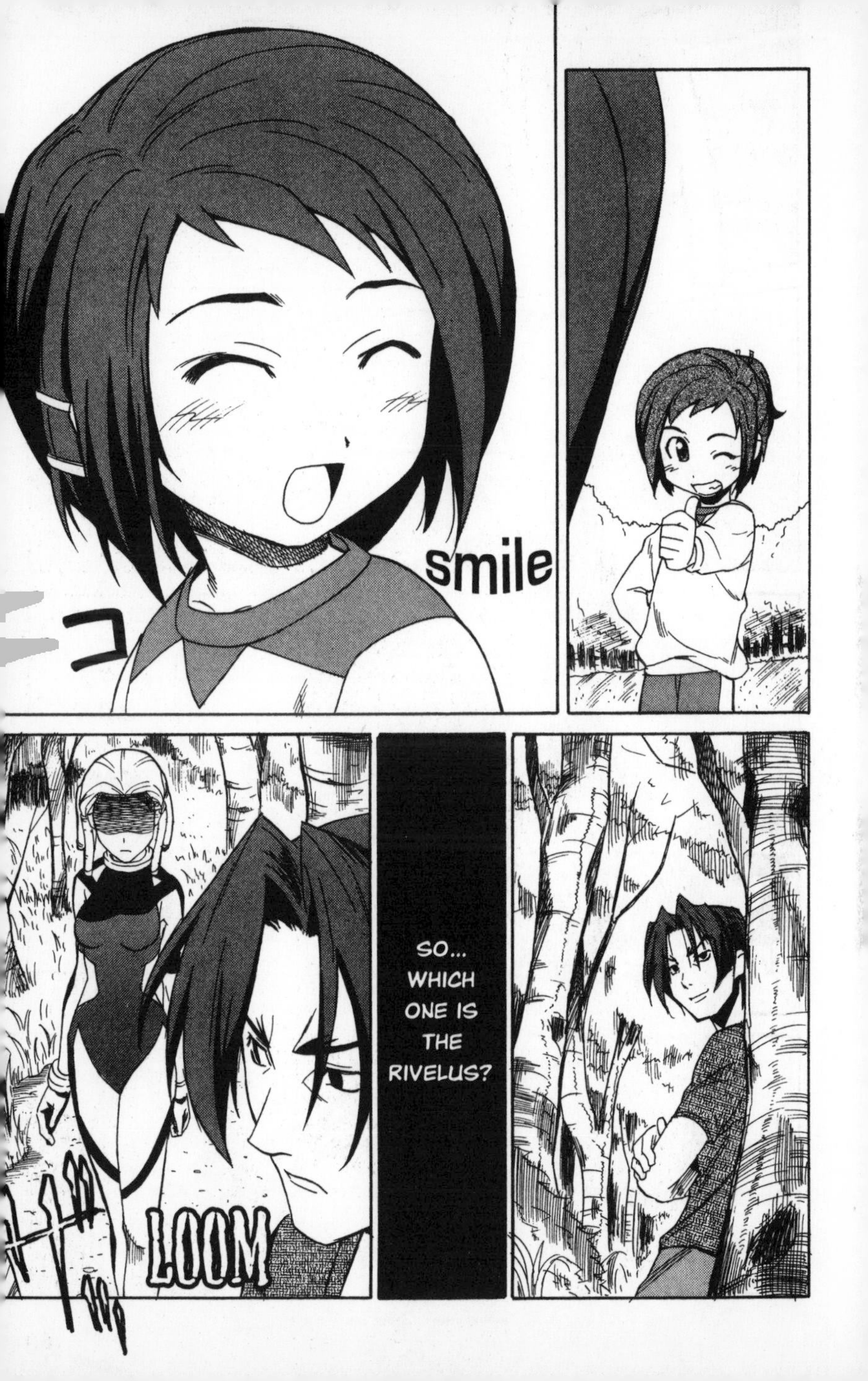
smile
LOOM
SO... WHICH ONE IS THE RIVELUS?

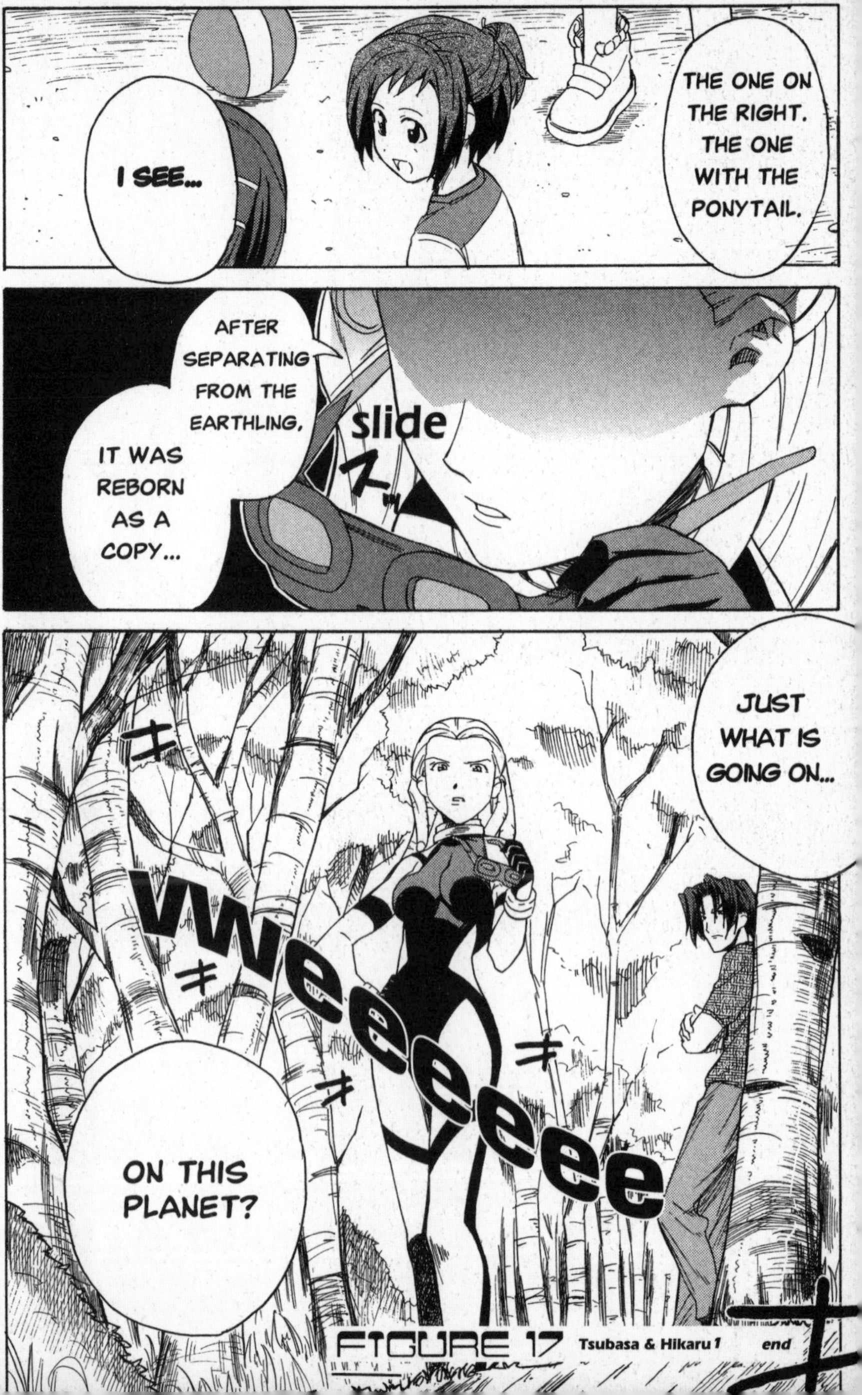
THE ONE ON THE RIGHT. THE ONE WITH THE PONYTAIL.
I SEE...
AFTER SEPARATING FROM THE EARTHLING,
IT WAS REBORN AS A COPY...
slide
JUST WHAT IS GOING ON...
vweeeeeee
ON THIS PLANET?
FIGURE 17 Tsubasa & Hikaru 1 end

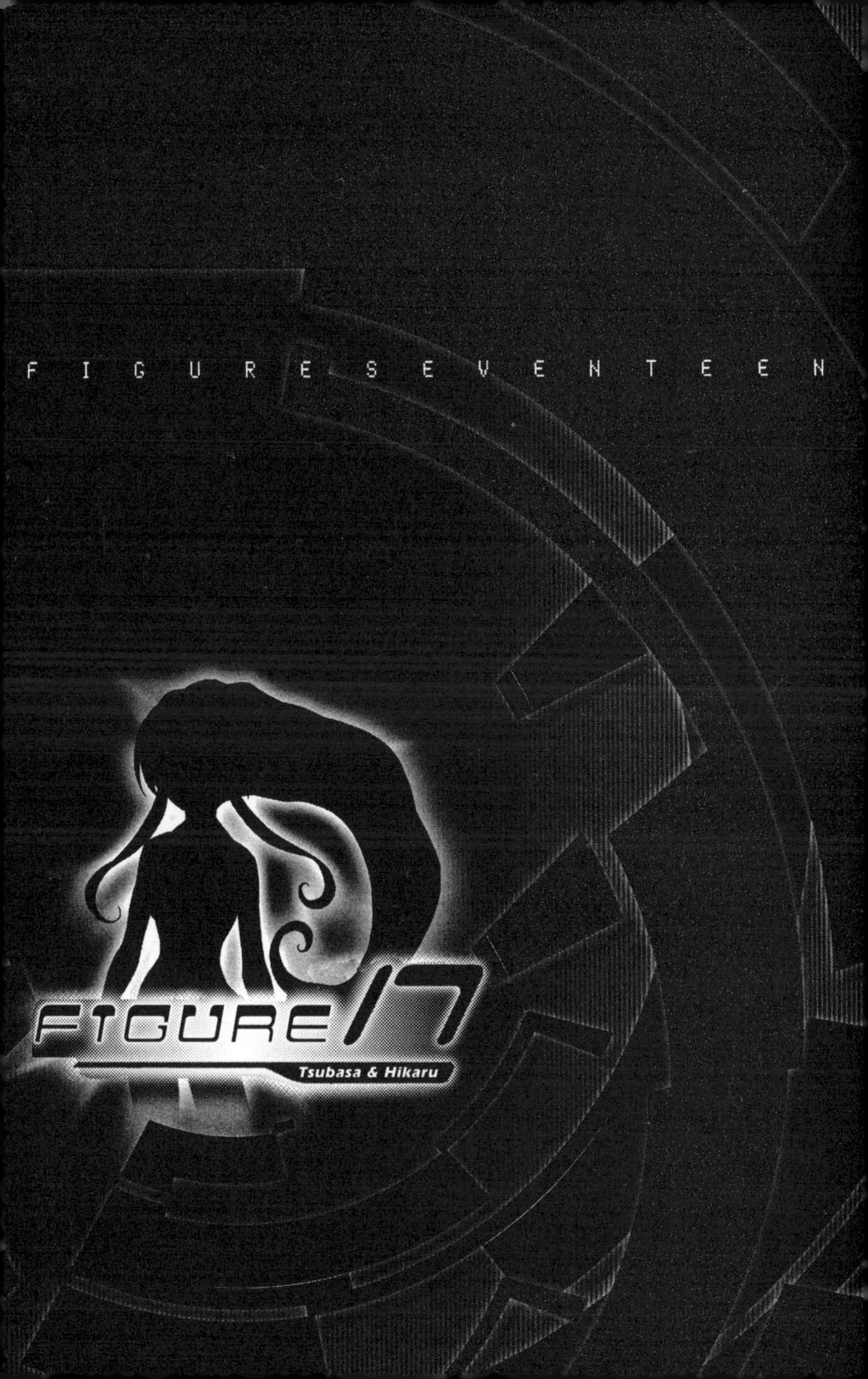
F I G U R E S E V E N T E E N
FIGURE 17
Tsubasa & Hikaru

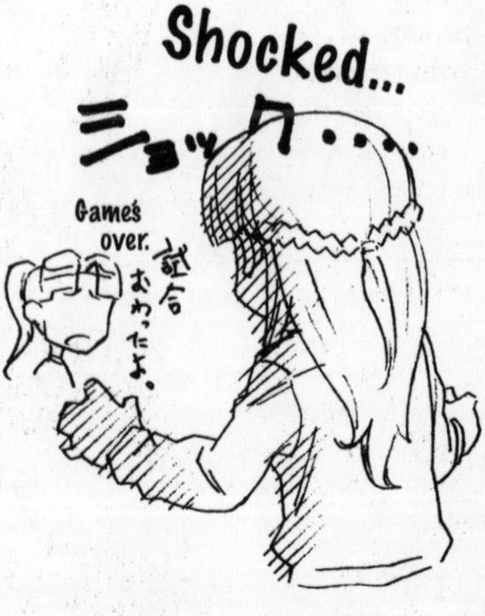
Shocked...
ショック…
Game's over.
試合おわったよ。

Figure 17 Extra

FIGURE 17

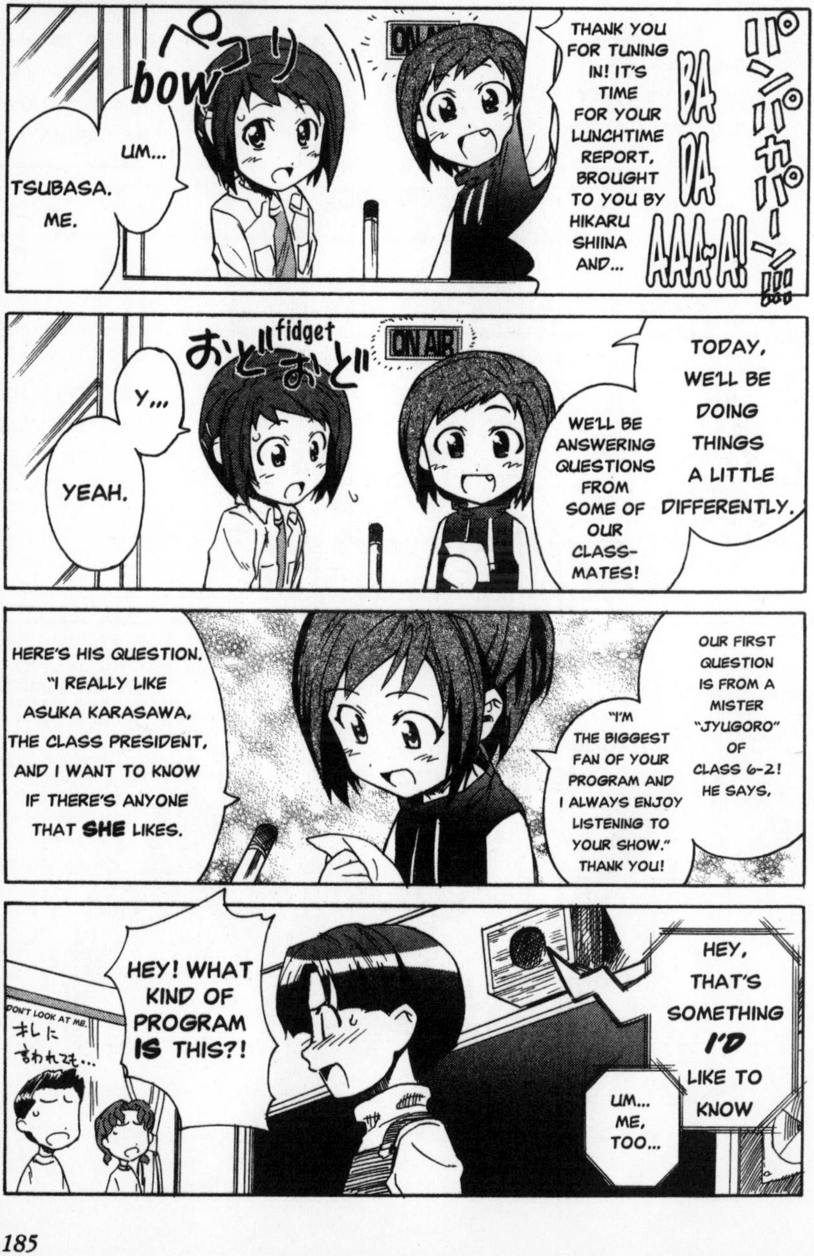

パンパカパーン!!
BA DA AAA-A!
THANK YOU FOR TUNING IN! IT'S TIME FOR YOUR LUNCHTIME REPORT, BROUGHT TO YOU BY HIKARU SHIINA AND...
ペコリ
bow
UM... TSUBASA. ME.
TODAY, WE'LL BE DOING THINGS A LITTLE DIFFERENTLY.
WE'LL BE ANSWERING QUESTIONS FROM SOME OF OUR CLASS-MATES!
ON AIR
おどおど
fidget
Y... YEAH.
OUR FIRST QUESTION IS FROM A MISTER "JYUGORO" OF CLASS 6-2! HE SAYS,
"I'M THE BIGGEST FAN OF YOUR PROGRAM AND I ALWAYS ENJOY LISTENING TO YOUR SHOW." THANK YOU!
HERE'S HIS QUESTION. "I REALLY LIKE ASUKA KARASAWA, THE CLASS PRESIDENT, AND I WANT TO KNOW IF THERE'S ANYONE THAT SHE LIKES.
HEY, THAT'S SOMETHING I'D LIKE TO KNOW
UM... ME, TOO...
HEY! WHAT KIND OF PROGRAM IS THIS?!
DON'T LOOK AT ME.
オレに言われても…

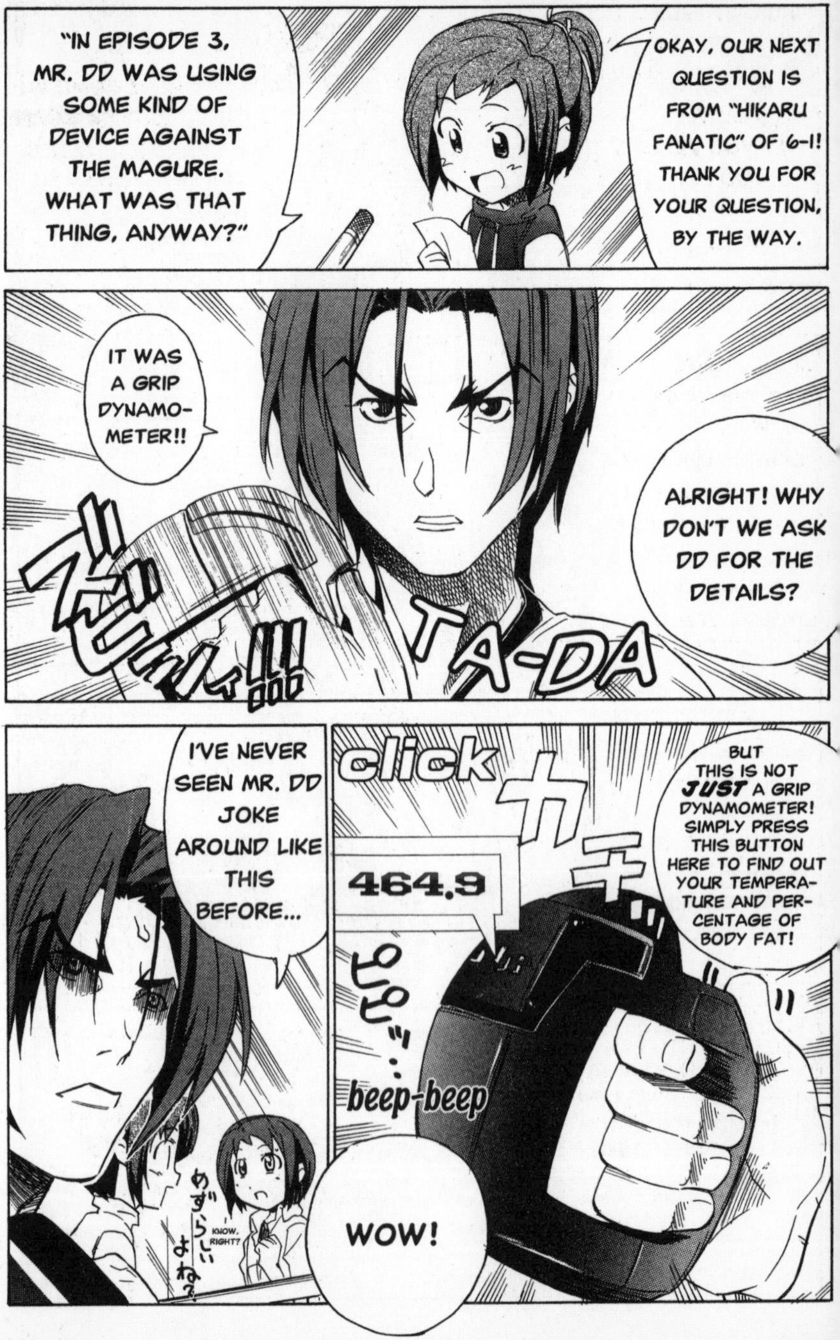
OKAY, OUR NEXT QUESTION IS FROM "HIKARU FANATIC" OF 6-1! THANK YOU FOR YOUR QUESTION, BY THE WAY.
"IN EPISODE 3, MR. DD WAS USING SOME KIND OF DEVICE AGAINST THE MAGURE. WHAT WAS THAT THING, ANYWAY?"
ALRIGHT! WHY DON'T WE ASK DD FOR THE DETAILS?
IT WAS A GRIP DYNAMO-METER!!
TA-DA
click
BUT THIS IS NOT JUST A GRIP DYNAMOMETER! SIMPLY PRESS THIS BUTTON HERE TO FIND OUT YOUR TEMPERA-TURE AND PER-CENTAGE OF BODY FAT!
464.9
beep-beep
WOW!
I'VE NEVER SEEN MR. DD JOKE AROUND LIKE THIS BEFORE...
KNOW, RIGHT?

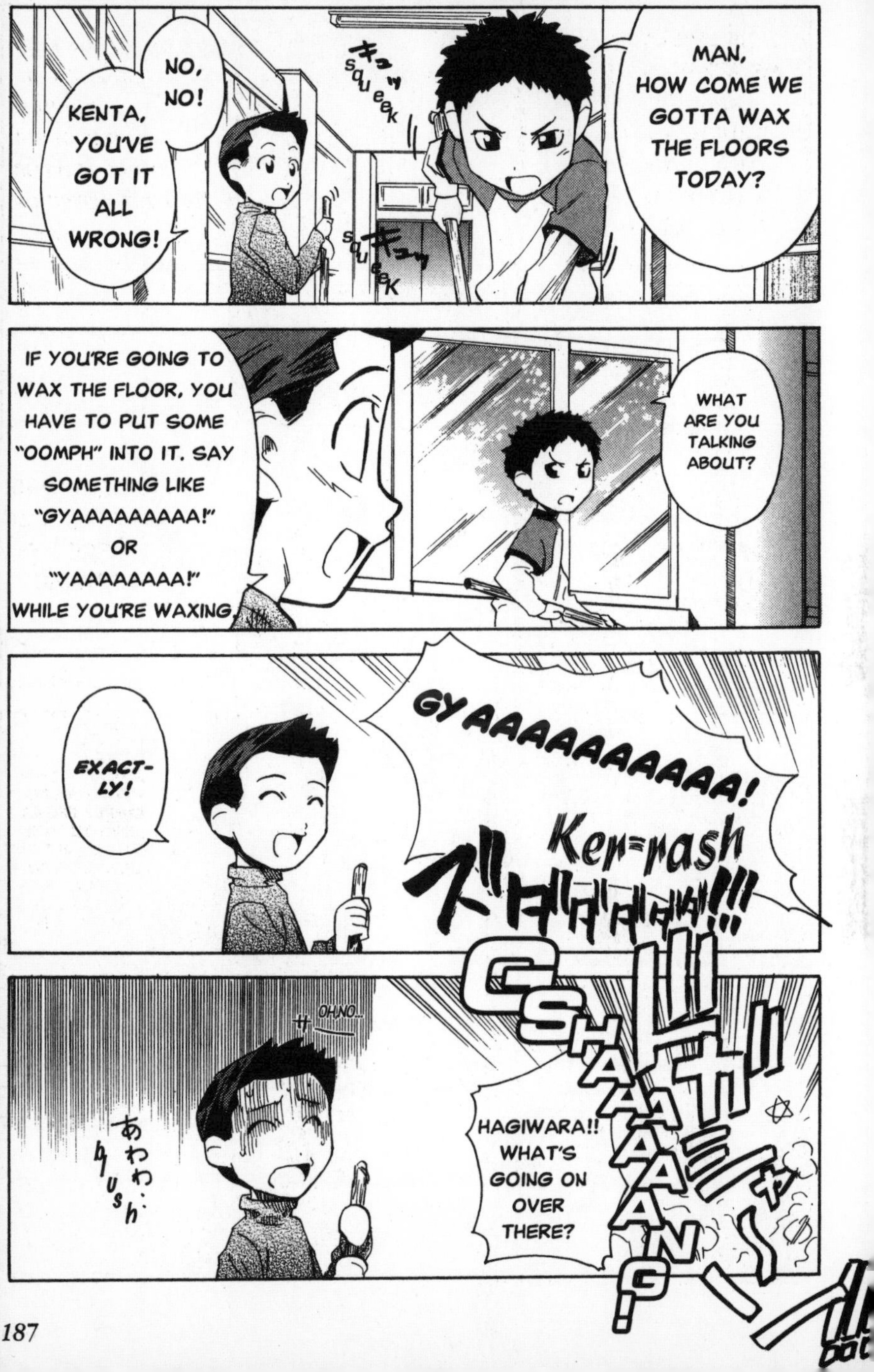
MAN, HOW COME WE GOTTA WAX THE FLOORS TODAY?
キュッ squeeek
キュッ squeeek
NO, NO! KENTA, YOU'VE GOT IT ALL WRONG!
WHAT ARE YOU TALKING ABOUT?
IF YOU'RE GOING TO WAX THE FLOOR, YOU HAVE TO PUT SOME "OOMPH" INTO IT. SAY SOMETHING LIKE "GYAAAAAAAAA!" OR "YAAAAAAAA!" WHILE YOU'RE WAXING.
GYAAAAAAAAAAAA!
Ker-rash
EXACTLY!
CSHAAAAAANG!
HAGIWARA!! WHAT'S GOING ON OVER THERE?
OH NO...
あわわ… flush

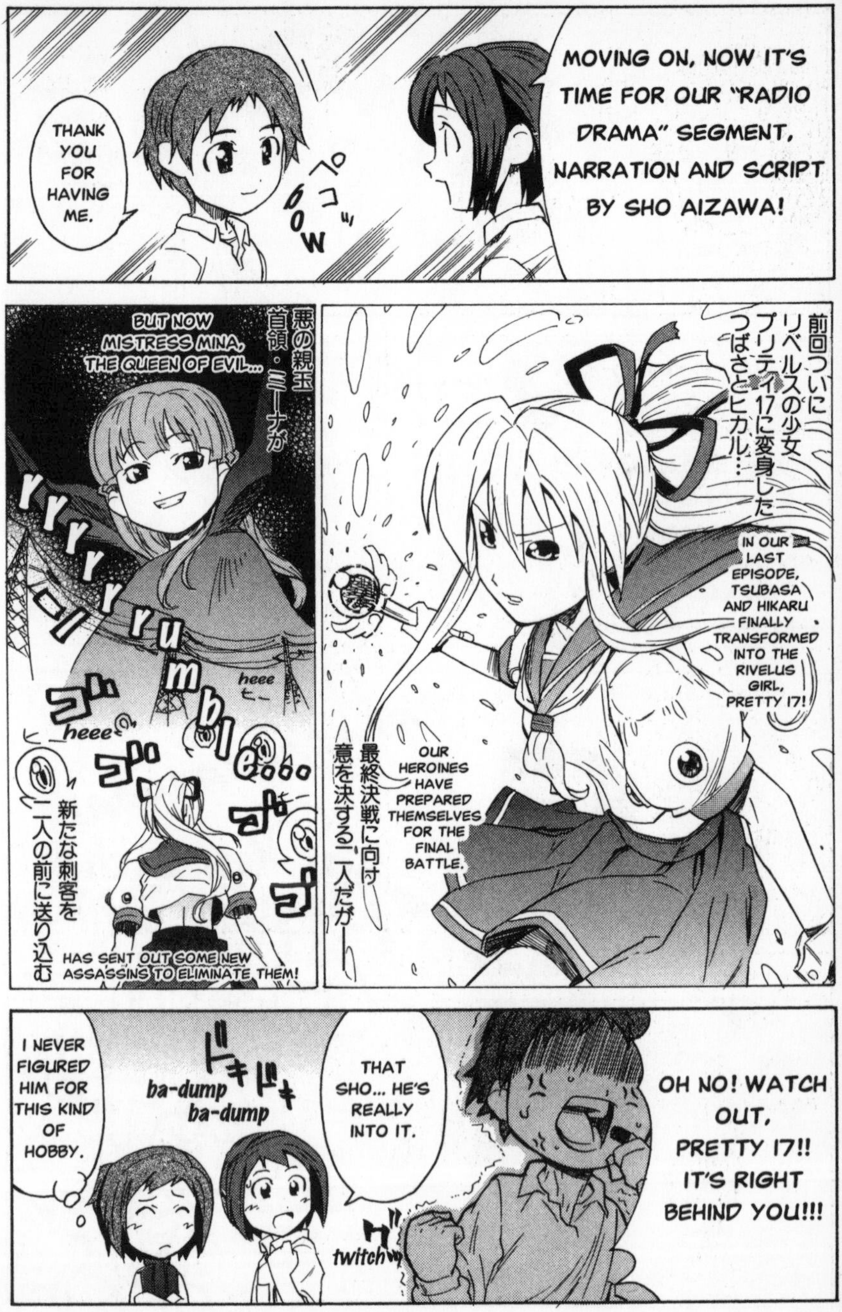
MOVING ON, NOW IT'S TIME FOR OUR "RADIO DRAMA" SEGMENT, NARRATION AND SCRIPT BY SHO AIZAWA!
ペコッ
bow
THANK YOU FOR HAVING ME.
前回ついに
リベルスの少女
プリティ17に変身した
つばさとヒカル…
IN OUR LAST EPISODE, TSUBASA AND HIKARU FINALLY TRANSFORMED INTO THE RIVELUS GIRL, PRETTY 17!
最終決戦に向け
意を決する二人だが—
OUR HEROINES HAVE PREPARED THEMSELVES FOR THE FINAL BATTLE.
悪の親玉
首領・ミーナが
BUT NOW MISTRESS MINA, THE QUEEN OF EVIL...
rrrrrrrumble...
heee
heee
新たな刺客を
二人の前に送り込む
HAS SENT OUT SOME NEW ASSASSINS TO ELIMINATE THEM!
OH NO! WATCH OUT, PRETTY 17!! IT'S RIGHT BEHIND YOU!!!
twitch
THAT SHO... HE'S REALLY INTO IT.
ドキドキ
ba-dump ba-dump
I NEVER FIGURED HIM FOR THIS KIND OF HOBBY.

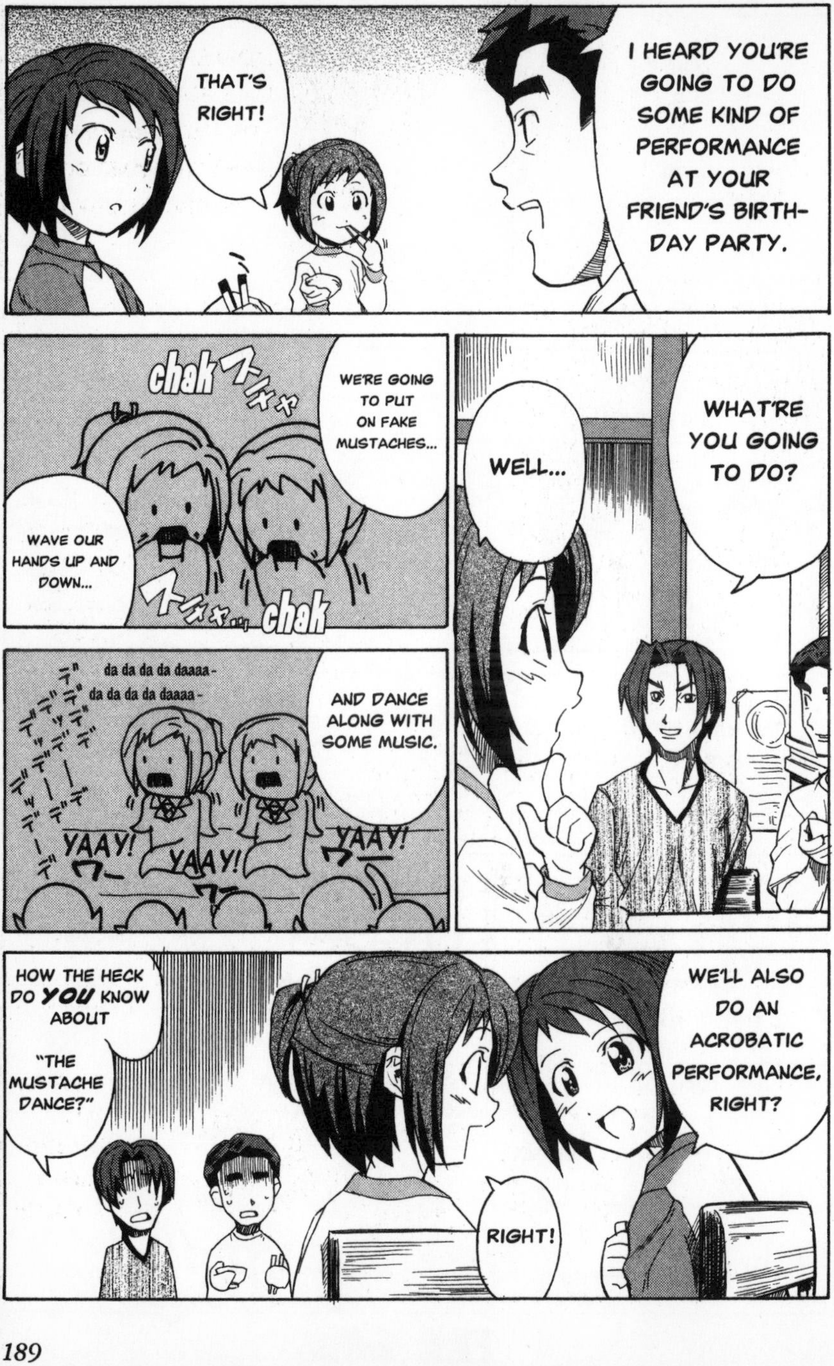

I HEARD YOU'RE GOING TO DO SOME KIND OF PERFORMANCE AT YOUR FRIEND'S BIRTH-DAY PARTY.
THAT'S RIGHT!
WHAT'RE YOU GOING TO DO?
WELL...
WE'RE GOING TO PUT ON FAKE MUSTACHES...
chak
WAVE OUR HANDS UP AND DOWN...
chak
AND DANCE ALONG WITH SOME MUSIC.
da da da da daaaa-
da da da da daaaa-
YAAY!
YAAY!
YAAY!
WE'LL ALSO DO AN ACROBATIC PERFORMANCE, RIGHT?
RIGHT!
HOW THE HECK DO ***YOU*** KNOW ABOUT "THE MUSTACHE DANCE?"

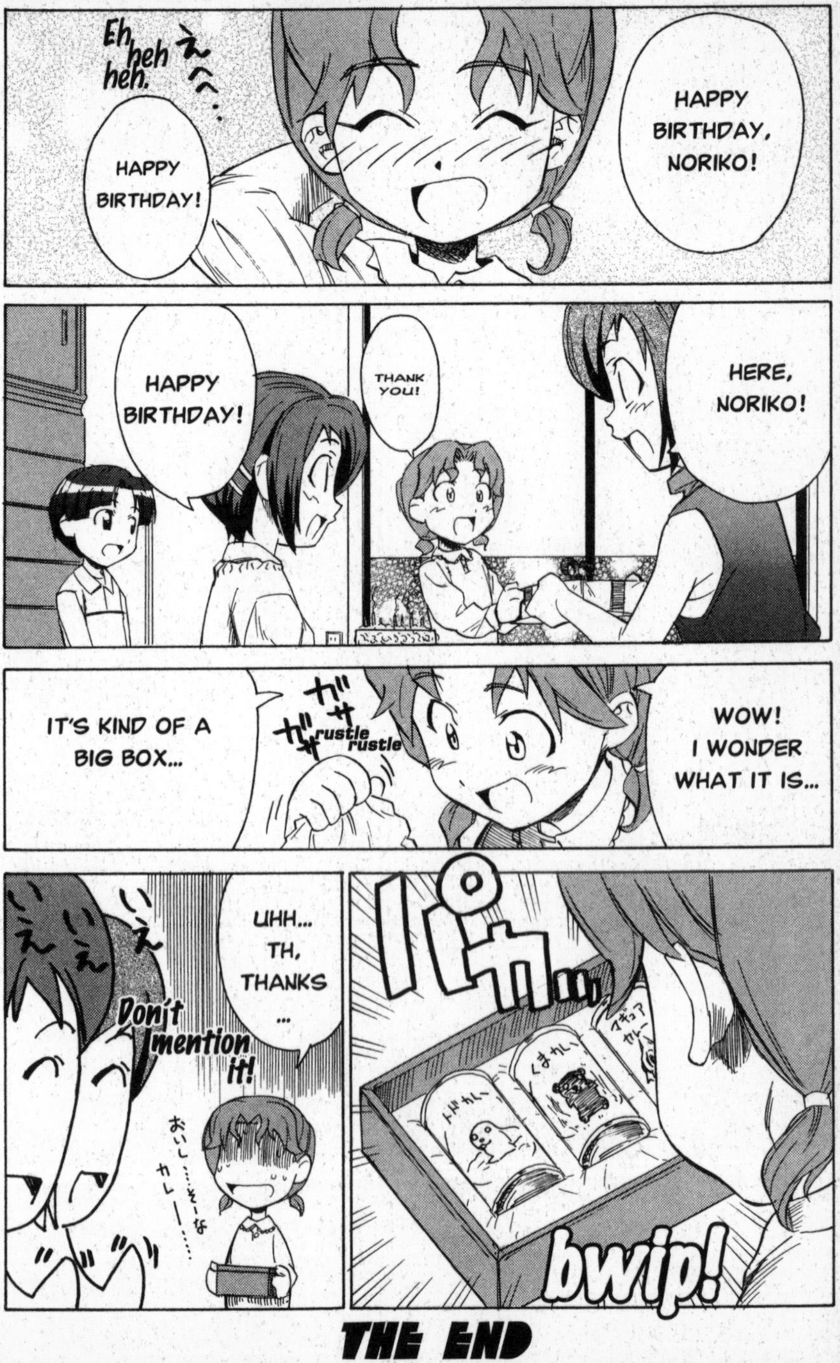
HAPPY BIRTHDAY, NORIKO!
Eh heh heh.
えへへ…
HAPPY BIRTHDAY!
HERE, NORIKO!
THANK YOU!
HAPPY BIRTHDAY!
WOW! I WONDER WHAT IT IS...
ガサガサ
rustle rustle
IT'S KIND OF A BIG BOX...
パカ…
bwip!
くまカレー
トドカレー
UHH... TH, THANKS ...
いえいえ
Don't mention it!
おいし……そーなカレー……

THE END

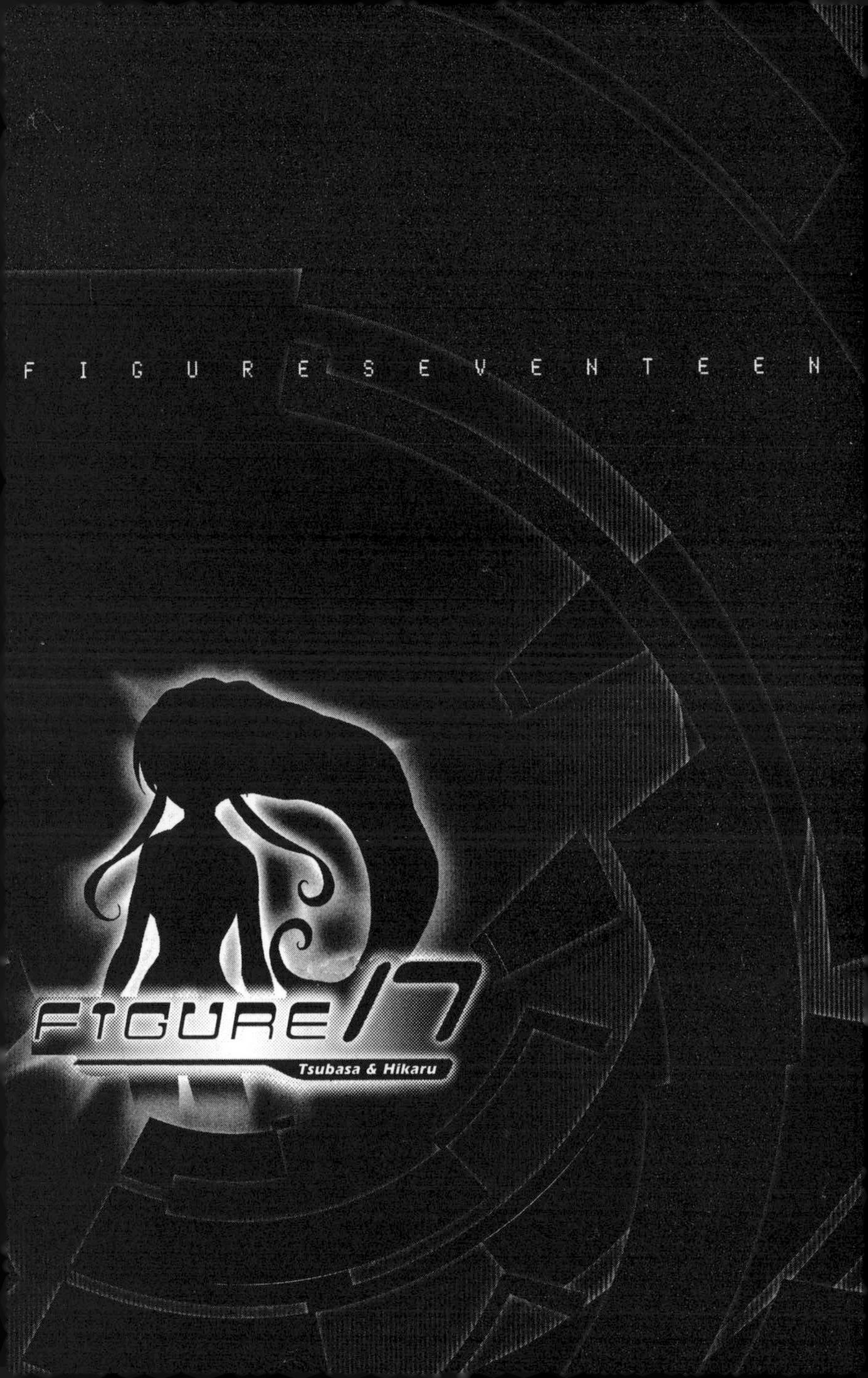
F I G U R E S E V E N T E E N
FIGURE 17
Tsubasa & Hikaru

FIGURE 17
VOLUME ONE

Original Story **Genco-Olm**
Script & Comic **Guy Nakahira**

© GUY NAKAHIRA 2001
© GENCO • OLM/FIGURE 17 COMMITTEE

First published in 2001 by Media Works Inc., Tokyo, Japan.
English translation rights arranged with Media Works Inc.

Translation Department Supervisor **JAVIER LOPEZ**
Translator **KAY BERTRAND**
Translation Staff **AMY FORSYTH, BRENDAN FRAYNE, EIKO McGREGOR**
Print Production Manager/Art Studio Manager **LISA PUCKETT**
Senior Designer **JORGE ALVARADO**
Art Production Manager **RYAN MASON**
Graphic Designer/Group Leader **SHANNON RASBERRY**
Graphic Artists **WINDI MARTIN, KRISTINA MILESKI, NATALIA MORALES,
GEORGE REYNOLDS, LANCE SWARTOUT, NANAKO TSUKIHASHI**
Graphic Intern **IVAN CURIEL**

International Coordinator **TORU IWAKAMI**
International Coordinator **ATSUSHI KANBAYASHI**

Publishing Editor **SUSAN ITIN**
Assistant Editor **MARGARET SCHAROLD**
Editorial Assistant **VARSHA BHUCHAR**
Proofreader **SHERIDAN JACOBS**
Research/ Traffic Coordinator **MARSHA ARNOLD**

President, C.E.O & Publisher **JOHN LEDFORD**

Email: editor@adv-manga.com
www.adv-manga.com
www.advfilms.com
For sales and distribution inquiries please call 1.800.282.7202

ADV MANGA™ is a division of A.D. Vision, Inc.
10114 W. Sam Houston Parkway, Suite 200, Houston, Texas 77099

English Text ©2004 published by A.D. Vision, Inc. under exclusive license.
ADV MANGA is a trademark of A.D. Vision, Inc.

ISBN: 1-4139-0019-4
First printing, February 2004
10 9 8 7 5 4 3 2 1
Printed in Canada

LETTER FROM THE ADV MANGA TRANSLATION STAFF

Dear Reader,

On behalf of the ADV Manga translation team, thank you for purchasing an ADV book. We are enthusiastic and committed to our work, and strive to carry our enthusiasm over into the book you hold in your hands.

Our goal is to retain the true spirit of the original Japanese book. While great care has been taken to render a true and accurate translation, some cultural or readability issues may require a line to be adapted for greater accessibility to our readers. At times, manga titles that include culturally-specific concepts will feature a "Translator's Notes" section, which explains noteworthy references to the original text.

We hope our commitment to a faithful translation is evident in every ADV book you purchase.

Sincerely,

Javier Lopez,
Lead Translator

Eiko McGregor

Kay Bertrand

Brendan Frayne

Amy Forsyth

TRANSLATOR'S NOTES

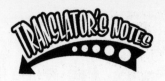

Figure 17 Volume 01

PG. 189 **The Mustache Dance**

This particular performance was a huge hit in Japan way back when. It's called the "Hige Dance," and was part of the Japanese TV show, "Hachiji-dayo! Zenin Shugo!" (1969-1985). Ken Shimura and Cha Kato wear Mario brothers-like mustaches and dance to music in a silly performance. Readers who don't know anything about this particular performance or the show, likely wouldn't have caught the reference.

PG. 190 **Sea Lion Curry**

Yes, there IS such a thing as sea lion curry. And bear curry. (No Magure curry, though).

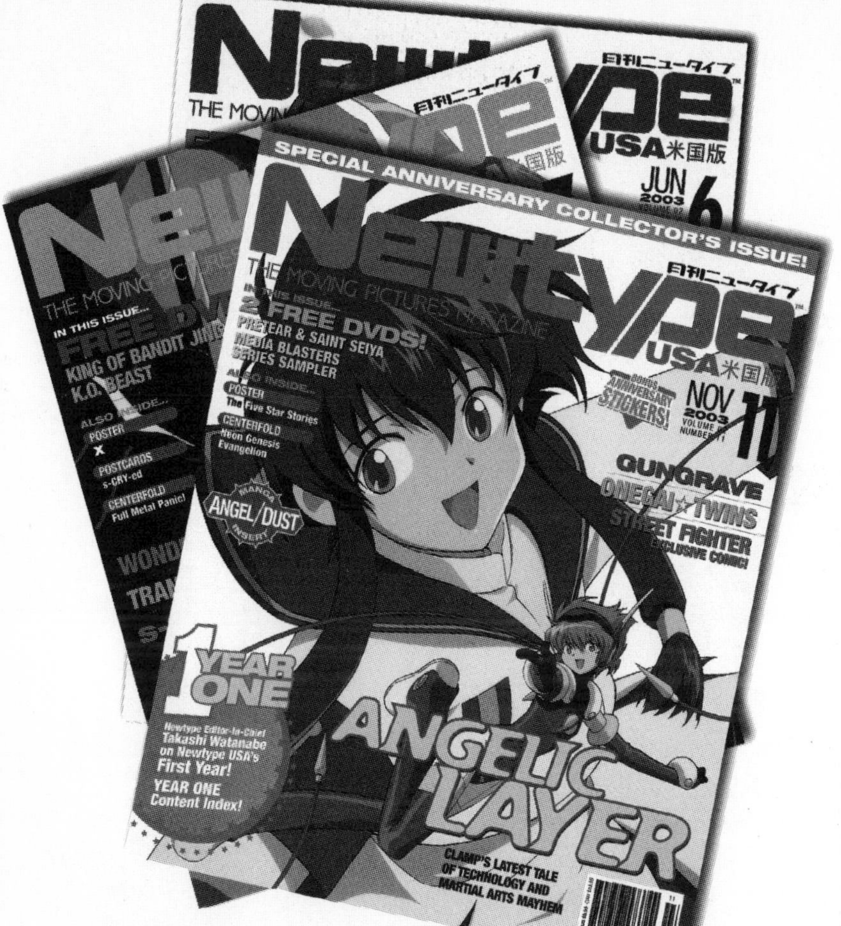
Newtype
THE MOVING PICTURES MAGAZINE
USA
JUN 2003 6
SPECIAL ANNIVERSARY COLLECTOR'S ISSUE!
IN THIS ISSUE...
2 FREE DVDS!
PRETEAR & SAINT SEIYA
MEDIA BLASTERS SERIES SAMPLER
ALSO INSIDE...
POSTER
The Five Star Stories
CENTERFOLD
Neon Genesis Evangelion
ANGEL/DUST
NOV 2003 11
GUNGRAVE
ONEGAI☆TWINS
STREET FIGHTER
EXCLUSIVE COMIC!
YEAR ONE
Newtype Editor-In-Chief Takashi Watanabe on Newtype USA's First Year!
YEAR ONE Content Index!
ANGELIC LAYER
CLAMP'S LATEST TALE OF TECHNOLOGY AND MARTIAL ARTS MAYHEM
IN THIS ISSUE...
KING OF BANDIT JING
K.O. BEAST
ALSO INSIDE...
POSTER
X
POSTCARDS
s-CRY-ed
CENTERFOLD
Full Metal Panic!

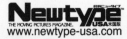

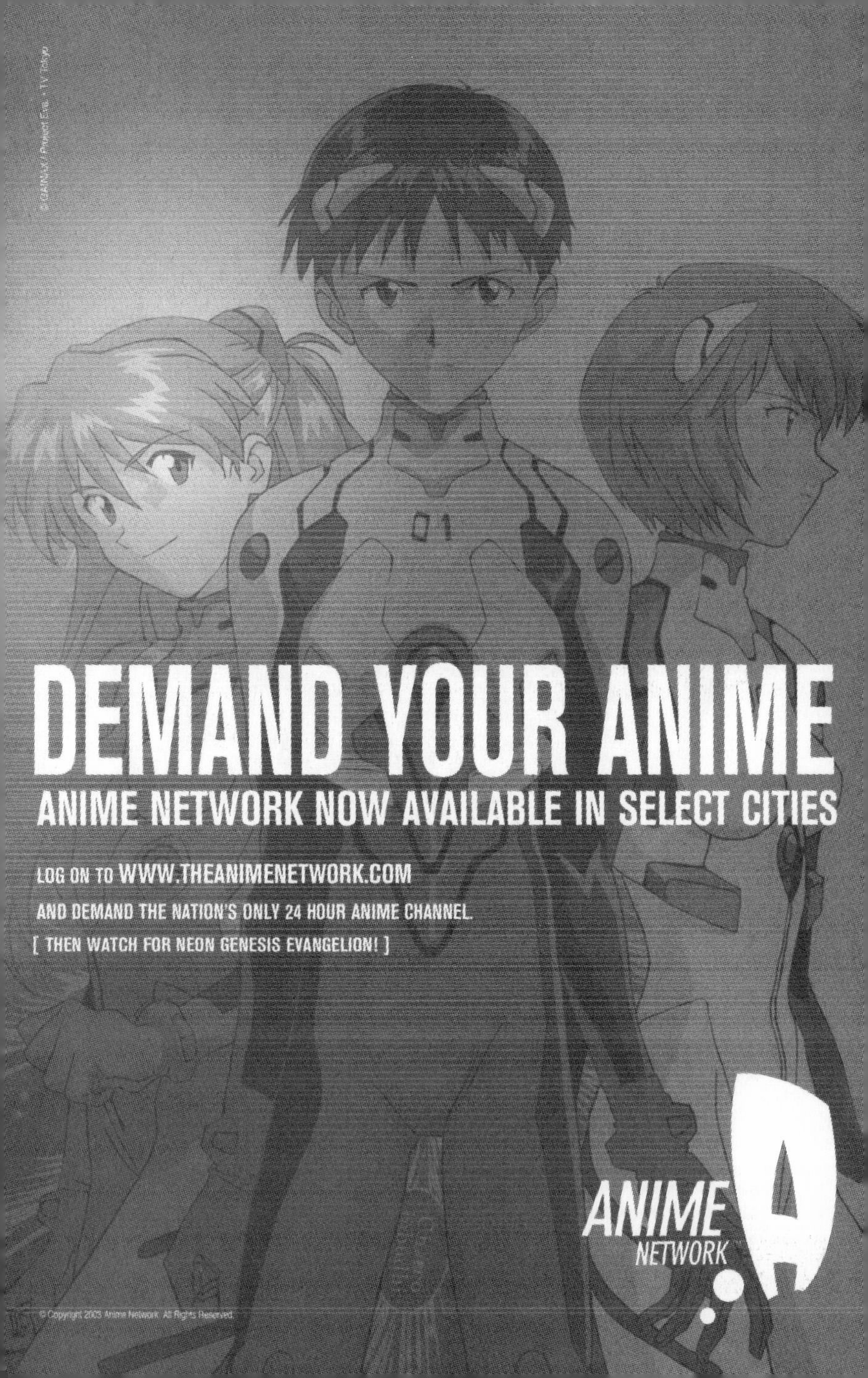

© GAINAX / Project Eva. • TV Tokyo
DEMAND YOUR ANIME
ANIME NETWORK NOW AVAILABLE IN SELECT CITIES
LOG ON TO WWW.THEANIMENETWORK.COM
AND DEMAND THE NATION'S ONLY 24 HOUR ANIME CHANNEL.
[THEN WATCH FOR NEON GENESIS EVANGELION!]
ANIME NETWORK
© Copyright 2003 Anime Network. All Rights Reserved.

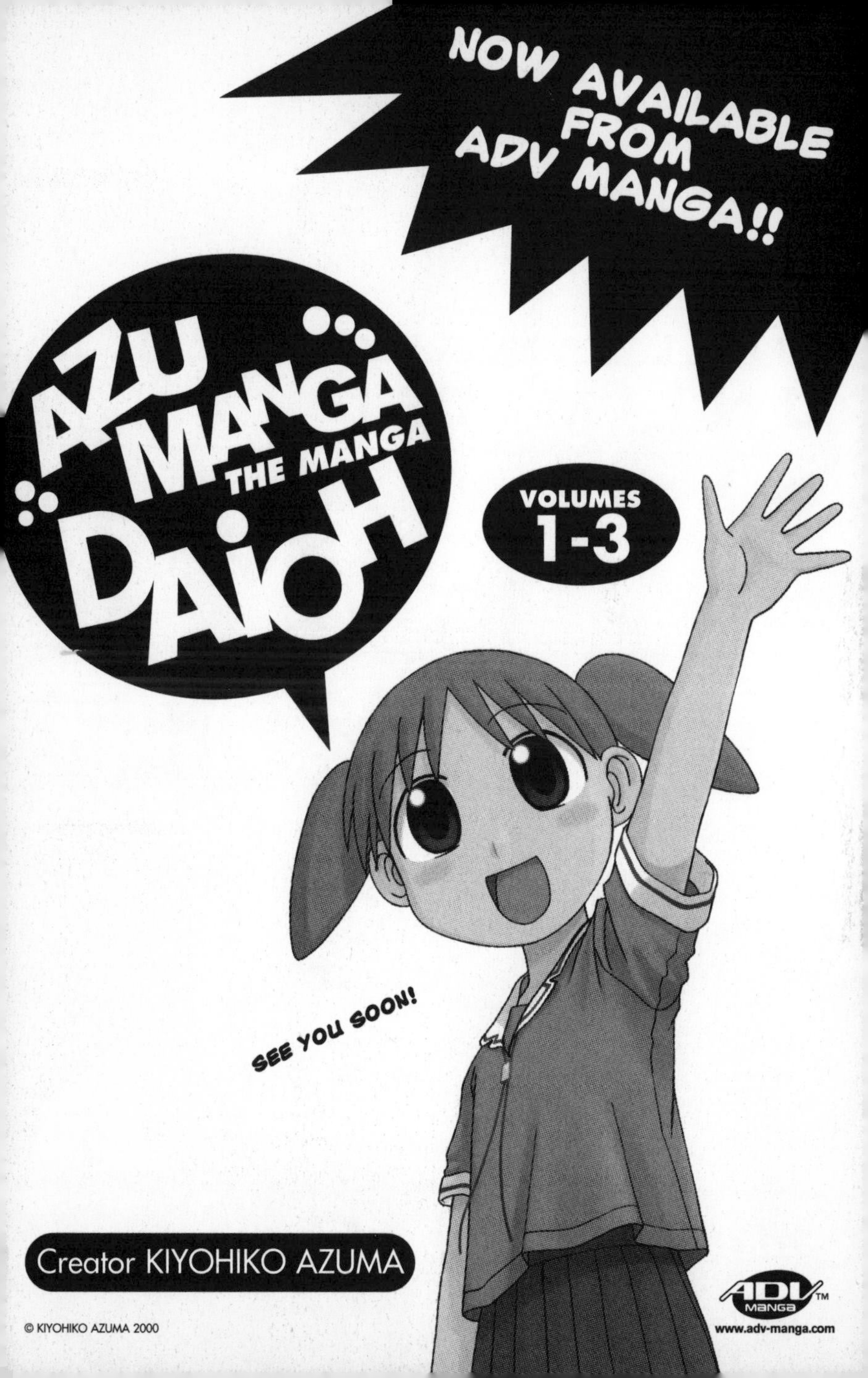
NOW AVAILABLE FROM ADV MANGA!!
AZU MANGA DAIOH
THE MANGA
VOLUMES 1-3
SEE YOU SOON!
Creator KIYOHIKO AZUMA
ADV Manga TM
© KIYOHIKO AZUMA 2000
www.adv-manga.com

The legendary video game series comes to exquisite
life in a brand new anime animated by GONZO
(Full Metal Panic) and directed by Mahiro Maeda
(The Animatrix: Second Renaissance)...

FINAL FANTASY: UNLIMITED

Welcome to Wonderland

COMING IN APRIL 2004

FIGURE 17

VOLUME 2

ORIGINAL STORY
GENCO•OLM
SCRIPT AND COMIC
GUY NAKAHIRA

WHEN HIKARU GETS INJURED IN BATTLE, TSUBASA HAS
DOUBTS ABOUT JUST HOW LONG SHE CAN GO ON FIGHTING.
THE RIFT BETWEEN TSUBASA AND HIKARU WIDENS AS
TSUBASA LOSES THE BOY SHE CARED FOR, AND ACCUSES
HIKARU OF NOT UNDERSTANDING BECAUSE *SHE ISN'T HUMAN!*

adv-manga.com

AVAILABLE WHEREVER ADV MANGA IS SOLD!

ADV MANGA™ ANIME SURVEY

PLEASE MAIL THE COMPLETED FORM TO: EDITOR – ADV MANGA
℅ A.D. Vision, Inc. 10114 W. Sam Houston Pkwy., Suite 200 Houston, TX 77099

Name: ______________________
Address: ______________________
City: State: Zip: ______________________

E-Mail: ______________________
Male ☐ Female ☐ Age: ______________________
Cable Provider: ______________________

☐ ***CHECK HERE IF YOU WOULD LIKE TO RECEIVE OTHER INFORMATION OR FUTURE OFFERS FROM ADV.***

1. Annual Household Income (*Check only one*)

- ☐ Under $25,000
- ☐ $25,000 to $50,000
- ☐ $50,000 to $75,000
- ☐ Over $75,000

2. How do you hear about new Anime releases? (*Check all that apply*)

- ☐ Browsing in Store
- ☐ Internet Reviews
- ☐ Anime News Websites
- ☐ Direct Email Campaigns
- ☐ Online forums (message boards and chat rooms)
- ☐ Carrier pigeon
- ☐ Other:__________
- ☐ Magazine Ad
- ☐ Online Advertising
- ☐ Conventions
- ☐ TV Advertising

3. Which magazines do you read? (*Check all that apply*)

- ☐ Wizard
- ☐ SPIN
- ☐ Animerica
- ☐ Rolling Stone
- ☐ Maxim
- ☐ DC Comics
- ☐ URB
- ☐ Polygon
- ☐ Original Play Station Magazine
- ☐ Entertainment Weekly
- ☐ YRB
- ☐ EGM
- ☐ Newtype USA
- ☐ SciFi
- ☐ Starlog
- ☐ Wired
- ☐ Vice
- ☐ BPM
- ☐ I hate reading
- ☐ Other:

4. Would you subscribe to digital cable if you could get a 24 hour/7 day a week anime channel (like the Anime Network)?
- ☐ Yes
- ☐ No

5. Would you like to see the Anime Network in your area?
- ☐ Yes
- ☐ No

6. Would you pay $6.99/month for the Anime Network?
- ☐ Yes
- ☐ No

7. What genre of manga and anime would you like to see from ADV?
(*Check all that apply*)
- ☐ adventure
- ☐ romance
- ☐ detective
- ☐ fighting
- ☐ horror
- ☐ sci-fi/fantasy
- ☐ sports

8. How many manga titles have you purchased in the last year?
- ☐ none
- ☐ 1-4
- ☐ 5-10
- ☐ 11+

9. Where do you make your manga purchases? (*Check all that apply*)
- ☐ comic store
- ☐ bookstore
- ☐ newsstand
- ☐ online
- ☐ other:_____
- ☐ department store
- ☐ grocery store
- ☐ video store
- ☐ video game store

10. What's your favorite anime-related website?
- ☐ advfilms.com
- ☐ anipike.com
- ☐ rightstuf.com
- ☐ animenewsservice.com
- ☐ animenewsnetwork.com
- ☐ animeondvd.com
- ☐ animenation.com
- ☐ animeonline.net
- ☐ planetanime.com
- ☐ other: _____

All information provided will be used for internal purposes only. We promise not to sell or otherwise divulge your information.